WHERE ARE THE LESSON FILES?

Purchase of this Classroom in a Book in any format gives you access to the lesson files you'll need to complete the exercises in the book.

You'll find the files you need on your **Account** page at peachpit.com on the **Registered Products** tab.

1 Go to www.peachpit.com/register.

2 Sign in or create a new account.

3 Enter the ISBN: 9780134664286.

4 Answer the questions as proof of purchase.

5 The lesson files can be accessed through the Registered Products tab on your Account page.

6 Click the Access Bonus Content link below the title of your product to proceed to the download page. Click the lesson file links to download them to your computer.

CONTENTS

GETTING STARTED

Adobe® Dreamweaver CC is the industry-leading web-authoring program. Whether you create websites for others for a living or plan to create one for your own business, Dreamweaver offers all the tools you need to get professional-quality results.

About Classroom in a Book

Adobe Dreamweaver CC Classroom in a Book® (2017 release) is part of the official training series for graphics and publishing software developed with the support of Adobe product experts.

The lessons are designed so you can learn at your own pace. If you're new to Dreamweaver, you'll learn the fundamentals of putting the program to work. If you are an experienced user, you'll find that Classroom in a Book teaches many advanced features, including tips and techniques for using the latest version of Dreamweaver.

Although each lesson includes step-by-step instructions for creating a specific project, you'll have room for exploration and experimentation. You can follow the book from start to finish or complete only those lessons that correspond to your interests and needs. Each lesson concludes with a review section containing questions and answers on the subjects you've covered.

TinyURLs

At several points in the book, I reference external information available on the Internet. The uniform resource locators (URLs) for this information are often long and unwieldy, so I have provided custom TinyURLs in many places for your convenience. Unfortunately, the TinyURLs sometimes expire over time and no longer function. If you find that a TinyURL doesn't work, look up the actual URL provided in the appendix.

Prerequisites

Before using *Adobe Dreamweaver CC Classroom in a Book (2017 release)*, you should have a working knowledge of your computer and its operating system. Be sure you know how to use the mouse, standard menus, and commands, as well as how to open, save, and close files. If you need to review these techniques, see the printed or online documentation included with your Windows or Mac operating system.

Conventions used in this book

Working in Dreamweaver means you'll be working with code. We have used several conventions in the following lessons and exercises to make working with the code in this book easier to follow and understand.

Code font

In many instructions, you will be required to enter HTML code, CSS rules, and properties and other code-based markup. To distinguish the markup from the instructional text, the entries will be styled with a code font, like this:

Examine the following code: `<h1>Heading goes here</h1>`

In instances where you must enter the markup yourself, the entry will be formatted in color, like this:

Insert the following code: `<h1>Heading goes here</h1>`

Strikethrough

In several exercises, you will be instructed to delete markup that already exists within the webpage or style sheet. In those instances, the targeted references will be identified with strikethrough formatting, like this:

Delete the following values:

```
margin: 10px 20px 10px 20px;
background-image: url(images/fern.png), url(images/stripe.png);
```

Be careful to delete only the identified markup so that you achieve the following result:

```
margin: 10px 10px;
background-image: url(images/fern.png);
```

Missing punctuation

HTML code, CSS markup, and JavaScript often require the use of various punctuation, such as periods (.), commas (,), and semicolons (;), among others, and can be damaged by their incorrect usage or placement. Consequently, I have omitted periods and other punctuation expected in a sentence or paragraph from an instruction or hyperlink whenever it may cause confusion or a possible error, as in the following two instructions:

Enter the following code: `<h1>Heading goes here</h1>`

Type the following link: `http://adobe.com`

Element references

Within the body of descriptions and exercise instructions, elements may be referenced by name or by class or id attributes. When an element is identified by its tag name, it will appear as `<h1>` or `h1`. When referenced by its class attribute, the name will appear with a leading period (`.`) in a code-like font, like this: `.content` or `.sidebar1`. References to elements by their id attribute will appear with a leading hash (#) and in a code font, like this: `#top`. This practice matches the way these elements appear in Dreamweaver's tag selector interface.

Windows vs. macOS instructions

In most cases, Dreamweaver performs identically in both Windows and macOS. Minor differences exist between the two versions, mostly because of platform-specific issues out of the control of the program. Most of these are simply differences in keyboard shortcuts, how dialogs are displayed, and how buttons are named. In most cases, screen shots were made in the macOS version of Dreamweaver and may appear different from your own screen.

Where specific commands differ, they are noted within the text. Windows commands are listed first, followed by the macOS equivalent, such as Ctrl+C/Cmd+C. Common abbreviations are used for all commands whenever possible, as follows:

Windows	macOS
Control = Ctrl	Command = Cmd
Alternate = Alt	Option = Opt

As lessons proceed, instructions may be truncated or shortened to save space, with the assumption that you picked up the essential concepts earlier in the lesson. For example, at the beginning of a lesson you may be instructed to "press Ctrl+C/Cmd+C." Later, you may be told to "copy" text or a code element. These should be considered identical instructions.

If you find you have difficulties in any particular task, review earlier steps or exercises in that lesson. In some cases if an exercise is based on concepts covered earlier, you will be referred to the specific lesson.

Installing the program

Before you perform any exercises in this book, verify that your computer system meets the hardware requirements for Dreamweaver, that it's correctly configured, and that all required software is installed.

If you do not have Dreamweaver, you will first have to install it from Creative Cloud. Adobe Dreamweaver must be purchased separately; it is not included with the lesson files that accompany this book. Go to **www.adobe.com/products/dreamweaver/tech-specs.html** to obtain the system requirements.

Go to **https://creative.adobe.com/plans** to sign up for Adobe Creative Cloud. Dreamweaver may be purchased with the entire Creative Cloud family or as a stand-alone app. Adobe also allows you to try Creative Cloud and the individual applications for 7 days for free.

Check out **www.adobe.com/products/dreamweaver.html** to learn more about the different options for obtaining Dreamweaver.

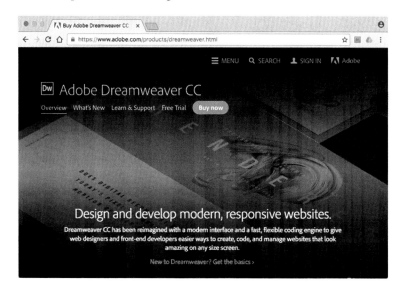

Updating Dreamweaver to the latest version

Although Dreamweaver is downloaded and installed on your computer hard drive, periodic updates are provided via Creative Cloud. Some updates provide bug fixes and security patches, while others supply amazing new features and capabilities.

The lessons in this book are based on Dreamweaver CC (2017 release) and may not work properly in any earlier version of the program. To check which version is installed on your computer, choose Help > About Dreamweaver in Windows or Dreamweaver > About Dreamweaver on the Macintosh. A window will display the version number of the application and other pertinent information.

 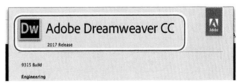

If you have an earlier version of the program installed, you will have to update Dreamweaver to the latest version. You can check the status of your installation by opening the Creative Cloud manager and logging in to your account.

 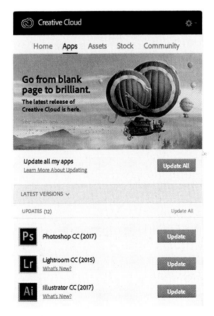

Windows   macOS

Check out **https://helpx.adobe.com/creative-cloud/help/download-install-trial.html** to learn how to download and install a limited-period trial of Creative Cloud to your computer or laptop.

Online Content

Your purchase of this Classroom in a Book includes online materials provided by way of your Account page on peachpit.com.

Lesson Files

To work through the projects in this book, you will need to download the lesson files from peachpit.com. You can download the files for individual lessons or it may be possible to download them all in a single file.

Web Edition

The Web Edition is an online interactive version of the book providing an enhanced learning experience. Your Web Edition can be accessed from any device with a connection to the Internet; it contains the following:

- The complete text of the book

- Hours of instructional video keyed to the text

- Interactive quizzes

In addition, the Web Edition may be updated when Adobe adds significant feature updates between major Creative Cloud releases. To accommodate the changes, sections of the online book may be updated or new sections may be added.

Accessing the Lesson Files and Web Edition

If you purchased an ebook from peachpit.com or adobepress.com, your Web Edition will automatically appear under the Digital Purchases tab on your Account page. Click the **Launch** link to access the product. Continue reading to learn how to register your product to get access to the lesson files.

If you purchased an ebook from a different vendor or you bought a print book, you must **register** your purchase on peachpit.com to access the online content:

1 Go to www.peachpit.com/register.

2 Sign in or create a new account.

3 Enter the ISBN **9780134664286**.

4 Answer the questions as proof of purchase.

5 The **Web Edition** will appear on the Digital Purchases tab on your Account page. Click the **Launch** link to access the product.

   The **Lesson Files** can be accessed through the Registered Products tab on your Account page. Click the Access Bonus Content link below the title of your product to proceed to the download page. Click the lesson file links to download them to your computer.

The files are compressed into ZIP archives to speed up download time and to protect the contents from damage during transfer. You must uncompress (or "unzip") the files to restore them to their original size and format before you use them with the book. Modern Mac and Windows systems are set up to open ZIP archives by simply double-clicking.

6 Do one of the following:

- If you downloaded **DWCC2017_lesson_files.zip**, unzipping the archive will produce a folder named **DWCC2017_Lesson_Files** containing all the lesson files used by the book.

- If you downloaded the lessons individually, create a new folder on your hard drive and name it **DWCC2017**. Unzip the individual lesson files to this folder. That way, all the lesson files will be stored in one location. Do not share or copy files between lessons.

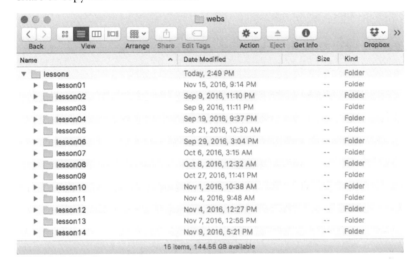

Note: The files are updated from time to time, so the date may be different than the one shown.

Recommended lesson order

The training in this book is designed to take you from A to Z in basic to intermediate website design, development, and production. Each new lesson builds on previous exercises, using supplied files and assets to create an entire website. I recommend you download all lesson files at once, and then perform each lesson in sequential order to achieve a successful result and the most complete understanding of all aspects of web design.

The ideal training scenario will start in Lesson 1 and proceed through the entire book to Lesson 15. Each lesson builds the skills and understanding necessary to complete subsequent tasks. We recommend that you do not skip any lessons, or even individual exercises. Although ideal, this method may not be a practicable scenario for every user. So, each lesson folder contains all the files needed to complete every exercise within it using partially completed or staged assets, allowing you to complete individual lessons out of order, if desired.

However, don't assume that the staged files and customized templates in each lesson represent a complete set of assets. It may seem that these folders contain duplicative materials. But these "duplicate" files and assets, in most cases, cannot be used interchangeably in other lessons or exercises. Doing so will probably cause you to fail to achieve the goal of the exercise.

For that reason, you should treat each folder as a stand-alone website. Copy the lesson folder to your hard drive, and create a new site for that lesson using the Site Setup dialog. Do not define sites using subfolders of existing sites. Keep your sites and assets in their original folders to avoid conflicts.

One suggestion is to organize the lesson folders in a single *web* or *sites* master folder near the root of your hard drive. But avoid using the Dreamweaver application folder. In most cases, you'll want to use a local web server as your testing server, which is described in Lesson 13, "Publishing to the Web."

Bonus material

We've provided additional material for Lessons 2 and 3 and a bonus Lesson 15 on the Peachpit website:

- Lesson 2, "HTML Basics Bonus"
- Lesson 3, "CSS Basics Bonus"
- Lesson 15, "Working with Web Animation and Video Bonus"

You will find these on your Account page once you register your book, as described earlier in "Accessing the Lesson Files and Web Edition."

On first launch

Right after installation or upon first launch, Dreamweaver CC will display several introduction screens. The program will first ask you if you are a new or experienced user of Dreamweaver.

As each screen appears, it guides you through the setup of the interface. Depending whether you using Windows or macOS, or select new or experienced user, several screens will show different options. You will choose your workspace and color theme. I used the lightest theme for the screen shots and the Standard workspace. Feel free to pick the theme color you prefer. All exercises in the book will work in any color theme.

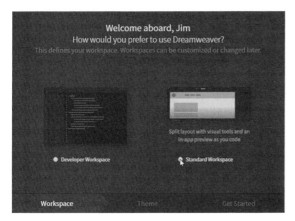

New User

Experienced User

As you work through the introductory screens, they may appear in a different sequence than shown here.

New User

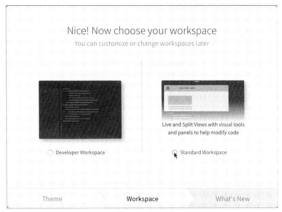

Experienced User

For experienced users, the Introduction screen will preview some of the new features added to the program. Review the new features or proceed to the final screen.

When you complete the setup, the final screen prompts you to get started. Depending on whether you are a new or experienced user, you may be directed to open a file; select a folder or proceed to the program interface.

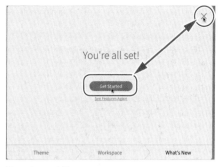

New User   Experienced User

Once you complete the introductory screens, Dreamweaver may prompt you to Sync Settings to the Creative Cloud. This feature allows you to back up and synchronize program preferences between two machines using your account. Click Advanced to access the Sync Settings in Preference. Click Disable Sync Settings to shut off synchronization. Click Sync Setting Now to synchronize your settings immediately.

Choosing the program color theme

If you purchased the book after you installed and launched Dreamweaver, you may be currently using a different color theme than the one pictured in most screen shots in the book. All exercises will function properly using any color theme, but if you want to configure your interface to match the one shown, complete the following steps.

1 Select Edit > Preferences in Windows or Dreamweaver CC > Preferences in macOS.

The Preferences dialog appears.

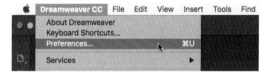

2 Select the **Interface** category.

3 Select the lightest color theme.

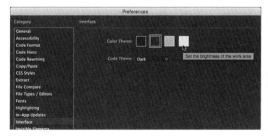

The interface changes to the new theme. Note how the Code theme changed too. But the changes are not permanent. If you close the dialog, the theme will revert to the original colors.

4   Click the Apply button.

The theme changes are now permanent.

5   Click the Close button.

Feel free to change the color theme at any time. Often users select the theme that works best in their normal working environment. The lighter themes work best in well-lighted rooms, while the darker themes work best in indirect or controlled lighting environments used in some design offices. All exercises will work properly in any theme color.

Setting up the workspace

Dreamweaver CC (2017 release) includes two main workspaces to accommodate various computer configurations and individual workflows. For this book, the Standard workspace is recommended.

1   If the Standard workspace is not displayed by default, you can select it from the Workspace drop-down menu on the upper-right side of the screen.

2   If the default Standard workspace has been modified—where certain toolbars and panels are not visible (as they appear in the figures in the book)—you can restore the factory setting by choosing Reset 'Standard' from the Workspace drop-down menu.

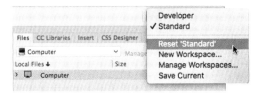

Workspace Layout options can also be accessed from the Window menu.

Most of the figures in this book show the Standard workspace. When you finish the lessons in this book, experiment with each workspace to find the one that you prefer, or build your own configuration and save the layout under a custom name.

For a more complete description of the Dreamweaver workspaces, see Lesson 1, "Customizing Your Workspace."

Defining a Dreamweaver site

In the course of completing the following lessons, you will create webpages from scratch and use existing files and resources that are stored on your hard drive. The resulting webpages and assets make up what's called your *local* site. When you are ready to upload your site to the Internet (see Lesson 13, "Publishing to the Web"), you publish your completed files to a web-host server, which then becomes your *remote* site. The folder structures and files of the local and remote sites are usually mirror images of one another.

The first step is to define your local site.

1 Launch Adobe Dreamweaver CC (2017 release) or later.

2 Open the Site menu.

The Site menu provides options for creating and managing standard Dreamweaver sites.

3 Choose New Site.

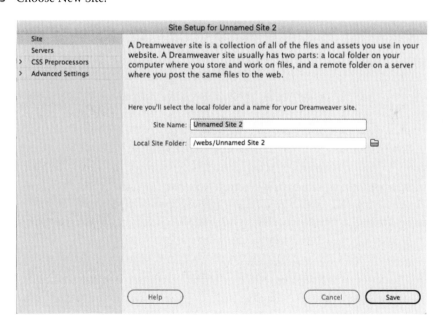

The Site Setup dialog appears.

◆ **Warning:** You must unzip the lesson files before you create your site definition.

To create a standard website in Dreamweaver, you need only name it and select the local site folder. The site name should relate to a specific project or client and will appear in the Files panel Site drop-down menu. This name is intended for your own purposes only; it will not be seen by the public, so there are no limitations to the name you can create. Use a name that clearly describes the purpose of the website. For the purposes of this book, use the name of the lesson you intend to complete, such as lesson01, lesson02, lesson03, and so on.

4   Type **lesson01** or another name, as appropriate, in the Site Name field.

● **Note:** The main folder that contains the site will be referred to throughout the book as the site root folder.

5   Next to the Local Site Folder field, click the Browse for Folder icon 📁.

The Choose Root Folder dialog appears.

6   Navigate to the appropriate folder containing the lesson files you downloaded from Peachpit.com (as described earlier) and click Select/Choose.

● **Note:** Lesson files must be decompressed prior to defining the site.

You could click Save at this time and begin working on your new website, but you'll add one more piece of handy information.

● **Note:** The folder that contains the image assets will be referred to throughout the book as the site default images folder or the default images folder.

7   Click the arrow next to the Advanced Settings category to reveal the categories listed there. Select Local Info.

Although it's not required, a good policy for site management is to store different file types in separate folders. For example, many websites provide individual folders for images, PDFs, videos, and so on. Dreamweaver assists in this endeavor by including an option for a Default Images folder.

Later, as you insert images from other locations on your computer, Dreamweaver will use this setting to automatically move the images into the site structure.

8 Next to the Default Images Folder field, click the Browse for Folder icon. When the dialog opens, navigate to the appropriate images folder for that lesson or site and click Select/Choose.

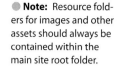 **Note:** Resource folders for images and other assets should always be contained within the main site root folder.

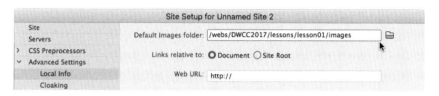

The path to the images folder appears in the Default Images Folder field. The next step would be to enter your site domain name in the Web URL field.

9 Enter **http://green-start.org** for the lessons in this book, or enter your own website URL, in the Web URL field.

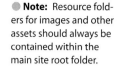 **Note:** The Web URL is not needed for most static HTML sites, but it's required for working with sites using dynamic applications or to connect to databases and a testing server.

You've entered all the information required to begin your new site. In subsequent lessons, you'll add more information to enable you to upload files to your remote and testing servers.

10 In the Site Setup dialog, click Save.
The Site Setup dialog closes.

In the Files panel, the new site name appears in the site list drop-down menu. As you add more site definitions, you can switch between the sites by selecting the appropriate name from this menu.

Whenever a site is selected or modified, Dreamweaver will build, or rebuild, a cache of every file in the folder. The cache identifies relationships between the webpages and the assets within sites and will assist you whenever a file is moved, renamed, or deleted to update links or other referenced information.

11 Click OK to build the cache, if necessary.

Setting up a site is a crucial first step in beginning any project in Dreamweaver. Knowing where the site root folder is located helps Dreamweaver determine link pathways and enables many sitewide options, such as orphaned-file checking and Find and Replace.

Checking for updates

Adobe periodically provides software updates. To check for updates in the program, choose Help > Updates in Dreamweaver. An update notice may also appear in the Creative Cloud update desktop manager.

For book updates and bonus material, visit your Account page on Peachpit.com and select the Lesson & Update Files tab.

Additional resources

Adobe Dreamweaver CC Classroom in a Book (2017 release) is not meant to replace documentation that comes with the program or to be a comprehensive reference for every feature. Only the commands and options used in the lessons are explained in this book. For comprehensive information about program features and tutorials, refer to these resources:

Adobe Dreamweaver Learn & Support: helpx.adobe.com/dreamweaver (accessible in Dreamweaver by choosing Help > Help And Support > Dreamweaver Support Center) is where you can find and browse tutorials, help, and support on Adobe.com.

Dreamweaver Help: helpx.adobe.com/support/dreamweaver.html is a reference for application features, commands, and tools (press F1 or choose Help > Help And Support > Dreamweaver Online Help). You can also download Help as a PDF document optimized for printing at helpx.adobe.com/pdf/dreamweaver_reference.pdf.

Adobe Forums: forums.adobe.com lets you tap into peer-to-peer discussions and questions and answers on Adobe products.

Resources for educators: www.adobe.com/education and edex.adobe.com offer a treasure trove of information for instructors who teach classes on Adobe software. You'll find solutions for education at all levels, including free curricula that use an integrated approach to teaching Adobe software and that can be used to prepare for the Adobe Certified Associate exams.

Also check out these useful links:

Adobe Add-ons: creative.adobe.com/addons is a central resource for finding tools, services, extensions, code samples, and more to supplement and extend your Adobe products.

Adobe Dreamweaver CC product home page: www.adobe.com/products/dreamweaver has more information about the product.

Adobe Authorized Training Centers

Adobe Authorized Training Centers offer instructor-led courses and training on Adobe products. A directory of AATCs is available at training.adobe.com/trainingpartners.

1 CUSTOMIZING YOUR WORKSPACE

Lesson overview

In this lesson, you'll familiarize yourself with the Dreamweaver CC (2017 release) program interface and learn how to do the following:

- Use the program Welcome screen
- Switch document views
- Work with panels
- Select a workspace layout
- Adjust toolbars
- Personalize preferences
- Create custom keyboard shortcuts
- Use the Property inspector
- Use the Extract workflow

 This lesson will take about 1 hour to complete. Download the project files for this lesson from the Lesson & Update Files tab on your Account page at www.peachpit.com, store them on your computer in a convenient location, and define a site based on the lesson01 folder, as described in the "Getting Started" section at the beginning of this book. Your Account page is also where you'll find any updates to the lessons or to the lesson files. Look on the Lesson & Update Files tab to access the most current content.

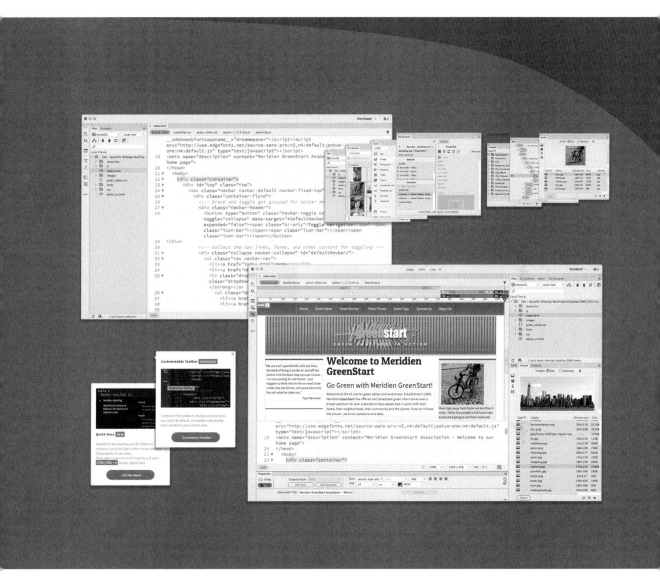

You'd probably need a dozen programs to perform all the tasks that Dreamweaver can do—and none of them would be as fun to use.

Touring the workspace

Note: Before you begin this lesson, download the lesson files and create a new website for lesson01 as described in the "Getting Started" section at the beginning of the book.

Dreamweaver is the industry-leading Hypertext Markup Language (HTML) editor, with good reasons for its popularity. The program offers an incredible array of design and code-editing tools. Dreamweaver offers something for everyone.

Coders love the range of enhancements built into the Code view environment, and developers enjoy the program's support for a variety of programming languages and code hinting. Designers marvel at seeing their text and graphics appear in an accurate What You See Is What You Get (WYSIWYG) depiction as they work, saving hours of time previewing pages in browsers. Novices certainly appreciate the program's simple-to-use and power-packed interface. No matter what type of user you are, if you use Dreamweaver, you don't have to compromise.

A	Menu bar	**F**	Document toolbar	**K**	CSS Designer
B	Document tab	**G**	Visual Media Query (VMQ) interface	**L**	Scrubber
C	Related files interface	**H**	Live/Design views	**M**	CC Libraries panel
D	Common toolbar	**I**	Files panel	**N**	Insert panel
E	New Feature guides	**J**	Workspace menu	**O**	DOM panel

P	Assets panel			
Q	Behaviors panel			
R	Code view			
S	Tag selectors			
T	Property inspector			

The Dreamweaver interface features a vast array of user-configurable panels and toolbars. Take a moment to familiarize yourself with the names of these components.

You'd think a program with this much to offer would be dense, slow, and unwieldy, but you'd be wrong. Dreamweaver provides much of its power via dockable panels and toolbars that you can display or hide and arrange in innumerable combinations to create your ideal workspace. In most cases, if you don't see a desired tool or panel, you'll find it in the Window menu.

This lesson introduces you to the Dreamweaver interface and gets you in touch with some of the power hiding under the hood. We don't spend a lot of time in the upcoming lessons teaching you how to perform basic activities within the interface; that's the intention of this lesson. So, take some time to go through the following descriptions and exercises to familiarize yourself with the basic operations of the program interface. Feel free to refer to this lesson any time you need a refresher on the program's many dialogs and panels and how they function.

Using the Start Screen

Once the program is installed and the initial setup is completed, you will see the new Dreamweaver Start Screen. This screen provides quick access to recent pages, easy creation of a range of page types, and a direct connection to several key Help topics. The Start Screen appears when you first start the program or when no other documents are open. The Start Screen has gotten a facelift in this version and deserves a quick review to check out what it offers. For example, it now has four main options: Recent Files, CC Files, Quick Start, and Starter Templates. Click the name of each option to access these features.

Recent Files

When you select the Recent Files options, Dreamweaver will provide a list of the files you last worked on. The list is dynamic. To reopen a file, simply click its name.

CC Files

The CC Files option shows a list of any files you have copied to your Creative Cloud Files folder that can be edited in Dreamweaver. This will include HTML, CSS, JavaScript, and text files among others. Files incompatible to Dreamweaver will simply be hidden from view.

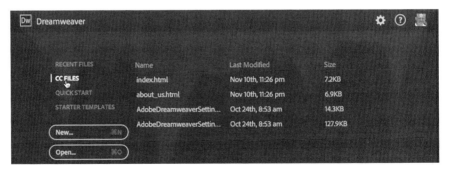

Quick Start

If the Quick Start tab looks familiar, it's because it has been around in one form or another for many versions of Dreamweaver. As it has always done, it provides instant access to a list of basic web-compatible file types, such as HTML, CSS, JS, PHP, and so on. Just click the file type to start a new document.

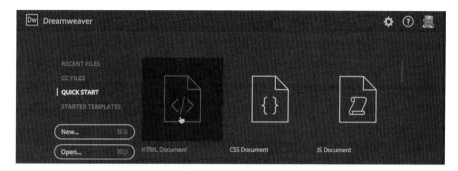

Starter Templates

The Starter Templates option enables you to access predefined starter templates that provide responsive styling to support smartphones and mobile devices, as well as starter layouts based on the popular Bootstrap framework.

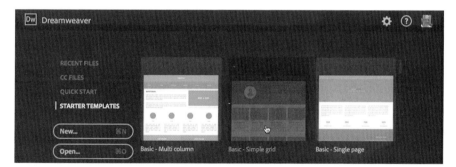

New and Open

The New and Open options enable you to access the New Document and Open dialogs, respectively. Previous users of Dreamweaver may be more comfortable using these options, which open familiar interfaces for creating new or opening existing documents. You can also use the keyboard shortcuts Ctrl+N/Cmd+N and Ctrl+O/Cmd+O.

Show All

When you select the Show All option in the Start Screen, you will see a list of help topics that provide guided tours and video overviews of the program overall as well as a selection of new tools and workflows that you may review. This option is updated dynamically as features are added to Dreamweaver or improved.

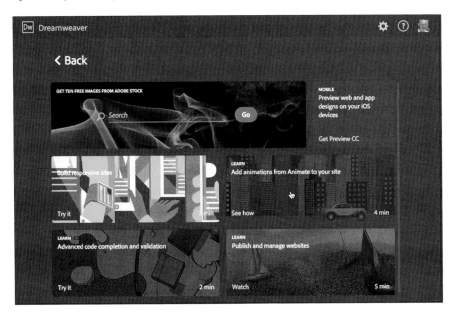

If you do not want to see the Start Screen any more, you can disable it by accessing the option in the General settings in Dreamweaver Preferences and deselecting the checkbox.

Exploring New Feature guides

In Dreamweaver CC, the New Feature guides will pop up from time to time as you access various tools, features, or interface options. The pop-ups will call your attention to new features or workflows that have been added to the program and provide handy tips to help you get the most out of them.

When a tip appears, it may provide more extensive information or a tutorial you can access by following the prompts within the pop-up window. When you are finished, you can then close the pop-up by clicking the Close icon in the upper-right corner of each tip. When you close the tip, it will not appear again. If desired, you can display the tips again by selecting Help > Reset Contextual Feature Tips.

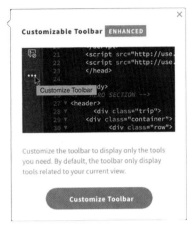

Working with toolbars

Some program features are so handy you may want them available all the time in toolbar form. Two of the toolbars—Document and Standard—appear horizontally at the top of the document window. The Common toolbar, however, appears vertically on the left side of the screen. You can display the desired toolbar by choosing it from the Window menu.

● **Note:** The Common toolbar is visible at all times. To access the other toolbars, you must have a file open. Open **index.html** from the lesson01 folder.

Document toolbar

The document toolbar appears at the top of the program interface and provides onscreen commands for switching views from Live, Design, Code, and Split views.

Document toolbar

Standard toolbar

When activated, the Standard toolbar appears between the Related Files interface and the document window and provides handy commands for various document and editing tasks, such as creating, saving, or opening documents; copying, cutting, and pasting content; and so on. You can display it by selecting Window > Toolbars > Standard.

Standard toolbar

Common toolbar

The Common toolbar was formerly known as the Coding toolbar in previous versions of Dreamweaver. In its old incarnation it appeared only in the Code view window, but now it is firmly ensconced full-time on the left side of the interface. It now provides a variety of tools for working with both code and HTML elements in all document view modes. The toolbar displays six tools by default in Live and Design views. Insert the cursor in the code window and you may see several more.

This toolbar is user customizable. You can add and remove tools by selecting the Customize Toolbar icon ⋯. Be aware that some tools will be displayed and active only when the cursor is active in the Code view window.

Common toolbar and dialog

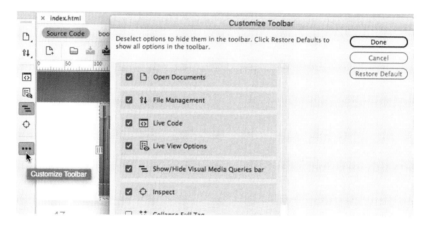

Switching and splitting views

Dreamweaver offers dedicated environments for coders and visual designers.

Code view

Code view focuses the Dreamweaver workspace exclusively on the HTML code and a variety of code-editing productivity tools. To access Code view, click the Code view button in the Document toolbar.

Code view

Design view

Design view shares the document window with Live view and focuses the Dreamweaver workspace on its WYSIWYG editor, which in the past provided a reasonable facsimile of the webpage as it would appear in a browser. However, with the advancements in CSS and HTML, Design view is no longer as WYSIWYG as it once was. Although it can be difficult to use, you'll find it does offer an interface that speeds up the creation and editing of your content. And, at the moment, it's also the only way to access certain Dreamweaver tools or workflows, as you will see in the upcoming lessons.

Design view

To activate Design view, choose it from the Design/Live views drop-down menu in the Document toolbar. Most HTML elements and basic CSS formatting will be rendered properly within Design view, with the major exceptions of CSS3 properties, dynamic content, interactivity such as link behaviors, video, audio, jQuery widgets, and some form elements. This may be the first version of Dreamweaver in which you spend more time in Live view than in Design view.

Live view

Live view is the default workspace of Dreamweaver CC. It speeds up the process of developing modern websites by allowing you to create and edit webpages and web content *visually* in a browser-like environment, and it supports and previews most dynamic effects and interactivity.

Live view

To use Live view, choose it from the Design/Live views drop-down menu in the Document toolbar. When Live view is activated, most HTML content will function as it would in an actual browser, allowing you to preview and test most dynamic applications and behaviors.

In previous versions of Dreamweaver, the content in Live view was not editable. This has all changed. You can edit text, add and delete elements, create classes and ids, and even style elements all in the same window. It's like working on a live webpage right inside Dreamweaver.

Live view is integrally connected to the CSS Designer, allowing you to create and edit advanced CSS styling and build fully responsive webpages without having to switch views or waste time previewing the page in a browser.

Split view

● **Note:** Split view can pair Code view with either Design or Live view.

Split view provides a composite workspace that gives you access to both the design and the code simultaneously. Changes made in either window update in the other in real time.

To access Split view, click the Split view button in the Document toolbar. Dreamweaver splits the workspace horizontally by default. When using Split view, you can display the Code view with either Live or Design view.

Split view (horizontal)

If desired, you can also split the screen vertically by selecting View > Split > Split Vertically. When the window is split, Dreamweaver also gives you options for how the two windows display. You can put the code window on the top, bottom, left, or right. You can even set up two code windows at the same time. You can find all these options in the View menu. Most screen shots in the book that show Split view show Design or Live view at the top or on the right.

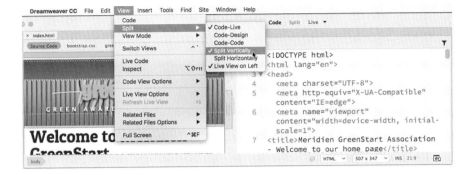

Split view (vertical)

Live Source Code

Live Source Code is an HTML code-troubleshooting display mode available whenever Live view is activated. To access Live Source Code, activate Live view and then click the Live Source Code icon <> in the Common toolbox at the left side of the document window. While active, Live Source Code displays the HTML code as it would appear in a live browser on the Internet and gives you a peek at how the code changes when the visitor interacts with various parts of the page.

● **Note:** If you do not see the Live Source Code icon, you may need to activate it. Select the Customize Toolbar icon in the Common toolbar and activate the Live Source Code tool.

You can see this interaction firsthand by clicking the *Green Events* menu item to open the drop-down menu. In Code view, you will see the class attribute of open is added to the menu interactively. The class is then removed when you close the menu. Without the live source code, you would not be able to see this interaction and behavior.

Live Source Code mode

Be aware that while Live Source Code is active, you will not be able to edit the HTML code, although you can still modify external files, such as linked style sheets. To disable Live Source Code, click the Live Source Code icon <> again to toggle the mode off.

Inspect mode

Inspect mode is a CSS troubleshooting display mode available whenever Live view is activated. It is integrated with the CSS Designer and allows you to rapidly identify CSS styles applied to content within the page by moving the mouse cursor over elements within the webpage. Clicking an element freezes the focus on that item.

The Live view window highlights the targeted element and displays the pertinent CSS rules applied or inherited by that element. You can access Inspect mode at any time by clicking the Live view icon ⊕ whenever an HTML file is open and then clicking the Inspect icon in the Common toolbar.

Inspect mode

Selecting a workspace layout

A quick way to customize the program environment is to use one of the prebuilt workspaces in Dreamweaver. These workspaces have been optimized by experts to put the tools you need at your fingertips.

Dreamweaver CC (2017 release) includes two prebuilt workspaces: Standard and Developer. To access these workspaces, choose them from the Workspace menu located at the upper-right side of the program window.

Standard workspace

The Standard workspace focuses the available screen real estate on the Design and Live view window. Standard is the default workspace for screen shots in this book.

Standard workspace

Developer workspace

Users who work mostly with code will want to use the Developer workspace because it optimizes the panels and windows to provide an effective workspace for coding.

Developer workspace

Working with panels

Although you can access most commands from the menus, Dreamweaver scatters much of its power in user-selectable panels and toolbars. You can display, hide, arrange, and dock panels at will around the screen. You can even move them to a second or third video display if you desire.

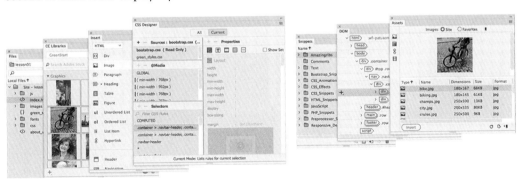

Standard panel grouping

The Window menu lists all the panels available in the program. If you do not see a desired panel on the screen, choose it from the Window menu. A checkmark appears next to its name in the menu to indicate that the panel is open. Occasionally, one panel may lie behind another on the screen and be difficult to locate. In such situations, simply choose the desired panel from the Window menu and the panel will rise to the top of the stack.

Minimizing panels

To create room for other panels or to access obscured areas of the workspace, you can minimize or expand individual panels in place. To minimize a stand-alone panel, double-click the tab containing the panel name. To expand the panel, click the tab once.

Minimizing a panel by double-clicking its tab

You can also minimize one panel within a stack of panels individually by double-clicking its tab. To open the panel, click once on its tab.

Minimizing one panel in a stack using its tab

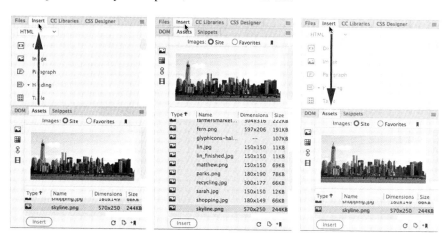

To recover more screen real estate, you can minimize panel groups or stacks down to icons by double-clicking the title bar. You can also minimize the panels to icons by clicking the double-arrow icon in the panel title bar. When panels are minimized to icons, you access any of the individual panels by clicking its icon or button. The selected panel will appear on the left or right of the icon, wherever room permits.

Collapsing a panel to icons or buttons

Closing panels and panel groups

Each panel or panel group may be closed at any time. You can close a panel or panel group in several ways; the method often depends on whether the panel is floating, docked, or grouped with another panel.

To close an individual panel that is docked, right-click in the panel tab and choose Close from the context menu. To close an entire group of panels, right-click any tab in the group and choose Close Tab Group. Both commands are also available from the panel menu.

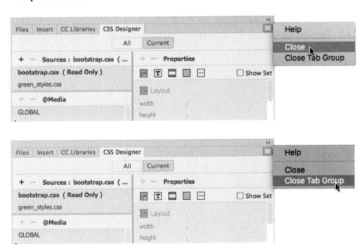

To close a floating panel or panel group, click the Close icon that appears in the left corner of the title bar of the panel or panel group. To reopen a panel, choose the panel name from the Window menu. Reopened panels will sometimes appear undocked. Feel free to dock them as desired.

Dragging

You can reorder a panel tab by dragging it to the desired position within the group.

Dragging a tab to change its position

Floating

A panel that is grouped with other panels can be floated separately. To float a panel, drag it from the group by its tab.

Pulling a panel out by its tab

To reposition floating panels, groups, and stacks in the workspace, simply drag them by the title bar. To pull out a single panel group when it's docked, grab it by the tab bar.

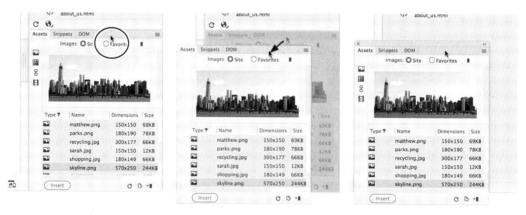

Dragging a whole docked panel group to a new position

Grouping, stacking, and docking

You can create custom groups by dragging one panel into another. When you've moved the panel to the correct position Dreamweaver highlights the area, called the *drop zone*, in blue. Release the mouse button to create the new group.

Creating new groups

In some cases, you may want to keep both panels visible simultaneously. To stack panels, drag the desired tab to the top or bottom of another panel. When you see the blue drop zone appear release the mouse button.

Creating panel stacks

Floating panels can be docked to the right, left, or bottom of the Dreamweaver workspace. To dock a panel, group, or stack, drag its title bar to the edge of the window on which you want to dock. When you see the blue drop zone appear, release the mouse button.

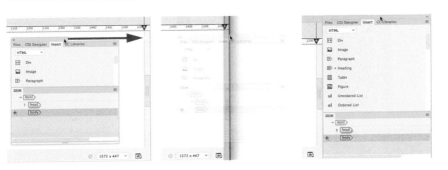

Docking panels

Personalizing Dreamweaver

As you continue to work with Dreamweaver, you'll devise your own optimal work-space of panels and toolbars for each activity. You can store these configurations in a custom workspace of your own naming.

Saving a custom workspace

To save a custom workspace, first create your desired configuration of panels, choose New Workspace from the Workspace menu, and then give it a custom name.

Saving a custom workspace

Working with Extract

Extract is a workflow that allows you to create CSS styles and image assets from a Photoshop-based mock-up. You can create your webpage design using text and linked or embedded image layers and post the file to Creative Cloud, where Dreamweaver can access the styles, colors, and images to help you build your basic site design. Select Window > Extract to access the Extract dialog.

Build your design in Photoshop using text, images, and effects stored in layers.

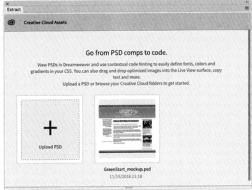

Post your file to your Creative Cloud online folder right inside Dreamweaver.

Access the various layers from the Extract panel inside Dreamweaver, copy styles and text, and even download image assets.

Try these features yourself by uploading **GreenStart_mockup.psd**, in the lesson01 resources folder, to your Creative Cloud account online folder. Go to helpx.adobe.com/creative-cloud/help/sync-files.html to learn how to upload files to your Creative Cloud account.

Creating custom keyboard shortcuts

Another powerful feature of Dreamweaver is the ability to create your own keyboard shortcuts as well as edit existing ones. Keyboard shortcuts are loaded and preserved independently of workspaces.

Is there a command you can't live without that doesn't have a keyboard shortcut or that uses one that's inconvenient? Create one of your own. Try this:

1   Choose Edit > Keyboard Shortcuts (Windows) or Dreamweaver CC > Keyboard Shortcuts (Mac OS).

    You cannot modify the default shortcuts. So, you have to create a list of your own.

2 Click the Duplicate Set icon 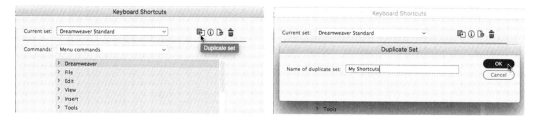 to create a new set of shortcuts.

> **Note:** The default keyboard shortcuts are locked and cannot be edited. But you can duplicate the set, save it under a new name, and modify any shortcut within that custom set.

3 Enter a name in the Name Of Duplicate Set field.
Click OK.

4 Choose Menu Commands from the Commands pop-up menu.

5 In the Commands window, choose File > Save All.

Note that the Save All command does not have an existing shortcut, although you'll use this command frequently in Dreamweaver.

6 Insert the cursor in the Press Key field.
Press Ctrl+Alt+S/Cmd+Opt+S.

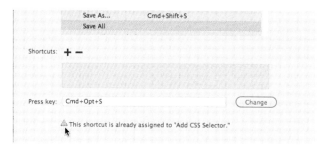

Note the error message indicating that the keyboard combination you chose is already assigned to a command. Although you could reassign the combination, let's choose a different one.

7 Press Ctrl+Alt+Shift+S/Ctrl+Cmd+S.

This combination is not currently being used, so let's assign it to the Save All command.

8 Click the Change button.

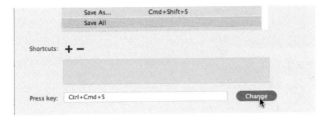

The new shortcut is now assigned to the Save All command.

9 Click OK to save the change.

You have created your own keyboard shortcut—one you can use in upcoming lessons.

Using the Property inspector

One tool vital to your workflow is the Property inspector. The Property inspector no longer appears at the bottom of either of the default workspaces. If it is not visible in your program interface, you can display it by selecting Window > Properties and then dock it to the bottom of the document window as described earlier. The Property inspector is context-driven and adapts to the type of element you select.

Using the HTML tab

Insert the cursor into any text content on your page and the Property inspector provides a means to quickly assign some basic HTML codes and formatting. When the HTML button is selected, you can apply heading or paragraph tags as well as bold, italics, bullets, numbers, and indenting, among other formatting and attributes. The Document Title metadata field is also available in the Property inspector in all views. Enter your desired Document Title in this field, and Dreamweaver adds it automatically to the document <head> section.

HTML Property inspector

Using the CSS tab

Click the CSS button to quickly access commands to assign or edit CSS formatting.

CSS Property inspector

Accessing image properties

Select an image in a webpage to access the image-based attributes and formatting controls of the Property inspector.

Image Property inspector

Accessing table properties

To access table properties, insert your cursor in a table and then click the table tag selector at the bottom of the document window.

Table Property inspector

Using the Related Files interface

Webpages are often built with multiple external files providing styling and programming assistance. Dreamweaver enables you to see all the files linked to, or referenced by, the current document by displaying the filenames in the Related Files interface at the top of the document window. This interface displays the name of any external file and will actually display the contents of each file—if it's available—when you simply select the filename in the display.

The Related Files interface lists all external files linked to a document.

To view the contents of the referenced file, click the name. If you are in Live or Design view, Dreamweaver splits the document window and shows the contents of the selected file in the Code view window. If the file is stored locally, you'll even be able to edit the contents of the file when it's selected.

Use the Related Files interface to edit locally stored files.

To view the HTML code contained within the main document, click the Source Code option in the interface.

Choose the Source Code option to see the contents of the main document.

Using tag selectors

One of the most important features of Dreamweaver is the tag selector interface that appears at the bottom of the document window. This interface displays the tags and element structure in any HTML file pertinent to the insertion point of, or selection by, the cursor. The display of tags is hierarchical, starting at the document root at the left of the display and listing each tag or element in order based on the structure of the page and the selected element.

The display in the tag selector interface mimics the structure of the HTML code based on your selection.

The tag selectors also enable you to select any of the elements displayed by simply clicking a tag. When a tag is selected, all the content and child elements contained within that tag are also selected.

Use the tag selectors to select elements.

The tag selector interface is closely integrated with the CSS Designer panel. You may use the tag selectors to help you style content or to cut, copy, paste, and delete elements.

The tag selector is closely integrated with the styling and editing of elements.

Using the CSS Designer

The CSS Designer is a powerful tool for visually creating, editing, and troubleshooting CSS styling. It allows you to create style sheets, media queries, and CSS rules. It provides hinting for selector creation and allows you to simplify or increase the specificity of a new selector by pressing the up or down arrow. The CSS Designer also enables you to identify the styling of any existing element in a webpage. All you have to do is select the element in the layout and click the Current button at the top of the panel.

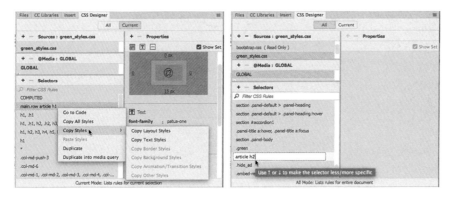

Copy and paste styles from one rule to another (left). Make selectors more or less specific by using the arrow keys (right).

The CSS Designer panel consists of four windows: Sources, @Media, Selectors, and Properties. The panel is responsive. When you widen the panel sufficiently, it will split into two columns as shown.

Sources

The Sources window allows you to create, attach, define, and remove internal embedded and external linked style sheets.

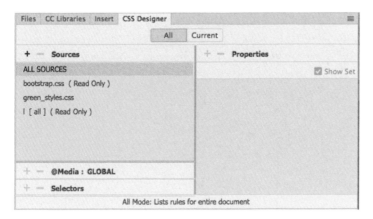

@Media

The @Media window is used to define media queries to support various types of media and devices.

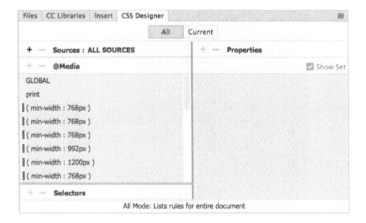

Selectors

The Selectors window is used to create and edit the CSS rules that format the components and content of your page. Once a selector, or rule, is created, you define the formatting you want to apply in the Properties window.

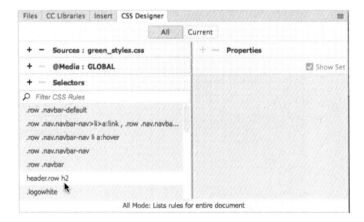

In addition to allowing you to create and edit CSS styling, the CSS Designer can also be used to identify styles already defined and applied and to troubleshoot issues or conflicts with these styles.

Properties

The Properties window features two basic modes. By default, the Properties window displays all available CSS properties in a list, organized in five categories: Layout ⬛, Text **T**, Borders ⬜, Background ▨, and More ⬛. You can scroll down the list and apply styling as desired.

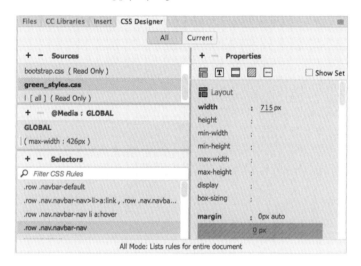

The second mode can be accessed by selecting Show Set at the upper-right corner of the panel. In this mode, the Properties pane will then filter the list to only the properties actually applied to the rule chosen in the Selectors window. In either mode, you can add, edit, or remove style sheets, media queries, rules, and properties.

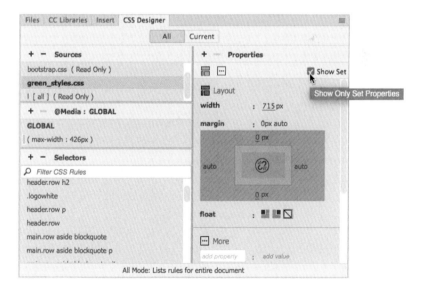

Selecting the Show Set option limits the property display to only the properties that are styled.

The Properties pane also features a COMPUTED option that displays the aggregated list of styles applied to the selected element. The COMPUTED option will appear anytime you select an element or component on the page. When you're creating any type of styling, the code created by Dreamweaver complies with industry standards and best practices.

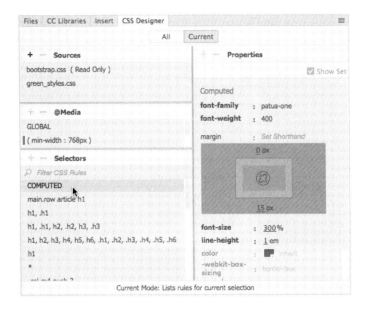

All and Current modes

In Dreamweaver CC (2015.1 release), the CSS Designer gained two additional modes, All and Current, that enable specific functions and workflows within the panel.

When the All button is selected, the panel allows you to create and edit CSS style sheets, media queries, rules, and properties. When the Current button is selected, the CSS troubleshooting functions are enabled, allowing you to inspect individual elements and assess existing styling properties applied to the selected element. In this mode, you are able to edit existing properties, but you're not allowed to add new style sheets, media queries, or rules. This interaction works the same way in all document views.

In addition to using the CSS Designer, you may also create and edit CSS styling manually within Code view while taking advantage of many productivity enhancements, such as code hinting and auto completion.

When the Current button is selected, the CSS Designer displays all styling associated with a selected element.

Using the Visual Media Query interface

The Visual Media Query (VMQ) interface appears above the document window. The VMQ interface allows you to visually inspect and interact with existing media queries, as well as create new ones on the fly using a simple point-and-click interface.

Open any webpage that is formatted by a style sheet with one or more media queries, and the VMQ interface will appear above the document window, displaying color-coded bars that specify the type of media query that has been defined. Media queries using only a max-width specification will be displayed in green. Media queries using only a min-width specification will be displayed in purple. Ones that use both will be displayed in blue. Clicking the Toggle Visual Media Query icon in the Common toolbar turns the VMQ display on and off.

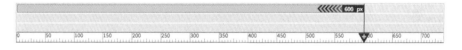

Max-width media query in the VMQ interface

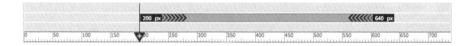

Min-width media query in the VMQ interface

Media using both max-width and min-width specifications

Using the DOM Viewer

The DOM Viewer has been vastly improved in Dreamweaver CC (2017 release). It allows you to view the Document Object Model (DOM) to quickly examine the structure of your webpage and now enables you to interact with it to select, edit, and move existing elements as well as to insert new ones.

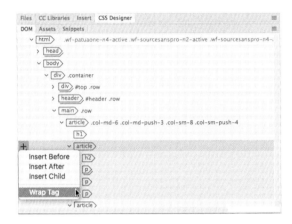

Using the heads-up displays

As Live view becomes the default workspace of Dreamweaver it has driven the development of new methods for editing and managing HTML elements. Dreamweaver CC provides a handful of heads-up displays (HUDs) whenever you select an element or a range of text that give you instant access to important properties and specifications.

Position Assist HUD

The Position Assist HUD appears whenever new elements are being inserted in Live view, using either the Insert menu or the Insert panel. Typically, the Position Assist HUD will offer the options Before, After, Wrap, and Nest. Depending on what type of element is selected and what item is targeted by the cursor, one or more of the options may be grayed out.

The Position Assist HUD allows you to control how elements and components are inserted in Live view.

Element HUD

The Element HUD appears whenever you select an element in Live view. It allows you to add class and id attributes, and by clicking the sandwich icon ▤, access the

Quick Property inspector, which enables you to change the format, add a hyperlink, and apply bold or italic or other styling.

The Element HUD enables you to quickly apply classes, ids, and links, as well as basic formatting.

Image HUD

The Image HUD appears when you select an image in Live view and provides access to the Quick Property Inspector that provides access to image source, alt text, width and height attributes, as well as a field to add a hyperlink.

The Image HUD gives you quick access to basic image attributes and enables you to add hyperlinks.

Text HUD

The Text HUD appears whenever you select a portion of text in Live view. The Text HUD allows you to apply bold <strong>, italic <em>, and hyperlink <a> markup to the selected text. Double-click the text to open the orange editing box. When you select some text, the Text HUD will appear. When you are finished editing the text, click just outside the orange box to complete the changes. Press Esc to cancel the changes and return the text to its previous state.

The Text HUD lets you apply bold, italics, and hyperlink markup to selected text.

Exploring, experimenting, and learning

The Dreamweaver interface has been carefully crafted over many years to make the job of webpage design and development fast and easy. It's a design in progress. It's always changing and evolving. If you think you already know the program, you're wrong. Install the latest version and check it out. Feel free to explore and experiment with various menus, panels, and options to create the ideal workspace and keyboard shortcuts to produce the most productive environment for your own purposes. You'll find the program endlessly adaptable, with power to spare for any task. Enjoy.

Review questions

1 Where can you access the command to display or hide any panel?

2 Where can you find the Code, Split, Design, and Live view buttons?

3 What can be saved in a workspace?

4 Do workspaces also load keyboard shortcuts?

5 What happens in the Property inspector when you insert the cursor into various elements on the webpage?

6 What feature in the CSS Designer makes it easy to build new rules from existing ones?

7 What is the purpose of the DOM Viewer?

8 Does the Element HUD appear in Design or Code views?

Review answers

1 All panels are listed in the Window menu.

2 The Code, Split, Design, and Live view buttons are components of the Document toolbar.

3 Workspaces can save the configuration of the document window, the open panels, and the panels' size and position on the screen.

4 No. Keyboard shortcuts are loaded and preserved independently of a workspace.

5 The Property inspector adapts to the selected element, displaying pertinent information and formatting commands.

6 The CSS Designer allows you to copy and paste styles from one rule to another.

7 The DOM Viewer allows you to visually examine the Document Object Model and select and insert new elements and edit existing ones.

8 No. HUDs are visible only in Live view.

2 HTML BASICS

Lesson overview

In this lesson, you'll familiarize yourself with HTML and learn the following:

- What HTML is and where it came from
- Frequently used HTML tags
- How to insert special characters
- What semantic web design is and why it's important
- New features and capabilities in HTML

 This lesson will take about 25 minutes to complete. This lesson does not have support files.

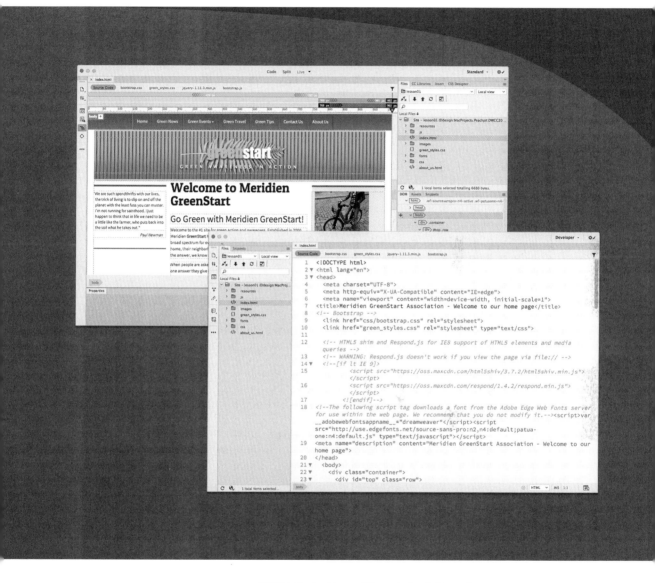

HTML is the backbone of the web, the skeleton of your webpage. Like the bones in your body, it is the structure and substance of the Internet, although it is usually unseen except by the web designer. Without it, the web would not exist. Dreamweaver has many features that help you access, create, and edit HTML code quickly and effectively.

What is HTML?

"What other programs can open a Dreamweaver file?" asked a student in one of my Dreamweaver classes. Although it might seem obvious to an experienced developer, this illustrates a basic problem in teaching and learning web design. Most people confuse the program with the technology. Some may assume that the extension .htm or .html belongs to Dreamweaver or Adobe. This isn't as unusual as it seems. Print designers are used to working with files ending with extensions such as .ai, .psd, .indd, and so on; it's just part of their jobs. They have learned over time that opening these file formats in a different program may produce unacceptable results or even damage the file.

On the other hand, the goal of the web designer is to create a webpage for display in a browser. The power and functionality of the originating program have little bearing on the resulting browser display because the display is completely contingent on the HTML code and how the browser interprets it. Although a program may write good or bad code, it's the browser that does all the hard work.

The web is based primarily on the HyperText Markup Language (HTML). The language and the file format don't belong to any individual program or company. In fact, it is a *non*proprietary, plain-text language that can be edited in any text editor, in any operating system, on any computer. Dreamweaver is, in part, an HTML editor, although it is much more than this. But to maximize the potential of Dreamweaver, it's vital that you have a good understanding of what HTML is and what it can (and can't) do. This lesson is intended as a concise primer on HTML and its capabilities. It will be a helpful foundation for understanding Dreamweaver.

Where did HTML begin?

HTML and the first browser were invented in 1989 by Tim Berners-Lee, a computer scientist working at CERN (Conseil Européen pour la Recherche Nucléaire, which is French for European Council for Nuclear Research), a particle physics laboratory in Geneva, Switzerland. He intended the technology as a means for sharing technical papers and information via the fledgling Internet that existed at the time. He shared his HTML and browser inventions openly as an attempt to get the scientific community at large and others to adopt them and engage in the development themselves. The fact that he did not copyright or try to sell his work started a trend for openness and camaraderie on the web that continues to this day.

CompuServe　　　TOP

```
 1 Instructions/user Information
 2 Find a Topic
 3 Communications/Bulletin Bds.
 4 News/Weather/Sports
 5 Travel
 6 The Electronic MALL/Shopping
 7 Money Matters & Markets
 8 Entertainment/Games
 9 Home/Health/Family
10 Reference/Education
11 Computers and Technology
12 Business/Other Interests

>_
```

The Internet before HTML looked more like MS-DOS or the macOS Terminal application. It had no formatting, no graphics, and no user-definable color.

The language that Berners-Lee created more than 27 years ago was a much simpler construct of what we use now, but HTML is still surprisingly easy to learn and master. At the time of this writing, HTML is now at version 5, officially adopted in October 2014. It consists of more than 120 *tags*, such as html, head, body, h1, p, and so on.

The tag is inserted between less-than (<) and greater-than (>) angle brackets, as in <p>, <h1>, and <table>. These tags are used to identify, or *mark up*, text and graphics to signal the browser to display them in a particular way. HTML code is considered properly *balanced* when the markup features both an opening (<...>) tag and a closing (</...>) tag, such as <h1>...</h1>.

When two matching tags appear this way, they are referred to as an *element*; an element encompasses any contents contained within the two tags, as well. Empty, or *void*, elements, like the horizontal rule, can be written in an abbreviated fashion using only one tag, such as <hr/>, essentially opening and closing the tag at the same time. In HTML5, empty elements can also be validly expressed without the closing slash, such as <hr>. Some web applications require the closing slash, so it's a good idea to check before using one form over the other.

Some elements are used to create page structures, others to structure and format text, and yet others to enable interactivity and programmability. Even though Dreamweaver obviates the need for writing most of the code manually, the ability to read and interpret HTML code is still a recommended skill for any burgeoning web designer. Sometimes it's the only way to find an error in your webpage. The ability to understand and read code may also become an essential skill in other fields as more information and content is created and disseminated via mobile devices and Internet-based resources.

Note: If you are dead set against learning how to read and write good HTML, you should check out Adobe Muse. This program allows you to create professional-looking webpages and complete websites using point-and-click techniques in a graphical user interface similar to Adobe InDesign while never exposing you to the code running behind the scenes.

Basic HTML code structure

Here you see the basic structure of a webpage:

Basic HTML Code Structure

Note: Go to the book's online resources at Peachpit.com for bonus hands-on exercises to gain some vital skills and experience writing and editing HTML code. See the "Getting Started" section at the beginning of the book for more details.

You may be surprised to learn that the text "Welcome to my first webpage" is the only thing from this code that displays in the web browser. The rest of the code creates the page structure and text formatting. Like an iceberg, most of the content of the actual webpage remains out of sight.

Frequently used HTML elements

HTML code elements serve specific purposes. Tags can create distinct objects, apply formatting, identify logical content, or generate interactivity. Tags that make their own space on the screen and stand alone are known as *block* elements; the ones that perform their duties within the flow of another tag are known as *inline* elements. Some elements can also be used to create *structural* relationships within a page, like stacking content in vertical columns or collecting several elements in logical groupings. Structural elements can behave like block or inline elements or do their work while entirely invisible to the user.

HTML tags

Table 2.1 shows some of the most frequently used HTML tags. To get the most out of Dreamweaver and your webpages, it helps to understand the nature of these elements and how they are used. Remember that some tags can serve multiple purposes.

Table 2.1 Frequently used HTML tags

TAG	DESCRIPTION
`<!--...-->`	Comment. Designates an HTML comment. Allows you to add notes within the HTML code that are not displayed within the browser.
`<a>`	Anchor. The basic building block for a hyperlink.
`<blockquote>`	Quotation. Creates a stand-alone, indented paragraph.
`<body>`	Body. Designates the document body. Contains the visible portions of the webpage content.
` `	Break. Inserts a line break without creating a new paragraph.
`<div>`	Division. Divides webpage content into discernible sections.
`<em>`	Emphasis. Adds semantic emphasis. Displays as italics by default in most browsers and readers.
`<form>`	Form. Designates an HTML form. Used for collecting data from users.
`<h1>` to `<h6>`	Headings. Creates headings. Implies semantic value. The default formatting is bold.
`<head>`	Designates the document head. Contains code that performs background functions, such as meta tags, scripts, styling, links, and other information not overtly visible to site visitors.
`<hr>`	Horizontal rule. Empty element that generates a horizontal line.
`<html>`	Root. Root element of most webpages. Contains the entire webpage, except in certain instances where server-based code must load before the opening `<html>` tag.
`<iframe>`	Inline frame. A structural element that can contain another document or load content from another website.
`<img>`	Image. Provides the source reference to display an image.
`<input>`	Input. Element for a form such as a text field.
`<li>`	List item. The content of an HTML list.
`<link>`	Link. Designates the relationship between a document and an external resource.
`<meta>`	Metadata. Additional information provided for search engines or other applications.

TAG	DESCRIPTION
`<ol>`	Ordered list. Defines a numbered list. List items display in a numbered sequence.
`<p>`	Paragraph. Designates a stand-alone paragraph.
`<script>`	Script. Contains scripting elements or points to an internal or external script.
`<span>`	Designates a section within an element. Provides a means to apply special formatting or emphasis to a portion of an element.
`<strong>`	Strong. Adds semantic emphasis. Displays as bold by default in most browsers and readers.
`<style>`	Style. Embedded or inline reference for Cascading Style Sheets (CSS) styling.
`<table>`	Table. Designates an HTML table.
`<td>`	Table data. Designates a table cell.
`<textarea>`	Text area. Designates a multiline text input element for a form.
`<th>`	Table header. Identifies a cell as containing a header.
`<title>`	Title. Contains the metadata title reference for the current page. Typically displayed in the browser tab or title bar.
`<tr>`	Table row. Structural element that delineates one row of a table from another.
`<ul>`	Unordered list. Defines a bulleted list. List items display with bullets by default.

HTML character entities

Text content is normally entered via a computer keyboard. But many characters don't appear on a typical 101-key input device. If a symbol can't be entered directly from the keyboard, it can be inserted within the HTML code by typing the name or numeric value referred to as an *entity*. Entities exist for every letter and character that can be displayed. Table 2.2 lists some popular entities.

⬤ **Note:** Some entities can be created using either a name or a number, as in the copyright symbol, but named entities may not work in all browsers or applications. So either stick to numbered entities or test the specific named entities before you use them.

Table 2.2 HTML character entities

CHARACTER	DESCRIPTION	NAME	NUMBER
©	Copyright	&copy;	&#169;
®	Registered trademark	&reg;	&#174;
™	Trademark		&#153;
•	Bullet		&#149;
–	En dash		&#150;
—	Em dash		&#151;
	Nonbreaking space		

Go to www.w3schools.com/html/html_entities.asp to see a complete list of entities with descriptions.

What's new in HTML5

Every new version of HTML has made changes to both the number and purpose of the tags that make up the language. HTML 4.01 consisted of approximately 90 tags. HTML5 has removed some of those HTML 4 tags from its specification altogether, and some new ones have been adopted or proposed.

Changes to the list usually revolve around supporting new technologies or different types of content models, as well as removing features that were bad ideas or ones infrequently used. Some changes simply reflect customs or techniques that have been popularized within the developer community over time. Other changes have been made to simplify the way code is created to make it easier to write and faster to disseminate.

HTML5 tags

Table 2.3 shows some of the important new tags in HTML5. The specification features nearly 50 new tags in total, while at least 30 old tags were deprecated. As you move through the exercises of this book, you will learn how to use many of these new HTML5 tags, as appropriate, to help you understand their intended role on the web. Take a few moments to familiarize yourself with these tags and their descriptions.

Table 2.3 Important new HTML5 tags

TAG	DESCRIPTION
`<article>`	Designates independent, self-contained content, which can be distributed independently from the rest of the site.
`<aside>`	Designates sidebar content that is related to the surrounding content.
`<audio>`	Designates multimedia content, sounds, music, or other audio streams.
`<canvas>`	Designates graphics content created using a script.
`<figure>`	Designates a section of stand-alone content containing an image or video.
`<figcaption>`	Designates a caption for a `<figure>` element.
`<footer>`	Designates a footer of a document or section.
`<header>`	Designates the introduction of a document or section.
`<hgroup>`	Designates a set of <h1> to <h6> elements when a heading has multiple levels.
`<main>`	Designates the main content of the webpage. This element must be unique to the document.
`<nav>`	Designates a section of navigation.
`<picture>`	Designates one or more resources for a webpage image to support the various resolutions available on smartphones and other mobile devices. This is a new tag that may not be supported in older browsers or devices.
`<section>`	Designates a section in a document.
`<source>`	Designates media resources for video or audio elements. Multiple sources can be defined for browsers that do not support the default file type.
`<video>`	Designates video content, such as a movie clip or other video streams.

Go to www.w3schools.com/tags/default.asp to see the complete list of HTML5 elements.

Semantic web design

Many of the changes to HTML were made to support the concept of *semantic web design*. This movement has important ramifications for the future of HTML, its usability, and the interoperability of websites on the Internet. At the moment, each webpage stands alone on the web. The content may link to other pages and sites, but there's really no way to combine or collect the information available on multiple pages or multiple sites in a coherent manner. Search engines do their best to index the content that appears on every site, but much of it is lost because of the nature and structure of old HTML code.

HTML was initially designed as a presentation language. In other words, it was intended to display technical documents in a browser in a readable and predictable manner. If you look carefully at the original specifications of HTML, it looks like a list of items you would put in a college research paper: headings, paragraphs, quoted material, tables, numbered and bulleted lists, and so on.

The element list in the first version of HTML basically identified how the content would be displayed. These tags did not convey any intrinsic meaning or significance. For example, using a heading tag displayed a particular line of text in bold, but it didn't tell you what relationship the heading had to the text that followed or to the story as a whole. Is it a title or merely a subheading?

HTML5 has added a significant number of new tags to help us add semantic meaning to our markup. Semantic tags, such as `<header>`, `<footer>`, `<article>`, and `<section>`, allow you for the first time to identify specific content without having to resort to additional attributes. The result is simpler code and less of it. But most of all, the addition of semantic meaning to your code allows you and other developers to connect the content from one page to another in new and exciting ways—many of which haven't even been invented yet. It's truly a work in progress.

New techniques and technology

HTML5 has also revisited the basic nature of the language to take back some of the functions that over the years have been increasingly handled by third-party plug-in applications and programming.

If you are new to web design, this transition will be painless because you have nothing to relearn and no bad habits to break. If you already have experience building webpages and applications, this book will guide you safely through some of these waters and introduce the new technologies and techniques in a logical and straightforward way. But either way, you don't have to trash all your old sites and rebuild everything from scratch.

Valid HTML 4 code will remain valid for the foreseeable future. HTML5 was intended to make web design easier by allowing you to do more with less work. So let's get started!

See www.w3.org/TR/2014/WD-html5-20140617 to learn more about HTML5.

See www.w3.org to learn more about HTML.

Review questions

1 What programs can open HTML files?

2 What does a markup language do?

3 HTML is composed of how many code elements?

4 What are the three main parts of most webpages?

5 What is the difference between block and inline elements?

6 What is the current version of HTML?

Review answers

1 HTML is a plain-text language that can be opened and edited in any text editor and viewed in any web browser.

2 A markup language places tags contained within brackets, as in < >, around plain-text content to pass information concerning structure and formatting from one application to another.

3 HTML5 contains more than 100 tags.

4 Most webpages are composed of three main sections: root, head, and body.

5 A block element creates a stand-alone element. An inline element can exist within another element.

6 HTML5 was formally adopted at the end of 2014. However, full support may take several more years. And, as with HTML 4, some browsers and devices may support the specification in differing ways.

3 CSS BASICS

Lesson overview

In this lesson, you'll familiarize yourself with CSS and learn the following:

- CSS (cascading style sheets) terms and terminology
- The difference between HTML and CSS formatting
- How the cascade, inheritance, descendant, and specificity theories affect the way browsers apply CSS formatting
- New features and capabilities of CSS3

 This lesson will take about 1 hour and 15 minutes to complete. If you have not already done so, download the project files for this lesson from the Lesson & Update Files tab on your Account page at www.peachpit.com, store them on your computer in a convenient location, and define a new site in Dreamweaver based on this folder, as described in the "Getting Started" section at the beginning of this book. Your Account page is also where you'll find any updates to the chapters or to the lesson files. Look on the Lesson & Update Files tab to access the most current content.

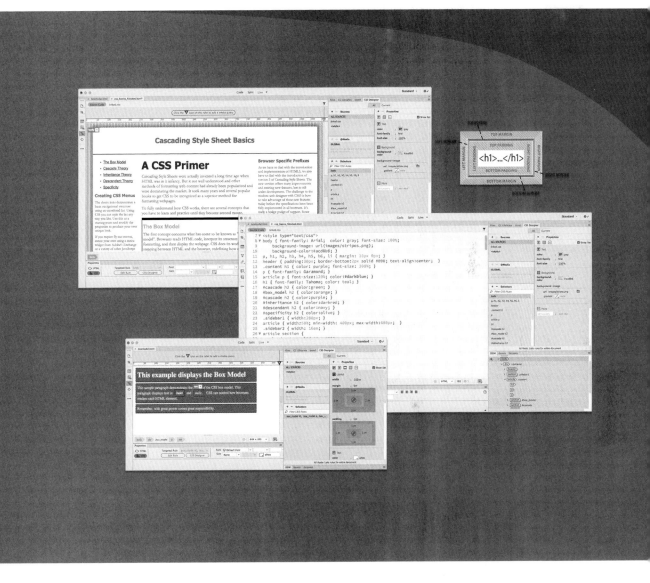

Cascading style sheets control the look and feel of a webpage. The language and syntax of CSS is complex, powerful, and endlessly adaptable. It takes time and dedication to learn and years to master, but a modern web designer can't live without it.

What is CSS?

Note: We removed much of the hands-on exercises and moved them to an online bonus lesson. Go to the book's online resources at Peachpit.com for bonus hands-on exercises to gain some vital skills and experience writing and editing CSS code. See the "Getting Started" section at the beginning of the book for more details.

HTML was never intended to be a design medium. Other than allowing for bold and italic, version 1 lacked a standardized way to load fonts or even format text. Formatting commands were added along the way—up to version 3 of HTML— to address these limitations, but these changes still weren't enough. Designers resorted to various tricks to produce the desired results. For example, they used HTML tables to simulate multicolumn and complex layouts for text and graphics, and they used images when they wanted to display typefaces other than Times or Helvetica.

HTML-based formatting was so misguided a concept that it was deprecated from the language less than a year after it was formally adopted in favor of cascading style sheets. CSS avoids all the problems of HTML formatting, while saving time and money too. Using CSS lets you strip the HTML code down to its essential content and structure and then apply the formatting separately, so you can more easily tailor the webpage to specific devices and applications.

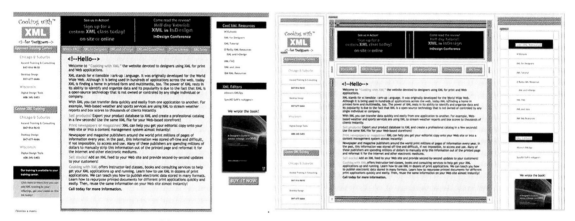

By adding cell padding and margins to the table structure in Dreamweaver (left), you can see how this webpage relies on tables and images to produce the final design (right).

HTML vs. CSS formatting

When comparing HTML-based formatting to CSS-based formatting, it's easy to see how CSS produces vast efficiencies in time and effort. In the following exercise, you'll explore the power and efficacy of CSS by editing two webpages, one formatted by HTML and the other by CSS.

Note: To save ink, screen shots in this and all subsequent lessons will be taken using a UI Brightness of 1.0 and the Light code-coloring theme. You are free to use the default dark UI and code theme if you prefer, or any custom setting. The program and lessons will perform identically in any UI color settings.

1 Launch Dreamweaver CC 2017 or later, if it's not currently running.

2 Create a new site based on the lesson03 folder, using instructions in the "Getting Started" section at the beginning of the book. Name the site **lesson03**.

3 Choose File > Open.

4 Navigate to the lesson03 folder, and open **html_formatting.html**.

5 Click the Split view button. If necessary, choose View > Split > Split Vertically to split the Code and Live view windows vertically, side by side.

Each element of the content is formatted individually using the deprecated `<font>` tag. Note the attribute `color="blue"` in each `<h1>` and `<p>` element.

⬤ **Note:** *Deprecated* means that the tag has been removed from future support in HTML but may still be honored by current browsers and HTML readers.

6 Replace the word `"blue"` with `"green"` in each line in which it appears. If necessary, click in the Live view window to update the display.

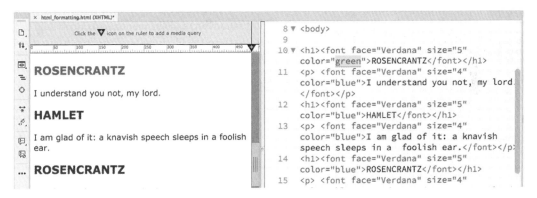

The text displays in green now in each line where you changed the color value. As you can see, formatting using the obsolete `<font>` tag is not only slow but prone to error. Make a mistake, like typing `greeen` or `geen`, and the browser will ignore the color formatting entirely.

7 Open **css_formatting.html** from the lesson03 folder.

8 If it's not currently selected, click the Split view button.

The content of the file is identical to the previous document, except that it's formatted using CSS. The code that formats the HTML elements appears in the `<head>` section of this file. Note that the code contains only two `color:blue;` attributes.

9 In the code h1 { color: blue; } select the word blue and type green to replace it. If necessary, click in the Live view window to update the display.

> **Note:** Dreamweaver usually defaults to Live view when you open or create a new page. If not, you can select it from the Document toolbar using the Live/Design drop-down menu.

In Live view, all the heading elements display in green. The paragraph elements remain blue.

10 Select the word blue in the code p { color: blue; } and type green to replace it. Click in the Live view window to update the display.

In Live view, all the paragraph elements have changed to green.

11 Close all files and do not save the changes.

> **Note:** To get a fuller appreciation of the power and capabilities of CSS, check out the hands-on, online CSS bonus lesson included with the book's lesson files. See the "Getting Started" section at the beginning of this book for details on how to download the bonus lessons.

In this exercise, CSS accomplished the color change with two simple edits, whereas the HTML <font> tag required you to edit every line. Now think how tedious it would be to go through thousands of lines of code and hundreds of pages on a site to make such a change. Is there any wonder why the W3C, the web standards organization that establishes Internet specifications and protocols, deprecated the <font> tag and developed cascading style sheets? This exercise highlights just a small sample of the formatting power and productivity enhancements offered by CSS unmatched by HTML alone.

HTML defaults

Since the beginning of the language, HTML tags came right out of the box with one or more default formats, characteristics, or behaviors. So, even if you did nothing, much of your text would already be formatted in a certain way in most browsers. One of the essential tasks in mastering CSS is learning and understanding these defaults and how they may affect your content. Let's take a look.

1. Open **html_defaults.html** from the lesson03 folder. If necessary, select Live view to preview the contents of the file.

    The file contains a range of HTML headings and text elements. Each element visually exhibits basic styling for traits such as size, font, and spacing, among others.

2. Switch to Split view. If necessary, choose View > Split > Split Vertically to split the Code and Live view windows side by side. In the Code view window, locate the <head> section and try to identify any code that may be formatting the HTML elements.

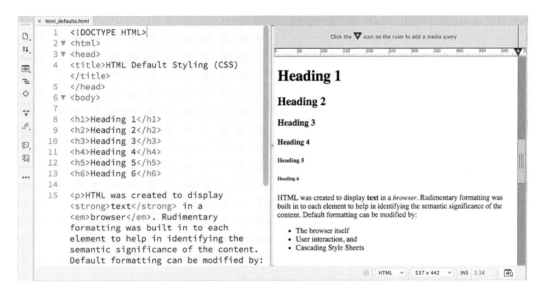

● **Note:** The Code and Live view windows can be swapped from top to bottom and left to right by selecting the option under the View menu. See Lesson 1, "Customizing Your Workspace," for more information.

A quick look will tell you that there is no overt styling information in the file, yet the text still displays different kinds of formatting. So where does the formatting come from? And, more importantly, what are the settings being used?

The answer is: It depends. In the past, HTML 4 elements drew characteristics from multiple sources. The first place to look is to the W3C. It created a default style sheet, which you can find at www.w3.org/TR/CSS21/sample.html. The style sheet defines the standard formatting and behaviors of all HTML elements. The browser vendors used this style sheet to base their default rendering of HTML elements. But that was before HTML5.

HTML5 defaults?

The last decade has seen a consistent movement on the web to separate "content" from its "styling." At the time of this writing, the concept of "default" formatting in HTML seems to be dead. According to specifications adopted by the W3C in 2014, there are no default styling standards for HTML5 elements. If you look for a default style sheet for HTML5 on w3.org—like the one noted for HTML 4—you won't find one. At the moment, there are no public moves to change this relationship, and browser manufacturers are still honoring and applying HTML 4 default styling to HTML5-based webpages. Confused? Join the club.

Note: If the current trends continue, the lack of an HTML5 default style sheet makes the development of your own site standards even more important.

The ramifications could be dramatic and wide-reaching. Someday, in the not too distant future, HTML elements may not display any formatting at all by default. That means understanding how elements are currently formatted is more important than ever so that you will be ready to develop your own standards if or when the need arises.

To save time and give you a bit of a head start, I pulled together Table 3.1, which contains some of the most common defaults:

Table 3.1 Common HTML defaults

ITEM	DESCRIPTION
Background	In most browsers, the page background color is white. The background of the elements <div>, <table>, <td>, <th>, and most other tags is transparent.
Headings	Headings <h1> through <h6> are bold and align to the left. The six heading tags apply differing font size attributes, with <h1> the largest and <h6> the smallest. Apparent sizes may vary between browsers.
Body text	Outside of a table cell, paragraphs—<p>, <li>, <dd>, <dt>—align to the left and start at the top of the page.
Table cell text	Text within table cells, <td>, aligns horizontally to the left and vertically to the center.
Table header	Text within header cells, <th>, aligns horizontally and vertically to the center (this is not standard across all browsers).
Fonts	Text color is black. The default typeface and font are specified and supplied by the browser, which in turn can be overridden by the user using the preference settings in the browser itself.
Margins	Spacing external to the element border/boundary is handled by margins. Many HTML elements feature some form of margin spacing. Margins are often used to insert additional space between paragraphs and to indent text, as in lists and block quotes.
Padding	Spacing within the box border is handled by padding. According to the default HTML 4 style sheet, no elements feature default padding.

Browser antics

The next task in developing your own styling standards is to identify the browser (and its version) that is displaying the HTML. That's because browsers frequently differ (sometimes dramatically) in the way they interpret, or render, HTML elements and CSS formatting. Unfortunately, even different versions of the same browser can produce wide variations from identical code.

Web design best practices dictate that you build and test your webpages to make sure they work properly in the browsers employed by the majority of web users in general—but especially the browsers preferred by your own visitors. The break-down of browsers used by your own visitors can differ quite a bit from the norm. They also change over time, especially now as more and more people abandon desktop computers in favor of tablets and smartphones. In August 2016, the W3C published the following statistics identifying the most popular browsers:

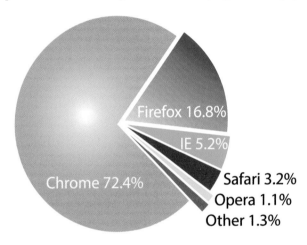

Although it's nice to know which browsers are the most popular among the general public, it's crucial that before you build and test your pages you identify the browsers your target audience uses.

Although this chart shows the basic breakdown in the browser world, it obscures the fact that multiple versions of each browser are still being used. This is impor-tant to know because older browser versions are less likely to support the latest HTML and CSS features and effects. To make matters more complicated, these statistics show trends for the Internet overall, but the statistics for your own site may vary wildly.

As HTML5 becomes more widely supported, the inconsistencies will fade, although they may never go away. Some aspects of HTML 4 and CSS 1 and 2 are still not universally agreed on to this day. It's vital that any styling or structure be tested carefully.

CSS box model

Browsers normally read the HTML code, interpret its structure and formatting, and then display the webpage. CSS does its work by stepping between HTML and the browser, redefining how each element should be rendered. It imposes an imaginary box around each element and then enables you to format almost every aspect of how that box and its contents are displayed.

The box model is a programmatic construct imposed by HTML and CSS that enables you to format, or redefine, the default settings of any HTML element.

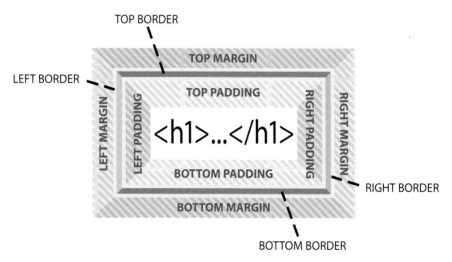

CSS permits you to specify fonts, line spacing, colors, borders, background shading and graphics, margins, and padding, among other things. Most of the time these boxes are invisible, and although CSS gives you the ability to format them, it doesn't require you to do so.

1 Launch Dreamweaver CC 2017 or later, if necessary.
   Open **boxmodel.html** from the lesson03 folder.

2 If necessary, click the Split view button to divide the workspace between the Code view and Live view windows.

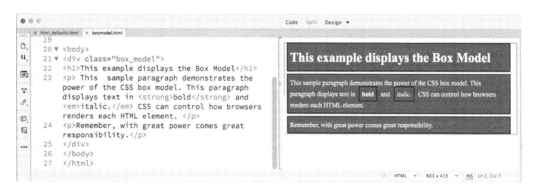

The file's sample HTML code contains a heading and two paragraphs with sample text formatted to illustrate some of the properties of the CSS box model. The text displays visible borders, background colors, margins, and padding. To see the real power of CSS, sometimes it's helpful to see what the page would look like without CSS.

3   Switch to Design view.

Choose View > Design View Options > Style Rendering > Display Styles to disable style rendering.

Note: The style rendering command is available only in Design view.

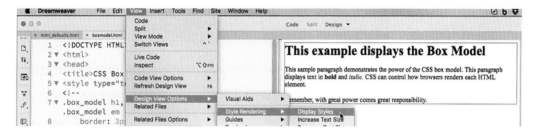

Dreamweaver now displays the page without any applied styling. A basic tenet in web standards today is the separation of the *content* (text, images, lists, and so on) from its *presentation* (formatting). Although the text now is not wholly unformatted, it's easy to see the power of CSS to transform HTML code. Whether formatted or not, this illustrates the importance of the structure and *quality* of your content. Will people still be enthralled by your website if all the wonderful formatting were pulled away?

4   Choose View > Design View Options > Style Rendering > Display Styles to enable the CSS rendering in Dreamweaver again.

5   Close all files and do not save changes.

The working specifications at www.w3.org/TR/css3-box describe how the box model is supposed to render documents in various media.

Applying CSS styling

You can apply CSS formatting in three ways: *inline* (on the element itself), *embedded* (in an internal style sheet), or *linked* (via an external style sheet). A CSS formatting instruction is known as a *rule*. A rule consists of two parts—a *selector* and one or more *declarations*. The selector specifies what element, or combination of elements, is to be formatted; declarations contain the styling information. CSS rules can redefine any existing HTML element, as well as define two custom element modifiers, named *class* and *id*.

A rule can also combine selectors to target multiple elements at once or to target specific instances within a page where elements appear in unique ways, such as when one element is nested within another.

These sample rules demonstrate some typical constructions used in selectors and declarations. The way the selector is written determines how the styling is applied and how the rules interact with one another.

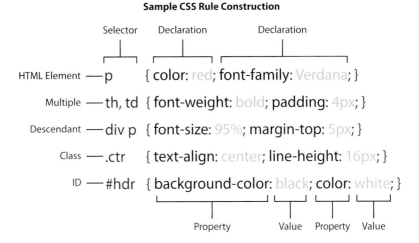

Applying a CSS rule is not a simple matter of selecting some text and applying a paragraph or character style, as in Adobe InDesign or Adobe Illustrator. CSS rules can affect single words, paragraphs of text, or combinations of text and objects. A single rule can affect an entire webpage, a single paragraph, or just a few words or letters. Basically, anything that has an HTML tag on it can be styled, and there is even an HTML tag specifically intended to style content that has no tag.

Many factors come into play when determining how a CSS rule performs its job. To help you better understand how it all works, the following sections illustrate four main CSS concepts, which I like to refer to as theories: cascade, inheritance, descendant, and specificity.

Note: I call them "theories" because they explain what is supposed to happen but may not in all cases, because of hardware or software inconsistencies in some browsers or devices.

Cascade theory

The cascade theory describes how the order and placement of rules in the style sheet or on the page affects the application of styling. In other words, if two rules conflict, which one wins out?

Take a look at the following rules that might appear in a style sheet:

```
p { color: red; }
p { color: blue; }
```

Both rules apply text color to the paragraph <p> tag. Since they are identical, they both cannot win. According to the cascade theory, the rule declared last, or closest to the HTML code, wins. The text would appear in blue.

CSS rule syntax: write or wrong

CSS is a powerful adjunct to HTML. It has the power to style and format any HTML element, but the language is sensitive to even the smallest typo or syntax error. Miss a period, comma, or semicolon and you may as well have left the code out of your page entirely. An error in one rule may cancel all the styling in subsequent rules or the entire style sheet.

For example, take the following simple rule:

```
p { padding: 1px;
    margin: 10px; }
```

It applies both padding and margins to the paragraph <p> element.

This rule can also be written properly without spacing as follows:

```
p{padding:1px;margin:10px;}
```

The spaces and line breaks used in the first example are unnecessary, merely accommodations for the humans who may write and read the code. Removing excess spacing is known as *minification* and is often used to optimize style sheets. Browsers and other applications processing the code do not need this extra space, but the same cannot be said of the various punctuation marks sprinkled throughout the CSS.

Use parentheses, ( ), or brackets, [ ], instead of braces, { }, and the rule (and perhaps your entire style sheet) is useless. The same goes for the use of colons, :, and semicolons, ;, in the code.

Can you catch the error in each of the following sample rules?

```
p { padding; 1px: margin; 10px: }
p { padding: 1px; margin: 10px; ]
p { padding 1px, margin 10px, }
```

Similar problems can arise in the construction of compound selectors too. For example, putting a space in the wrong place can change the meaning of a selector entirely.

The rule `article.content { color: #F00 }` formats the <article> element and all its children in this code structure:

```
<article class="content"><p>...</p></article>
```

On the other hand, the rule `article .content { color: #F00 }` would ignore the previous HTML structure altogether and format only the <p> element in the following code:

```
<article class="content"><p class="content">...</p></article>
```

A tiny error can have dramatic and far-reaching repercussions. To keep their CSS and HTML functioning properly, good web designers keep their eyes peeled for any little error, misplaced space, or punctuation mark. As you work through the following exercises, keep a careful eye on all the code for any similar errors. As mentioned in the "Getting Started" section at the beginning of this book, some instructions in this book may omit an expected period or other punctuation in a sentence on purpose when including it might cause confusion or possible code errors.

When you try to determine which CSS rule will be honored and which formatting will be applied, browsers typically honor the following order of hierarchy, with the fourth one being the most powerful:

1. Browser defaults.

2. External or embedded style sheets. If both are present, the one declared last supersedes the earlier entry in conflicts.

3. Inline styles (within the HTML element itself).

4. Styles with the value attribute `!important` applied.

Inheritance theory

The inheritance theory describes how an element can be affected by one or more rules at the same time. Inheritance can affect rules of the same name as well as rules that format parent elements—ones that contain other elements. Take a look at the following code:

```
<article>
    <h1>Pellentesque habitant</h1>
    <p>Vestibulum tortor quam</p>
    <h2>Aenean ultricies mi vitae</h2>
    <p>Mauris placerat eleifend leo.</p>
    <h3>Aliquam erat volutpat</h3>
    <p>Praesent dapibus, neque id cursus.</p>
</article>
```

The code contains various headings and paragraph elements and one parent element `<article>` that contains them all. If you wanted to apply blue to all the text, you could use the following set of CSS rules:

```
h1 { color: blue;}
h2 { color: blue;}
h3 { color: blue;}
p { color: blue;}
```

That's a lot of code all saying the same thing, something most web designers typically want to avoid. This is where inheritance comes into play to save time and effort. Using inheritance, you can replace all four lines of code with the following:

```
article { color: blue;}
```

That's because all the headings and paragraphs are children of the `article` element; they each inherit the styling applied to their parent, as long as there are no other rules overriding it. Inheritance can be of real assistance in economizing on the amount of code you have to write to style your pages. But it's a two-edged sword. As much as you can use it to style elements intentionally, you also have to keep an eye out for unintentional effects.

Descendant theory

Inheritance provides a means to apply styling to multiple elements at once, but CSS also provides the means to target styling to specific elements.

The descendant theory describes how formatting can target specific elements based on their position relative to other elements. This technique involves the creation of a selector name that identifies a specific element, or elements, by combining multiple tags and, in some cases, id and class attributes.

Take a look at the following code:

```
<section><p>The sky is blue</p></section>
<div><p>The forest is green.</p></div>
```

Notice how both paragraphs contain no intrinsic formatting or special attributes, although they do appear in different parent elements. Let's say you wanted to apply blue to the first line and green to the second. You would not be able to do this using a single rule targeting the <p> tag alone. But it's a simple matter using descendant selectors, like these:

```
section p { color: blue;}
div p { color: green;}
```

See how two tags are combined in each selector? The selectors identify a specific kind of element structure to format. One targets p tags that are children of `section` elements, the other children of `div` elements. It's not unusual to combine multiple tags within a selector to tightly control how the styling is applied.

In recent years, a set of special characters has been developed to hone this technique to a fine edge. Check out www.w3schools.com/cssref/css_selectors.asp to see the full set of special selector characters and how to use them. But be careful using these special characters. Many of them were only added in the last few years and still have limited support.

Specificity theory

Conflicts between two or more rules are the bane of most web designers' existence and can waste hours of time in troubleshooting CSS formatting errors. In the past, designers would have to spend hours manually scanning style sheets and rules one by one trying to track down the source of styling errors.

Specificity describes how browsers determine what formatting to apply when two or more rules conflict. Some refer to this as *weight*—giving certain rules higher priority based on order (cascade), proximity, inheritance, and descendant relationships. One way to make it easier to understand a selector weight is by giving numeric values to each component in the name.

For example, each HTML tag gets 1 point, each class gets 10 points, each id gets 100 points, and inline style attributes get 1000 points. By adding up the component values within each selector, its specificity can be calculated and compared to another, and the higher specific weight wins.

Calculating specificity

Can you do the math? Look at the following list of selectors and see how they add up. Look through the list of rules appearing in the sample files in this lesson. Can you determine the weight of each of those selectors and figure out which rule is more specific on sight?

```
* (wildcard)  { } 0 + 0 + 0 + 0     =     0 points
h1            { } 0 + 0 + 0 + 1     =     1 point
ul li         { } 0 + 0 + 0 + 2     =     2 points
.class        { } 0 + 0 + 10 + 0    =    10 points
.class h1     { } 0 + 0 + 10 + 1    =    11 points
a:hover       { } 0 + 0 + 10 + 1    =    11 points
#id           { } 0 + 100 + 0 + 0   =   100 points
#id.class     { } 0 + 100 + 10 + 0  =   110 points
#id.class h1  { } 0 + 100 + 10 + 1  =   111 points
style=" "     { } 1000 + 0 + 0 + 0  =  1000 points
```

As you have learned in this lesson, CSS rules often don't work alone. They may style more than one HTML element at a time and may overlap or inherit styling from one another. Each of the theories described so far has a role to play in how CSS styling is applied through your webpage and across your site. When the style sheet is loaded, the browser will use the following hierarchy—with the fourth one being the most powerful—to determine how the styles are applied, especially when rules conflict:

1. Cascade

2. Inheritance

3. Descendant structure

4. Specificity

Of course, knowing this hierarchy doesn't help much when you are faced with a CSS conflict on a page with dozens or perhaps hundreds of rules and multiple style sheets. Luckily, Dreamweaver has several tools that can help you in this endeavor. The first one we'll look at is named Code Navigator.

Code Navigator

Code Navigator is a tool within Dreamweaver that allows you to instantly inspect an HTML element and assess its CSS-based formatting. When activated, it displays all the embedded and externally linked CSS rules that have some role in formatting a selected element, and it lists them in the order of their cascade application and specificity. Code Navigator works in all Dreamweaver-based document views.

1 If necessary, open **css_basics_finished.html** from the lesson03 folder.

2 Switch to Split view, if necessary.

Depending on the size of your computer display, you may want to split the screen horizontally to see the width of the entire page.

3 Select View > Split > Split Horizontally.

The screen shot shows the Live view window on top.

4 In Split view, observe the CSS code and the structure of the HTML content. Then, note the appearance of the text in the Live view window.

The page contains headings, paragraphs, and lists in various HTML5 structural elements, such as `article`, `section`, and `aside`, styled by CSS rules appearing in the `<head>` section of the code.

5 In Live view, insert the cursor into the heading "A CSS Primer".
Press Ctrl+Alt+N/Cmd+Opt+N.

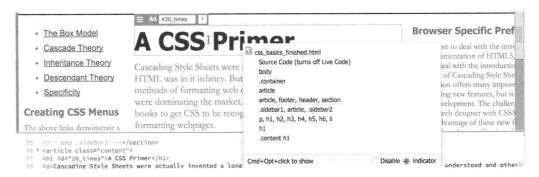

A small window appears, displaying a list of eight CSS rules that apply to this heading. This is how you access Code Navigator in Live view. You can also right-click any element and select Code Navigator from the Context menu.

If you position the pointer over each rule in turn, Dreamweaver displays any properties formatted by the rule and their values. The rule with the highest specificity (most powerful) is at the bottom of the list.

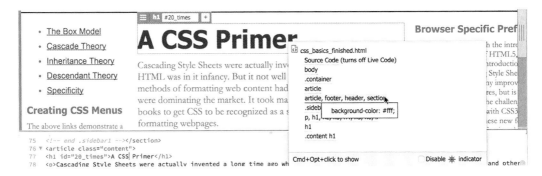

Unfortunately, Code Navigator doesn't show styling applied via inline styles, so you'll have to check for these types of properties separately and calculate the effect of inline styles in your head. Otherwise, the sequence of rules in the list indicates both their cascade order and their specificity.

When rules conflict, rules farther down in the list override rules that are higher up. Remember that elements may inherit or combine styling from one or more rules, and default styling—that which is not overridden—may still play a role in the final presentation. Unfortunately, Code Navigator doesn't show what, if any, default styling characteristics may still be in effect.

The .content h1 rule appears at the bottom of the Code Navigator window, indicating that its specifications are the most powerful ones styling this element. But many factors can influence which of the rules may win. Sometimes the specificity of two rules is identical; then, it's simply the order (cascade) in which rules are declared in the style sheet that determines which one is actually applied.

As described earlier, changing the order of rules can often affect how the rules work. There's a simple exercise you can perform to determine whether a rule is winning because of cascade or specificity.

6 In the Code view window, click the line number for the .content h1 rule.

7 Press Ctrl+X/Cmd+X to cut the line.

8 Insert the cursor at the beginning of the style sheet (line 8).
Press Ctrl+V/Cmd+V to paste the line at the top of style sheet.

9 Click in the Live view window to refresh the display, if necessary.

The styling did not change.

10 Insert the pointer into the text of the heading "A CSS Primer" and activate Code Navigator as you did in step 5 or by right-clicking on the element.

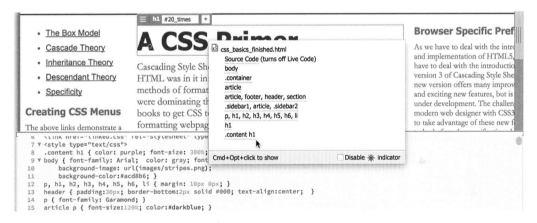

Although the rule was moved to the top of the style sheet—the weakest position—the order of the rules in Code Navigator did not change. In this case, the cascade was not responsible for the power of the rule. The .content h1 selector has a specificity higher than either the body or h1 selector. In this instance, it would win no matter where it was placed in the code. But its specificity can change by simply modifying the selector.

11 Select and delete the .content class notation from the .content h1 selector.

⬤ **Note:** Don't forget to delete the leading period indicating the class name.

▶ **Tip:** Code Navigator may be disabled by default. To have it display automatically, deselect the Disable option in the Code Navigator window when it's visible.

12 Click in the Live view window to refresh the display, if necessary.

Did you notice how the styling changed? The "A CSS Primer" heading reverted to the color teal, and the other h1 headings scaled to 300 percent. Do you know why this happened?

13 Insert the pointer in the "A CSS Primer" heading and activate Code Navigator.

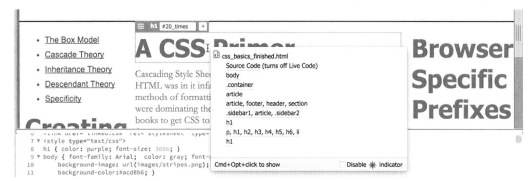

Code Navigator shows two h1 rules styling the headings. By removing the class notation from the selector, the rule you edited now has equal value to the other h1 rule, but since it is the first one declared, it loses precedence by virtue of its cascade position.

14 Using Code Navigator, examine and compare the rules applied to the headings "A CSS Primer" and "Creating CSS Menus."

Code Navigator shows the same rules applied to both.

By removing the .content class from the selector, the rule no longer targets only h1 headings in the <article class="content"> element; it's now styling all h1 elements on the page.

15 Choose Edit > Undo to restore the .content class to the h1 selector. Refresh the Live view display.

All the headings return to their previous styling.

16 Insert the pointer in the heading "Creating CSS Menus" and activate Code Navigator.

The heading is no longer styled by the `.content h1` rule.

17 Choose File > Save All.

Is it starting to make more sense? If not, it will—over time. Until then, just remember that the rule appearing last in Code Navigator has the most influence on any particular element.

● **Note:** Code Navigator doesn't display inline CSS rules. Since most CSS styling is not applied this way, it's not much of a limitation, but you should still be aware of this blind spot if you work with Code Navigator.

CSS Designer

Code Navigator was introduced in Dreamweaver CS4 and has been an invaluable aid for troubleshooting CSS formatting. Yet the latest tool in Dreamweaver's CSS arsenal is much more than a good troubleshooting aid. CSS Designer not only displays all the rules that pertain to any selected element but also allows you to create and edit CSS rules at the same time.

When you use Code Navigator, it shows you the relative importance of each rule, but you still have to assess the effect of all the rules to determine the final result. Since some elements can be affected by a dozen or more rules, this can be a daunting task for even a veteran web coder. CSS Designer eliminates this pressure altogether by providing a Properties window that computes the final CSS display for you. Best of all, unlike Code Navigator, CSS Designer can even compute the effects of inline styles.

1 Open **css_basics_finished.html** in Split view.

2 If necessary, choose Window > CSS Designer to display the panel.

The CSS Designer panel features four windows: Sources, @Media, Selectors, and Properties. Feel free to adjust the heights and widths of the windows as needed. The panel is also responsive: It will even take advantage of any extra screen space by splitting into two columns if you drag out the edge.

3 Select or insert the cursor in the heading "A CSS Primer."

The CSS Designer has two basic modes: *All* and *Current*. When the All mode is engaged, the panel allows you to review and edit all existing CSS rules and create new rules. In Current mode, the panel allows you to identify and edit the rules and styling already applied to a selected element.

4 If necessary, click the Current button in the CSS Designer panel.

When the Current mode is active, the panel displays the CSS rules that are affecting the heading. In the CSS Designer, the most powerful rules appear at the top of the Selectors window, the opposite of Code Navigator.

5 Click the rule `.content h1` in the Selectors panel.

By default, the Properties window of CSS Designer lists the properties you can style for this element. The list is not exhaustive, but it contains most of the properties you will need.

Showing a seemingly endless list of properties can be confusing as well as inefficient. For one thing, it makes it difficult to differentiate the properties assigned from those that aren't. Luckily, CSS Designer allows you to limit the display to only the properties currently applied to the selected element.

6 Click the Show Set option in the CSS Designer panel menu to enable it, if necessary.

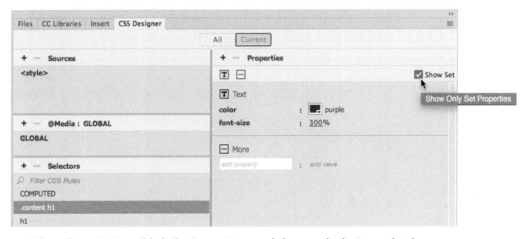

When Show Set is enabled, the Properties panel shows only the items that have been set in that rule.

7 Select each rule that appears in the Selectors window and observe the properties of each. To see the expected result of all the rules combined, select the COMPUTED option.

The COMPUTED option analyzes all the CSS rules affecting the element and generates a list of properties that should be displayed by browsers or HTML readers. By displaying a list of pertinent CSS rules and then computing how the CSS should render, CSS Designer does Code Navigator one step better. But it doesn't stop there. Although Code Navigator allows you to select a rule and then edit it in Code view, CSS Designer lets you edit the CSS properties right inside the panel itself. Best of all, CSS Designer can compute *and* edit inline styles too.

8 Select COMPUTED in the Selectors window.

In the Properties window, select the `color` property `purple`.

Enter **red** in the field and press Enter/Return to complete the change.

> **Tip:** Double-click to edit the text-based color name. You can also select colors by using the color picker.

The heading displays in red. What you may not have noticed is that the change you made was entered directly in the rule that contributed the styling in the first place.

9 In the Code view window, scroll to the embedded style sheet and examine the `.content h1` rule.

As you can see, the color was changed within the code and added to the proper rule.

10 Save all files.

CSS Designer is like an amalgam of Code Navigator and Dreamweaver's old CSS Styles panel. In upcoming exercises, you'll get the chance to experience all aspects of CSS Designer as you learn more about cascading style sheets.

Multiples, classes, and ids, oh my!

By taking advantage of the cascade, inheritance, descendant, and specificity theories, you can target formatting to almost any element anywhere on a webpage. But CSS offers a few more ways to optimize and customize the formatting and increase your productivity even further.

Applying formatting to multiple elements

To speed things up, CSS allows you to apply formatting to multiple elements at once by listing each in the selector, separated by commas. For example, the formatting in these rules:

```
h1 { font-family:Verdana; color:gray; }
h2 { font-family:Verdana; color:gray; }
h3 { font-family:Verdana; color:gray; }
```

can also be expressed like this:

```
h1, h2, h3 { font-family:Verdana; color:gray; }
```

Using CSS shorthand

Although Dreamweaver will write most of the CSS rules and properties for you, at times you will want, or need, to write your own. All properties can be written out fully, but many can also be written using a shorthand method. Shorthand does more than make the job of the web designer easier; it reduces the total amount of code that has to be downloaded and processed. For example, when all properties of margins or padding are identical, such as:

```
margin-top:10px;
margin-right:10px;
margin-bottom:10px;
margin-left:10px;
```

the rule can be shortened to `margin:10px;`

When the top and bottom and left and right margins or padding are identical, like this:

```
margin-top:0px;
margin-right:10px;
margin-bottom:0px;
margin-left:10px;
```

it can be shortened to `margin:0px 10px;`

But even when all four properties are different, like this:

```
margin-top:20px;
margin-right:15px;
margin-bottom:10px;
margin-left:5px;
```

● **Note:** Shorthand specifications are entered in clockwise fashion starting with the top property.

they can still be shortened to `margin:20px 15px 10px 5px;`

In these three examples, you can see clearly how much code can be saved using shorthand. There are way too many references and shorthand techniques to cover here. Check out http://tinyurl.com/shorten-CSS to get a full description.

Throughout the book I'll use common shorthand expressions wherever possible; see if you can identify them as we go.

Creating class attributes

So far, you've learned that you can create CSS rules that format specific HTML elements and ones that can target specific HTML element structures or relationships. In some instances, you may want to apply unique formatting to an element that is already formatted by one or more existing rules. To accomplish this, CSS allows you to make your own custom class and id attributes.

Class attributes may be applied to any number of elements on a page, whereas id attributes can appear only once per page. If you are a print designer, think of classes as being similar to a combination of Adobe InDesign's paragraph, character, table, and object styles all rolled into one. Class and id names can be a single word, an abbreviation, any combination of letters and numbers, or almost anything, but they may not contain spaces. In HTML 4, ids could not start with a number, although there doesn't seem to be any similar restrictions in HTML5. For backward compatibility you should probably avoid starting class and id names with numbers.

Although there's no strict rule or guideline on how to create them, classes should be more general in nature, and ids should be more specific. Everyone seems to have an opinion, but at the moment there is no absolutely right or wrong answer. However, most agree that they should be descriptive, such as `"co-address"` or `"author-bio"` as opposed to `"left-column"` or `"big-text"`. This will especially help to improve your site analytics. The more sense Google and other search engines can make of your site's structure and organization, the higher your site will rank in the search results.

To declare a CSS class selector, insert a period before the name within the style sheet, like this:

```
.content
.sidebar1
```

Then, apply the CSS class to an entire HTML element as an attribute, like this:

```
<p class="intro">Type intro text here.</p>
```

or to individual characters or words using the `<span>` tag, like this:

```
<p>Here is <span class="copyright">some text formatted
differently</span>.</p>
```

Creating id attributes

Note: The use of id attributes has changed dramatically with the introduction of HTML5 semantic elements. Although they can still be used for the purposes of styling content, most designers and developers are using them more for site navigation.

HTML designates id as a unique attribute. Therefore, any id should be assigned to no more than one element per page. In the past, many web designers used id attributes to style or identify specific components within the page, such as the header, the footer, or specific articles. With the advent of HTML5 elements—header, footer, aside, article, and so on—the use of id and class attributes for this purpose became less necessary. But ids can still be used to identify specific text elements, images, and tables to assist you in building powerful hypertext navigation within your page and site. You will learn more about using ids this way in Lesson 12, "Working with Navigation."

To declare an id attribute in a CSS style sheet, insert a number sign, or hash mark, before the name, like this:

```
#cascade
#box_model
```

Here's how you apply the CSS `id` to an entire HTML element as an attribute:

```
<div id="cascade">Content goes here.</div>
<div id="box_model">Content goes here.</div>
```

or to a portion of an element:

```
<p>Here is <span id="copyright">some text</span> formatted
differently.</p>
```

CSS3 features and effects

CSS3 has more than two dozen new features. Many have already been implemented in all the modern browsers and can be used today; others are still experimental and are supported less fully. Among the new features, you will find

- Rounded corners and border effects
- Box and text shadows
- Transparency and translucency
- Gradient fills
- Multicolumn text elements

You can implement all these features and more via Dreamweaver. To give you a quick tour of some of the coolest features and effects brewing, I've provided a sample of CSS3 styling in a separate file.

1   Open **css3_demo.html** from the lesson03 folder.
    Display the file in Split view and observe the CSS and HTML code.

    Some of the new effects can't be previewed directly in Design view. You'll need to use Live view or a browser to get the full effect.

2   If necessary, activate Live view to preview all the CSS3 effects.

The file contains a hodgepodge of features and effects that may surprise and even delight you—but don't get too excited. Although many of these features are already supported in Dreamweaver and will work fine in modern browsers, there's still a lot of older hardware and software out there that can turn your dream site into a nightmare. And there's at least one additional twist.

Some of the new CSS3 features have not been standardized, and certain browsers may not recognize the default markup generated by Dreamweaver. In these instances, you may have to include specific vendor commands to make them work properly, such as -ms-, -moz-, and -webkit-. If you look carefully in the code of the demo file, you'll be able to find examples of these within the CSS markup. Can you think of ways for using some of these effects in your own pages?

CSS3 overview and support

The Internet doesn't stand still for long. Technologies and standards are evolving and changing constantly. The members of the W3C have been working diligently to adapt the web to the latest realities, such as powerful mobile devices, large flat-panel displays, and HD images and video—all of which seem to get better and cheaper every day. This is the urgency that currently drove the development of HTML5 and CSS3.

Many of these new standards have not been officially defined yet, and browser vendors are implementing them in varying ways. But don't worry. The latest version of Dreamweaver has been updated to take advantage of the latest changes, and it provides many new features based on these evolving standards. This includes ample support for the current mix of HTML5 elements and CSS3 formatting. As new features and capabilities are developed, you can count on Adobe to add them to the program as quickly as possible using Creative Cloud.

As you work through the lessons that follow, you will be introduced to and actually implement many of these new and exciting techniques in your own sample pages.

Additional CSS support

CSS formatting and application is so complex and powerful that this short lesson can't cover all aspects of the subject. For a full examination of CSS, check out the following books:

- *Bulletproof Web Design: Improving Flexibility and Protecting Against Worst-Case Scenarios with HTML5 and CSS3 (3rd Edition)*, Dan Cederholm (New Riders Press, 2012) ISBN: 978-0-321-80835-6

- *CSS3: The Missing Manual (4th Edition)*, David Sawyer McFarland (O'Reilly Media, 2015) ISBN: 978-1-491-91805-0

- *HTML and CSS: Visual QuickStart Guide (8th Edition)*, Elizabeth Castro and Bruce Hyslop (Peachpit Press, 2014) ISBN: 978-0-321-92883-2

- *Stylin' with CSS: A Designer's Guide (3rd Edition)*, Charles Wyke-Smith (New Riders Press, 2012) ISBN: 978-0-321-85847-4

Review questions

1 Should you use HTML-based formatting?

2 What does CSS impose on each HTML element?

3 True or false? If you do nothing, HTML elements will feature no formatting or structure.

4 What four "theories" affect the application of CSS formatting?

5 True or false? CSS3 features are all experimental, and you shouldn't use them at all.

Review answers

1 No. HTML-based formatting was deprecated in 1997 when HTML 4 was adopted. Industry best practices recommend using CSS-based formatting instead.

2 CSS imposes an imaginary box on each element. This box, and its content, can then be styled with borders, background colors and images, margins, padding, and other types of formatting.

3 False. Even if you do nothing, many HTML elements feature default formatting.

4 The four theories that affect CSS formatting are cascade, inheritance, descendant, and specificity.

5 False. Many CSS3 features are already supported by modern browsers and can be used right now.

4 WEB DESIGN BASICS

Lesson overview

In this lesson, you'll learn the following:

- The basics of webpage design
- How to create page thumbnails and wireframes
- How to use Adobe Photoshop to generate site image assets automatically

 This lesson will take about 30 minutes to complete. If you have not already done so, download the project files for this lesson from the Lesson & Update Files tab on your Account page at www.peachpit.com, store them on your computer in a convenient location, and define a new site in Dreamweaver based on this folder, as described in the "Getting Started" section at the beginning of this book. Your Account page is also where you'll find any updates to the chapters or to the lesson files. Look on the Lesson & Update Files tab to access the most current content.

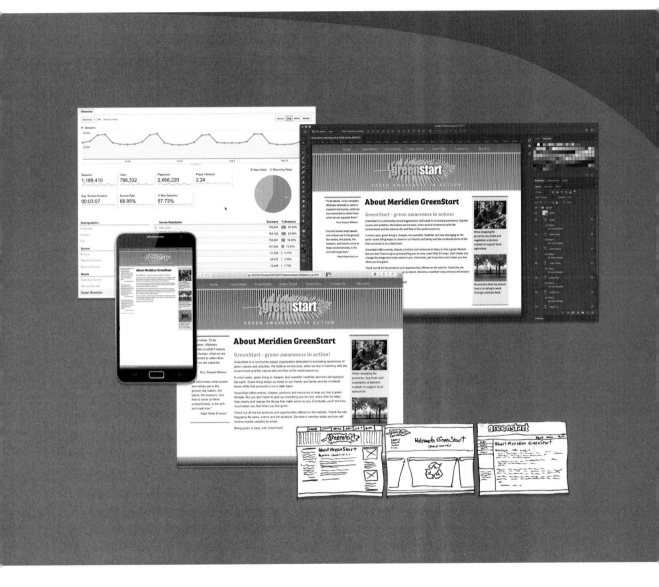

Whether you use thumbnails and wireframes, Photoshop, or just a vivid imagination, Dreamweaver can quickly turn your design concepts into complete, standards-based CSS layouts.

Developing a new website

Before you begin any web design project for yourself or for a client, you need to answer three important questions:

- What is the purpose of the website?
- Who is the audience?
- How do they get here?

What is the purpose of the website?

Will the website sell or support a product or service? Is your site for entertainment or games? Will you provide information or news? Will you need a shopping cart or database? Do you need to accept credit card payments or electronic transfers? Knowing the purpose of the website tells you what type of content you'll be developing and working with and what types of technologies you'll need to incorporate.

Who is the audience?

Is the audience adults, children, seniors, professionals, hobbyists, men, women, everyone? Knowing *who* your audience will be is vital to the overall design and functionality of your site. A site intended for children probably needs more animation, interactivity, and bright, engaging colors. Adults will want serious content and in-depth analysis. Seniors may need larger type and other accessibility enhancements.

A good first step is to check out the competition. Is there an existing website performing the same service or selling the same product? Are they successful? You don't have to mimic others just because they're doing the same thing. Look at Google and Yahoo—they perform the same basic service, but their site designs couldn't be more different from one another.

How do they get here?

This sounds like an odd question when speaking of the Internet. But just as with a brick-and-mortar business, your online customers can come to you in a variety of ways. For example, are they accessing your site on a desktop computer, laptop, tablet, or cellphone? Are they using high-speed Internet, wireless, or dial-up service? What browser are they most likely to use, and what is the size and resolution of the display? These answers will tell you a lot about what kind of experience your customers will expect. Dial-up and cellphone users may not want to see a lot of graphics or video, whereas users with large flat-panel displays and high-speed connections may demand as much bang and sizzle as you can send at them.

So where do you get this information? Some you'll have to get through painstaking research and demographic analysis. Some you'll get from educated guesses based on your own tastes and understanding of your market. But a lot of it is actually available on the Internet itself. W3Schools, for one, keeps track of tons of statistics regarding access and usage, all updated regularly:

- http://w3schools.com/browsers/default.asp provides information about browser statistics.

- http://w3schools.com/browsers/browsers_os.asp gives the breakdown on operating systems. In 2011, W3Schools started to track the usage of mobile devices on the Internet.

- http://w3schools.com/browsers/browsers_display.asp lets you find out the latest information on the resolution, or size, of screens using the Internet.

If you are redesigning an existing site, your web-hosting service itself may provide valuable statistics on historical traffic patterns and even the visitors themselves. If you host your own site, you can incorporate third-party tools, such as Google Analytics and Adobe Omniture, into your code to do the tracking for you for free or for a small fee.

As of the fall of 2016, Windows still dominates the Internet (80 to 85 percent), with most users favoring Google Chrome (73 percent), followed by Firefox (16 percent), with various versions of Internet Explorer (5 percent) a distant third. The vast majority of browsers (99 percent) are set to a resolution higher than 1024 pixels by 768 pixels. If it weren't for the rapid growth in usage of tablets and smartphones for accessing the Internet, these statistics would be great news for most web designers and developers. But designing a website that can look good and work effectively for both flat-panel displays and cellphones is a tall order.

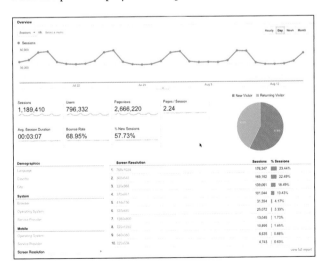

Analytics provides comprehensive statistics on the visitors to your site. Google Analytics, pictured here, is a popular choice.

Responsive web design

Each day, more people are using cellphones and other mobile devices to access the Internet. Some people may use them to access the Internet more frequently than they use desktop computers. This presents a few nagging challenges to web designers. For one thing, cellphone screens are a fraction of the size of even the smallest flat-panel display. How do you cram a two- or three-column page design into a meager 300 to 400 pixels? Another problem is that mobile device manufacturers have dropped support for Flash-based content on their devices.

Until the last few years, web design usually required that you target an optimum size (height and width in pixels) for a webpage and then build the entire site on these specifications. Today, that scenario is becoming a rare occurrence. Now, you are presented with the decision to build a site that either can scale to any size display (responsive) or can morph to support a few target display types for desktop and mobile users (adaptive).

Your own decision will be based in part on the content you want to provide and on the capabilities of the devices accessing your pages. Building an attractive website that supports video, audio, and other dynamic content is hard enough without throwing in a panoply of different display sizes and device capabilities. The term *responsive web design* was coined, in a book of the same name (2011), by a Boston-based web developer named Ethan Marcotte. In it he describes the notion of designing pages that can adapt to multiple screen dimensions automatically. As you work through the following lessons, you will learn many techniques for responsive web design and implement them in your site and asset design.

Many of the concepts of print design are not applicable to the web, because you are not in control of the user's experience. For example, print designers know in advance the page size for which they are designing. The printed page doesn't change when you rotate it from portrait to landscape. On the other hand, a page carefully designed for a typical flat panel is basically useless on a cellphone.

Scenario

For the purposes of this book, you'll be working to develop a website for Meridien GreenStart, a fictitious community-based organization dedicated to green investment and action. This website will offer a variety of products and services and require a broad range of webpage types, including dynamic pages using technologies such as jQuery, which is a form of JavaScript.

Your customers come from a wide demographic that includes all ages and educational levels. They are people who are concerned about environmental conditions and who are dedicated to conservation, recycling, and the reuse of natural and human resources.

Your marketing research indicates that most of your customers use desktop computers or laptops, connecting via high-speed Internet services. You can expect to get 20 to 30 percent of your visitors exclusively via cellphone and other mobile devices, and much of the rest will be using mobile from time to time.

To simplify the process of learning Dreamweaver, we'll focus on creating a fixed-width desktop site design first. In Lesson 7, "Designing for Mobile Devices," you'll learn how to adapt your fixed-width design to work with smartphones and tablets.

Working with thumbnails and wireframes

After you have nailed down the answers to the three questions about your website purpose, customer demographic, and access model, the next step is to determine how many pages you'll need, what they will do, and what they will look like.

Creating thumbnails

Many web designers start by drawing thumbnails with pencil and paper. Think of thumbnails as a graphical shopping list of the pages you'll need to create for the website. Thumbnails can help you work out the basic navigation structure for the site. Draw lines between the thumbnails showing how navigation will connect them.

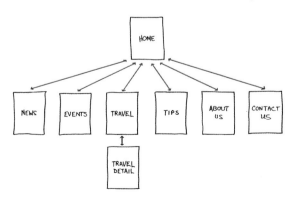

Thumbnails list the pages that need to be built and how they are connected to each other.

Most sites are divided into levels. Typically, the first level includes all the pages in your main navigation menu—the ones a visitor can reach directly from the home page. The second level includes pages you can reach only through specific actions or from specific locations, say from a shopping cart or product detail page.

Creating a page design

Once you've figured out what your site needs in terms of pages, products, and services, you can then turn to what those pages will look like. Make a list of components you want or need on each page, such as headers and footers, navigation, and areas for the main content and the sidebars (if any). Put aside any items that won't be needed on every page. What other factors do you need to consider? If mobile devices are going to be an important consideration of your design identity, will any of the components be required or optional for these devices? Although many components can be simply resized for mobile screens, some will have to be completely redesigned or reimagined.

Identifying the essential components for each page helps you create a page design and structure that will meet your needs.

1. Header (includes banner and logo)
2. Footer (copyright info)
3. Horizontal navigation (for internal reference, i.e., Home, About Us, Contact Us)
4. Main content (one-column with chance of two or more)

Do you have a company logo, business identity, graphic imagery, or color scheme you want to match or complement? Do you have publications, brochures, or current advertising campaigns you want to emulate? It helps to gather them all in one place so you can see everything all at once on a desk or conference table. If you're lucky, a theme will rise organically from this collection.

Desktop or mobile

Once you've created your checklist of the components that you'll need on each page, sketch out several rough layouts that work for these components. Depending on your target visitor demographics, you may decide to focus on a design that's optimized for desktop computers or one that works best on tablets and smartphones.

Most designers settle on one basic page design that is a compromise between flexibility and sizzle. Some site designs may naturally lean toward using more than one basic layout. But resist the urge to design each page separately. Minimizing the number of page designs may sound like a major limitation, but it's key to producing a professional-looking site that's easy to manage. It's the reason why some professionals, such as doctors and airline pilots, wear uniforms. Using a consistent page design, or template, conveys a sense of professionalism and confidence to your visitor. While you're figuring out what your pages will look like, you'll have to address the size and placement of the basic components. Where you put a component can drastically affect its impact and usefulness.

In print, designers know that the upper-left corner of a layout is considered one of the "power positions," a place where you want to locate important aspects of a design, such as a logo or title. This is because in western culture we read from left to right, top to bottom. The second power position is the lower-right corner, because this is the last thing your eyes will see when you're finished reading.

Unfortunately, in web design this theory doesn't hold up for one simple reason: You can never be certain how the user is seeing your design. Are they on a 20-inch flat panel or a 3-inch wide smartphone?

In most instances, the only thing you can be certain of is that the user can see the upper-left corner of any page. Do you want to waste this position by slapping the company logo here? Or make the site more useful by slipping in a navigational menu? This is one of the key predicaments of the web designer. Do you go for design sizzle, workable utility, or something in between?

Creating wireframes

After you pick the winning design, wireframing is a fast way to work out the structure of each page in the site. A wireframe is like a thumbnail, but bigger, that sketches out each page and fills in more details about the components, such as actual link names and main headings, but with minimal design or styling. This step helps to anticipate problems before you smack into them when working in code.

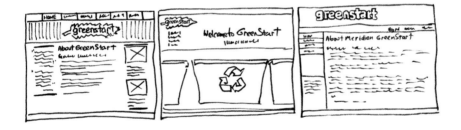

Wireframes allow you to experiment with page designs quickly and easily without wasting time with code.

Once the basic concepts are worked out, many designers take an extra step and create a full-size mock-up or "proof of concept" using a program like Photoshop or even Adobe Illustrator. It's a handy thing to do because you'll find that some clients just aren't comfortable giving an approval based only on pencil sketches. The advantage here is that all these programs allow you to export the results to full-size images (JPEG, GIF, or PNG) that can be viewed in a browser as if they were finished webpages. Such mock-ups are as good as seeing the real thing but may take only a fraction of the time to produce.

The wireframe for the final design should identify all components and include specific information about content, color, and dimensions.

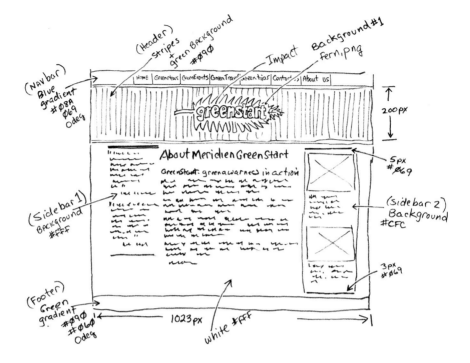

To demonstrate how a graphics program could be used to build such a mock-up, I created a sample webpage layout using Photoshop and saved it into the Lesson 4 resources folder. Let's take a look.

1   Launch Photoshop CC or higher.

2   Open **GreenStart_mockup.psd** from the lesson04/resources folder.

The Photoshop file contains a complete mock-up of the GreenStart site design, which is composed of various vector-based design components as well as image assets stored in separate layers. Note the use of colors and gradients in the design.

In addition to creating graphical mock-ups, Photoshop has tricks geared specifically for web designers. So you can see these features firsthand, I've provided a bonus online lesson where you can learn how to use Photoshop to create your web image assets from this file. Check out the "Getting Started" section at the beginning of the book to learn how to access the bonus lesson.

Note: You should be able to open this file with any version of Photoshop CC or higher. Be aware if you use a version different from the one pictured, the panels and menu options may appear different.

Note: The mock-up uses fonts from Typekit, Adobe's online font service. To view the final design properly in Photoshop, you will need to download and install these fonts. Typekit fonts are included in your subscription to Creative Cloud.

Review questions

1 What three questions should you ask before starting any web design project?

2 What is the purpose of using thumbnails and wireframes?

3 Why is it important to create a design that takes into account smartphones and tablets?

4 What is responsive design, and why should Dreamweaver users be aware of it?

5 Why would you use Photoshop, Illustrator, or other programs, like Adobe Fireworks to design a website?

Review answers

1 What is the purpose of the website? Who is the audience? How did they get here? These questions, and their answers, are essential in helping you develop the design, content, and strategy of your site.

2 Thumbnails and wireframes are quick techniques for roughing out the design and structure of your site without having to waste lots of time coding sample pages.

3 Mobile device users are one of the fastest-growing demographics on the web. Many visitors will use a mobile device to access your website on a regular basis or exclusively. Webpages designed for desktop computers often display poorly on mobile devices, making the websites difficult or impossible to use for these mobile visitors.

4 Responsive design is a method for making the most effective use of a webpage, and its content, by designing it to adapt to various types of displays and devices automatically.

5 Using Photoshop, Illustrator, or Fireworks, you can produce page designs and mock-ups much faster than when designing in code with Dreamweaver. Designs can even be exported as web-compatible graphics that can be viewed in a browser to get client approval.

5 CREATING A PAGE LAYOUT

Lesson overview

In this lesson, you'll learn how to do the following:

- Examine the chosen page design and evaluate the use of the predefined layouts provided by Dreamweaver.

- Work with the Visual Media Query interface.

- Create a new layout using the BootStrap framework.

- Modify the layout structure to use HTML5 semantic elements.

 This lesson will take about 90 minutes to complete. If you have not already done so, download the project files for this lesson from the Lesson & Update Files tab on your Account page at www.peachpit.com, store them on your computer in a convenient location, and define a new site in Dreamweaver based on this folder, as described in the "Getting Started" section at the beginning of this book. Your Account page is also where you'll find any updates to the chapters or to the lesson files. Look on the Lesson & Update Files tab to access the most current content.

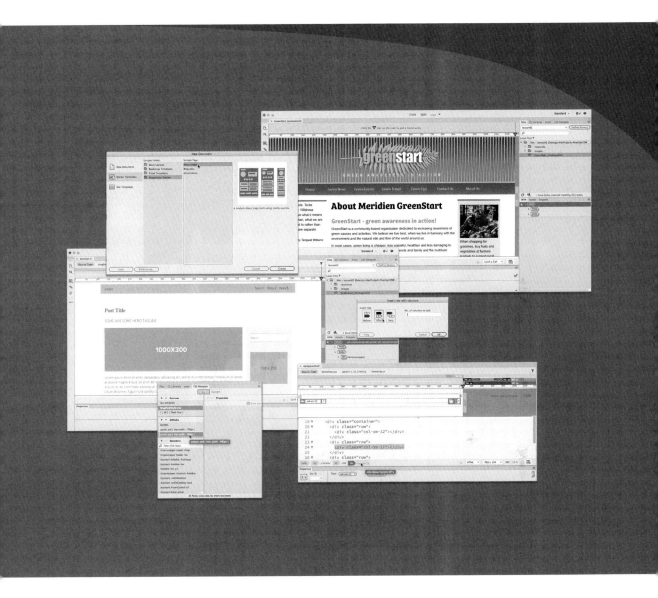

Whether you are designing a single page or an entire website, Dreamweaver provides all the tools you need to complete the project on time and under budget.

Evaluating page design options

In the previous lesson, you went through the process of identifying the pages, components, and structures you would need for a specific website. The selected design balances those needs against a variety of other factors, such as the types of visitors that may come to the site and their means of connecting to it. In this lesson, you will learn how to break down a graphical mock-up into actual HTML structures and components and then build that basic layout in code.

Since there are almost unlimited ways to build a particular design, we'll concentrate on building a simple structure that uses the minimum number of HTML5 semantic elements. This will produce a page design that will be the easiest to implement and maintain.

Let's start by taking a look at the mock-up created in Lesson 4.

1 Open **GreenStart_mockup.html** from the lesson05 folder.

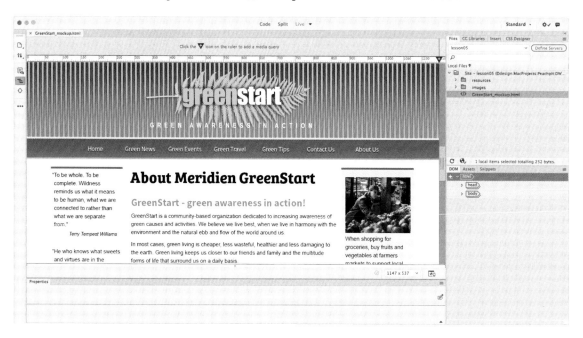

This file contains an image depicting the final mock-up of the GreenStart site design. The design can be broken down into basic components, such as header, footer, navigation, main, and sidebar content elements. If you diagrammed this scheme over the mock-up, it might look like the following figure.

Navigation   Header

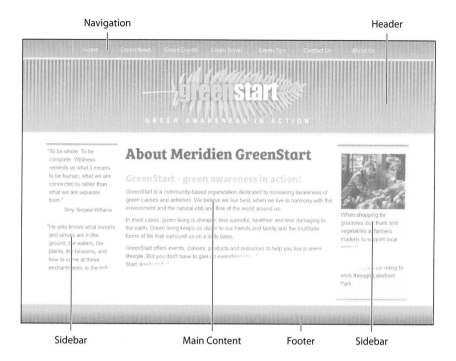

Sidebar   Main Content   Footer   Sidebar

Once you identify the basic page component scheme, you could then break down the diagram into basic HTML elements, like the following.

`<div class="sidebar1">`   `<div class="header">`   `<div class="nav">`

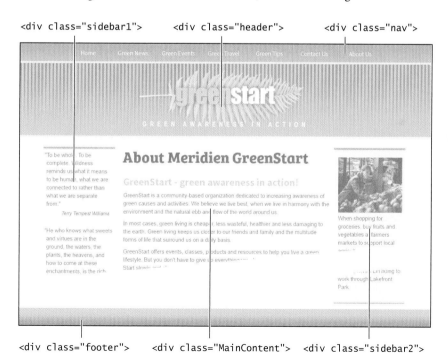

`<div class="footer">`   `<div class="MainContent">`   `<div class="sidebar2">`

Although the `<div>` element is perfectly acceptable and still in wide use as a page component, it is a holdover from HTML 4 and comes with some disadvantages. For example, it makes the underlying code more complex by requiring the use of class, and/or id, attributes to help delineate the various components within the design.

Today, web designers are instead using the new HTML5 elements to simplify their designs and to add semantic meaning to their code. If you substitute the `<div>` elements with HTML5 structures, it's easy to see how much simpler the layout can be.

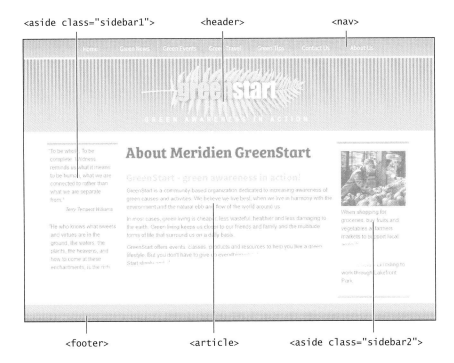

Now that the page has been diagrammed and broken down into its components, you could start creating the basic structure right away. But before you spend any time creating the new layout by hand, Dreamweaver may offer better alternatives.

2   Close **GreenStart_mockup.html**.

In the next exercise, you'll review some layout options provided by Dreamweaver.

Working with predefined layouts

Dreamweaver has always tried to offer the latest tools and workflows to all web designers, regardless of their skill level. For example, over the years, the program has provided a selection of predefined templates and various page components to make the task of building and populating webpages fast and easy. Often the first step of building a website was to see whether one of these predefined layouts matched your needs or whether your needs could be adapted to one of the available designs.

Dreamweaver CC (2017 release) continues this tradition by providing sample CSS layouts and frameworks that you can adapt to many popular types of projects. You can access these samples from the File menu.

1 Choose File > New.

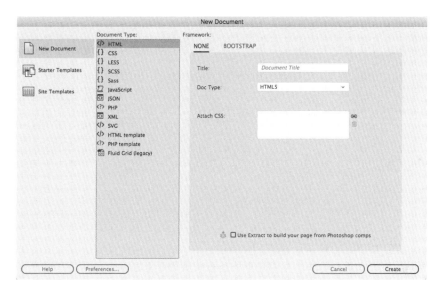

The New Document dialog appears. Dreamweaver allows you to build a wide spectrum of web-compatible documents besides those built using HTML, CSS, and JavaScript. The New Document dialog displays many of these document types, including PHP, XML, and SVG. Predefined layouts, templates, and frameworks can also be accessed from this dialog.

At the time of this writing, Dreamweaver CC (2017 release) offers three basic layouts, six Bootstrap templates, four email templates, and three responsive starter layouts. The exact number and features of these layouts may change over time through automatic updates via Creative Cloud. The changes to this list may occur without notice or fanfare, so keep your eyes peeled for new options in this dialog.

All the featured starter templates have responsive designs built using HTML5-compatible structures and will help you gain valuable experience with this evolving standard. Unless you need to support older browsers (such as IE5 and 6), there's little to worry about when using these newer designs. Let's check out the options.

2 In the New Document dialog, choose Starter Templates > Responsive Starters.

The Starter Templates window of the New Document dialog displays three choices: About Page, Blog Post, and eCommerce.

3 Select **About Page**. Observe the preview image in the dialog.

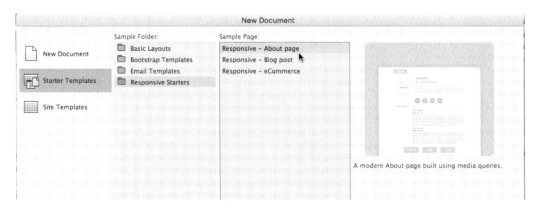

An image appears showing the design of a webpage that will adapt automatically to desktops, tablets, and smartphones.

4 Select Blog Post.

The preview image changes to depict the new design.

5 Select each of the design options in turn. Observe the preview image in the dialog.

Each template offers a design appropriate for specific applications. None of the templates is identical to our chosen design, but Blog Post is the closest fit. Let's take a firsthand look.

6 Select Blog Post again.

Click Create.

A new, untitled document appears in the workspace based on the starter layout. Before working in any document, it's a good idea to save it.

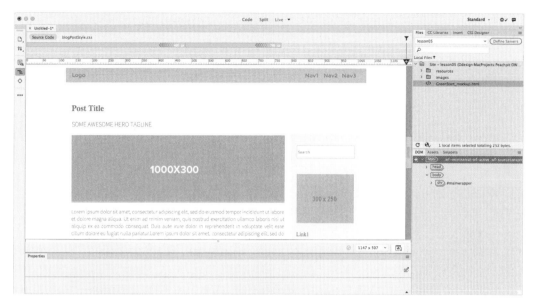

7   Select File > Save.

The Save As dialog appears.

8   Name the page **page1.html** and click Save to save the page into the root folder for lesson05.

The file is saved to the site folder. At the same time Dreamweaver creates a BlogPostAssets folder and inserts some files in it to support the starter layout.

Dreamweaver designed this page for use for blog posts. The new page is populated with placeholders for text, images, and even menu items. To use it, you simply swap out these placeholders with your own words and pictures.

Another attribute of this layout, which is not readily apparent at this moment, is that it has been built right out of the box to be fully responsive. Dreamweaver enables you to test this functionality right inside the program.

Live view is the default workspace for most functions in Dreamweaver. It offers an accurate display of all page components, styling, and even interactivity. You may still switch to Design or Code view for various operations, but you'll find that Live view provides most of the tools and functionality you'll ever need in one place.

9   If necessary, switch to Live view.

▶ **Tip:** When saving documents, Dreamweaver may initially open a folder you previously accessed and not the site root folder. You can click the Site Root button in the dialog to target the site folder selected and displayed in the Files panel.

● **Note:** The support files may not appear immediately in the Files panel.

10 Drag the Scrubber to the left to make the document window narrower.

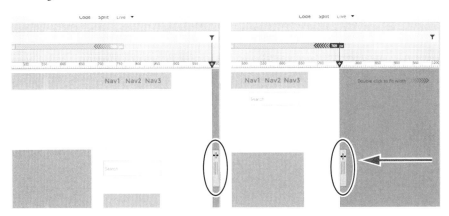

As the document window narrows, some of the components resize or reformat to adapt to the smaller window. Note that some elements actually change positions within the layout. When the window narrows below 480 pixels, the content displays in a single column.

11 Drag the Scrubber to the right to make the document window wider.

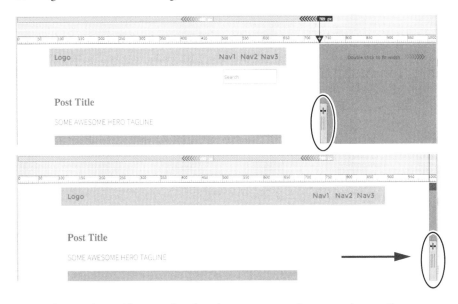

As the window widens, notice that the content continues to adapt to the screen until it automatically resumes its original layout and formatting.

Did you notice that the layout changed abruptly at certain widths? These changes were caused by *media queries* that control the application of the CSS styling. To help you work with media queries, Dreamweaver CC (2017 release) offers the *Visual* Media Queries interface, which should be visible at the top of the document window when you are in Live view.

Introducing the Visual Media Queries interface

The Visual Media Queries (VMQ) interface allows you to identify and interact with media queries instantly using the cursor.

1   If necessary, click the Toggle Visual Media Queries Bar icon in the toolbox on the left side of the screen.

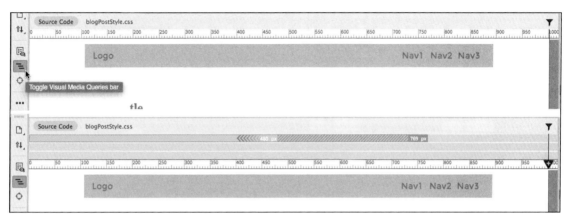

The toolbar displays two media queries settings for this document.

2   Position the cursor over the first media query.

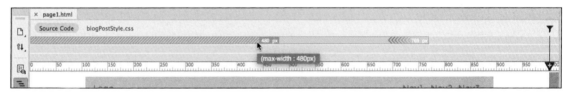

A tooltip appears, identifying that the media query is set for a max-width of 480 pixels.

3   Position the cursor over the second media query.

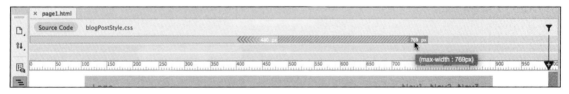

The second media query is set for a max-width of 769 pixels. The interface displays the existing settings using numbers and colors so you can see the specifications instantly. You can use the cursor to activate or switch between each media query.

VMQ enables you to see the differences

Media queries enable your webpage and its content to adapt to a variety of different types of screens and devices. They do this by loading custom style sheets created just for specific screen sizes, devices, or even orientations. Later, you'll learn more about media queries, how they work, and how to create them. For now, let's just review how the Visual Media Queries interface works.

The VMQ interface identifies all media queries defined on the page or within style sheets linked to it. The media queries are displayed in color based on their specifications.

Media queries that define only a minimum width are displayed in purple.

Media queries that define only a maximum width are displayed in green.

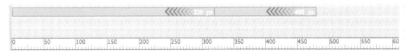

Media queries that define both minimum and maximum widths are displayed in blue.

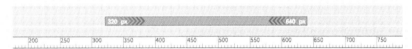

The Dreamweaver workspace is fully responsive and will display the specific CSS styling appropriate to the screen size and orientation within the CSS Designer. To display the styling associated with a specific media query, simply click the media query notation in the @Media pane of CSS Designer.

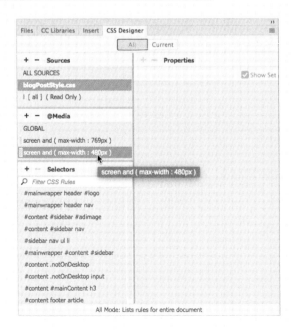

4 Click the cursor to the left of the number 480 in the VMQ interface.

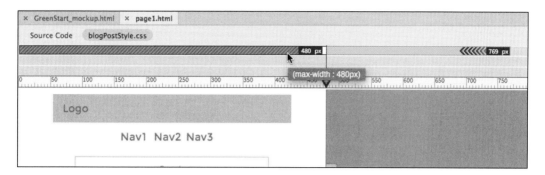

The document window narrows instantly to 480 pixels. The content adapts to the window size based on the applicable CSS styles.

5 Click the cursor to the left of the number 769 in the Visual Media Queries interface.

The document window widens to 769 pixels. To return to full size, you can drag the Scrubber to the right edge of the window or double-click in the gray area to the right of the Scrubber.

6 Double-click in the gray area on the right side of the Scrubber.

The document window opens to the full size of the workspace.

If you examine the current layout and compare it to our chosen site design, the Blog Post layout is not similar enough to be easily adaptable. The same is true of the other responsive starter layouts. Perhaps the Bootstrap templates offer a closer fit.

7 Close **page1.html**. Do not save changes, if prompted.

In the next exercise, you'll learn how to build a custom layout using the Bootstrap framework.

Introducing Bootstrap

The Bootstrap templates are predefined layouts using the Bootstrap framework. Bootstrap is a set of open source tools that help you quickly build websites and web applications that are fully responsive.

Created by Twitter, Bootstrap was released to the public in 2011 and quickly became one of the most popular frameworks in use. It has now been incorporated into Dreamweaver.

Note: Don't click directly on the number itself because it will open a field that allows you to edit the width setting.

Note: To see the page and CSS styling properly, the program and document window should be 1200 pixels in width or larger.

Before you begin this exercise, you should have already defined a site based on the lesson05 folder.

1 Select File > New.

The New Document dialog appears.

2 Select Starter Templates > Bootstrap Templates in the New Document dialog.

The Sample Page window displays six templates based on the Bootstrap framework. A preview of the layout appears when you select the template name.

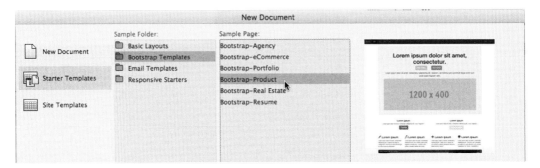

3 Select each layout option and compare the preview to the proposed site design.

None of the templates are close enough to the proposed design to warrant trying to use one as the basis for the new site. Instead, you'll see what all the hype is about Bootstrap firsthand by using it to create your own template from scratch.

4 Select the New Document tab in the New Document dialog.

5 Select HTML in the Document Type window.

6 Select the Bootstrap framework.

7 For Bootstrap CSS, select Create New.

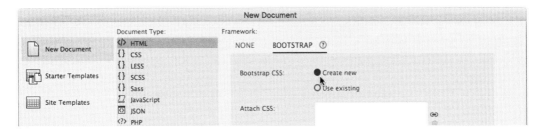

8 Deselect the Design option Include a Pre-built Layout.

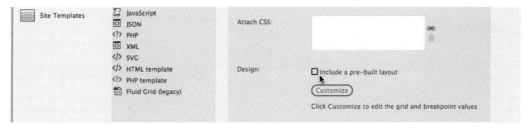

9 Click the Customize button.

The Customize options allow you to change the number of columns, the gutter width, or the predefined screen sizes. For this layout, you will leave the default settings as they are, but if you use Bootstrap in the future, you should make sure these numbers reflect the needs of your site and its visitors.

10 Click Create.

A new, untitled document appears in the document window.

11 Select File > Save. Name the file **mylayout.html** and click Save.

⬤ **Note:** The supporting JavaScript and CSS files for various frameworks, like Bootstrap, are updated from time to time and may be different from the ones shown in this chapter.

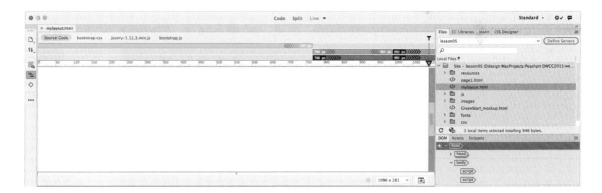

Although the file seems to be entirely empty, lots of things are already going on. You can see that the VMQ interface displays at least six media queries and that the Related files interface shows one CSS and two JavaScript files. But you've only started. The next step is to add some basic structures.

Creating a layout with Bootstrap

Underlying all the power and flexibility of Bootstrap is a basic grid system of rows and columns. This concept harkens back to the earlier days of web design, before the advent of CSS, when we would use tables to cobble together our layouts. The only way to impose order on our webpages was to organize our text and pictures into table rows and cells.

No, we're not going back to the bad old days. Tables were not responsive. Although they could scale up or down in size, they would not automatically adapt to the screen and knew nothing about mobile devices. Instead, the rows and columns of Bootstrap have been carefully engineered to work in most modern browsers and devices.

The first step in Bootstrap is to identify the basic grid structure you need to build, or impose, on the proposed site design. This should be quite easy when you examine the mock-up. Start by marking up the content that would be grouped together in rows, as in the following figure.

Next, identify the columns within the content. Remember that the columns are divvied up in the rows you already created.

You will use the Insert panel to build this structure.

1 If necessary, open **mylayout.html** in Split view. Click in the Live view window.

The <body> element is selected in the window.

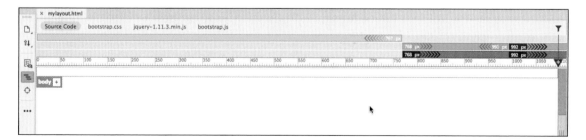

2 Display the Insert panel. If it's not visible on the screen, you can select it from the Window menu.

3 In the Insert panel, select **Bootstrap Components** from the drop-down menu.

The panel displays a list of 26 main items and more than 80 subitems supported by the framework. Although the list is not exhaustive of all the possible Bootstrap components and widgets, it's a good start. And, whatever you can't find in the Insert panel can always be added by hand manually using the Code window.

4 Click the **Container** item at the top of the panel.

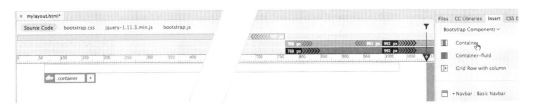

Note: If you instead prefer to create a site that automatically scales to every screen width, use the Container-fluid item in the panel.

This option inserts in the page a fixed-width `<div>` element. In Bootstrap it is, by default, 1170 pixels wide in a full-screen browser on a desktop computer. On smaller screens or devices, this container will display at various smaller fixed widths or scale as necessary to fit the screen.

Once you've established your overall container, you can start creating the row and column scheme devised earlier, but first you will target the default page width.

Note: To see all the media queries, the document window will have to be at least 1100 pixels in width.

5 Click the *Small* media query (min-width 768 pixels) in the VMQ.

The document window resizes to match the dimensions of the media query. Targeting a specific width first determines what classes the Bootstrap framework automatically assigns to the components when you add columns to the rows.

6   Click the **Grid Row with Column** item in the Insert panel.

The Insert Row with Columns dialog appears.

7   Click the **Nest** option, which inserts the row inside the container element created in step 4.

Enter **1** in the No. of Columns to Add field. Click OK.

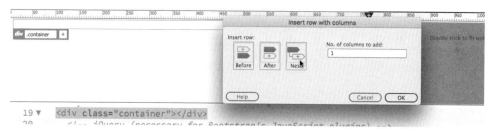

In the Code window, you can see that Dreamweaver inserted two `<div>` elements, one with a class of `row` and the other with a class of `col-sm-12`, nested one inside the other in the initial container. Since the *Small* media query was targeted in step 5, the class says `sm`. *Medium* classes will say `md`, and *Large* classes will say `lg`.

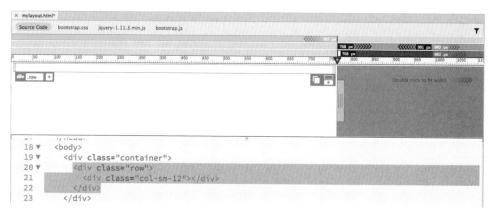

The structure doesn't look very remarkable, but this is the key to the power of Bootstrap. These classes apply predefined styles to the elements that will allow them to adapt to different screens and devices. By adding more classes or manipulating the existing ones, you can provide different types of formatting and behaviors as desired.

As complex and elaborate as Bootstrap might be, one aspect of this scheme is easy to understand. If you remember what you saw in the New Document dialog, the Bootstrap specifications called for 12 columns in the grid. The class `col-sm-12` speaks to this grid by telling the `<div>` to be *12 columns* wide on *small* devices. A small device is considered to be a tablet at least 768 pixels wide. But don't let that fool you. It's important to know that some Bootstrap classes, like this one, are based on inheritance theory and format elements even on larger devices. In other words, this class will continue to format the page unless another class overrides the styling.

As we work through this layout and the upcoming lessons, you will learn how to add to the main components other Bootstrap classes that will specify their behavior in each target environment you want to support. The first row will hold the main site navigation menu. Let's continue building this layout by adding a new row for the page header next.

8 Click the **Grid Row with Column** item again.

The Insert Row with Columns dialog appears. The first row should still be selected.

9 Enter **1** for the number of columns.

Select **After**, which will insert a row after the current one. Click OK.

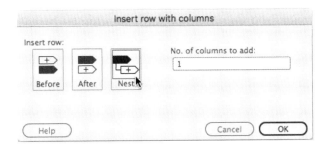

Note: Pay close attention to where the new element appears in the responsive structure. Make sure the new row appears separate and below the first but wholly inside the container element.

A new row is created, inserted after the first. The second is a duplicate of the first and will eventually hold the header and company logo. You'll add that later, but now let's create the next row.

10 Insert another Grid Row with Column as in step 8.

In the Insert Row with Columns dialog, enter **3** this time for the number of columns and select After.

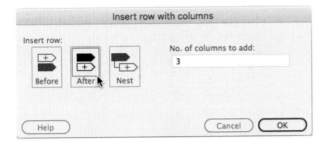

11 Click OK.

A new row appears with three nested `<div>` elements. The new elements have a class of `col-sm-4`. Because 4 divides into 12 three times, the new elements form three columns that divide the available space into three equal parts. Later, you will modify these classes to change the widths and the relationships of these elements to one another. But let's finish the layout first. There's one more row needed for the page footer.

```
19 ▼      <div class="container">
20 ▼        <div class="row">
21             <div class="col-sm-12"></div>
22          </div>
23 ▼        <div class="row">
24             <div class="col-sm-12"></div>
25          </div>
26 ▼        <div class="row">
27             <div class="col-sm-4"></div>
28             <div class="col-sm-4"></div>
29             <div class="col-sm-4"></div>
30          </div>
31       </div>
```

12 Repeat steps 8 and 9 to create a row with one column.

A new row is added for the last row, which will hold the footer. The basic Bootstrap structure for the site design is now complete.

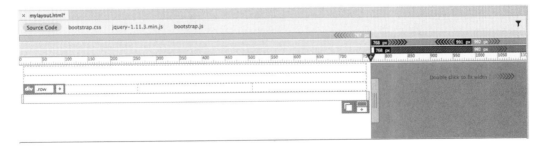

13 Save the file. If you are continuing to the next exercise, leave **mylayout.html** open, but close any other open documents, if necessary.

In the upcoming exercises, you will modify the basic layout to add HTML5 elements and content placeholders for the site template.

Adding semantic elements to Bootstrap

As you can see from the previous exercise, Bootstrap relies heavily on the `<div>` element. There's nothing wrong with this technique, since the framework can't intuit the purpose of the elements in the rows and columns and automatically add the appropriate tags. But as a generic container, the `<div>` element conveys no semantic value or other information to search engines or other web applications.

Once you have created your basic structure, it makes sense to go back and swap out these generic structures with HTML5 semantic elements that more closely match your intended usage or content model. Dreamweaver makes it easy to edit structural elements.

1 If necessary, launch Dreamweaver CC (2017 release) or later.
Open **mylayout.html** from the lesson05 folder.

The file has a basic Bootstrap structure containing four rows, three with one column and one with three columns.

2 Select Split view so that the workspace displays the Code and Live view windows at the same time.

The Bootstrap borders, rows, and columns should be visible in the Live view window as faint blue lines. Since we're going to add a dedicated navigation menu to the first row later, let's start on the second row.

3 Click in the second row of the layout and examine the tag selector at the bottom of the document window.

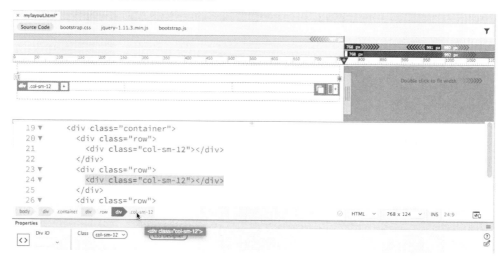

● **Note:** If you are an experienced user of Dreamweaver, you may expect to see your cursor inserted in the document window. Live view does not enable direct editing of your text and images as in Design view. You will learn the proper techniques for creating and editing text in Live view later in this lesson.

Dreamweaver selects one of the elements in the row and displays the blue heads-up display (HUD) interface.

Depending on where or how you click, you might select the row itself or the column nested within it. You can determine which element is selected by looking at the class name displayed in either the HUD or the tag selectors. If it displays `div.row`, it indicates you have selected a row, whereas `div.col-sm-12` means you have a column selected. The selected element will be highlighted in blue in the tag selectors interface.

4 Click the tag selector for `div.row`.

5 Press Ctrl+T/Cmd+T to activate the Quick Tag Editor.

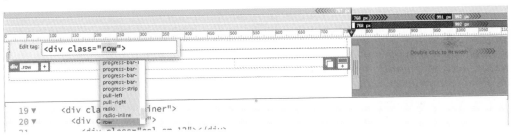

The Quick Tag Editor appears, populated by the code for the row element. If you recall from the original page diagram, this element should be designated as an HTML5 `<header>`.

6 Edit the element code as highlighted:

`<header class="row">`

Edit tag: `<header class="row">`

7 Press Enter/Return twice to complete the change.

The structure is now updated to use the new `header` element.

8 Repeat steps 4 through 7 to edit the third row as highlighted:

`<main class="row">`

This row also contains three columns: one `article` element and two sidebars, or `aside` elements.

9 Click the third row.

The HUD appears for `main.row`.

Tip: You can also use the DOM viewer to select the column element.

10 Press the down arrow key once.

You can use the up and down arrows keys in Live view to change the selection focus on consecutive elements in the HTML code. The first `div.col-sm-4` element in the row should be selected. We'll refer to this element as Sidebar 1 from this point on.

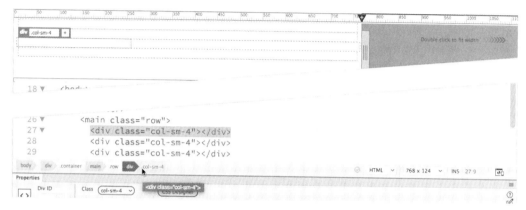

11 Press Ctrl+T/Cmd+T.

Edit the element as highlighted:

`<aside class="col-sm-4">`

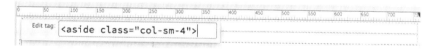

12 Click the third row and press the down arrow twice to select the second column in `main.row`.

Edit the column element as highlighted:

`<article class="col-sm-4">`

13 Edit the third column as highlighted:

`<aside class="col-sm-4">`

We'll refer to this element as Sidebar 2.

14 Edit the fourth row as highlighted:

```
<footer class="row">
```

15 Save the file.

```
19 ▼ <div class="container">
20 ▼ <div class="row">
21   <div class="col-sm-12"></div>
22   </div>
23 ▼ <div class="row">
24   <header class="col-sm-12"></header>
25   </div>
26 ▼ <main class="row">
27   <aside class="col-sm-4"></aside>
28   <article class="col-sm-4"></article>
29   <aside class="col-sm-4"></aside>
30   </main>
31   <footer class="row">
32   <div class="col-sm-12"></div>
33   </footer>
34   </div>
```

The layout has now been updated to use HTML5 semantic elements. In the next lesson, you'll learn how to add some basic content and to format various elements.

Review questions

1 Does Dreamweaver provide any design assistance for beginners?

2 What advantages do you get from using a responsive starter layout?

3 What does the Visual Media Queries (VMQ) interface do?

4 What do the colors in the VMQ signify?

5 How does the Scrubber work in conjunction with the VMQ?

6 Why should you consider using Bootstrap for your next website?

7 True or false: You have to use one of the six predefined templates if you want to use Bootstrap.

8 Why should you replace the <div> elements created by Bootstrap with HTML5 semantic elements?

Review answers

1 Dreamweaver CC (2017 release) provides three basic layouts, six Bootstrap layouts, four email layouts, and three responsive starter layouts.

2 Responsive starter layouts help you jump-start the design of a site or layout by providing a finished layout complete with predefined CSS and placeholder content.

3 The VMQ interface provides a visual representation of the existing media queries in a file and allows you to create new media queries and interact with them in a point-and-click interface.

4 The colors displayed indicate whether the media query is defined with min-width specifications, max-width specifications, or a combination of both.

5 The Scrubber allows you to quickly preview the page design at varying screen sizes to test the predefined media queries and pertinent styling.

6 Bootstrap is one of the most popular frameworks for building responsive websites. It provides a comprehensive set of tools and components that allow you to build a site that adapts automatically to various screen sizes and devices in a fraction of the time you would need otherwise.

7 False. Dreamweaver provides tools and a workflow that allow you to easily build your own Bootstrap layout from scratch.

8 The `<div>` element conveys no semantic value or other information to search engines and other applications. Semantic elements may improve your ranking by making it easier for search engines to identify your site structure and content.

6

WORKING WITH A WEB FRAMEWORK

Lesson overview

In this lesson, you'll learn how to do the following:

- Insert and format new content and components into a Bootstrap-based layout

- Use the CSS Designer to identify applied CSS formatting

- Create advanced CSS background and gradient effects

- Access and use web-hosted fonts

 This lesson will take about 3 hours and 30 minutes to complete. If you have not already done so, download the project files for this lesson from the Lesson & Update Files tab on your Account page at www.peachpit.com, store them on your computer in a convenient location, and define a new site in Dreamweaver based on this folder, as described in the "Getting Started" section at the beginning of this book. Your Account page is also where you'll find any updates to the lessons or to the lesson files. Look on the Lesson & Update Files tab to access the most current content.

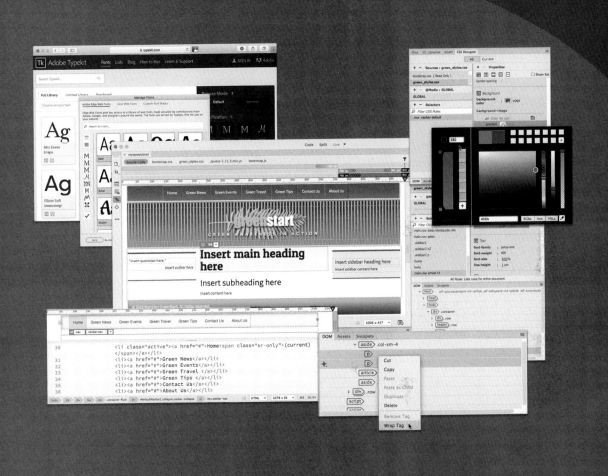

Dreamweaver has incorporated many advanced functions and components from various web frameworks, such as jQuery and Bootstrap, to speed up and simplify the process of developing fully functional, mobile-friendly websites, much of it without having to write a single line of code.

Creating a navigation menu

If you start at the top of the webpage and work down, the first element to address is the navigation menu. The site mock-up we used in Lesson 5, "Creating a Page Layout," sports a horizontal navigation menu with seven links. It may seem odd to start the page with a menu, but in recent years this has become a common practice with many web designers for some practical reasons.

Note: The site design mock-up is included in the file set for Lesson 6. Feel free to open GreenStart_mockup.html to refresh your memory of the design and components.

Menus have been shifted to the top of the page to enhance support for various screen dimensions and mobile devices. By using a simple CSS trick, you can freeze the menu so that the content will scroll underneath it, making the menu visible and accessible to visitors at all times.

In this exercise, you will insert a navigation menu and set it up for the seven pages shown in the site thumbnails in Lesson 5. We don't have seven pages to link to yet, but you can create simple placeholder links for the final content. In Lesson 11, "Working with Navigation," you'll add actual functioning links.

Tip: If you are working on a smaller display such as a laptop, to get the most out of the Dreamweaver interface you should consider using a second external monitor or display.

1   If necessary, open **mylayout.html** from the lesson06 folder in Live view. To perform most of the tasks described within this exercise, the document window should be displayed at a width of 1100 pixels or greater.

2   Select the first row of the Bootstrap layout.

    The Element HUD appears. Two elements comprise the first row. It's important that you select the correct element to build the navigation menu.

3   Select the `div.col-sm-12` tag selector.

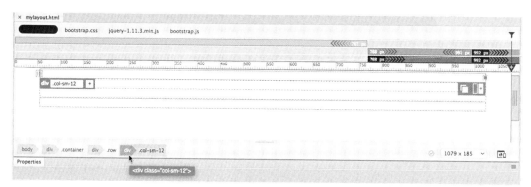

This `<div>` element is inserted as a responsive Bootstrap element. The class `col-sm-12` formats the element to occupy all 12 columns in the grid, or the entire width of the container. The Bootstrap navbars are designed to be responsive out of the box, so this element is redundant and may cause undesirable interference. You will replace this element with the navbar.

4 Press Delete.

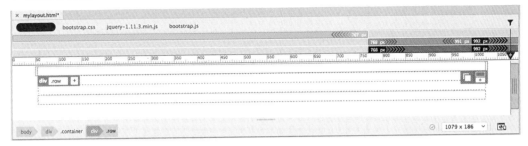

The `<div.col-sm-12>` is removed. When an element is deleted, Dreamweaver leaves the cursor at the position of that element. So, this is the perfect time to insert the navbar.

5 Display the Insert panel. Select the Bootstrap Components category.

The Bootstrap Components category offers two types of navigational elements: complete navigational menu bars, or *navbars*, and standalone navigational menu components. In this situation, you'll use one of the complete navbars.

6 In the Navbar item drop-down menu, click **Basic Navbar**. The position-assist dialog appears.

7 Click **Nest**.

A predefined Bootstrap navbar appears in the first row.

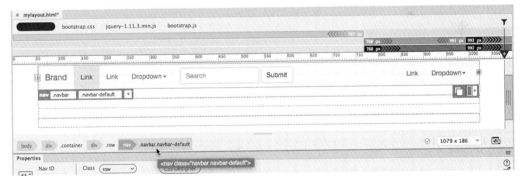

The navbar comprises two separate navigation menus with drop-down components, a search field with a button as well as a menu header. The current design doesn't require all of these items. So, any element that's not needed should be deleted. The safest method to select and delete HTML elements is via the tag selector interface.

8 In Live view, click the Dropdown menu on the right side of the navbar in Live view.

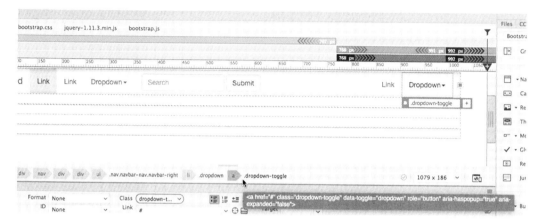

The HUD appears, focusing on the a tag. Observe the tag selector interface. Can you identify the parent element to the right-side menu?

9 Select the `ul.nav.navbar-nav.navbar-right` tag selector.

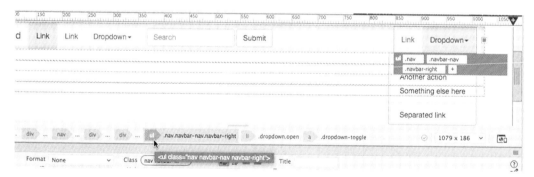

The entire menu on the right side of the navbar is selected, displaying the HUD.

> ● **Note:** Tag selectors can be finicky, you may have to click the tag selector more than once to select the entire element.

10 Press Delete.

The menu is removed. Next, you'll remove the search field and button.

11 Click the search field or button.

As before, the HUD appears, identifying the selected element. If you examine the tag selectors, you should be able to track down the parent structure. It helps to know that search fields need to be inserted in an HTML `<form>` element.

12 Select `form.navbar-form.navbar-left` in the tag selector interface and press Delete.

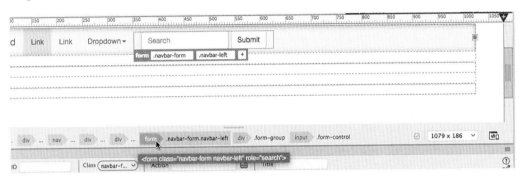

The search field and button are removed. The current design doesn't call for a drop-down menu. If you need one later, it's a simple matter to add one. Drop-down menus are usually built from a sublist inserted into an existing menu item.

13 Click the Dropdown menu and observe the tag selectors.

Dreamweaver will focus on the `a` tag in the parent `<li>`. In Live view, the drop-down menu should open, displaying the sublinks contained within the menu. Deleting the parent will remove the entire structure.

14 Select `li.dropdown` and press Delete.

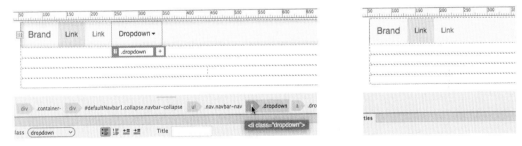

The drop-down menu is removed, leaving two of the original links and the word *Brand.* At first you might think that the word is simply another link in the remaining menu. But take a quick look using the tag selectors and you will see the truth.

15 Click one of the Link items in the menu, examine the tag selectors, and then click the word *Brand*.

If you compare the structures, you should see that the Link items are contained within nav.nav.navbar-nav, while the word *Brand* is actually in nav.navbar-header. In Bootstrap, the Brand element could be used for your company name to provide a handy link back to your home page, or perhaps for a page or section title. Like the other elements, it's unneeded in this layout. You need to remove the text as well as any link markup.

16 Select the a.navbar-brand tag selector and press Delete.

All the unneeded components have now been removed. Next, you will replace the generic link placeholders with ones that match the site design and learn how to make new Link items.

17 Click the first Link item to select it.

The blue HUD appears focused on the a tag. You can edit text directly in Live view, but you need to know a simple trick to make it editable.

18 Double-click the first Link item.

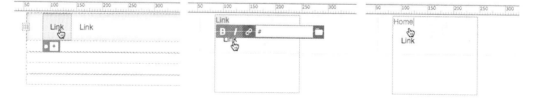

The blue HUD disappears and is replaced by a plain orange box, indicating that the content of the <a> is now in text-editing mode.

19 Select the text *Link* and type **Home** to replace it.

The text for the new link destination appears on the screen, but the change is not permanent yet. Looking at the Code window, you will not see the text you just typed. If you press the Esc key or click in the Code window, the new text may be discarded altogether.

20 Click just outside the orange box.

The new link text now appears in the button.

21 Repeat steps 18 and 19 to change the remaining Link item to **Green News** and save the file.

The two predefined links now match the menu items from the design mock-up, but you still need to create five more items. The good thing about using unordered lists as the underlying structure for menus is that Dreamweaver makes it easy to insert new list items.

Adding new items to a navigation menu

In this exercise, you will learn how to insert new items in the navigation menu. Links can be added in any view mode, although the techniques differ.

1 In Live view, click the *Green News* link.
Select the li tag selector.

2 Choose Window > Insert to display the Insert panel.
In the HTML category, click the **List Item** option.

The position-assist interface appears.

3 Click **After**.

A new list item appears with placeholder text.

4 Select the placeholder text *Content for li Goes Here*.
Type **Green Events** to replace it and click outside the orange box to commit the change.

The new item appears beside the previous ones, but it's not formatted like the other links. You might be able to figure out what's wrong using Live view, but in this case, the problem can be identified faster in Code view.

5 Click the <li> tag selector for the new link item and switch to Code view.
Observe the menu items and compare the first two to the new one.

Can you identify the difference? In fact, there are a few. For one thing, the first item features a class of `active` as well as a `<span>` element containing text intended for screen readers (`class="sr-only"`). But the only thing the first two share that the last item lacks is the hyperlink placeholder markup `<a href="#">`.

Since this is the only meaningful difference between the list items, you can rightly assume that the `<a>` markup is conveying at least part of the menu styling. To make *Green Events* look like the other menu items, you have to add a hyperlink to it, too, or at least a similar placeholder.

6   Select the text *Green Events* in Code view.
    In the Property inspector Link field, type # and press Enter/Return.

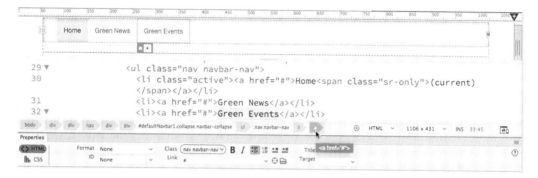

The `<a href="#">` notation is added to the text so that the menu item now features the same markup as the others.

7   Switch to Split view.

    The new item now looks like the others. New menu items can also be added by typing.

▶ **Tip:** Double-click to edit the text element. Click outside the orange editing box to finalize the content.

8   In Live view, insert the cursor at the end of the text *Green Events* and press Enter/Return to create a new line.

    It may not be apparent in Live view, but Dreamweaver is creating a new `<li>` element in the background. But unlike using the Insert panel, this method doesn't add any placeholder text.

9   Type **Green Travel** and select the text.

    The text HUD appears focused on the selection. The HUD offers a Quick Link feature.

10 Click the Link icon in the HUD.

    A link field appears next to the HUD.

11 Enter # and press Enter/Return.

Click outside the orange editing box.

The new *Green Travel* link is complete. You can also add menu items in Code view.

12 Switch to Code view.

In this view, you can choose from several methods for creating a new list item. For example, you can type out the entire element manually, use the Insert panel as in step 2, or use copy and paste.

13 Insert the cursor in the *Green Travel* link.

Select the li tag selector.

By using the <li> element, Dreamweaver selects the link markup as well as the text.

14 Choose Edit > Copy or press Ctrl+C/Cmd+C.

15 Click at the end of the </li> tag.

The cursor is outside the current <li> element. Although there's no need to insert a new line in the code, it keeps the markup consistent and easier to read.

16 Press Enter/Return to insert a new line.

Choose Edit > Paste or press Ctrl+V/Cmd+V.

```
32          <li><a href="#">Green Events</a></li>
33          <li><a href="#">Green Travel </a></li>
34 ▼        <li><a href="#">Green Travel </a></li>
35      </ul>
```

A duplicate version of the *Green Travel* list item appears.

17 Select the duplicate text *Green Travel*.

Type **Green Tips** to replace it.

The new menu item is complete and already contains the link # placeholder.

18 Using any of the methods described earlier, create two more menu items for the links *Contact Us* and *About Us*.

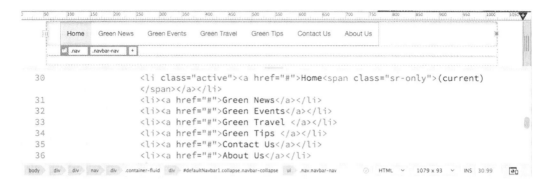

```
30    <li class="active"><a href="#">Home<span class="sr-only">(current)
      </span></a></li>
31    <li><a href="#">Green News</a></li>
32    <li><a href="#">Green Events</a></li>
33    <li><a href="#">Green Travel </a></li>
34    <li><a href="#">Green Tips </a></li>
35    <li><a href="#">Contact Us</a></li>
36    <li><a href="#">About Us</a></li>
```

19 Save the file. If necessary, switch to Split view.

There are seven items in the menu now. Before you can format the menu, though, you'll have to correct some inconsistencies in its basic structure. These differences entail the attributes class (`active`) and the screen reader text (`sr-only`) noted earlier. Let's discard both of them.

Cleaning up Bootstrap components

Your newly modified Bootstrap menu has some inconsistent code structures in the new menu. In this exercise, you'll clean up these inconsistencies.

1 If necessary, open **mylayout.html**.
Switch to Split view.

2 Examine the code of the horizontal menu.

The menu is constructed using an unordered list with seven list items. In Live view you can see that the *Home* link is formatted differently from the rest. The most obvious difference between this link and the others is the class attribute `active`.

3 Select and delete the attribute ~~class="active"~~ from the first <li> element in Code view.

Once the class is deleted from the *Home* link, the formatting of the button will match the others. The last step is to remove the screen reader text.

4 Select and delete the element ~~`<span class="sr-only">(current)</span>`~~ from the first `<li>` element.

```
<ul class="nav navbar-nav">
    <li><a href="#">Home<span class="sr-only">(current)</span></a></li>
    <li><a href="#">Green News</a></li>
```

```
<ul class="nav navbar-nav">
    <li><a href="#">Home</a></li>
    <li><a href="#">Green News</a>
```

5 Save the file.

All the links in the menu are now formatted identically. It's common when using predefined or third-party components that you will have to modify the original structure and formatting to conform to your own content or project requirements.

Working with the CSS Designer

In the upcoming exercises in this lesson, you'll learn how to use the CSS Designer to inspect the existing CSS and create new rules to complete the basic site template design. Before you proceed, it's vital to your role as a designer to understand and identify any existing structure and formatting of a page so that you can effectively complete your tasks.

It's always a good idea when using any predefined components or frameworks to take a few minutes to examine the underlying HTML and CSS to understand what role they perform in the current document. It will also be a good opportunity to familiarize yourself with the CSS Designer and how to use it properly.

1 Open **mylayout.html** from the lesson06 folder in Live view, if necessary.

2 Choose Window > CSS Designer to display it, if necessary.

Note: CSS Designer should be a default component of the Design workspace, but sometimes users close panels unintentionally. Dreamweaver will remember any customizations you perform to the interface. If necessary, you can open it by choosing Window > CSS Designer.

The CSS Designer has four panes that display different aspects of the CSS structure and styling: *Sources, @Media, Selectors,* and *Properties.* Depending on how wide the panel is, it will display in one or two columns. The latest version of CSS Designer also features two distinct modes: *All* and *Current.* At this moment you should ensure that the All mode is enabled.

3 Click the All button in the CSS Designer, if necessary.

▶ **Tip:** If the pane is collapsed, you can open it by clicking its name. You may also need to resize the individual panes to create a more effective display.

The Sources pane now displays all style sheets embedded or linked to the page. You should see two notations: ALL SOURCES and bootstrap.css.

4 Select ALL SOURCES in the Sources pane.

The @Media and Selectors panes display all the media queries and selector names defined in any listed style sheet. The All mode will be helpful in tracking down a specific rule and where it's defined. By selecting an item in either pane, the CSS Designer will identify its location by highlighting its source in bold.

5 Select the rule `a:active, a:hover` in the Selectors pane.
In the Properties pane, deselect the Show Set option, if necessary.

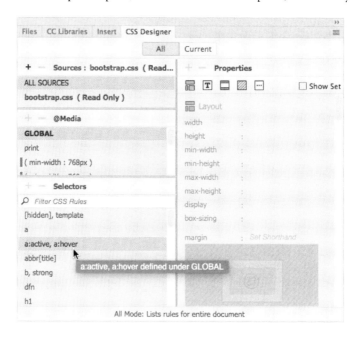

Note that the name bootstrap.css in the Sources pane and GLOBAL in the @Media pane are now bolded. The bolding indicates that `a:active, a:hover` is defined in the **bootstrap.css** style sheet as a global rule. This behavior works even in the other panes.

6 Select the first (`min-width 768`) media query in the @Media window. Observe the changes in the CSS Designer display.

Note that **bootstrap.css** is still selected but the Selectors pane now shows only one name: `.lead`. This indicates that only one rule is defined within the selected media query.

7 Select the `.lead` rule in the Selectors pane.

The Properties pane displays the CSS properties defined in the rule. Depending on its configuration, you may not see which property or properties are set.

8 If necessary, select the Show Set option in the Properties pane.

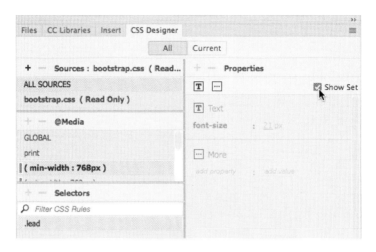

When Show Set is enabled, the Properties pane displays only the properties modified by the rule. In this case, the .lead rule sets the font-size property to 21 px.

You may also notice that the Properties pane and the settings are grayed out. This indicates that the properties are noneditable. If you look at the Sources pane, you can see that the **bootstrap.css** style sheet is marked as (Read Only). Since the page is based on the Bootstrap framework, Dreamweaver prevents you from modifying and potentially damaging its predefined styling. The styling contained within it is complex and full of interdependencies. It's recommended that any changes or overrides be made in your own custom style sheet.

At the moment, there is no custom style sheet. Before you can style the structure or content of the new page and site, you'll have to add a new editable style sheet. You can create the style sheet directly in the CSS Designer.

9 Click the Add CSS Source ✚ icon in the CSS Designer.

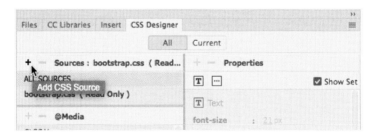

A drop-down menu appears that allows you to create a new CSS file, attach an existing CSS file, or define a style sheet embedded within the page code.

Reading no writing

The Bootstrap style sheet is formatted as a read-only file to prevent you from making accidental changes to the framework's complex styling. From time to time as you work in your pages, a warning message may appear at the top of the screen indicating that the file is read-only. You can dismiss the message by clicking the icon on the right side. It also provides an option to make the file writable. You're advised to resist the temptation.

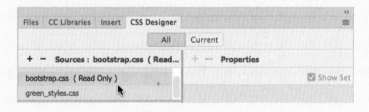

10 Choose **Create A New CSS File** from the drop-down menu.

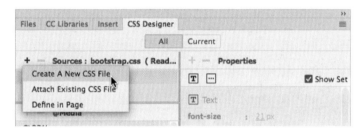

The Create A New CSS File dialog appears.

11 Type **green_styles.css** in the Create A New CSS File dialog. Click OK to create the style sheet reference.

When you click OK, a reference to the new style sheet is added to the CSS Designer Sources pane. The CSS file has not actually been created yet, but a link has been added to the <head> section of the page, and the file will be created automatically as soon as you create your first custom rule.

12 Click **green_styles.css** in the Sources pane.

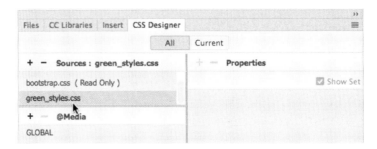

The @Media and the Selectors panes are both empty. This means there are no CSS rules or media queries yet. You have a blank slate on which you can make any design additions or modifications. Since you will not change the Bootstrap CSS directly, this style sheet will be the means you use to make its structure and content bend to your wishes.

13 Click the item "Green News" in the navbar.

If you examine the tag selectors, you will notice that the menu items are composed of `<a>`, `<li>`, and `<ul>` elements contained in a couple of `<div>` elements and a `<nav>`.

● **Note:** The Current mode limits the display to only the CSS affecting the element selected in the document window.

14 Click the Current button. Observe the CSS Designer.

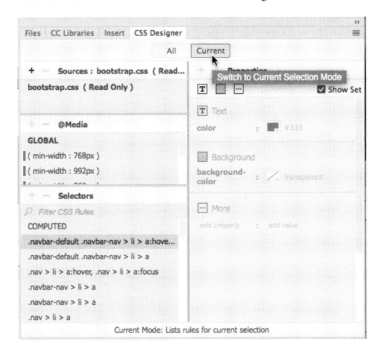

The panes in the CSS Designer change, displaying the media queries and selectors that format the selected element. A close inspection of the Sources pane tells you that only the **bootstrap.css** file holds any of these rules. Then, a look at the Selectors pane shows you the names of the rules that provide some sort of styling to the `<a>` or `<li>` elements themselves or to their surrounding structure.

15 Click the All button.

The CSS Designer changes to show all rules again.

16 Select each rule in the Selectors pane, starting at the top of the list. Observe the Properties pane as each rule is highlighted, but keep your eyes peeled for other changes in the workspace.

As you inspect each rule, you will see the Properties pane change to display the formatting applied by each one. When you click a rule that affects an element in the layout, Live view highlights the element or elements in blue.

As you can see, CSS Designer can be used in a variety of ways to identify the styling applied to a specific element as well as to identify the element affected by a specific rule. It can also help you create and name the CSS rules.

Note: Remember you learned in Lesson 3, "CSS Basics," that some HTML elements have default styling. Default properties will not be shown in the CSS Designer.

Hyperlink pseudo-classes

The `<a>` element (hyperlink) provides five states, or distinct behaviors, that can be modified by CSS using what are known as pseudo-classes. A pseudo-class is a CSS feature that can add special effects or functionality to certain selectors, such as the `<a>` anchor tag.

- The `a:link` pseudo-class creates the default display and behavior of the hyperlink and in many cases is interchangeable with the `a` selector in CSS rules. But the `a:link` is *more* specific and will override specifications assigned to a less-specific selector if both are used in the style sheet.

- The `a:visited` pseudo-class formats the link after it has been visited by the browser. This resets to default styling whenever the browser cache, or history, is deleted.

- The `a:hover` pseudo-class formats the link when the cursor passes over it.

- The `a:active` pseudo-class formats the link when the mouse clicks it.

- The `a:focus` pseudo-class formats the link when accessed via keyboard as opposed to mouse interaction.

When used, the pseudo-classes must be declared in the order listed here to be effective. Remember, whether declared in the style sheet or not, each state has a set of default formats and behaviors.

Styling a navigational menu

Menus typically exhibit at least two basic behaviors, or looks: a static, or default, state and a rollover, or hover, state. All the formatting is controlled by CSS. See the sidebar "Hyperlink pseudo-classes" for more information on these and other hyperlink behaviors.

Tip: Not sure how wide your window is? The ruler should be visible at the top of the document window whenever Live view is selected.

1   Open **mylayout.html** in Live view, if necessary.
Maximize the program to fill the computer display.
The document window must be wider than 1024 pixels.

The navigation menu was created from a Bootstrap component and comes with basic predefined styling provided by the Bootstrap default style sheet, which is locked. Any styles you create will be added to the **green_styles.css** file. The new styles will reset or override the predefined specifications or create new ones from scratch. The first step is to add a background color to the entire menu.

2   Select any menu item.
Examine the tag selectors to identify the structure of the menu.

The menu is built by inserting an <a> element within an unordered list. The list is contained within the navbar element you created using a Bootstrap component. The formatting is coming from some aspect of the menu you inserted. To create a background color for the entire navbar, you first need to identify the rule that applies the current formatting.

3   Click the Current button in the CSS Designer.

The Selectors pane displays a list of rules that are applying some sort of styling to the navbar or menu items.

Note: You may not be able to select Show Set until a rule is selected.

4   Select the Show Set option, if necessary.

5   Start at the top of the Selectors list and click each rule. Examine the properties assigned by each and look for any that assign background colors or background gradients.

The first rule applies a background color of `transparent`. Although this is the correct CSS property, you can see that the background of the navbar has some sort of shading or gradient. There must be another rule applying a background setting. Keep looking.

Next, you will come across a rule that formats the `a:hover` and `a:focus` states of the menu links. Although this is another valid background property, the `a:hover` and `a:focus` selectors will format only the actual hyperlinks themselves. There still has to be another rule that formats the entire navbar. Keep looking.

Finally, more than 20 rules down the list you will find `.navbar-default`, which applies a background color of `#f8f8f8`. To reset the styling and apply a background to match the site design, you have to make a new rule that has equal or greater specificity.

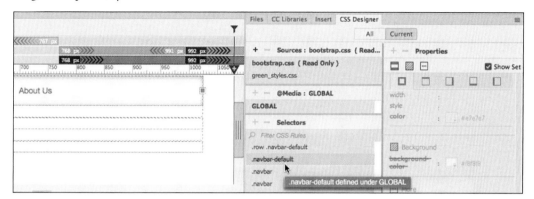

6   Select the `.navbar-default` tag selector.

The HUD appears around the entire navbar.

7   In the CSS Designer, click the All button.
Select **green_styles.css** in the Sources pane.
Click the Add Selector **+** icon.

A suggested selector name appears in the window. You can accept the suggested selector name or create your own. In this case, you need to create a rule to override the rule `.navbar-default`. As you learned in Lesson 3, adding another tag or class to a selector increases its specificity.

8   Edit the name to
`.row .navbar-default`

Be mindful of the space and leading dot (.).

9   Press Enter/Return twice to complete the selector.

10 In the CSS Designer, deselect Show Set.

Only when Show Set is deselected does the Properties pane display the list of all available CSS specifications. The list is organized into five categories, which can be accessed quickly by clicking their icons: Layout ⊞, Text **T**, Border ▭, Background ▨, and More ⋯.

11 Click the Background category ▨ icon.

The Properties pane focuses on the Background category.

12 In the Background category, click the Background-color color picker.

The color picker window opens. The color picker enables you to select colors in several ways. You can choose a color by sight by using the various visual tools or by entering the color by number, using RGB, Hex, or HSL values.

Note: When using hex number shorthand, Dreamweaver may rewrite it to the full number.

13 Enter #069 in the **background-color** property.
Press Enter to complete the color selection.

The background color changes from light gray to dark blue. The `background-color` property covers the older browsers that don't support CSS3 specifications.

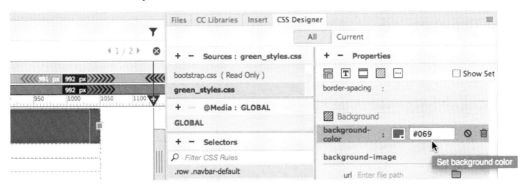

14 Choose File > Save All.

By using the Save All command, Dreamweaver will create the **green_styles.css** file in the site root folder. In the next exercise, you'll add some advanced styling.

Creating a CSS gradient

Element background styling can include colors, images, and gradients. Dreamweaver makes defining CSS gradients a point-and-click process.

Tip: CSS properties can be entered manually or by using the various menus, checkboxes, and color pickers. Feel free to turn Show Set on and off to access your favorite workflow or method.

1 If necessary, select the rule `.row .navbar-default` in **green_start.css**. Deselect the Show Set option, if necessary.

2 In the `background-image` property, click the gradient color picker.

The Gradient color picker provides an easy way to set CSS gradients. To choose a color, you first click the stop icon at the top or bottom of the gradient and then enter the desired color number in the field using RGBa, Hex, or HSLa color models. Or you can pick a color by eye using the visual display.

3 Set #069 as the **top** gradient color stop.
Set #08A as the **bottom** gradient color stop.
Set Linear Gradient Angle to 180 degrees.
Press Enter/Return to complete the gradient.

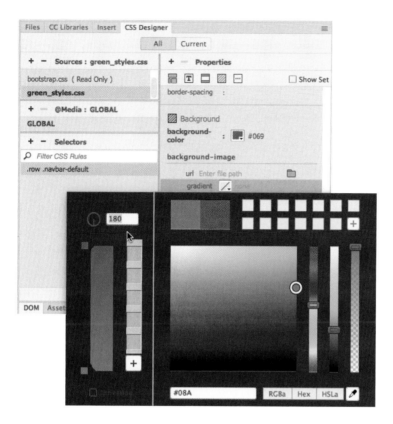

4 Choose File > Save All.

The gradient background supersedes the solid background color. The new background color is nice, but it makes the menu buttons hard to see. They could use some definition of their own, such as adding some lines, or borders, between them.

Adding borders to menu items

Most menus differentiate individual options by either separating the items or by adding borders between them.

1 Select one of the menu items.

The HUD displays the a tag. It's always a good policy before creating a new rule or property to check for properties in the existing rules that are performing the same task. Menu styling can be applied using either <li> or <a> elements.

2 In the CSS Designer, click the Current button and enable the Show Set option again.

▶ **Tip:** You can also right-click the file tab and select Save All from the context menu or use the keyboard shortcut you created in Lesson 1, "Customizing Your Workspace."

3 Check the existing rules for border properties applied to <li>, <a>, or <ul> elements.

Since there are no visible borders between the menu items, you're probably safe creating a new rule. A check of the existing rules shows that a few apply borders to the entire navbar, but none do so for the individual menu items. Let's apply the border to the <a> element.

The new rule will be inserted in your custom style sheet.

4 Click the All button.

5 In the Sources pane, select **green_styles.css**.

6 Click the Add New Selector icon ✚.

A suggested selector appears in the Selectors pane.

● **Note:** The greater-than symbols you see in the selector name indicate that the rule is targeting only the immediate children of the preceding element rather than any descendant.

7 Delete the entire selector and enter the following:
```
.row .nav.navbar-nav > li > a
```

By adding `.row` to the selector, it will supersede any default formatting and specifically target only this `nav` element. It will also preclude the rule from unintentionally formatting other menus you may insert in the layout later.

8 Add the following properties to the new rule:
```
border-top: solid 1px #0AE
border-right: solid 1px #037
border-bottom: solid 1px #037
border-left: solid 1px #0AE
```

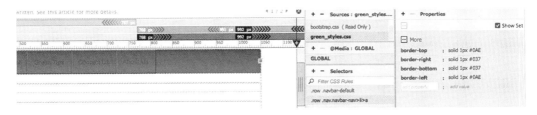

9 Choose File > Save All.

By alternating the border colors this way, it produces a three-dimensional effect on the menu buttons. Another common step is to add styling to various dynamic behaviors of menu items.

Adding dynamic styling

The main feature of the navigation menu is the hyperlink. It features five distinct states: link, visited, hover, active, and focus, in that order. See the sidebar "Hyperlink pseudo-classes" for a full description of hyperlink behaviors and states.

When links appear in the body of a webpage, the link and visited states are usually formatted separately, but in a menu you want them to be identical. The selector `.row .nav.navbar-nav > li > a` created in the previous exercise already targets the default state of the hyperlink. But you'll need to add the *visited* reference to the name to cover both behaviors.

1 In **green_style.css**, double-click the selector name:

`.row .nav.navbar-nav > li > a`

The selector name becomes editable.

2 Select the entire name and copy it.

3 Insert the cursor at the end of the selector, type `:link,` and press Ctrl+V/Cmd+V to paste the copied selector.

4 At the end of the new name, type `:visited` and press Enter/Return as needed to complete the name.

● **Note:** Don't forget the comma between selectors. You can also add a space, but it's not necessary.

● **Note:** It's not required to add the `:link` markup to the default link name, but it increases the specificity of the rule.

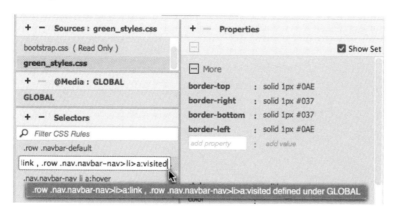

The new selector targets the link and visited states of the menu items. Check your selector name to make sure you did not accidentally add spaces to the pseudo-classes.

5 Deselect the Show Set option.

In the Text category, enter #FFC in the color property.

The link names appear in light yellow.

The :hover pseudo-class is responsible for styling links whenever the cursor is positioned over them. Normally, you'll see this behavior simply as the cursor turning into the pointer icon, but for this dynamic menu let's apply different background and text colors to create what's known as a *rollover* effect.

6 Click the Add Selector icon. Select the new name and press Ctrl+V/Cmd+V to replace it with the selector you copied in step 2.

7 At the end of the name, type :hover
Press Enter/Return twice to create the new selector.

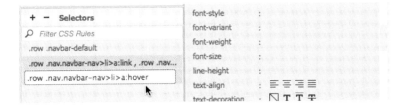

As with the other pseudo-classes, there should be no space after the a: tag.

8 In the background-image property, click the gradient color picker.

9 Set #069 as the **top** gradient color stop.
Set #08A as the **bottom** gradient color stop.
Set Linear Gradient Angle to 0 degrees.
Press Enter/Return to complete and apply the gradient.

The new gradient is a mirror image of the one created in the previous exercise.

10 In the Text category, enter #FFF in the **color** property.

You can test the effect in Live view.

11 Position the cursor over any of the menu items.

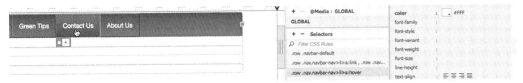

The gradient background flips vertically and the text color displays in white, providing a good contrast from the default menu state.

12 Choose File > Save All.

The navigation menu is nearly complete. The last step is to center the menu horizontally within the navbar itself.

Centering the navigation menu

Bootstrap enables you to create complex menu and navigation components with a minimum of effort, but it doesn't provide unlimited styling options. For one thing, the framework offers two basic alignment options for horizontal menus: aligned to the left or justified across the entire structure. Aligning the menu to the center of the navbar, as in our proposed site design, will require you to step away from the framework defaults and create your own custom styling.

The first step is to set a fixed width on the menu.

1 Create a new selector in **green_styles.css** named
`.row .nav.navbar-nav`

2 In the `width` property, enter `715px`

This width allows the menu to fit on one line but still function properly in the responsive structure. Now that you have set the element width, you can center it using a simple CSS trick.

3 In the `margin` property, enter the shorthand:
`0px auto`

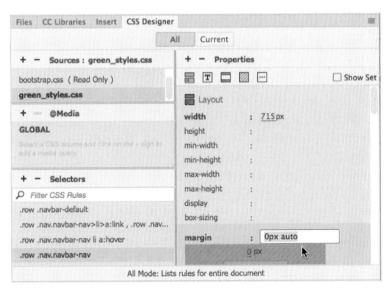

● **Note:** The menu width is derived from the Bootstrap CSS, which sets a maximum of 750 pixels for the menu before it collapses to an icon. You will work with mobile design in Lesson 7, "Designing for Mobile Devices."

The shorthand applies zero pixels of margin to the top and bottom of the menu and equal amounts of spacing to the left and right. This setting should center the element, but the menu isn't moving. When styling doesn't work as expected, use CSS Designer to identify the issue.

4 Select Show Set in CSS Designer.

Select the COMPUTED option in the Selectors pane.

5 Click the Current button in CSS Designer and examine the properties styling the menu.

Some properties are displayed in gray and some in black, indicating which items are editable and which are not. One of the uneditable Bootstrap rules sets a `float:left` property. You can cancel it out using the rule created in step 1.

6 Select the All button in CSS Designer.
Select the `.row .nav .navbar-nav` rule you created in step 1.

When the Show Set option is enabled, you can still edit the properties and values in the CSS Designer or even create new ones. When Show Set is enabled, you don't see a list to choose from, so you have to know what property you want to enter in the open field.

7 Insert the cursor in the empty field in the More section at the bottom of the Properties pane.

8 Type `float` and press the Tab key.

Note how the hinting menu appears and filters the available options as you type. As with the HTML hinting menu, feel free to select the property using your mouse or keyboard once the menu appears.

9 Type or select **none** in the value field.

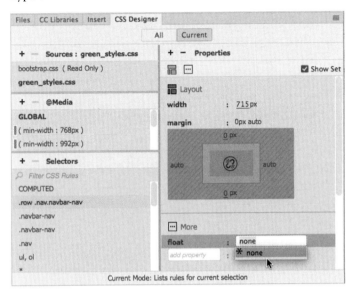

The menu centers in the navbar. There's one last tweak you need to make. If you look closely at the second row, you will see that there is spacing below the navbar. If you examine the rules affecting this element, you will find a bottom margin of 20 pixels applied via one of the Bootstrap rules: `.navbar`.

10 Create a selector named `.row .navbar`

Create the property `margin-bottom` and enter `0px`.

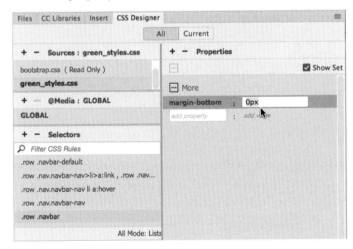

The space below the navbar is removed. The navigation placeholder is now complete.

11 Choose File > Save All.

The next task is to fill in the content area. First, you'll insert new placeholder content in the left <aside> element.

Creating header content

If you follow the site design mock-up as your guide, the <header> is composed of several components, including the company name, the motto, a logo graphic, and a graphical background.

The entire effect could be reproduced by using a single image, but that image would have to be quite large to support large desktop displays. A single image would also be the least flexible option, not to mention the least accessible. Instead, we'll stretch your CSS skills by building a composite design combining text and a few background effects. This technique will allow the design to be more adaptable to various devices, such as cellphones and tablets. Let's start by adding the text.

1   If necessary, open **mylayout.html** from the lesson06 folder in Split view, with Live view enabled.

2   Click the second row of the Bootstrap structure.
    Select the header.col-sm-12 tag selector.

3   Open the Insert panel.
    Select the HTML tab from the drop-down menu.

    The HTML tab provides an easy way to insert all sorts of standard HTML elements.

4   In the Headings drop-down menu, select **H2**.

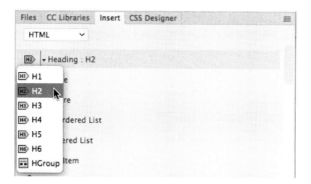

The position-assist interface appears. This interface enables you to choose where the new element will be inserted: *before*, *after*, *nested* within the current selection, or *wrapped* around the selection.

5 Select **Nest**.

A new `<h2>` element appears within the `<header>` filled with placeholder text.

6 Double-click the placeholder text.

The blue HUD disappears and is replaced by a plain orange box.

7 Select the text and type **greenstart** in all lowercase.

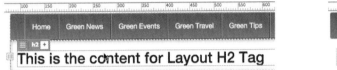 

The company name replaces the placeholder text. Now let's add the company motto.

8 Press Enter/Return to create a new line.
Type **GREEN AWARENESS IN ACTION** in all uppercase.

The motto appears in a new `<p>` element, but the change is not permanent yet.

9 Click the cursor just outside the orange editing box.

⬤ **Note:** Exiting editing mode may take a moment. Be patient.

 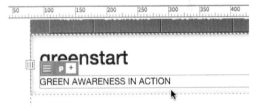

The orange box disappears. The heading and the motto are now a permanent part of the header.

10 Save the file.

The text has been entered but still needs to be formatted.

Formatting type

In this exercise, you will format the text within the `<header>` element.

1 Click the text *greenstart* to select the h2 element.

2 Select the All button again in the CSS Designer.

3 Select **green_styles.css** in the Sources pane.

4 Click the Add New Selector **+** icon.

The selector name `.row .col-sm-12 h2` appears in the Selectors pane.
A selector written this way would affect `<h2>` elements inserted into the first,
second, and fourth rows of the current layout. To target the styling more nar-
rowly, a bit of tweaking is required.

5 Edit the selector as shown: `header.row h2`
Press Enter/Return twice to complete the selector.

This new name will target only `<h2>` headings that are inserted into `<header>`
elements with a class of `row`. Note that the Properties pane has a light gray
background, indicating that this rule is fully editable.

6 Deselect the Show Set option in the Properties pane.

7 Click the Text category **T** icon.

The Properties pane focuses on the Text properties. You'll set some basic styling
now and come back to this element later to add more styling to the header.

8 Click the Set Color ⬚ icon to open the Color Picker pop-up window.

9 Select Hex and enter `#0F0` in the color field.
Press Enter/Return to close the color picker window.

The text changes the color to a bright green.

10 Click the value field to the right of the **font-family** property.

A pop-up window appears showing nine groups of typeface names and several design categories, such as sans-serif and monospace. You'll explore and learn more about how to use fonts later, but for the moment let's just pick one of the predefined font groups.

11 Select this group: `Impact, Haettenschweiler, "Franklin Gothic Bold", "Arial Black", sans-serif`

The <h2> is now formatted by the font Impact.

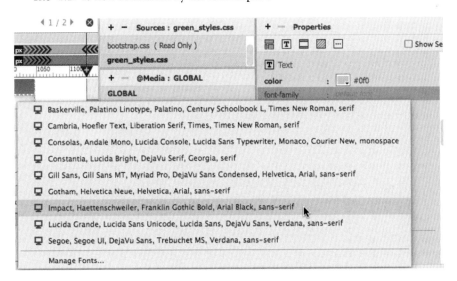

Defining values

Values can be expressed in one or two parts in the Properties pane. When the value comes in two parts, numeric values are entered on the left side, and the measurement system (px, em, %) is entered, or selected, on the right. Single-part values (center, left, right, and so on) can be selected from the right side of the field or entered manually.

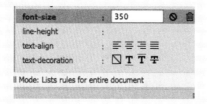 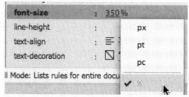

Predefined values (center, middle, top) or measurement systems can be selected from a hinting menu that pops up when Show Set is deselected. When Show Set is selected, the hinting menu may not appear for some properties, and the values must be entered in full, manually.

You may enter the value and measurement system all at once at any time by double-clicking the field and typing them in using the keyboard.

12 Double-click the `font-size` property value field and enter `350%`

> 💧 **Note:** Font sizes based on percentage are factored from the size of the body element. Check out the bonus online lessons on CSS Basics for more details.

13 In the `text-align` property, select `center`.

The text moves to the center of the `<header>`. The text is hard to read in such a bright color, but a drop shadow can improve the legibility.

14 In the `text-shadow` property, enter the following specifications:
```
h-shadow: 0px
v-shadow: 5px
blur: 5px
color: rgba(0,0,0,0.40)
```

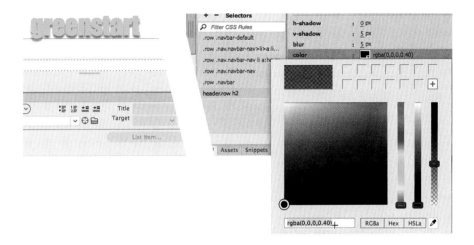

A drop shadow appears behind the heading.

The last bit of styling is to format the letters of "start" in white. This will require a custom class.

Creating custom classes

You can apply CSS styling to any distinct element, such as div, h1, p, a, and so on. When you want to apply formatting to a string of text that has no tag of its own, you need to use the <span> tag. When the styling can't be targeted using the structure of the code itself, the use of a class or id attribute is warranted.

In this exercise, you will create a custom class to apply white to a portion of the logo.

1 Double-click the text *greenstart* to enter text-editing mode in Live view.

   The blue Element HUD is replaced by the orange editing box.

2 Select the letters "start".

3 Press Cmd+T/Ctrl+T to activate the Quick Tag Editor.

   The Quick Tag Editor appears. It should default to Wrap tag mode.

4 Type <span> and press Enter/Return twice to complete the tag.

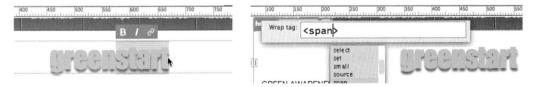

The blue HUD, displaying the span tag, replaces the editing box. There is no existing formatting to call on, so you'll have to create a new class.

5   Click the Add Class/ID icon in the HUD for the `span` tag.

6   Type `.logowhite` to create a new class name.

After you type the leading period (.) to start the class name, Dreamweaver will display a list of existing classes for you to choose from. As you continue to type, the list is filtered to names that match. If the list disappears as you type, it means the class name doesn't already exist.

7   Press Enter/Return to create the class.

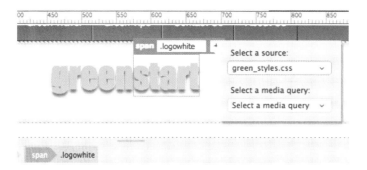

A CSS Source HUD appears allowing you to pick the style sheet and media query into which you can insert the new class. Since **bootstrap.css** is a read-only file, the menu should default to **green_styles.css**. At the moment, there are no media queries in **green_style.css**, so the class will be entered as a global style by default.

Note: If **green_styles.css** does not appear in the source menu, select it manually.

8   Press Enter/Return to complete the creation of the class `logowhite`.

9   Select **green_styles.css** in the Sources pane. Select `.logowhite` in the Selectors pane.

10   Select the Text category icon in the Properties pane.

11   In the `color` property, type `#FFF` and press Enter.

The letters "start" appear in white. The logo is complete. Now, let's format the association motto. As with the heading, the process starts with a selection.

12   Click the text *GREEN AWARENESS IN ACTION* in the `<header>` element.

The blue Element HUD should appear around the `<p>` element.

13 If necessary, select **green_styles.css** in Sources.

14 Click the Add Selector icon.

The name `.row .col-sm-12 p` appears in the Selectors pane.

15 Change the selector to `header.row p`
Press Enter/Return twice to complete the name.

The new selector will target only <p> elements in the <header>.

16 Click the Text category 𝐓 icon in the CSS Designer, if necessary.

17 In the `font-family` property, select `Lucida Grande, Lucida Sans Unicode, Lucida Sans, DejaVu Sans, Verdana, sans-serif`.

18 In the `font-weight` property, enter `bold`

19 In the `text-align` property, select `center`.

20 In the `text-shadow` property, enter the following specifications:
`h-shadow: 0px`
`v-shadow: 3px`
`blur: 5px`
`color: rgba(0,0,0,0.50)`

21 In the `letter-spacing` property, enter `0.5em`

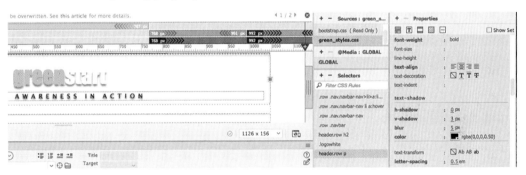

The spacing between the letters expands.

22 In the `color` property, enter #FFF

The motto now displays in white with a drop shadow. The styling of the header text is complete.

23 Choose File > Save All.

Next, you'll learn how to add background effects to the element.

Adding a background image

In this exercise, you will add the first of two background images to the `<header>` element, and then use CSS to adjust its size and position.

1 If necessary, open **mylayout.html** from the lesson06 folder and switch to Live view.

2 Select or open the CSS Designer.

3 Click the second row of the Bootstrap structure.
Select the `header.row` tag selector.

4 Click the All button in the CSS Designer.

5 Select **green_styles.css** in the Sources pane.

When **green_styles.css** is selected, the Selectors pane displays only the rules that appear in that style sheet.

6 Click the Add Selector ✚ icon .

The selector name `.container .row` appears in the Selectors pane. As you have seen several times now, the suggested selector name is too generic to be useful here. It would format every element with the class of `row`, which includes all four rows of the layout. In this case, you want to format only the `<header>`.

7 Edit the selector name to say `header.row`
Press Enter/Return as needed to complete the name.

This new selector appears in the CSS Designer and will specifically target only the header row. The first thing you should do is add a little breathing room above and below the header text. In the past, designers would often set a fixed height to elements like this. But the trend is to stay away from hard measurements so that the design can adapt more responsively to various display types and screen sizes. One popular technique is to add padding to an element, which will allow it to expand naturally.

8 Click the Layout category 🔲 icon .

9 In the padding property, enter **20px 0px**

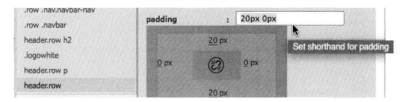

The header increases in height 40 pixels in total.

If you remember from Lesson 3, you can abbreviate CSS values using shorthand. This property applies 20 pixels of padding to the top *and* bottom of the header and zero (0) pixels left and right. Now, let's insert a background image.

10 Click the Background category ▨ icon.

In the background-image section, click in the URL field.

11 Click the Browse 📁 icon next to the URL field.

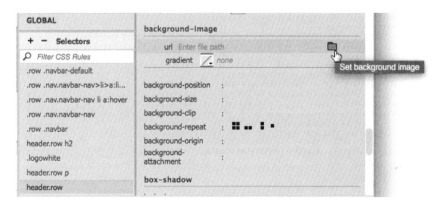

12 In the Select Image Source dialog, navigate to the default images folder.

13 Select **fern.png** and click Choose/Open.

Background images repeat both vertically and horizontally by default. This image is too tall to repeat vertically, but, depending on your screen size, at least two ferns appear left to right.

14 In the **background-repeat** property, choose the `no-repeat` option.

The background image now appears once in the `<header>` element, aligned to the left side. The background specifications can also control the size and alignment of background images.

15 In the `background-size` property, select % from the **height** (right side) value field.

▶ **Tip:** If you find the process of dragging to set the values too difficult, you may enter them via the keyboard by double-clicking the field.

When you set the measurement system, the value defaults to zero (0). If only one value is set, the other value is set to `auto` by default. For the background-size property, a percentage value scales the image based on the size of the parent element. In the Properties pane, you can enter the value via the keyboard or by using the mouse.

16 Position the cursor over the height value field. Drag to the right to increase the value to 80%.

The image will scale to 80 percent of the height of the `<header>` element.

17 In the `background-position` property, select `center` from the **horizontal** (left side) and **vertical** (right side) value fields.

The image appears centered vertically, but it seems slightly off-center horizontally.

18 In the `background-position` property, select % from the **horizontal** (left side) field.

The field defaults to zero (0).

19 Click the field and drag to the right to increase the setting to **47%**.

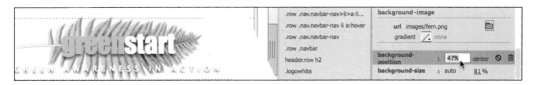

The fern image is now visually centered vertically and horizontally in the `<header>`.

20 Select File > Save All.

In addition to the background image, you can apply other background effects, such as solid colors and even gradients. Since gradients are a new CSS3 specification, it's recommended that you always add a solid color to the background to support browsers or devices that don't support gradients.

Adding other background effects

In this exercise, you will add a `background-color` property to the `<header>` element.

1 If necessary, open **mylayout.html** in Live view and open the CSS Designer.

2 Click the All button in the CSS Designer.
Select **green_styles.css** in the Sources pane.

3 Select the `header.row` rule.
In the `background-color` property, enter **#090**

⬤ **Note:** Hexadecimal colors can be written in shorthand, like #090, when the numbers are in matched pairs, such as #009900. Be aware, however, that any time you enter such shorthand expressions, Dreamweaver may arbitrarily rewrite them in full or swap them with RGB values.

The background color of the header changes to green. This color setting is a fallback option if the browser doesn't display the other background effects.

Let's take the background one step further by adding a third effect to create the vertical stripes, as shown in the mock-up. CSS3 allows you to apply multiple background images to an element. It even allows you to apply individual specifications to each effect. Unfortunately, although the CSS Designer can apply both an image and a color to the background, it provides only one set of source, size, and positioning specifications. But don't worry. Whenever the CSS Designer lets you down, you can always resort to Code view.

4 Right-click the `header.row` rule.

A context menu appears.

5 Select **Go To Code** from the menu.

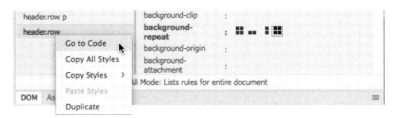

The Code view window appears in Split view focused on the first `header.row` rule in the linked style sheet.

The reference to **fern.png** appears in the `background-image` property. To get the stripes to appear behind this effect, you'll have to add the new specifications after it. Be sure each new specification is separated with a comma and ends with a semicolon.

> ▶ **Tip:** Don't forget to add the comma (,) between each specification. They won't work properly without it.

6 Modify the following properties:
```
background-image: url(images/fern.png), url(images/stripe.png);
background-repeat: no-repeat, repeat-x;
background-size: auto 80%, auto auto;
background-position: 47% center, left top;
```

> ● **Note:** CSS properties in your code may appear in a different order than that pictured. Be sure to edit the correct properties.

```
45 ▼ header.row {
46       padding: 20px 0px;
47       background-image: url(images/fern.png), url(images/stripe.png);
48       background-repeat: no-repeat, repeat-x;
49       background-size: auto 80%, auto auto;
50       background-position: 47% center, left top;
51       background-color: #090;
```

The stripes appear and repeat horizontally across the header. By using a small graphic that repeats across the element, you are minimizing the size of the graphics that must be downloaded to create this effect. In the odd chance that the stripes graphic is not displayed, the header will display the solid green color applied in step 3.

The last additions to the header are the yellow borders at the top and bottom.

7 In the CSS Designer, select Show Set.

Select the `header.row` rule.

Create a new `border-top` property and enter
`5px solid #FD5`

A yellow border appears above the menu.

8 Create a new `border-bottom` property and enter
`5px solid #FD5`

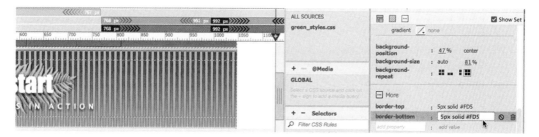

9 Choose File > Save All.

The basic design of the `<header>` element for desktop or GLOBAL environments is now complete. The text, logo, and background effects will require some custom specifications for smaller screens, but we'll address that task in Lesson 7. Next, we'll start building some placeholders for the main and sidebar content.

> **Tip:** In some cases, you may need to refresh the document window display manually to see the effects of the CSS.

Building semantic content

The left column of the `<main>` element will be used for environmentally themed quotations. In the past, you might display quotations like any other paragraph, but to follow web standards under HTML5, you'll want to build these quotations using semantic elements. Unlike normal paragraph text, the value of a quotation is usually based on the perceived reputation of the author or source. HTML provides several elements designed specifically to identify this type of content.

1 If necessary, open **mylayout.html** in Live view.

2 Click the third row in the Bootstrap structure.

The HUD appears on the `main.row` element. The `<aside>` element appears as the first column in the row. You can change the focus of the HUD to the next consecutive element in a selection using the up or down arrow keys.

3 Press the down arrow.

The focus of the HUD changes to `aside.col-sm-4`. First, you'll insert the placeholders for the quotation and citation, and then you'll wrap them with a semantic structure.

> **Note:** At the time of this writing, there is a bug in Dreamweaver that prevents users from selecting child elements within a Bootstrap structure based on the `<main>` tag using the mouse. By the time you read this, you may be able to click and select such elements.

4 Open the Insert panel and select the HTML category.

5 Click the **Paragraph** item. Select **Nest**.

A <p> element appears in the column with placeholder text.

6 Select the placeholder text *This is the content for Layout P Tag* and delete it.

● **Note:** Don't forget the quotation marks.

7 Type **"Insert quotation here."** and press Enter/Return to create a new paragraph.

8 Type **Insert author here** and click outside the orange box to complete the elements.

Next, you'll wrap the two paragraphs in a semantic tag specifically designed for quotations.

Using the DOM viewer

Semantically, web-based quotations should be based on the <blockquote> element. You'll need to put both paragraphs into a blockquote, but, unfortunately, you can't do this directly in Live view. It's hard to select more than one element at a time. So, this is perfect time to introduce you to the DOM panel.

1 Choose Window > DOM to display the DOM panel, if necessary.

The DOM panel displays the Document Object Model, or the schematic view, of your webpage content. This schematic lists the various tags in the page, diagramming the actual structure visually. But it's not just a pretty picture; the DOM panel also provides important features to help you work with these elements while you are in Live view.

2 In the Live view window, click the first paragraph in the sidebar section.

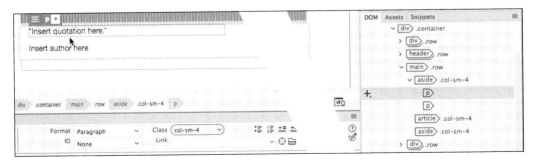

Note how the DOM panel highlights a p tag in the structure in blue. As you select various elements in Live view or Code view, the panel will identify the element and how it appears in the overall code structure. The interactive behavior also works the other way around.

3   Click several tags in the DOM panel and observe the Live view window.

The HUD appears in Live view on each element selected. This is not a new behavior to Dreamweaver, the DOM panel was introduced previously, but new features have been added to the panel that enable you to now edit the elements in brand-new ways.

4   In Live view, click the first quotation placeholder.

The p element in the DOM panel is highlighted.

5   Holding the Shift key, click the p tag immediately below the highlighted element in the DOM panel.

The HUD disappears in Live view as both elements are highlighted in the DOM panel. As you can see, there's no way to select multiple elements in Live view. But obviously the DOM panel has no problems doing so. You can also use the panel to add new elements and structures to the code.

6   Right-click the selection.
    Click Wrap Tag in the Context menu.

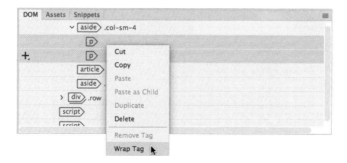

A new div element appears wrapping the selection. Note how the element field is still open and editable.

7   Type blockquote

As you type, a hinting menu appears and filters the options down to the desired tag. Feel free to use the arrow key or the mouse to select the tag you want.

8 Press Enter/Return twice to select and complete the element.

The `blockquote` element now wraps both paragraphs. When completed, the default styling of the `<blockquote>` element automatically formats the content, indenting the text on the left and right. Such indentation is typical of material quoted within a research paper and may be desirable in the main content area, when it appears with paragraphs of regular text, but it's totally unnecessary standing alone in the `<aside>` element. To modify the styling, you'll need to create a new CSS rule.

9 In CSS Designer, click the All button.
Create a new selector in **green_styles.css**:
```
main.row aside blockquote
```

The Show Set option should still be active from the previous exercise.

10 Create the following properties in the new rule:
```
margin: 0px 0px 20px 0px
padding: 0px
```

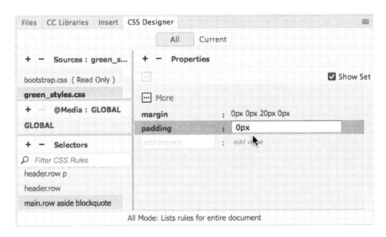

Typically, a blockquote should contain a quotation, either in one or more paragraphs, and an element providing the source or citation. Like `<blockquote>`, the `<cite>` element provides the correct semantic structure in this situation. You can also use the DOM panel to edit existing tags.

11 In the DOM panel, double-click the second p tag.

12 Type `cite` to replace the p tag.
Press Enter/Return twice to complete the edit.

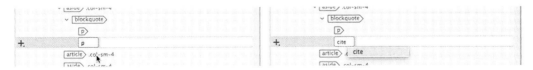

If you look carefully, you can see that the opening quotation mark in the first paragraph is indenting the first line of text slightly, leaving the text in the two paragraphs misaligned. A technique used by professional typesetters actually *outdents* such items to produce a *hanging* quotation mark.

13 Create a new selector in **green_styles.css**:

```
main.row aside blockquote p
```

14 Create the following properties:

```
margin: 0px 0px 5px 0px
padding: 0px .5em
text-indent: -1em
```

You can see now that the two lines of text are aligned, while the quotation mark is shifted to the left slightly. The effect on multiline quotations will be visually appealing.

Now you'll create a new rule to style the author name.

15 Create a new selector:

```
main.row aside blockquote cite
```

16 Create the following properties in the new rule:

```
display: block
padding: 0px 10px
font-style: italic
text-align: right
```

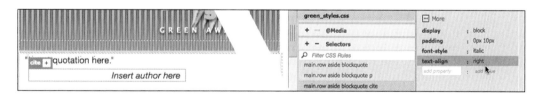

The quotation placeholder is complete and semantically designed. To remain semantically correct, each new quotation should be inserted into its own `<blockquote>` element.

The last task is to add the top and bottom borders shown in the site design.

17 Create a new selector: `main.row aside`

This rule will format both the left and right columns at once.

18 Add the following properties to the new rule:

```
border-top: solid 5px #069
border-bottom: solid 3px #069
margin: 1em 0px
padding: 1em 0px
```

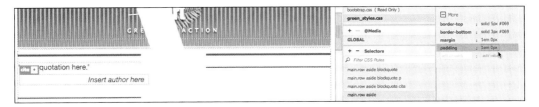

This rule formats both `<aside>` elements, which now display blue borders on the top and bottom.

19 Choose File > Save All.

The placeholder for the first column is complete. Next, you'll address the `article` element in the center of page.

Inserting main content placeholders

The layout will feature the main content in the center column. Content is usually introduced with HTML heading elements. The most important content would use the `<h1>` element, the most important heading. In the past, typically only one `<h1>` would appear on each page, since logically speaking a page could have only one most important heading.

However, with the introduction of the new semantic elements, many web professionals are actually using `<h1>` elements to introduce each major section or article that may appear on a page. For this design, you'll start with one `<h1>` and use more if warranted.

1 Click the center of the third row in the Bootstrap structure.

The HUD appears should focus on the `<main class="row">` element. In the DOM panel, the `main` element is highlighted.

2 In the DOM panel, select the `article` element.

The DOM panel also enables you to insert new content.

3 Click the Add Element ✚ icon in the highlighted row of the DOM panel.

A drop-down menu appears.

4 Select Insert Child.

A new `div` element appears below the `article` and indented to the right, indicating that it's a child element.

5   Type `h1` and press Enter twice.

A new h1 element appears in the layout complete with placeholder text.

6   Select the placeholder text.
Type **Insert main heading here** to replace the text.

7   Press Enter/Return to create a new line.
Type **Insert subheading here** and press Enter/Return.

8   Type **Insert content here** and click outside the orange editing box.

You have now created one heading and two new placeholder paragraphs. The first paragraph should be converted to an <h2> element.

9   Click the first paragraph "Insert subheading here". The HUD appears focused on the p element.

10   In the Property inspector, select Heading 2 from the Format drop-down menu.

> ▶ **Tip:** If the Property inspector is not visible, you can display it by choosing Window > Properties. Most people like to dock it to the bottom of the document window.

The paragraph is converted to an <h2> element. The placeholders for the center content area are complete. You'll format them later.

11   Save all files.

Now, let's add placeholders and formatting to the right column.

Creating custom element classes

The right column of the layout will contain materials related to the main content. As you can see from the site design, the element has a background color. You already have a rule that formats both `<aside>` elements, but in this case, the background will apply only to the right column.

Although you need to target styling only to the right column, there's no obvious structural difference between the two elements other than their position in the layout. This makes it difficult to apply unique formatting to either `aside` element. In such situations, the easiest method is to create a custom CSS class. First, you need to add a class attribute to the element. There are several ways you can do this, but using the HUD in Live view is fast and easy.

1 Open **mylayout.html** in Live view.

2 Click between the blue borders in the right column of the third row.

The HUD appears focused on the `aside.col-sm-4`. At the moment, this structure is identical to the first column.

3 Click the Add Class/ID ⊞ icon in the HUD.

A blank text field appears beside the existing class `col-sm-4`.

4 Type `.sidebar2` and press Enter/Return.

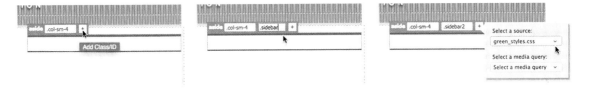

The CSS Source HUD appears allowing you to specify where the new class will be inserted. If **green_styles.css** does not appear in the source menu, select it manually.

▷ **Tip:** Another way to target formatting to a specific element when there is more than one in the same structure is to use a CSS pseudo-class, such as first-child or last-child. Check out http://tinyurl.com/pseudo-class for more information.

5 Press Enter/Return to complete the operation. You may also need to click away from the HUD to complete the operation.

If you look at the **green_styles.css** reference in the CSS Designer, you will see the new class `.sidebar2`. The class will allow you to apply styling to the right column that differs from the left.

6 Select `.sidebar2` in the Selectors pane.
Create the following properties:
`background-color: #CFC`
`padding: 0px 10px`

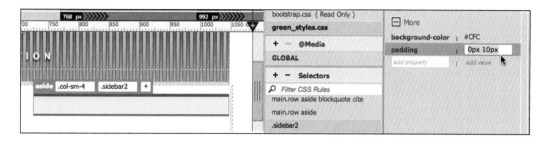

A light-green background color appears in the right column. Let's add some placeholder text.

7 Using the Insert panel, add an <h2> element to the right column using the Nest option.

8 Select the placeholder text.
Type **Insert sidebar heading here** to replace it.

9 Press Enter/Return to create a new paragraph.
Type **Insert sidebar content here** on the new line.
Click outside the orange editing box to complete the placeholders.

10 Create a new selector: `.sidebar2 h2`

11 Create the following properties in the new rule:
`margin-top: 10px`
`margin-bottom: 5px`
`padding: 0px 10px`
`font-size: 130%`
`line-height: 1.4em`

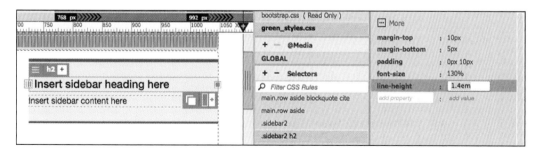

12 Create a new selector: `.sidebar2 p`

13 Create the following properties in the new rule:

```
margin-bottom: 5px
padding: 0px 10px
line-height: 1.3em
```

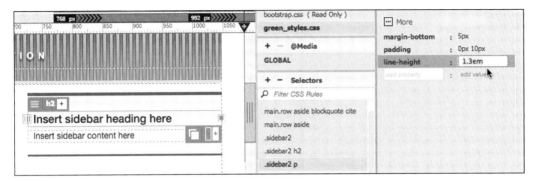

14 Save all files.

The right column is complete. Before moving on to the `<footer>`, you need to adjust the spacing of the three columns in the main content row. Currently, the three columns are equal in width, but in the site design the left and right columns are narrower than the center one. Since the widths are determined by the pre-defined Bootstrap classes, changing the relationship of these elements is simply a matter of changing their class names.

Managing Bootstrap component width

Bootstrap is based on a 12-column vertical grid system. Elements inserted into a layout conform to this grid by occupying some fraction of it. The amount of space an element uses is typically represented by a number that appears in the class attribute. For example, the three columns in the third row all have a class of `col-sm-4`. Since 4 divides into 12 three times, each column occupies one-third of the screen. By adjusting these class names, you should be able to change the width of each element.

▶ **Tip:** To achieve the expected results in this exercise, the document window should be at least 1100 pixels wide.

1 Open **mylayout.html** in Live view, if necessary.

At the moment, all three columns have the same class name and are equal in width.

2 Click the first column of the third row, in Live view.

The HUD appears focused on one of the elements in `aside.col-sm-4`.

3 Click the `aside.col-sm-4` tag selector.

The HUD focuses on `aside.col-sm-4`. You can edit the class name directly in the HUD.

4 Click the class name .col-sm-4 in the HUD.

Change the class name to .col-sm-3 and press Enter/Return.

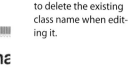

Note: Be careful not to delete the existing class name when editing it.

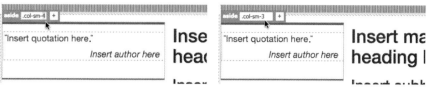

The width of the first column narrows. The other columns shift to the left, leaving open space on the right side of the third row. The HUD is still focused on the first column.

5 Click Sidebar 2.

The HUD focuses on one of the elements in aside.col-sm-4.sidebar2.

6 If necessary, select the tag selector for aside.col-sm-4.sidebar2.

7 Change the class name to .col-sm-3.sidebar2 and press Enter/Return.

The right column narrows. In total, the entire row is now occupying only 10 of the 12 columns in the grid. You can leave these settings this way, add more space between the columns, or simply add the space to the main content section.

8 Click the heading "Insert main heading here".

The HUD focuses on the h1 element.

9 Click the tag selector for article.col-sm-4.

Change the class name to .col-sm-6 and press Enter/Return.

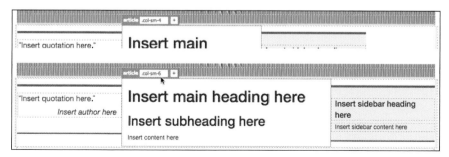

The center column widens to take up the empty space. The three columns are now using the entire width of the main container.

10 Save all files.

Later, you will learn more about how you can control the responsive behavior of your layout using Bootstrap classes. This will enable your layout to adapt to various screen sizes and devices automatically.

To complete the basic layout you only have to add some placeholder text to the footer and some formatting.

Inserting HTML entities

In this exercise, you will insert a generic copyright statement that includes an HTML entity and format the footer.

1 Open **mylayout.html** from the lesson06 folder, if necessary.

The file contains a four-row Bootstrap layout with various placeholder content and formatting, but the fourth row is still empty.

2 Click the fourth row of the layout.

The Element HUD appears focused on `div.col-sm-12`.

The site design shows the footer containing a copyright symbol. This character is one of many that you might want to use in your website but that you can't type directly using the keyboard. To insert a copyright character, you will use an HTML entity. But before you can insert the copyright character, you first need to insert a paragraph element to hold it.

3 Choose Insert > Paragraph and nest a new paragraph in the footer.

Dreamweaver inserts a `<p>` element into the footer, complete with placeholder text. To insert the entity, you will have to switch to Design or Code view. This particular command does not work in Live view.

4 Switch to Split view.
Locate the `<footer>` element and the new placeholder text in Code view.

5 Select the placeholder text *This is the content for Layout P Tag* and delete it.

Be sure you don't delete the `<p> </p>` tags. The cursor should be positioned between tags.

6 Choose Insert > HTML > Character > Copyright.

In Live view the copyright symbol © appears in the footer. In Code view you should see the named entity `&copy;` in the code. Since the cursor is already inserted in this location, let's finish the footer placeholder text.

◆ **Warning:** You may discover that you can sometimes insert special characters directly by typing a keyboard shortcut without using an entity. This is not a recommended practice.

7 Press the spacebar to insert a space.

Type **2017 Meridien GreenStart. All rights reserved.**

```
67 ▼        <footer class="row">
68 ▼          <div class="col-sm-12">
69 ▼            <p>This is the content for Layout P Tag</p>
70             </div>
71          </footer>
```

```
67 ▼        <footer class="row">
68 ▼          <div class="col-sm-12">
69              <p>&copy; 2017 Meridien GreenStart. All rights reserved.</p>
70             </div>
71          </footer>
```

▶ **Tip:** Modify the copyright date as necessary when you create a new page or update the content.

8 In the CSS Designer, select **green_styles.css** and create a new selector named `footer`

9 Create the following properties:

`padding: 1em 0px`
`background-color: #090`
`color: #FFC`

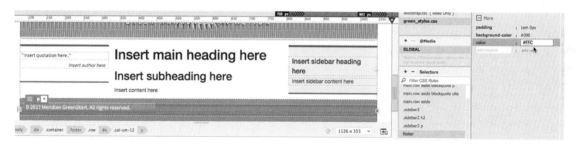

10 Deselect the Show Set option.

11 In the **background-image** property, click the gradient color picker.

12 Set #060 as the **top** gradient color stop.

Set #0C0 as the **bottom** gradient color stop.

Set the Linear Gradient Angle to 0 degrees.

Press Enter/Return to complete the gradient.

The footer displays a gradient that shifts from light green to dark green.

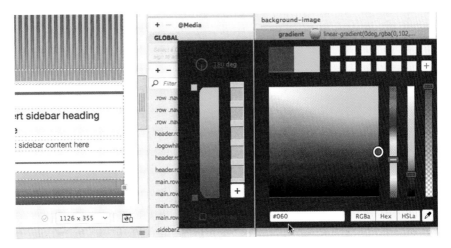

13 Save all files.

You've completed the basic structure and added placeholders to all the elements. You've even formatted some of the elements and content. The last task you'll accomplish will be to implement a global theme for the site design that will establish the basic design and usage of type within the site.

Creating global type styles

Most of the content of your site will be represented in text. Text is displayed in the web browser using digitized typefaces. Based on designs developed and used for centuries on the printing press, these typefaces can evoke all sorts of feelings in your visitors, ranging from security to elegance to sheer fun and humor.

Some designers may use multiple typefaces for different purposes throughout a site. Others select a single base typeface that may match their normal corporate themes or culture. CSS gives you tremendous control over page appearance and the formatting of text. In the last few years, there have been many innovations in the way typefaces are used on the web. The following exercises describe and experiment with these methods.

Face vs. font: Know the difference?

People throw the terms *typeface* and *font* around all the time as if they were interchangeable. They are not. Do you know the difference? *Typeface* refers to the design of an entire family of letterforms. *Font* refers to one specific design. In other words, a typeface is usually composed of multiple fonts. Typically, a typeface will feature four basic designs: regular, italic, bold, and bold-italic. When you choose a font in a CSS specification, you usually choose the regular format, or font, by default.

When a CSS specification calls for italic or bold, the browser will normally load the italic or bold versions of the typeface automatically. However, you should be aware that many browsers can actually generate italic or bold effects when these fonts are not present or available. Purists resent this capability and go out of their way to define rules for italic and bold variations with specific calls to italic and bold versions of the typefaces they want to use. But in the end, if the font is not installed, the browser cannot display it.

Using Edge Web Fonts

The first choice for most web designers is selecting the base typeface that will display their content. In this exercise, you will see how easy it is to use web fonts to apply a global site typeface by editing a single rule. There's no need to be intimidated about using web fonts—everything you need to implement this technology is built right into Dreamweaver CC.

> **Note:** Edge Web Fonts and other types of hosted fonts are rendered properly in Dreamweaver only in Live view with an active Internet connection.

1 If necessary, open **mylayout.html** in Live view.

2 In the CSS Designer, select **green_styles.css**.
   Create a new selector named body

3 In the Properties pane, deselect the Show Set option, if necessary.

   The pane now displays all CSS specifications.

4 Click the Text category **T** icon.

   The pane display focuses on CSS Properties for text.

5 Click to open the `font-family` property.

A window appears showing nine predefined Dreamweaver font groups, or *stacks*. You can select one of these or create one of your own. Are you wondering why you don't see the entire list of fonts installed on your computer?

The answer is a simple but ingenious solution to a problem that has nagged web designers from the beginning. Until recently, the fonts you see in your browser were not actually part of the webpage or the server; they were supplied by the computer browsing the site.

Although most computers have many fonts in common, they don't always have the same fonts and users are free to add or remove fonts at will. So, if you choose a specific font and it isn't installed on the visitor's computer, your carefully designed and formatted webpage could immediately and tragically appear in Courier or some other equally undesirable typeface.

For most people, the solution has been to specify fonts in groups, or *stacks*, giving the browser a second, third, and perhaps fourth (or more) choice to default to before it picks for itself (egads!). Some call this technique *degrading gracefully*. Dreamweaver CC (2017 release) offers nine predefined font groups.

As you can see, the predefined font stacks are pretty limited. If you don't see a combination you like, you can click the Manage Fonts option at the bottom of the Set Font Family pop-up menu and create your own.

But before you start building your own group, remember this: Go ahead and pick *your* favorite font, but then try to figure out what fonts are installed on your visitors' computers or devices and add them to the list too. For example, you may prefer the font Hoefelter Allgemeine Bold Condensed, but the majority of web users are unlikely to have it installed on their computers. By all means, select Hoefelter as your first choice; just don't forget to slip in some of the more tried-and-true, or *web-safe*, fonts, such as Arial, Helvetica, Tahoma, Times New Roman, Trebuchet MS, Verdana, and, finally, a design category like serif or sans serif.

In the last few years, a new trend has been gaining momentum to use fonts that are actually hosted on the site or by a third-party service. The reason for the popularity is obvious: Your design choices are no longer limited to the dozen or so fonts from which everyone can choose; you can choose among thousands of designs and develop a unique look and personality that was nearly impossible in the past. But don't think you can use just *any* font.

Licensing restrictions prohibit many fonts from web-hosted applications altogether. Other fonts have file formats that are incompatible with phones and tablets. So, it's important to look for fonts that are designed and licensed for web applications. Today, multiple sources exist for web-compatible fonts. Google and Font Squirrel are two such sources, and they even provide some free fonts for the budget-minded. Luckily, as a subscriber to Adobe Creative Cloud, you have access to two new services: Adobe Typekit and Adobe Edge Web Fonts.

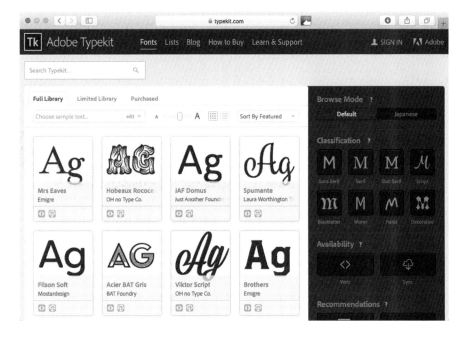

Web-hosted fonts offer a vast variety of design options.

Typekit is a web-hosted subscription service that offers both print and web fonts. You can subscribe to the service even if you don't have Creative Cloud, but as a subscriber you can access many of the available fonts for free. Adobe Edge Web Fonts is a free service that provides only web fonts, hence its name, and is powered by Typekit. The best thing about Edge Web Fonts is that you can access it directly inside Dreamweaver.

6 At the bottom of the font stack window, click Manage Fonts.

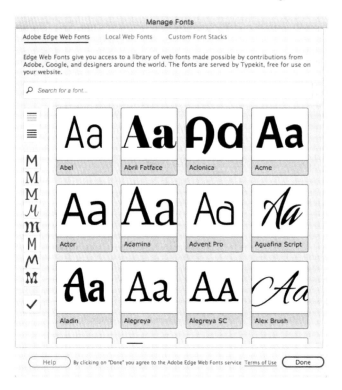

The Manage Fonts dialog gives you three options (tabs) for using web fonts: Adobe Edge Web Fonts, Local Web Fonts, and Custom Font Stacks. The first two tabs provide access to a new technique for using custom fonts on the web. Adobe Edge Web Fonts supports the Edge Web Fonts service to access hundreds of fonts in multiple design categories right inside the program. Local Web Fonts allows you to define the use of fonts that you can buy or find free on the Internet and host on your own website. Custom Font Stacks enables you to build font stacks using either the new web-hosted fonts, the various web-safe fonts, or a combination of both. For the site's base font, let's pick one from Edge Web Fonts.

The tab for Adobe Edge Web Fonts displays samples of all the fonts available from the service. You can filter the list to show specific designs or categories of fonts.

7 In the Manage Fonts dialog, select the option "List of fonts recommended for Headings."

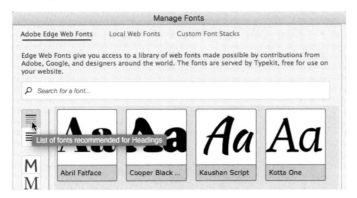

The window shows a list of fonts that are typically used for headings and titles. Some designers like to use the same font for both headings and paragraph text.

8 Select the option "List of fonts recommended for Paragraphs," directly below the option for headings.

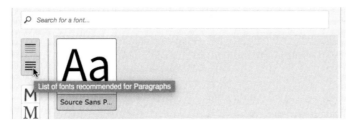

Only one font is displayed: Source Sans Pro. Since this font works well for headings and paragraph text, it's a perfect choice for the site's base font. By applying it to the body rule, it will automatically be applied to headings and paragraphs throughout the site.

9 Click the font sample displayed in the Manage Fonts dialog.
Click Done to close the panel.

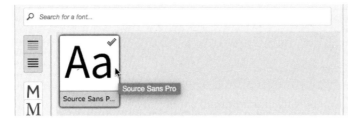

A blue checkmark appears on the sample of Source Sans Pro. Once you click Done, Dreamweaver will add the font to the CSS Designer interface and write any code needed in your page to use it in your CSS specifications.

10 Click the **font-family** property again.

When the Font Stack dialog opens, you will see source-sans-pro at the bottom of the list.

11 Select `source-sans-pro`.

12 In the `font-weight` property, select 400.

Source Sans Pro appears in the font-family property for the body rule. In most cases, the change in the layout will be instantaneous. The entire page, both headings and paragraph text, should now display Source Sans Pro.

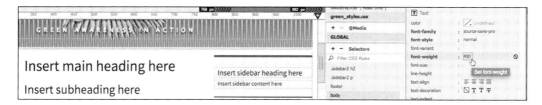

If you don't see the new font, you may not have a live connection to the Internet at this moment. Because Edge Web Fonts are hosted on the Internet, you won't be able to see them until you establish a live connection or upload this page to a live web server. You will learn how to upload pages to the Internet in Lesson 13, "Publishing to the Web."

13 Save all files.

As you can see, using Edge Web Fonts on your website is really easy. But don't be fooled into thinking they're any less problematic than old-fashioned font stacks. In fact, even if you want to use Edge Web Fonts as your primary font source, the best practice would be to include them in a custom font stack of their own.

Introducing web-hosted fonts

The latest trend around the Internet is the increasing popularity of custom type-faces. For years, we've been stuck with the familiar but faded presence of the same web-safe fonts gracing most of our websites: Arial, Tahoma, Times New Roman, Trebuchet MS, Verdana, and so on. To use a less common typeface, your options were to chance fate and flirt with font substitution or to render the custom typeface as a graphic (and all that entails).

If the concept of web fonts is new to you, you're not alone. At the time of this writing, "web fonts" had only been in existence a little over seven years and only started to gain widespread popularity for the last six.

The basic concept is relatively simple: The desired font is copied to your website or linked to it from a common web server. Then, the browser loads the font and caches it, as needed.

Here are some handy links to learn more about the new trend in web fonts:

* Adobe Edge Web Fonts: https://edgewebfonts.adobe.com

* Adobe Typekit: https://typekit.com

Here are some other font services:

* Google Web Fonts: https://fonts.google.com

* Font Squirrel: www.fontsquirrel.com

* MyFonts.com: www.myfonts.com

Building font stacks with web-hosted fonts

If you're lucky, your web-hosted fonts will display every time for every user. But luck can run out, and it's better to be safe than sorry. In the previous exercise, you accessed and selected a font from Edge Web Fonts and applied it to the base font of the body rule. In this exercise, you'll build a custom stack anchored on your chosen web font to provide the necessary fallback support for safety's sake.

1 Open **mylayout.htm**l in Live view, if necessary.

2 In the CSS Designer, select the body rule.

3 In the Text category, select the **font-family** property.

   The Font stack dialog appears.

4 Choose Manage Fonts.

5 In the Manage Fonts dialog, click the Custom Font Stacks tab.

Note: Once you have the font-family property specified in a preexisting rule, you can access the Manage Fonts dialog. If no font-family setting is already present, you may need to deselect the Show Set option.

Note: Whenever typing a font name manually, you must spell the font name correctly. Any typos will cause the font to fail to load.

6 In the Available Fonts list, locate **source sans pro**.

Click the << button to move the font to the Chosen Fonts list.

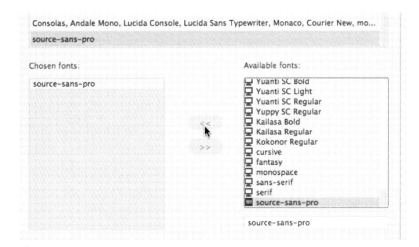

If you cannot find a font in the list, you can type the name in the text field at the bottom of the dialog and press the << button.

Note: Not all font formats are universally supported across all computers and devices. Make sure your chosen font is supported within your desired audience.

7 Repeat step 6 to add **Trebuchet MS**, **Verdana**, **Arial**, **Helvetica**, and **sans-serif** to the Chosen Fonts list.

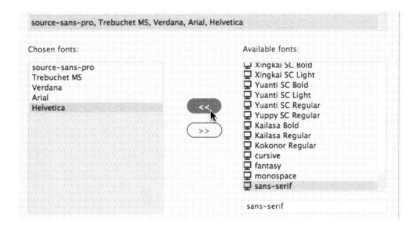

Feel free to add more web or web-safe fonts to your list as desired. If any fonts you want to use are not installed on your computer, type the names into the text field, and then add them to the stack using the << button.

8 Click Done.

9 In the **font-family** property, select your new custom font stack.

The page display should not change; Source Sans Pro is still the primary font in the list. But the new font stack, based on the new font from Edge Web Fonts, will ensure that your text will be formatted in all contingencies.

10 Save all files.

Now you've learned how to specify the style, or look, of your text content. Next, you'll learn how to control the size of the text.

● **Note:** Edge Web Fonts and other hosted fonts require the use of JavaScript. Some visitors may turn off JavaScript in their browser.

Specifying font size

Font size can convey the relative importance of the content on the page. Headings are typically larger than the text they introduce. In your working document, the content is divided into three areas: the main content and the two sidebars. In this exercise, you will learn how to set the base font size and then manage the size of the text in other areas of the page to add emphasis as desired.

1 Open **mylayout.html** in Live view, if necessary.

2 Select the body rule in **green_styles.css**.

3 In the **font-size** property, enter **14px**

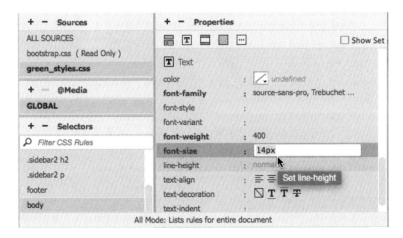

Setting the size of the body rule is a common practice for many web designers. This is designed to reset the base font size to a size that should be optimum for most visitors. You can also adjust the size as necessary for various devices and screen sizes using media queries.

4 Insert the cursor in the text "Insert main heading here."

If you look at the Selectors pane, you will see that you have not yet created a rule to specifically format this heading. Let's create one now.

5 Create a new selector in **green_styles.css** named
`main.row article h1`

Since the `<h1>` element is the main heading of the page, you should design it to stand out from the rest of the text and headings. This can be done in a variety of ways, using color, using size, or picking a great typeface.

6 Add **Patua One** from Edge Web Fonts as you did earlier with Source Sans Pro.

● **Note:** In this rule formatting the h1, you added only a single font. You may think you should have to build a custom font stack, but you don't. That's because the stack created earlier will be inherited by default if this font doesn't display properly.

7 Create the following properties for the `h1` rule:
```
margin-top: 0px
margin-bottom: 15px
font-family: patua-one
font-size: 300%
line-height: 1em
```

The main heading reformats and increases in size.

The sidebars contain text that is related to, but not semantically as important as, the main content. Reducing the size of this content provides a visual distinction to the layout. You created rules earlier in this lesson to format these items.

8 In **green_styles.css,** select the rule `main.row aside`.

9 Create the following property: `font-size: 95%`

The text in the right column has resized, but the quotation placeholder in the left column has not changed. When a rule does not format an element, it means one or more other rules are conflicting with it. This will be a common problem when you use predefined templates or frameworks, like Bootstrap. You can use the CSS Designer to troubleshoot the conflict.

10 Click the text "Insert quotation here" in the left column.

The HUD appears, focused on the p element.

11 Select the Current button in the CSS Designer, examine the list of rules, and identify any that format font-size properties for `blockquote` elements.

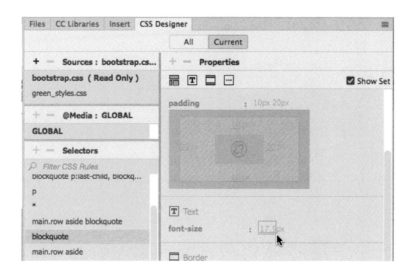

A `blockquote` rule in the **bootstrap.css** file is applying a font-size property of `17.5px` and applying a 5px gray border on the left. Luckily, you created a selector earlier that should be able to override this styling.

12 In **green_styles.css**, select:
`main.row aside blockquote`

13 Create the following new properties in the rule:
`font-size: 100%`
`border: none`

The new property resets the size of the `blockquote` contents to the default font size. That means the property you created in step 9 can function properly now. The basic page layout for desktop media is complete.

14 Save all files.

Congratulations1 You created a workable basic page layout for your project template and inserted additional components, placeholder text, and headings; modified existing CSS formatting; and created new rules. In upcoming lessons, you will continue to work on this file to tweak the CSS and Bootstrap structure to make it work on all mobile devices and then set it up as the primary site template.

Review questions

1 Why should you insert images into the element as a background property?

2 What is the advantage of using Bootstrap components in your layout?

3 Can you edit the styling of a Bootstrap element directly?

4 How does the CSS Designer assist in troubleshooting your website layout?

5 If a character does not appear on your keyboard, such as a copyright symbol, how is it possible to use this element on your webpage?

6 Can you use any font to create a font stack?

7 Why should you consider using web-hosted fonts?

Review answers

1   By inserting graphics as a background image, you leave the container free for other content and gain additional flexibility when designing for mobile devices.

2   Bootstrap components are built to be responsive out of the box, allowing you to create complex structures that support a variety of screen sizes and devices with minimum effort.

3   No. The Bootstrap style sheet is locked, but you can easily create styles in your own style sheet to format or override default styling.

4   The CSS Designer serves as a CSS detective, allowing you to investigate what CSS rules are formatting a selected element and how they are applied.

5   HTML provides code entities for all characters that you may want to use on your webpage but that you cannot type from the keyboard. Many are available directly from Dreamweaver's Insert menu.

6   Technically, yes, you can declare any font name in your CSS rules. However, normally the font will load only if the visitor has that font installed on their computer. Today, many designers are hosting custom fonts on their own sites or using third-party font-hosting services. But if you use third-party fonts on your site, be sure to check that they're licensed for web use.

7   Web-hosted fonts provide thousands of uniquely designed typefaces, many of them free, that can enhance the design and personality of your website.

7 DESIGNING FOR MOBILE DEVICES

Lesson overview

In this lesson, you'll edit and adapt cascading style sheets and CSS3 media queries in Dreamweaver for mobile devices and learn how to do the following:

• Edit and manipulate a Bootstrap framework to adapt to different types of mobile devices

• Create and edit a media query for mobile and handheld devices, such as tablets and smartphones

• Select and target CSS rules within specific media queries

• Configure page components to work with mobile devices

• Preview this page in Dreamweaver

 This lesson will take about 1 hour and 45 minutes to complete. If you have not already done so, download the project files for this lesson from the Lesson & Update Files tab on your Account page at www.peachpit.com. Store them on your computer in a convenient location, and define a new site based on the lesson07 folder, as described in the "Getting Started" section at the beginning of this book. Your Account page is also where you'll find any updates to the lessons or to the lesson files. Look on the Lesson & Update Files tab to access the most current content.

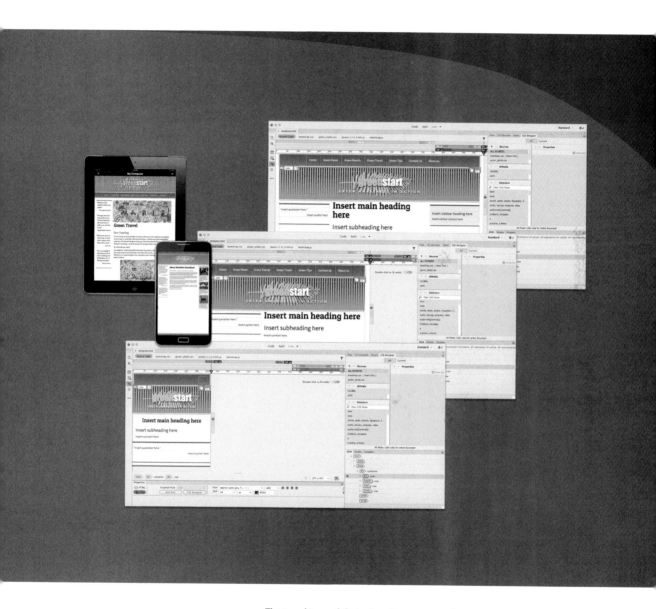

The trend toward designing sites to respond automatically to mobile devices and smartphones continues to grow exponentially. Dreamweaver has powerful tools to get your site mobile-ready.

Responsive design

The Internet of the 90s was never conceived for smartphones and tablets. For the first decade, the most difficult challenge a programmer or developer had to worry about was the size and resolution differences between 13- and 15-inch computer monitors. For years, resolutions and screen sizes only got *larger*.

Today, the chances that some or all of your visitors are using a smartphone or tablet to access your site are increasing daily. Statistics show that starting in 2014, more people were using mobile devices to access the Internet than using desktop computers, and that number has been increasing steadily ever since.

Mobile-first design

One concept that is starting to gain traction today is known as *mobile-first* design. It assumes that sites that aren't optimized for phones and tablets will shed users and traffic in this new environment.

This technique actually starts with a design for mobile devices, such as smartphones, and then adds content and structure for larger devices and computers. In some cases, the site content is actually minimized so that it loads and performs in an optimal fashion; then other content can be injected using JavaScript and databases for computers and more powerful devices. In the end, the decision to design for desktop or mobile first should be based on your site's demographics and analytics.

How your site deals with smartphones and mobile devices depends on whether you're adapting an existing site or developing a new one from scratch. For an existing site, you first have to create a basic design for the site's main components. Then, you have to work through each page, one at a time, to individually assess existing components—such as images and tables—that do not inherently adapt to the specific environment.

For new websites, the typical approach is to build in the adaptability as you create the overall design, and then build each page to achieve maximum flexibility. In either case, to support a truly mobile design, be aware that some site components may need to be replaced, left out of the final design altogether, or swapped out live by JavaScript or by the media query itself. For the time being, there is no single solution to all responsive issues, and many solutions are still in development.

Whether you design for desktop or mobile first, you still need to learn how to build designs that respond to all devices. To help web designers adapt pages and content to this changing landscape, two basic tools were created: *media type* and *media query*. These functions enable browsers to identify what size and type of device is accessing the webpage and then load the appropriate style sheet, if one exists.

Media type properties

The media type property was added to the CSS2 specifications and adopted in 1998. It was intended to address the proliferation of noncomputer devices that were able to access the web and web-based resources at that time. The media type is used to target customized formatting to reformat or optimize web content for different media or output.

● **Note:** In Lesson 4, "Web Design Basics," and Chapter 5, "Creating a Page Layout," you created the basic design for the website as it should appear on a standard desktop computer display based on the screen media type.

In all, CSS includes ten individually defined media types, as shown in **Table 7.1**.

Table 7.1 Media type properties

PROPERTY	INTENDED USE
all	All devices. "All" is the default media type if one is not specified in the code.
aural	Speech and sound synthesizers.
braille	Braille tactile feedback devices.
embossed	Braille printers.
handheld	Handheld devices (small screen, monochrome, limited bandwidth).
print	Documents viewed onscreen in print preview mode and for printing applications.
projection	Projected presentations.
screen	Primarily for color computer screens.
tty	Media using a fixed-pitch character grid, such as Teletypes, terminals, or portable.
tv	Television-type devices (low resolution, color, limited-scrollability screens, sound available).

Although the media type property works fine for desktop screens, it never really caught on with browsers used on cellphones and other mobile devices. Part of the problem is the sheer variety of devices in all shapes and sizes. Add to this smorgasbord an equally diverse list of hardware and software capabilities, and you've produced a nightmare environment for the modern web designer. But all is not lost.

Media queries

A media query is a newer CSS development that enables the webpage to inter-actively determine what formatting to use based on not only what kind of device (media type) is displaying the page but also on what dimensions and orientation it's using. Once the browser knows the type or size of the device it has encountered, it reads the media query to know how to format the webpage and content. This process is as fluid and continuous as a precision dance routine, even allowing the visitor to switch orientations during a session and have the page and content adapt seamlessly without other intervention. The key to this ballet is the creation of style sheets optimized for specific browsers, specific devices, or both.

Media query syntax

Like the CSS it controls, a media query requires a specific syntax to work properly in the browser. It consists of one or more media types and one or more expressions, or media features, which a browser must test as true before it applies the styles it contains. Currently, Dreamweaver supports 22 media features. Others are being tested or are still under development and may not appear in the interface, but you can add them manually to the code, if necessary.

The media query cre-ates a set of criteria to determine whether a specific set of rules contained within it is applied in a webpage.

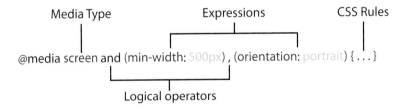

You can create media queries in a variety of ways. For example, they can be designed to work exclusively—by completely resetting the existing styling—or in tandem—by inheriting some styles and modifying specifications only as necessary. The latter method requires less CSS code and is typically more efficient. We will favor that method in the upcoming exercises and for the sample site design.

To learn more about media queries and how they work, check out www.w3schools.com/cssref/css3_pr_mediaquery.asp.

Adapting the site to different screen sizes

The GreenStart site design was based on a predefined Bootstrap layout that was created to be responsive out of the box. The Bootstrap framework provides a complex style sheet complete with numerous media queries and CSS rules to accommodate a wide variety of browsers and devices. Using a framework like

Bootstrap shortens the development time and allows you to concentrate on your content, instead of on technical issues.

In Lesson 6, "Working with a Web Framework," you fleshed out a Bootstrap layout with placeholder content based on your site design. This content will form the foundation of the site template, which you will use later to build pages for your site. At the moment, the page is partially responsive. In this exercise, you will learn how to tap into Bootstrap's built-in styles and media queries to make the page fully responsive.

Working with the responsive Scrubber

Before you can learn how to manipulate the Bootstrap framework for various screen sizes, it helps to identify how the current layout responds to changing screen sizes. The Scrubber tool was added to the previous release of Dreamweaver. It enables you to change the width of your document viewport so you can interact with the style sheets and media queries defined in the page and actually simulate different device or browser widths right inside Dreamweaver. In the past, to change the viewport you had to manipulate the whole program interface, dragging the edge of the document window or whole program to see a reaction in the page. Now, the Scrubber gives you that capability without having to change the entire program window.

1 Define a site based on the lesson07 folder as described in the "Getting Started" section at the beginning of the book.

2 Open **mylayout.html** from the lesson07 folder in Live view.

3 Maximize the program to fill the entire display; the program window should be displayed at a minimum of 1200 pixels in width to display and test all the media queries contained in the Bootstrap CSS.

The page displays the basic site design, complete with text placeholders and graphical treatments for the header and footer.

4 Drag the Scrubber to the left to decrease the width of the document window.

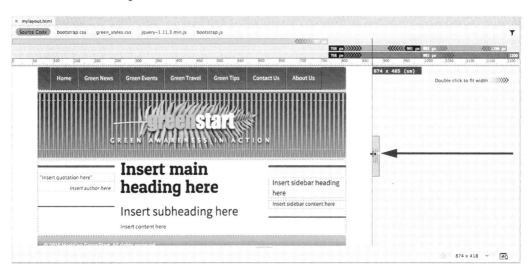

As the window narrows, the layout adapts to the changes. At first, the columns in the main content area share the row side by side. When the screen narrows below 768 pixels, the layout completely changes; all the elements stack vertically one atop the other, and the navigation menu collapses to an icon. The collapse coincides with the beginning of the final media query displayed in the VMQ interface at the top of the document window.

5 Stop dragging the Scrubber when the width reaches 320 pixels. Observe how the structure and content reacts to this screen width.

This is the width of the original iPhone and one of the narrowest smartphone screens you will want to support.

6   Drag the Scrubber to the right to increase the width of the document window.

Tip: Dreamweaver displays the current screen size just below the VMQ interface as you drag the Scrubber.

As the window widens, the content and structure resume their original styling. As you can see, the Bootstrap structure that you created is already fairly responsive, although there are a few things you will probably want to tweak.

For example, as the page narrows, the content continues to divide the space into the three-column layout. When the page narrows below 900 pixels, it gets unappealingly tight. Although the columns adjust properly for the tighter space, you may want to change the basic structure or content. One technique designers use in this situation is to hide content when there's no room for it or when it doesn't make sense to show it in a specific way or in a specific screen size.

Since the first column is intended for quotations and other inspiring messages, it's not essential to the purpose of the page or the site. Hiding it is one solution to the issue. Luckily, Bootstrap provides a simple solution.

Hiding Bootstrap elements

In this exercise, you will learn how to use predefined Bootstrap styles to hide unwanted content on small screens.

1   If necessary, open **mylayout.html** from the lesson07 folder in Live view.

2   Make sure the Scrubber is positioned fully to the right side of the document window and the document window is wider than 900 pixels.

The change can be made when the screen is at any width, but displaying the correct window size makes it easier to select the desired elements and styling and confirm the proper effect.

3   Click the Small media query in the VMQ.

The Scrubber jumps to the media query displayed in the VMQ. The three columns appear very tight at this width; headlines and text break into short lines, which may adversely affect readability.

4 Click the first column of the third row.

Select the `aside.col-sm-3` tag selector.

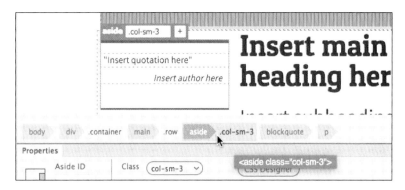

The HUD appears focused on the `<aside>` element.

Bootstrap provides various CSS styles to format elements at specific screen sizes. The framework classifies these sizes as *large* (desktop screens larger than 1200 pixels), *medium* (screens from 992 to 1199 pixels), *small* (screens from 768 to 991 pixels), and *extra-small* (screens below 768 pixels).

The class assigned to the `<aside>` (`col-sm-3`) styles the element for small screens. The styling will be inherited for larger screen sizes, but for smaller screen sizes there is no styling applied so the elements revert to CSS defaults. To hide the element on small screens, you need to add a second predefined Bootstrap class.

> **Note:** When you assign the class, the element will have two distinct classes assigned to it. In Bootstrap, it is common to see two or more classes assigned to structural elements.

5 Click the Add Class/ID icon ⊞ in the HUD.

A text field appears in the HUD.

6 Type `.hidden-sm` and press Enter/Return to complete the class.

A hinting menu appears as you type. After you select the desired class, Dreamweaver assigns it to the element. The element disappears from the layout.

> **Note:** This hinting menu is responsive to the screen width and the active media query. It may not show classes pertinent to other media queries.

7 Drag the Scrubber to the right to the Medium Bootstrap media query (992 to 1199 pixels).

The `<aside>` element reappears. Two classes appear on the element. This class is designed to hide elements on small screens. If the document width is from 768 to 991 pixels, the first column will disappear from the row. At 992 pixels, it reappears. Let's see what happens on extra-small screens.

8 Drag the Scrubber to the left until the document window is less than 768 pixels wide.

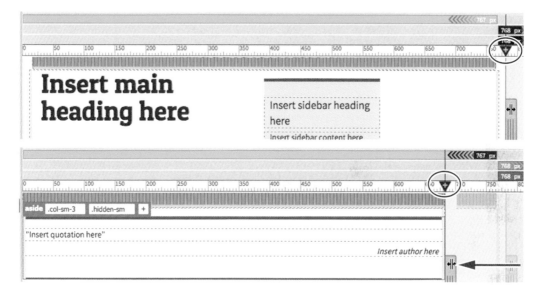

The `<aside>` disappears and then reappears back in the layout when the page drops below 767 pixels in width. Did you notice how the quotations reappeared at the top of the document in the Extra Small media query? The class `hidden-sm` hides the element only on small screens.

Hiding the element on small screens solves the original spacing issue when you have three columns. But on extra-small screens, the position of the element creates a new problem. It appears at the top of the page, pushing the main content down the screen where it may not be immediately visible on smaller devices. You could hide the element again on extra-small screens, but this is a problem that calls for a more imaginative solution.

In this case, the quotations are not too large or unwieldy to display; they just appear in the wrong place at the wrong time, or at the wrong screen size.

In situations like this, Bootstrap may offer a better alternative than hiding the element: You can *move* it. To learn how to rearrange the elements in your layout, you'll first have to remove the `hidden-sm` class.

Mobile-ready vs. mobile-optimized

Hiding elements, such as the first sidebar, is not an ideal solution in all situations. If you find yourself hiding an inordinate amount of content or you see that you have a large number of visitors via phones and tablets, you may want to consider creating a separate, mobile-*optimized* site.

A mobile-optimized site is often hosted on a subdomain, such as mobile. yourdomain.com, and contains pages designed specifically for mobile devices. These sites not only reduce page size, they may also select, or filter, content appropriate for the specific device. For example, some sites remove images, tables, video, and other large elements that don't scale down very well.

Obviously, producing two or more completely different sites can drastically increase design and maintenance costs, especially if the content changes on a regular basis. It's also not the best plan for optimizing your search engine ranking.

Instead, another option is to create your website based on an online database or content management system (CMS), such as Drupal, Joomla, or WordPress. A CMS can dynamically create pages as needed based on a template and style sheets with no additional effort. These systems enable you to design mobile-optimized templates that can automatically adapt to various devices and be programmed to deliver only content appropriate for those devices.

On sites that aren't made using a CMS, you may have to figure out a different solution. Hiding elements is good in some situations. But hiding an element doesn't prevent it from downloading. A hidden video or image still takes up valuable bandwidth on your visitors' devices and may cost them in minutes or data charges. Some designers take a mobile-first strategy and actually remove the undesirable content entirely from the page, making the pages and site work optimally on mobile devices. Then, they use JavaScript or other techniques to *inject* videos or large images into the layout but only on screens or devices that can handle it.

9 Select the `aside.col-sm-3.hidden-sm` tag selector.

The HUD appears focused on the `<aside>` element.

10 Position the cursor over the class `.hidden-sm`. Click the Remove Class/ID icon ✕.

The class is removed from the element.

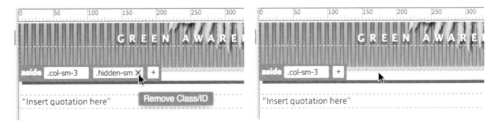

11 Save the file.

Before you can solve this "mobile" design challenge, you'll have to adjust the way you think about how elements are ordered and structured. You have to discard old-fashioned notions of form and function.

Creating a mobile-first structure

In this exercise, you will change the basic structure of the layout to create a mobile-first design.

1 Open **mylayout.html** in Live view, if necessary.

2 Make sure the document window is wider than 767 pixels and that the Scrubber is positioned against the right side of the window.

3 Drag the Scrubber to the Extra Small media query (767 pixels or less).

The content of the layout stacks vertically. The quotations appear at the top.

To build the mobile-first scheme, you have to adjust the current layout by moving the quotations to a location that will be more appropriate on extra-small screens. Then, by using a Bootstrap function, you will adjust the display of the elements for small screens before finally restoring the original design for larger screens and devices.

The process starts by moving the first column to a different position in the code structure. You could move the elements in Code view, but in this case you'll use the DOM panel.

4 If necessary, open the DOM panel by choosing Window > DOM. Resize the window as necessary to see the document structure.

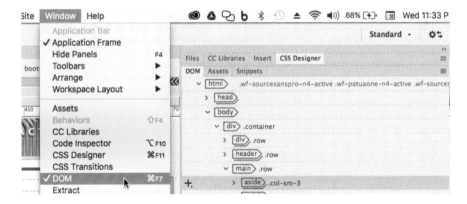

In Lesson 6 you learned that the DOM panel could create and edit elements in the layout; you can also use the DOM panel to move elements.

5 Select the `aside.col-sm-3` tag selector.
Observe the DOM panel display.

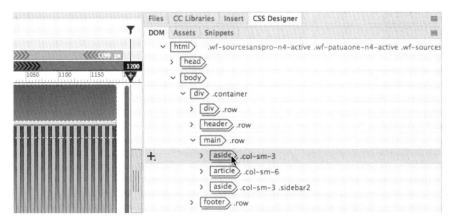

The `<aside>` element is highlighted. The diagram shows the parent `<main>` element and its three children. Notice that the child elements are indented in the structure. To move an element, simply drag it to the desired position in the schematic.

6 Drag the first `<aside>` element below the `<article>` element.

● **Note:** Dragging elements in the DOM panel requires a careful eye and a steady hand. It's easy to mess up the first few times you try. Take your time and check the code to make sure you put the element in the right spot. You can undo any errors by pressing Ctrl+Z/Cmd+Z.

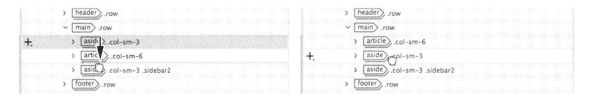

A green line appears indicating where the element will be inserted. If done properly, the element will appear below the `<article>` and be indented identically. The quotations now appear below the main content in the document window. The new arrangement puts the important content where it belongs on extra-small screens, but it has created a new problem on larger screens.

7 Drag the Scrubber to, or click, the Small media query (768 to 991 pixels).

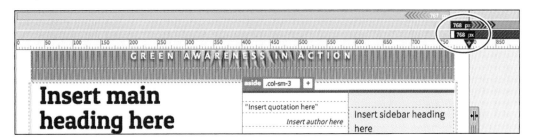

When the Scrubber moves into the Small media query, the three-column layout reappears, but now the quotations are displayed to the right of the main content. To restore the original look of the layout, you have to use a special Bootstrap function that is supplied within the predefined CSS.

8 If necessary, select the `aside.col-sm-3` tag selector for the quotations' column.

9 Using the HUD, add the following class:
`.col-sm-pull-6`

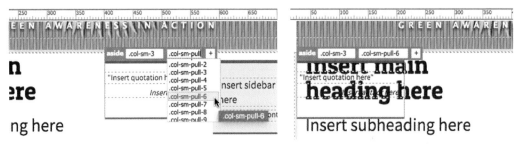

The `pull` function shifts the quotations back to the left side of the row, but it's overlapping the main content. To correct this problem, you can use a `push` function to move the main content to its original position in the center of the layout.

10 Click the `<h1>` element. *Insert main heading here.*
Select the `article.col-sm-6` tag selector.
Add the class `.col-sm-push-3`

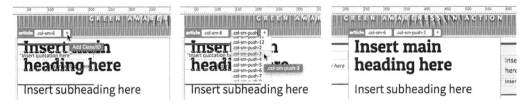

The main content section moves back to the center. All three columns are back in their original positions, but with an important *mobile-first* difference.

11 Drag the Scrubber to the left until the document window is narrower than 768 pixels.

Below 768 pixels the content displays in a single column again. The quotations appear below the main content. Through some Bootstrap magic you have created a layout that automatically adapts to mobile screens by shifting elements to more appropriate positions depending on the size of the screen.

12 Save the file.

Although you have solved one of the original challenges, the three columns still look a bit too tight on small screens. It would look better and less crowded in a two-column layout.

Manipulating column widths in Bootstrap

The great thing about Bootstrap is that it makes it easy to change the widths of columns at different screen sizes. In this exercise, you will create a two-column layout on small screens and then switch back to three columns at larger sizes.

1 Open **mylayout.html** in Live view if necessary.

2 Click the Medium screen media query (992 to 1199 pixels) in the VMQ.

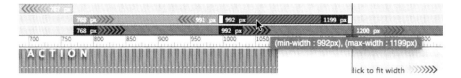

The Scrubber jumps to the selected media query. It may stop at the beginning or end of the screen range, but the CSS applies to the entire range, so it doesn't really matter where it stops. The important concept here is that setting the screen to the correct size before you begin allows you to see the results immediately.

Before you can change the layout, you have to understand how it was created in the first place. In Lesson 5, you built the three-column layout by manipulating the default Bootstrap class `col-sm-4` applied to each element in the row. The number indicates how many grid columns the element will use. By changing the number "4," you manipulated the widths of the columns to take space away from the `<aside>` elements and give more to the main content.

You may have noticed that the class has the letters `sm` in the name. This indicates that it applies to the Small media query. Some Bootstrap classes limit styling to a specific range of screen sizes, while others are designed for their styles to be inherited. In this instance, column widths are inherited in the larger screens sizes unless you reset the size with another class.

To change the number of columns displayed in different screen sizes, you simply have to change the existing classes or add additional ones. Since you want to keep the current layout on larger screens, the first change will be a minor one.

3   Click the quotation placeholder in Sidebar 1.
    Select the `aside.col-sm-3.col-sm-pull-6` tag selector for the first column.

4   In the HUD, edit the class name as highlighted:
    `.col-md-3`

This change makes the class start formatting on Medium screens. You'll have to change the `pull` function too.

5   In the HUD, edit the class name as highlighted:
    `.col-md-pull-6`

This change pulls the element into the first column for medium screens. You need to make the same changes for the other columns.

6   Select the second column. Change the classes for the main content element to:
    `.col-md-6` and `.col-md-push-3`

7   Change the class for Sidebar 2 to:
    `.col-md-3`

Nothing changes. The layout remains the same as before, which means the new classes are doing their job. The layout is ready now for medium and larger screens. But let's check out what happens on smaller screens.

8 Click the Small screen media query.

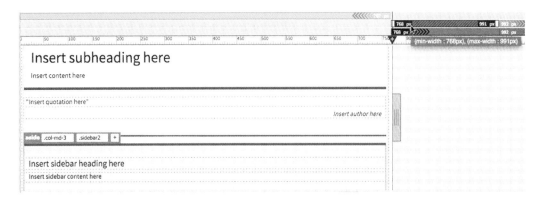

The document window resizes. The layout reformats into a single column, as it had done for the extra-small screens. This is because none of the Bootstrap classes are currently formatting these elements. To create the new column layout, you'll need to add new classes to each element.

9 Click the text "Insert main heading here."
Select the `article.col-md-6.col-md-push-3` tag selector.

On small screens, you want two columns on the first line and Sidebar 2 on the second line. You'll split the first line, with one-third for the quotations and two-thirds for the main content.

10 Add a new class to the `article`: `.col-sm-8`

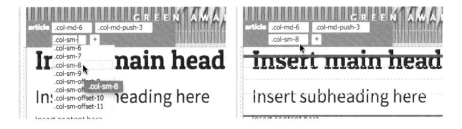

The main content section resizes to two-thirds of the screen width. Let's push the column to the right side of the row.

▷ **Tip:** Press Enter/Return to complete each new class.

11 Add a new class to the `article` element:
`.col-sm-push-4`

The column shifts to the right side of the row. Next, you'll deal with the quotations column, but you need to select Sidebar 1 first. This may be difficult to do in the document window with the columns overlapping as they are now. Whenever you have trouble selecting an element, remember you can always use the DOM panel.

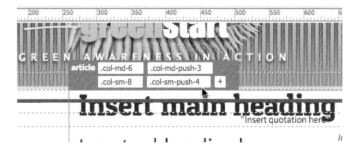

12 Click the `aside` element representing Sidebar 1.

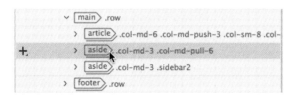

13 Add a new class to the `aside`: `.col-sm-4`

The column occupies four column grids but is still aligned to the right.

14 Add another new class to the `aside`: `.col-sm-pull-8`

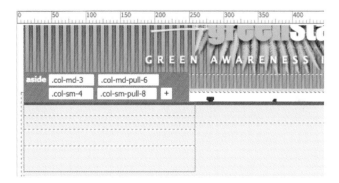

The column shifts back to the left edge, but Sidebar 2 is obscuring the first row. That's because nothing is formatting the column at this screen size and, since it isn't floating, it's trying to rise up to take the place of the other two elements. You can get it back into the mix by adding the proper class.

15 Use the DOM panel again to select the aside element for Sidebar 2.

16 Add the following class: `.col-sm-8`

The new class resizes the column. It now matches the width of the main content area and has shifted down below it. But, the column is aligned to the left. Let's match the alignment of the main content column.

17 Add another class to Sidebar 2: `.col-sm-push-4`

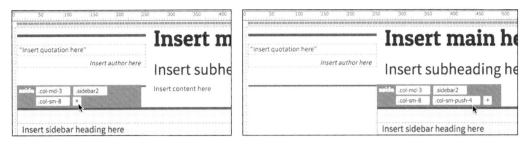

Sidebar 2 now aligns to the main content area. The styling of the new structure is complete. Let's see how it responds now to different screen sizes.

18 Drag the Scrubber left and right to test the styling at different screen widths.

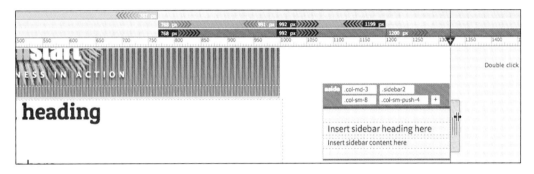

On small and extra-small screens, the layout looks fine. When the Scrubber hits the medium media query, the elements shift back to one row, but there's a problem. Sidebar 2 was OK originally, but now it appears far to the right edge of the screen. To get it back into the layout, you need to add a `push` function.

19 Add the following class to the `aside` element Sidebar 2:
`.col-md-push-0`

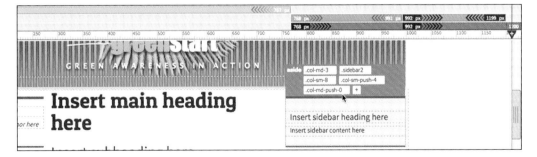

Sidebar 2 now fits back into the layout.

20 Drag the Scrubber left and right and observe the layout.

The layout shifts from one, to two, to three columns interactively as you change the width of the window. The layout works perfectly now, responding to all screen sizes smoothly. Overall, the structure looks fine, but the content could use a few tweaks on smaller screens. When the screen width gets to the smallest size, the logo in the header seems too big and actually extends beyond the edges of the screen. We will address this later in this lesson.

21 Save the file.

In the remaining exercises, you will learn how to style elements at different screen sizes by creating a custom media query and adding CSS rules to it.

Working with media queries

As you learned earlier, a media query is a method you can use to target styling to specific screen sizes, orientations, and devices. The Bootstrap framework provides predefined style sheets and JavaScript to make the underlying page structure responsive out of the box. In most cases, you only have to add your own style sheets and media queries to deal with conflicts with your page content or with specific design requirements. Whenever you start a project with predefined resources, it's a good idea to inspect the basic structure and the elements that format it.

Identifying media queries

The `<header>` consists of several elements and CSS effects. Take a moment to identify the styling that has already been created for mobile devices and what it does.

1 If necessary, launch Dreamweaver CC (2017 release) or later. Maximize the program to fill the entire screen.

2 Open **mylayout.html** from the lesson07 folder in Live view.

3 Choose Window > CSS Designer, if necessary, to display the panel. Click the All button.

4 Adjust the CSS Designer to display in two columns while maintaining a screen width of 1024 pixels or wider, if possible.

Setting up the CSS Designer in two columns makes working with and editing CSS easier.

5 Select ALL SOURCES.

Note: If your screen is too small to display the CSS Designer in two columns, you will still be able to complete the exercise.

6 Examine the @Media pane and note the existing media queries.

The window shows a list of media queries for a variety of screen sizes and applications.

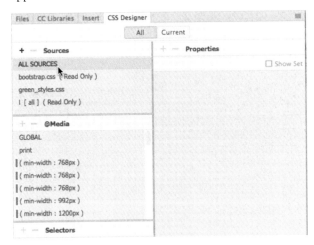

7 Click the first few media queries and observe the Sources pane display.

The **bootstrap.css** file is highlighted in bold, indicating that the selected media query is defined within that file. In fact, there are more than 60 media queries defined. The nature of a predefined framework is to anticipate all the needs and usage of basic HTML elements as well as any provided components and format them to work in any foreseeable environment or application. The rest is up to you.

8 Click the GreenStart logo.
Select the header.row tag selector.
Click the Current button.

The list of media queries is shorter, showing only the styles affecting the <header> element.

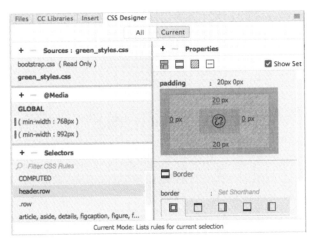

9 Drag the Scrubber to the left. Observe the text "Green Awareness in Action." When the words break to two lines, stop dragging the Scrubber.

● **Note:** The place at which the text breaks may differ in Windows than in macOS. This illustrates an issue mentioned earlier about how different browsers, devices, and even operating systems display HTML differently.

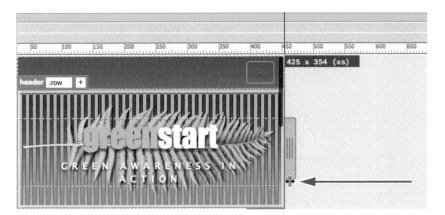

The motto breaks to two lines at approximately 425 pixels. Also note that the logo is filling the screen from left to right. If you added a new rule to adjust the formatting of this element, it would apply to the element at all screen sizes. That's because CSS rules are applied to all screen states unless limited by a media query, which is the meaning of the word GLOBAL in the @Media pane of CSS Designer. Since the Bootstrap media queries are locked, you'll need to create the new rule in the **green_styles.css** file.

10 Drag the Scrubber to the right until the motto appears on one line (between 426 to 438 pixels).

● **Note:** If your text doesn't display on one line, keep dragging to the right until it does, and then adjust the media query accordingly.

The motto should be displayed on one line. Dreamweaver allows you to create a new media query right in the document window. In the next exercise, you'll learn how to create your own custom media query.

Creating a custom media query

Once you identify the dimension that needs some special handing, Dreamweaver makes it easy to create new media queries. In the previous exercise, you moved the Scrubber to the last position where the motto displayed in one line.

1 Click the Add Media Query icon at the top of the Scrubber.

● **Note:** The purpose of the media query is to keep the motto on one line. Your pixel position may differ from the one described here or pictured in subsequent screen shots. Substitute your measurement in the following exercises, as necessary.

A Media Query Definition dialog appears. The max-width field is already popu-lated with the pixel position of your Scrubber (between 426 and 438 pixels). The min-width field is empty. That means this media query will apply to screens starting at this width and smaller. Using the max-width property means that none of the styles contained within it will affect any devices or displays wider than that designated. Make sure that the file name **green_styles.css** appears in the source pull-down menu.

● **Note:** If **green_styles.css** does not appear in the pull-down menu automatically, select it manually.

2 Click OK to create the media query.
If necessary, open the CSS Designer.

3 Click the All button.
Click **green_styles.css** in the Sources panel.

A new (`max-width`) media query has been added to the style sheet. You will use this media query to tweak the header and other elements on small screens.

4 Save all files.

Testing, testing

You have created a new custom media query designed to adjust the styling of specific elements in the layout at certain screen sizes. Although you chose a screen width that works for your own operating system and hardware, this measurement may not be correct for all visitors. The most crucial step in any web design project should be the testing regimen you use to confirm the effectiveness of your styling specifications. The media query or the rules contained within it may need to be adjusted so they work for the vast majority of visitors. In some cases, you may need to build separate media queries and rules for specific types of devices or browsers to deal with the variations in display. No website should be rolled out without testing the styling and content in multiple browsers on Mac and PC and on multiple devices.

Adding rules to a custom media query

CSS rules contained within a media query are used to reset or reformat elements based on the size, orientation, or type of device displaying your webpage. In this exercise, you will add rules to the new media query.

1 Open **mylayout.html** in Live view, if necessary.

2 Ensure the program is maximized to the full extent of the computer display.

3 Adjust the CSS Designer to display in two columns while maintaining a screen width of 1024 pixels or wider, if possible. Click the All button.

4 Click the new media query displayed in the VMQ interface (max-width 426 pixels).

> **Note:** From this point on I will refer to the width of my media query. If yours is different please substitute the width of yours instead.

The Scrubber repositions to 426 pixels. The motto should display in one line.

5 Drag the Scrubber to 320 pixels.

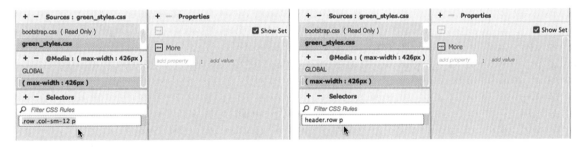

This is the width of the iPhone classic and probably the smallest device you will have to support. The motto breaks to two lines.

6 Click the motto "GREEN AWARENESS IN ACTION."

The motto is highlighted, displaying the HUD focused on the p tag. When adding new rules, it's vital that the rule be inserted into the correct style sheet and media query. The following technique will ensure that your rules get into the proper location every time in the CSS Designer.

7 Select **green_styles.css** in Sources.
Select (`max-width:426px`) in @Media.
Click the Add Selector icon ✚ in Selectors.

The selector `.row .col-sm-12 p` appears in the Selectors pane.

● **Note:** You created an identical rule in the global settings of the CSS file in Lesson 5.

8 Edit the selector name to `header.row p` and press Enter/Return as needed to complete the name.

9 Add the following property to the new rule:
`letter-spacing: .1em`

The motto narrows to fit on one line.

10 Drag the Scrubber to the right. Observe the header.

The motto remains narrow until the screen width exceeds 426 pixels. Then it expands to its original settings.

11 Save all files.

Next you'll adjust the size of the logo.

Copying and pasting CSS properties

In this exercise, you will learn how to create CSS styling by copying and pasting properties from one rule to another.

1 Drag the Scrubber to 320 pixels.
   Click in the `<header>` element in the second row of the layout.
   Select the `header.row` tag selector.

2 Click the All button in the CSS Designer, if necessary.

   The `<header>` has a complex set of properties creating the background effects. Writing a new rule to tweak the `<header>` on small devices might be a challenge for some designers. But instead of writing the new rule from scratch, you'll use a feature of the CSS Designer that will make the job fast and easy.

3 Select **green_styles.css** in Sources.

   The Selectors pane shows all the rules contained in the file. To narrow down the list to the rules affecting the `<header>`, use the Current button.

4 Click the Current button.

   The selectors list shows only the rules affecting the `<header>` in **green_style.css**. The `header.row` rule is at the top of the list.

5 Select `header.row` in Selectors.

   When the rule is selected, **green_styles.css** and GLOBAL are bolded, indicating where the rule is located. The Properties pane displays the current settings of the element stored by this rule. The CSS Designer enables you to copy some or all of the styles within one rule and paste them into a new or existing rule.

6 Right-click the `header.row` rule.

A context menu appears. Note the options for copying some or all of the properties in the rule.

7 Choose Copy Styles > Copy Background Styles.

8 Click the All button.

The All button must be selected to create new rules.

9 Select **green_styles.css** in Sources.
Select (max-width:426px) in @Media.
Click the Add Selector icon in Selectors.

The name .container .row appears in the Selectors pane.

10 Edit the name to header.row and press Enter/Return as needed to complete the selector.

The new selector appears in the window. The Properties pane is empty. The new rule has no styling applied to it.

11 Right-click header.row in Selectors.
In the context menu, select **Paste Styles**.

The background styles you copied in steps 6 and 7 are pasted into the new rule. The Properties pane is populated with the background styling from the original header.row rule.

There are now two rules formatting the <header>. Since the original rule is a global specification—it formats the element at all screen sizes—there's no need to keep any property that isn't going to format smaller screens. You need only the ones that will reset the logo's size. Let's delete the redundant properties.

12 Select the new header.row rule.
Select the Show Set option in Properties, if necessary.

The Properties pane displays all the specifications that were copied and pasted into the new rule. Beside the fields that allow you to add or edit CSS properties, each setting in the window also provides options to disable or delete the value.

13 Position the cursor over the `background-color` property.

When the cursor moves over the property, Dreamweaver highlights it. The Disable icon ⊘ and the Delete icon 🗑 appear to the right.

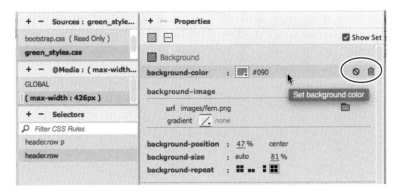

14 Click the Delete icon 🗑.

The background-color property is removed.

15 Delete all background properties except `background-size`.

The new rule now styles only the background size. At the moment, the setting is still identical to the one in the original rule. You can use this last property to reformat the `<header>` on screens smaller than 426 pixels, but remember it contains multiple settings to format the different components of the background.

16 Right-click the rule `header.row`.
Select **Go to Code** from the context menu.

Dreamweaver switches to Split view and loads **green_style.css** in the Code window. The window is focused on the `header.row` rule in the media query `@media (max-width: 426px)`.

17 Edit the declaration as highlighted:

```
background-size: 75% auto, auto auto;
```

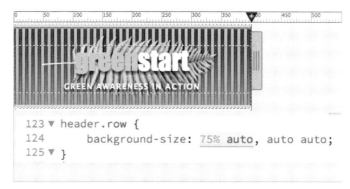

```
123 ▼ header.row {
124        background-size: 75% auto, auto auto;
125 ▼ }
```

Live view updates the `<header>` display, scaling the logo to fit the width of the screen. The new settings will prevent the logo from getting too big on the smaller screens.

18 Save all files.

The last step is to tweak the text styles to fit the content better on smaller screens.

Completing the mobile design

In this exercise, you'll wrap up the mobile design by overriding some of the existing rules to make the text fit better on the smaller window.

1 Open **mylayout.html** in Live view.
Adjust the screen width to 400 pixels to activate the new media query.

The logo and headings in the `<article>` element seem too large for the smaller screen. They take up too much space.

2 Open the CSS Designer, if necessary.
Select **green_styles.css** > (max-width:426px) > header.row

You can adjust all the text sizes in the `<header>` with a single property.

3 Create the following properties:

```
padding: 10px 0px
font-size: 90%
```

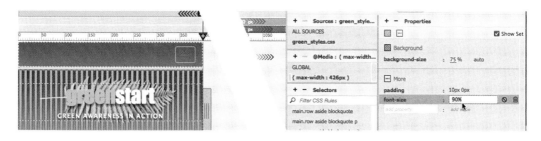

The logo text and motto scale down in size along with the height of the
`<header>`. Since you've adjusted the size of one element, why stop now?

4 Create a new rule: `main.row article h1`

● **Note:** Make sure
that the new rules all
go in your custom
media query.

5 Add the following properties:
   `padding-top: 15px`
   `font-size: 185%`
   `line-height: 1.1em`
   `text-align: center`

6 Create a new rule: `main.row article h2`

7 Add the following properties:
   `font-size: 150%`
   `line-height: 1.1em`

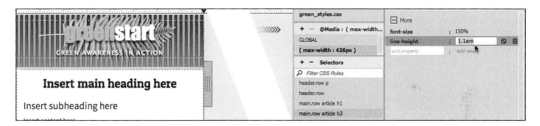

The h1 and h2 headings now fit the smaller screens better.

8 Save all files.

The basic page layout is complete and adapted to mobile screens. In the next
lesson, you will turn this layout into a Dreamweaver template, which will allow
you to create pages based on the site design quickly and easily.

More information on media queries

To learn more about media queries and how to work with them, check out the following links:

- *Adobe*: tinyurl.com/adobe-media-queries

- *W3C Consortium*: tinyurl.com/w3c-media-queries

- *Smashing Magazine*: tinyurl.com/media-queries-smashing

Congratulations! You've successfully modified a predefined mobile-ready layout and adapted it to your site design requirements. Although it's hard to imagine what amazing new features may come along, one thing you can be sure of is that Dreamweaver will continue to be at the forefront of web development. With support for media queries and other responsive techniques, the program continues to innovate and be a leader in the industry.

Review questions

1 What's the purpose of a media type?

2 What are media queries?

3 How do media queries target a specific device or screen size?

4 What's the difference between a mobile-ready and mobile-optimized site design?

5 Do you have to worry about CSS inheritance when using media queries?

6 In a mobile device, what happens to the webpage display if you rotate the device?

Review answers

1 A media type identifies what type of device is accessing the webpage, such as a screen, printer, Braille reader, and so on.

2 Media queries are a CSS3 specification for loading style sheets interactively, based on the screen dimensions and other characteristics of the device viewing the webpage.

3 Media queries include a logical expression that instructs the browser what style sheet to load, based on screen and device characteristics.

4 Mobile-ready sites adapt the existing design to various screen sizes using media queries and custom style sheets. Mobile-optimized sites build duplicate sites using subdomains and content created especially for each environment.

5 Yes. But bear in mind that media queries can be written to format exclusively or in conjunction with other media queries or style sheets. By allowing a base set of styles to be inherited, you can save on the total amount of CSS that needs to be created by the designer and downloaded by the user.

6 By rotating the device, you are changing the width of the screen and its orientation. Both factors can be used to load various style sheets or rules to format the page components and content differently.

8 WORKING WITH TEMPLATES

Lesson overview

In this lesson, you'll learn how to work faster, make updating easier, and be more productive. You'll learn how to do the following:

- Create a Dreamweaver template
- Insert editable regions
- Produce child pages
- Update templates and child pages

 This lesson will take about 1 hour and 15 minutes to complete. If you have not already done so, download the project files for this lesson from the Lesson & Update Files tab on your Account page at www.peachpit.com, store them on your computer in a convenient location, and define a new site based on the lesson08 folder as described in the "Getting Started" section at the beginning of this book. Your Account page is also where you'll find any updates to the lessons or to the lesson files. Look in the Lesson & Update Files tab to access the most current content.

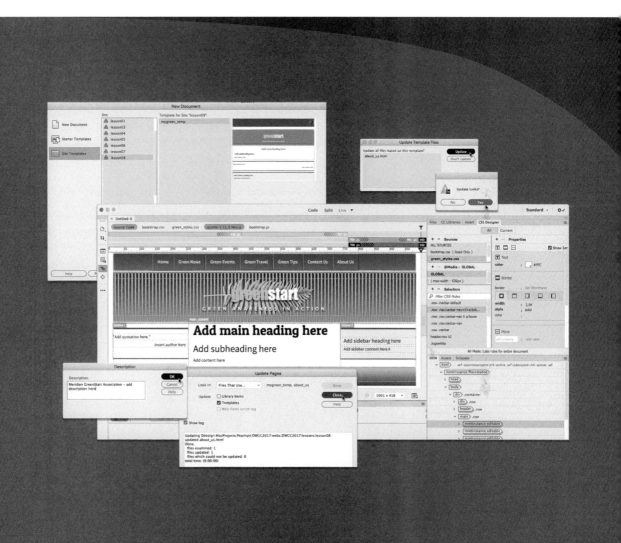

Dreamweaver's productivity tools and site-management
capabilities are among its most useful features for a
busy designer.

Creating a template from an existing layout

Note: Create a new site based on the lesson08 folder before beginning the lesson.

A template is a type of master page from which you can create related child pages. Templates are useful for setting up and maintaining the overall look and feel of a website while providing a means for quickly and easily producing site content. A template is different from a regular HTML page; it contains areas that are editable and other areas that are not. Templates enable a workgroup environment in which page content can be created and edited by several team members while the web designer controls the page design and the specific elements that must remain unchanged.

Although you can create a template from a blank page, converting an existing page into a template is far more practical and also far more common. In this exercise, you'll create a template from your existing layout.

1 Launch Dreamweaver CC (2017 release) or later.

2 Open **mylayout.html** from the lesson08 folder. Switch to Design view.

Note: Design view will often not display the layout accurately in the document window, and some of the responsive styling may not work as expected. Make good use of the DOM panel and your tag selectors if you have any doubt what element you are selecting.

The first step in converting an existing page to a template is to save the page as one. Most of the work creating a template must be completed in Design or Code view. The template options will not be accessible within Live view.

3 Choose File > Save as Template.

The Save As Template dialog appears.

4 If necessary, choose lesson08 from the Site pop-up menu. Leave the Description field empty. Type **mygreen_temp** in the Save As field. Click Save.

Tip: Adding the suffix "temp" to the filename helps to visually distinguish this file from others in the site folder display, but it's not a requirement.

Note: A dialog may appear, asking about saving the file without defining editable regions; just click Yes to save anyway. You'll create editable regions in the next exercise.

An untitled dialog appears, asking whether you want to update links.

Templates are stored in their own folder, Templates, which Dreamweaver automatically creates at the site root level.

5 Click Yes to update the links.

Since the template is saved in a subfolder, updating the links in the code is necessary so that they will continue to work properly when you create child pages later. Dreamweaver automatically resolves and rewrites links as necessary when you save files anywhere in the site.

Although the page still looks exactly the same, you can identify that it's a template by the file extension **.dwt** displayed in the document tab, which stands for Dreamweaver template.

A Dreamweaver template is *dynamic*, meaning that the program maintains a connection to all pages within the site that are derived from the template. Whenever you add or change content within the dynamic regions of the template and save it, Dreamweaver passes those changes to all the child pages automatically, keeping them up-to-date. But a template shouldn't be completely dynamic. Some sections of the page should contain areas where you can insert unique content. Dreamweaver allows you to designate these areas of the page as *editable regions*.

Inserting editable regions

When you create a template, Dreamweaver treats all the existing content as part of the master design. Child pages created from the template would be exact duplicates, and all the content would be locked and uneditable. This setup is great for repetitive features of the design, such as the navigation components, logos, copyright, contact information, and so on, but the downside is that it stops you from adding unique content to each child page. You get around this barrier by defining *editable regions* in the template. Dreamweaver creates two editable regions automatically, one for the `<title>` element and another for metadata or scripts that need to be loaded in the `<head>` section of the page; you have to create the rest.

First, give some thought to which areas of the page should be part of the template and which should be open for editing. At the moment, three sections of your current layout need to be editable: both the main content area and `<aside>` elements.

1 Open **mygreen_temp.dwt** from the lesson08 templates folder in Design view, if necessary. Maximize the program window to fill the entire screen.

2 Insert the cursor in the heading text *Insert main heading here*. Click the `article` tag selector.

Dreamweaver selects the entire `<section>` element.

Note: The template workflow currently works only in Design and Code views. You will not be able to perform any of these tasks in Live view.

3 Choose Insert > Template > Editable Region.

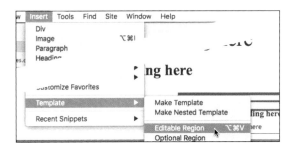

4 In the New Editable Region dialog, type **main_content** in the Name field. Click OK.

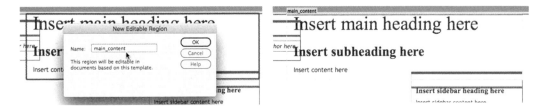

Each editable region must have a unique name, but no other special conventions apply. However, keeping the name short and descriptive is a good practice. The name is used solely within Dreamweaver and has no other bearing on the HTML code. In Design view, you will see the new region name in a blue tab above the designated area identifying it as an editable region. In Live view, the tabs are orange.

You also need to add an editable region to the two `aside` elements Sidebar 1 and Sidebar 2. Each of these sidebar regions contains text placeholders that you will be able to customize on each page.

5 Insert the cursor in Sidebar 1.
Click the `aside` tag selector.

6 Choose Insert > Template > Editable Region.

7 In the New Editable Region dialog, type **sidebar1** in the Name field. Click OK.

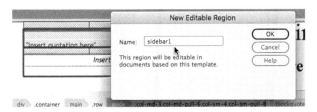
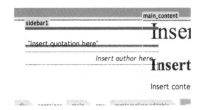

8 Insert the cursor in Sidebar 2.
Click the `aside` tag selector.

9 Choose Insert > Template > Editable Region.

10 In the New Editable Region dialog, type **sidebar2** in the Name field. Click OK.

11 Save the file.

Once you have set up the visible components of the template, you should turn your attention to areas that are hidden from most visitors.

Inserting metadata

A well-designed webpage includes several important components that users may never see. One such item is the *metadata* that is often added to the `<head>` section of each page. Metadata is descriptive information about your webpage or the contents it contains that is often used by other applications, like the browser or a search engine.

Adding metadata—for instance, a piece of data such as *title*—is not only a good practice, it's vital to your ranking and presence in the various search engines. Each title should reflect the specific content or purpose of the page. But many designers also append the name of the company or organization to help build more corporate or organizational awareness. By adding a title placeholder with the company name in the template, you will save time typing it in each child page later.

1 If necessary, open **mygreen_temp.dwt** in Design view.

2 In the Document Title field of the Property inspector, select the placeholder text *Untitled Document*.

Many search engines use the page title in the listings of a search result. If you don't supply one, the search engine will pick one of its own. Let's replace the generic placeholder with one geared for this website.

3 Type **Meridien GreenStart Association - Add Title Here** to replace the text. Press Enter/Return to complete the title.

Tip: If the Property inspector is not visible, you can display it by choosing Window > Properties.

Tip: The Document Title field is available in the Property inspector in all views.

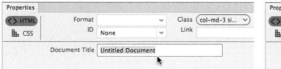 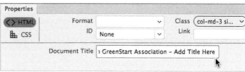

Along with the title, the other piece of metadata that usually appears in these search results is the page *description*. A description is a type of summary of a page that succinctly describes the contents in 25 words or less. Over the years, web developers have tried to drive more traffic to their sites by writing misleading titles and descriptions or outright lies. But be forewarned—most search engines have become wise to such tricks and will actually demote or even blacklist sites that use these tactics.

To achieve the highest ranking with the search engines, make the description of the page as accurate as possible. In many cases, the contents of the title and the description metadata will appear verbatim in the results page of a search.

4 Choose Insert > HTML > Description.

An empty Description dialog appears.

5 Type **Meridien GreenStart Association - add description here**. Click OK.

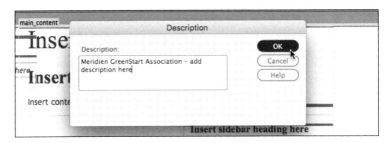

Dreamweaver has added the two metadata elements to the page. Unfortunately, only one of them was implemented properly in the template.

6 Switch to Code view. Locate and examine the `<title>` tag in the code and the surrounding markup.

```
7    <!-- TemplateBeginEditable name="doctitle" -->
8 ▼ <title>Meridien GreenStart Association - Add Title Here</title>
9    <!-- TemplateEndEditable -->
```

In most cases, the `<title>` will appear around line 8. Notice how the title appears between two comments that delineate an "editable" portion of the template named `"doctitle"`. This item was added correctly.

7 Locate and examine the `<meta>` tag containing the `"description"` and the surrounding markup.

```
21   <!-- TemplateBeginEditable name="head" -->
22   <!-- TemplateEndEditable -->
23 ▼ <meta name="description" content="Meridien GreenStart Association - add
     description here">
24   </head>
```

You should find the description near the end of the `<head>` section, around line 23. This element is not contained in an *editable* section of the template. This means that this metadata will be locked on all child pages and you will not be able to customize it for that page.

Luckily, Dreamweaver comes to the rescue by providing an editable section designed for metadata just like this. In this case, it can't even get any more convenient—you'll find it just above the description delineated by the HTML comment markup `<!-- TemplateBeginEditable name="head" -->`. To make the description metadata editable, you'll need to move it into this section.

8 Click the line number containing the entire description, or select the entire `<meta>` element using the cursor.

The `<meta>` tag and its contents should occupy a single line of the markup.

9 Press Ctrl+X/Cmd+X to cut this code into memory.

10 Insert the cursor at the end of the comment `<!--TemplateBeginEditable name="head"-->` (around line 21).

11 Press Enter/Return to insert a new line.

12 Click the line number of the new blank line.
Press Ctrl+V/Cmd+V to paste the description `<meta>` element.

The description is now contained within the editable template region named "head".

```
21    <!-- TemplateBeginEditable name="head" -->
22 ▼  <meta name="description" content="Meridien GreenStart Association - add
      description here">
23    <!-- TemplateEndEditable -->
```

13 Choose File > Save.

You now have three editable regions—plus editable metadata for the title and description—that you can change as needed when you create new child pages using this template.

14 Choose File > Close.

Now it's time to learn how to use your new template.

Producing child pages

Child pages are the *raison d'être* for Dreamweaver templates. Once a child page has been created from a template, only the content within the editable regions can be modified in the child page. The rest of the page remains locked within Dreamweaver. It's important to remember that this behavior is supported only within Dreamweaver and a few other HTML editors. Be aware: If you open the page in a text editor, like Notepad or TextEdit, the code is fully editable.

Creating a new page

The decision to use Dreamweaver templates for a site should be made at the beginning of the design process so that all the pages in the site can be made as child pages of the template. In fact, that was the purpose of the layout you've built up to this point: to create the basic structure of your site template.

1 Launch Dreamweaver CC (2017 release) or later, if necessary.

The template workflow functions only in Design and Code views. You can also access site templates from the New Document dialog.

2 Choose File > New, or press Ctrl+N/Cmd+N.

The New Document dialog appears.

3 In the New Document dialog, select the Site Templates option.
Select lesson08 in the Site list, if necessary.
Select **mygreen_temp** in the Template For Site "lesson08" list.

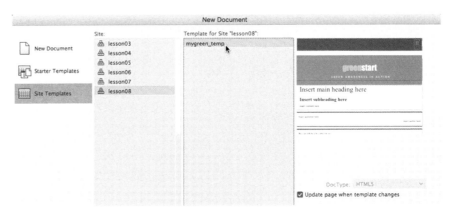

4 Select the Update Page When Template Changes option, if necessary.
Click Create.

Dreamweaver creates a new page based on the template.

5 If necessary, switch to Design view.

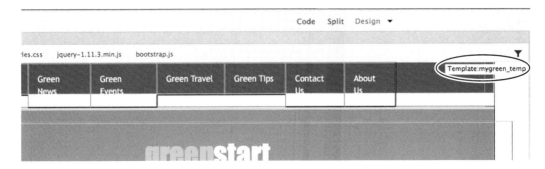

Typically, Dreamweaver defaults to the last document view (Code, Design, or Live) you were using for the new document. In Design view, you will see the name of the template file displayed in the upper-right corner of the document window. Before modifying the page, you should save it.

6 Choose File > Save.

The Save As dialog appears.

7 In the Save As dialog, navigate to the site root folder. Name the file **about_us.html** and click Save.

The child page has been created. When you save the document in the site root folder, Dreamweaver updates all links and references to external files. The template makes it easy to add new content.

Adding content to child pages

When you create a page from a template, only the editable regions can be modified.

1 Open **about_us.html** in Design view, if necessary.

You'll find that many of the features and functionality of templates work properly only in Design view, although you should be able to add or edit content in the editable regions from Live view.

2 Position the cursor over each area of the page. Observe the cursor icon.

When the cursor moves over certain areas of the page, such as the header, horizontal menu, and footer, the Locked icon appears. These areas are uneditable regions that are locked and cannot be modified within the child page inside Dreamweaver. Other areas, such as `sidebar1` and the main content section, can be changed.

> **Tip:** The Save As dialog provides a handy button to take you to the site root with a single click. Feel free to use it in any exercise, as needed.

> ◆ **Warning:** If you open a template in a text editor, all the code is editable, including the code for the noneditable regions of the page.

3 Open the Property inspector, if necessary.
In the Title field, select the placeholder text *Add Title Here.*
Type **About Meridien GreenStart** and press Enter/Return.

4 In the `main_content` region, select the placeholder text *Insert main heading here.* Type **About Meridien GreenStart** to replace the text.

▶ **Tip:** To add a little editorial flair, use the command Insert > HTML > Character > Em Dash to replace the hyphen in the heading with a long dash.

5 Select the placeholder text *Insert subheading here.*
Type **GreenStart - green awareness in action!** to replace the text.

6 In the Files panel, double-click **aboutus-text.rtf** in the lesson08 resources folder to open the file.

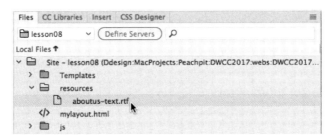

Dreamweaver opens only simple, text-based file formats, such as .html, .css, .txt, .xml, .xslt, and a few others. When Dreamweaver can't open the file, it passes the file to a compatible program, such as Word, Excel, WordPad, TextEdit, and so on. The file contains content for the main content section.

7 Press Ctrl+A/Cmd+A to select all the text.
Press Ctrl+C/Cmd+C to copy the text.

8 Switch back to Dreamweaver.

9 Insert the cursor in the placeholder text *Insert content here.*
Select the p tag selector.

10 Press Ctrl+V/Cmd+V to paste the text.

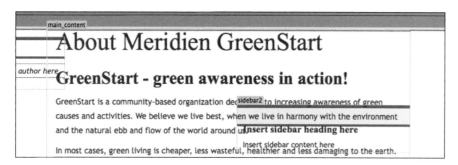

The placeholder text is replaced by the new content. You can also add content to the sidebar elements.

11 Open **sidebars08.html** in Design view from the site root folder.

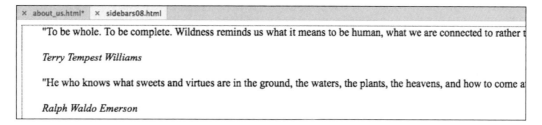

The file contains content for each sidebar. The top half is composed of three environmentally themed quotations, and the bottom half is composed of environmental tips and news.

12 Insert the cursor in the first paragraph and examine the tag selectors.

The tag selectors indicate a structure identical to what you created for the quotations column in Lesson 6, "Working with a Web Framework," but unformatted by the CSS. Let's use this content to replace the existing sidebar placeholders.

13 Click the `aside` tag selector.

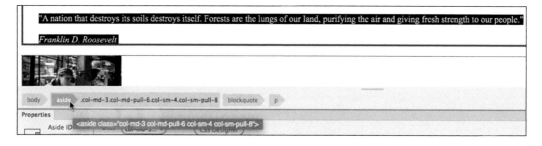

The tag selector shows the same Bootstrap class structure used in the template.

14 Press Ctrl+X/Cmd+X to cut the element into memory.

15 Select the **about_us.html** document tab.

The child page appears in the document window again.

16 Insert the cursor into Sidebar 1.
Select the `aside` tag selector.

17 Press Ctrl+V/Cmd+V to replace the sidebar placeholder.

The replacement content appears, formatted somewhat by the external CSS file.

18 Select the **sidebars08.html** document tab.

Tip: You may find it difficult to identify and select Sidebar 2 because of the inaccurate way Design view renders the page. To achieve success, be sure to use the correct tag selectors.

19 Repeat steps 12 through 17 to replace the Sidebar 2 placeholder.

All three editable regions have now been populated with content.

20 Close **sidebars08.html**.
Do not save the changes.

By not saving the changes, you preserve the content in the file if you want to repeat the exercise later.

21 Switch to Live view to preview the page.

The CSS styling kicks in again, and the page design and columns now render properly. Although you can't see the template name in the upper-right corner anymore, the names of the editable regions now display in orange tabs above their corresponding element.

22 Save the file.

You have populated the editable regions with text and pictures, but they can hold any type of web-compatible content, including tables, video, banner ads, and more. From time to time, content inserted into a template will require some additional styling via CSS.

For example, notice that the images and text in the right column are touching the left and right edges of the column. If the element had no background color, this would not be an issue. But normally you would want the text and other content to be moved slightly off these edges.

Formatting content in editable regions

Often content inserted into the editable regions will need to have custom styling created for it to help it adapt to the layout itself or to various screen sizes that may be encountered. In this exercise, you will create some new rules to format the picture and text in Sidebar 2.

1 Open **about_us.html** in Live view, if necessary. Maximize the program window to the full size of the computer display. Ensure that the document window and Scrubber show the page at least 1024 pixels in width.

Before you create any CSS rules, you should examine the structure of the element you want to style.

2 Select the first image in Sidebar 2.

The HUD appears focused on the `img` tag. The image appears in a semantic structure using the `<section>` and `<figure>` elements.

3 In the CSS Designer, select the All button.
Select **green_styles.css** > GLOBAL.
Click the Add Selector icon.

The selector `section figure img` appears in the Selectors window. This selector would format the image, but you'll want to limit the effect to Sidebar 2 to prevent unintended consequences.

4 Edit the selector name to say this:
`.sidebar2 section figure img`

By adding the class `sidebar2` to the selector name, only images appearing in this specific structure will be targeted.

5 Create the following properties in the new rule:
`margin: 0px auto`
`display: block`

The images in Sidebar 2 align to the center of the column. Setting *auto* margins on the left and right forces elements toward the center. But this alone will not achieve the desired result. Images are considered inline elements, which ignore margin settings. Setting `display: block` allows images to honor the specifications.

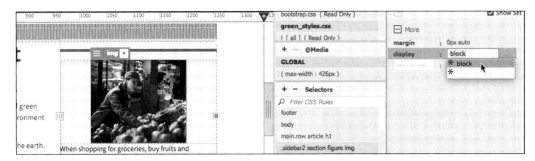

6 Select the caption below the first image in Sidebar 2.

The HUD appears focused on the `figcaption` element.

7 Choose **green_styles.css** > GLOBAL.
Click the Add Selector icon.

The selector `section figure figcaption` appears in the Selectors window. Let's limit this selector as you did the previous one.

8 Edit the selector name to say this:

`.sidebar2 section figure figcaption`

9 Create the following property:

`margin: 5px 10px 15px 10px`

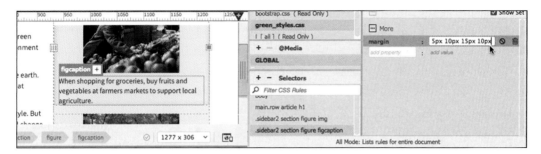

The captions are now indented on the left and right and exhibit more space at the top and bottom. Other custom styling may be needed as you create more pages, but for now you're finished.

10 Save all files.

11 Choose File > Close All.

Once you have created child pages and added content, there will come a time when you need to add or change a menu item, update the header or footer, or otherwise modify the content in the base template.

Updating a template

Templates can automatically update any child pages made from that template. But only areas outside the editable regions will be updated. Let's make some changes in the template to learn how templates work.

1 Choose Window > Assets.

The Assets panel appears. If it appears floating freely in the document window, you can dock it with the CSS Designer panel. The Assets panel gives you immediate access to a variety of components and content within your website folders.

2 In the Assets panel, click the Templates category icon. If no templates appear in the list, click the Refresh icon **C** at the bottom of the Assets panel.

The panel displays a list of site templates and a preview window. The name of your template appears in the list.

> ▶ **Tip:** The Template category in the Assets panel does not appear when a document is open in Live view. Switch to Design or Code view, if necessary, to access this category.

3 Right-click **mygreen_temp** and choose Edit from the context menu.

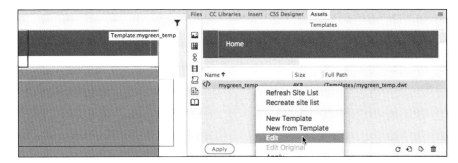

The template opens.

4 Make sure the document window is at least 768 pixels in width. Switch to Design view, if necessary.

5 In the navbar, select the text *Home*. Type **Green Home** to replace the text.

7 In the horizontal menu, select the text *Green News*. Type **Headlines** to replace the text.

8 Select and replace the text *Insert* with the word **Add** wherever it appears in the `main_content`, `sidebar1`, and `side_region2` editable regions.

9 Switch to Live view.

You can now clearly see the changes to the menu and content areas. In the template, the entire page is editable.

10 Save the file.

The Update Template Files dialog appears. The filename **about_us.html** appears in the update list. This dialog will list all files based on the template.

11 Click Update. The Update Pages dialog appears.

12 Select the Show Log option.

The window displays a report detailing which pages were successfully updated and which ones were not.

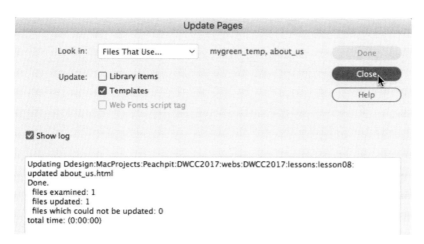

13 Close the Update Pages dialog.

14 Choose File > Open Recent > **about_us.html**.

Observe the page and note any changes.

The changes made to the horizontal menu in the template are reflected in this file, but the changes to the sidebars and main content areas were ignored, and the content you added to both areas earlier remains unaltered.

As you can see, you can safely make changes and add content to the editable regions without worrying that the template will delete all your hard work. At the same time, the boilerplate elements of the header, footer, and horizontal menu all remain consistently formatted and up-to-date, based on the status of the template.

15 Click the document tab for **mygreen_temp.dwt** to switch to the template file.

16 Switch to Design view.

17 Delete the word *Green* from the *Green Home* link in the horizontal menu. Change the word *Headlines* back to **Green News**.

18 Save the template and update the related files.

19 Click the document tab for **about_us.html**. Observe the page and note any changes.

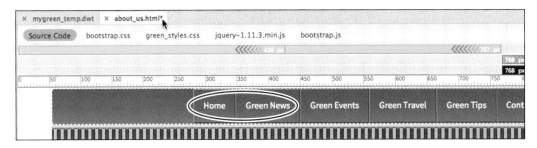

The horizontal menu has been updated. Dreamweaver even updates linked documents that are open at the time. The only concern is that the changes have not been saved; the document tab shows an asterisk, which means the file has been changed but not saved.

If Dreamweaver or your computer were to crash at this moment, the changes would be lost; you would have to update the page manually or wait until the next time you make changes to the template to take advantage of the automatic update feature.

20 Save and close all files.

Dreamweaver's templates help you build and automatically update pages quickly and easily. In the upcoming lessons, you will use the newly completed template to create files for the project site. Although choosing to use templates is a decision you should make when first creating a new site, it's never too late to use them to speed up your workflow and make site maintenance faster and easier.

> **Tip:** If an open page has been changed during the update, it will be updated by Dreamweaver and show an asterisk in the document tab by its name.

> **Tip:** Always use the Save All command whenever you have multiple files open that may have been updated by a template. In most cases, it's better to update when your files are all closed so that they are saved automatically.

Review questions

1 How do you create a template from an existing page?

2 Why is a template "dynamic"?

3 What must you add to a template to make it useful in a workflow?

4 How do you create a child page from a template?

5 Can templates update pages that are open?

Review answers

1 Choose File > Save as Template and enter the name of the template in the dialog to create a .dwt file.

2 A template is dynamic because Dreamweaver maintains a connection to all pages created from it within a site. When the template is updated, it passes any changes to the locked areas of the child pages and leaves the editable regions unaltered.

3 You must add editable regions to the template; otherwise, unique content can't be added to the child pages.

4 Choose File > New, and in the New Document dialog, select Site Templates. Locate the desired template, and click Create. Or right-click the template name in the Assets > Template category, and choose New From Template.

5 Yes. Open pages based on the template are updated along with files that are closed. The only difference is that files that are open are not automatically saved after being updated.

9 WORKING WITH TEXT, LISTS, AND TABLES

Lesson overview

In this lesson, you'll create several webpages from your new template and work with headings, paragraphs, and other text elements to do the following:

- Enter heading and paragraph text
- Insert text from another source
- Create bulleted lists
- Create indented text
- Insert and modify tables
- Spellcheck your website
- Search and replace text

This lesson will take about 3 hours to complete. If you have not already done so, download the project files for this lesson from the Lesson & Update Files tab on your Account page at www.peachpit.com, store them on your computer in a convenient location, and define a new site based on the lesson09 folder as described in the "Getting Started" section of this book. Your Account page is also where you'll find any updates to the lessons or to the lesson files. Look on the Lesson & Update Files tab to access the most current content.

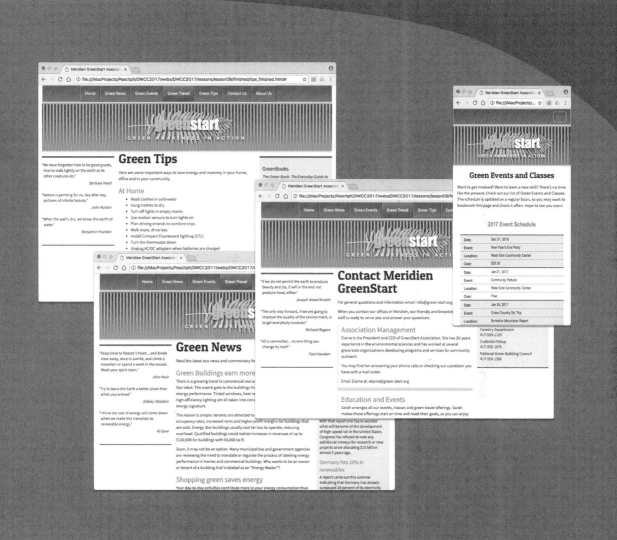

Dreamweaver provides numerous tools for creating, editing, and formatting web content, whether it's created within the program or imported from other applications.

Previewing the completed file

To get a sense of the files you will work on in the first part of this lesson, let's preview the completed pages in a browser.

1 Launch Adobe Dreamweaver CC (2017 release) or later, if necessary.
   If Dreamweaver is already running, close any open files.

2 Define a new site for the lesson09 folder, as described in the "Getting Started" section at the beginning of the book.
   Name the new site **lesson09**.

3 If necessary, press F8 to open the Files panel.
   Select lesson09 from the site drop-down list.

   Dreamweaver allows you to open one or more files at the same time.

4 Open the lesson09/finished folder.

● **Note:** To open consecutive files, hold the Shift key before selecting.

5 Select **contactus_finished.html**.
   Hold Ctrl/Cmd, and then select **events_finished.html**, **news_finished.html**, and **tips_finished.html**.

   By holding Ctrl/Cmd before you click, you can select multiple non-consecutive files.

6 Right-click any of the selected files.
   Choose Open from the context menu.

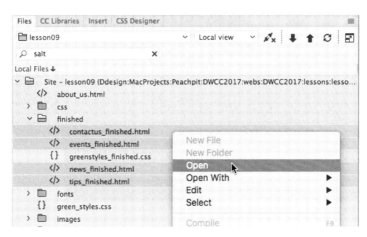

All four files open. Tabs at the top of the document window identify each file.

7 Click the **news_finished.html** tab to bring that file to the top, and switch to Live view if necessary.

⬤ **Note:** Be sure to use Live view to preview each of the pages.

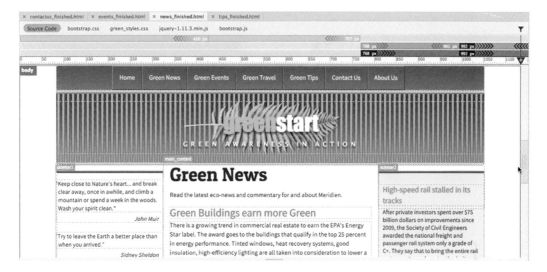

Note the headings and text elements used.

8 Click the **tips_finished.html** document tab to bring that file to the top.

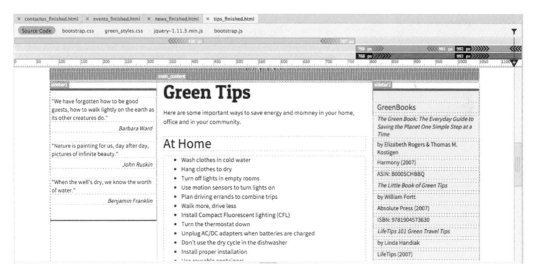

Note the bulleted list elements used.

9 Click the **contactus_finished.html** tab to bring that file to the top.

Note how text elements are indented and formatted.

10 Click the **events_finished.html** tab to bring that file to the top.

Note the two HTML-based tables used. The design employs techniques that allow the tables to adapt to tablets and smartphones.

11 Drag the Scrubber to the left.

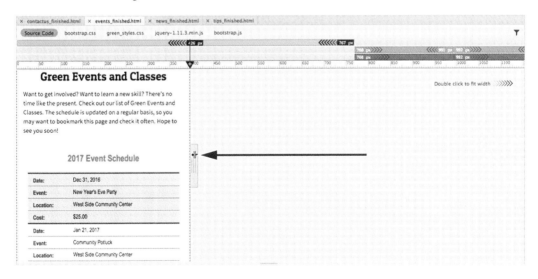

As the screen narrows, the media queries apply styles to reformat the content and layout. Note how the tables themselves drastically alter their appearance and structure to fit the smaller screens.

12 Choose File > Close All.

In each of the pages, there are a variety of elements used, including headings, paragraphs, lists, bullets, indented text, and tables. In the following exercises, you will create these pages and learn how to format each of these elements.

Creating and styling text

Most websites are composed of large blocks of text with a few images sprinkled in for visual interest. Dreamweaver provides a variety of means for creating, importing, and styling text to meet any need. In the following exercises, you will learn a variety of techniques for working with and formatting text.

Importing text

In this exercise, you'll create a new page from the site template and then insert heading and paragraph text from a text document.

1 Choose Window > Assets to display the Assets panel.
Select the Templates category icon 📄. Right-click **mygreen_temp** and choose New From Template from the context menu.

> **Tip:** The Assets panel may open as a separate, floating panel. To save screen space, feel free to dock the panel on the right side of the screen, as shown in Lesson 1, "Customizing Your Workspace."

> **Note:** The Templates tab of the Asset panel appears only in Design and Code views when documents are open. You will also be able to see it and select a template when no document is open.

A new page is created based on the site template.

2 Save the file as **news.html** in the site root folder.

It's a good idea when you first create a file that you immediately update or replace the various metadata placeholder text elements in the new page. These items are often overlooked or forgotten in all the hubbub around creating the text and images for the main content. First, you'll update the page title.

3 If necessary, choose Window > Properties to display the Property inspector.

> **Tip:** The Property inspector may not be visible in the default workspace. You can access it in the Window menu and dock it to the bottom of the screen.

4 In the Document Title field, select the placeholder text *Add Title Here*. Type **Green News** and press Enter/Return to complete the title.

Each page also has a meta description element, which provides valuable information about your page content to search engines. You'll have to edit it in Code view.

5 Switch to Code view.

The meta description should appear around line 22.

6 Scroll to editable region in the <head> section, around line 22.

7 Select the text *add description here* and type:
Read the latest eco-news and commentary for and about Meridien

Once the metadata is updated, you can start working on the main content.

8 In the Files panel, double-click **green_news.rtf** in the lesson09/resources folder.

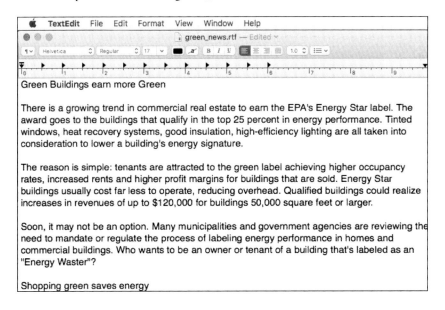

Dreamweaver automatically launches a program compatible to the file type selected. The text is unformatted and features extra lines between each paragraph. These extra lines are intentional. For some reason, Dreamweaver swaps out single paragraph returns for <br> tags when you copy and paste them from another program. Adding a second return forces Dreamweaver to use paragraph tags instead.

This file contains four news stories. After you move the stories to the webpage, you're going to create semantic structures, as you did for the quotation placeholders. As explained earlier, semantic web design attempts to provide a context for your web content so that it will be easier for users and web applications to find the information and reuse it, as necessary.

9 In the text editor or word-processing program, insert the cursor in the text *Green Buildings earn more Green.* Press Ctrl+A/Cmd+A.

All the text is highlighted.

10 Press Ctrl+C/Cmd+C to copy the text.
Close **green_news.rtf**. Do not save any changes.

▶ **Tip:** When you use the clipboard to bring text into Dreamweaver from other programs, you can now use Live or Design view if you want to honor the paragraph returns.

11 Switch back to Dreamweaver.

12 Switch to Live view, if necessary.

13 Select the text *Add main heading here.*
Type **Green News** to replace it.

▶ **Tip:** Remember you have to double-click an element in Live view to enter editing mode.

14 Select the heading *Add subheading here.*

The HUD appears focused on the h2 element.

15 Press Delete.

The placeholder is deleted.

16 Select the text *Add content here.*
Type **Read the latest eco-news and commentary for and about Meridien**.

The placeholder appears in the orange editing box.

17 Click outside the orange box.

The change is complete.

18 Click the newly edited text to display the HUD.

Press Ctrl+V/Cmd+V to paste the text from the clipboard.

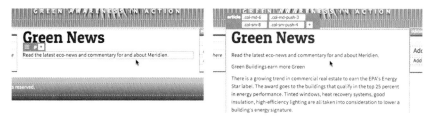

▶ **Tip:** Remember this technique when you want to paste multiple paragraphs into Live view.

The text from **green_news.rtf** appears in the layout preserving the various paragraph elements.

19 Save the file.

Although a human visitor would be able to distinguish where one story ends and another begins, there currently is no differentiation between them within the existing code. Adding semantic structures should be your goal whenever possible. This is encouraged not only to support accessibility standards but also to improve your SEO ranking at the same time.

Creating semantic text structures

In this exercise, you will insert HTML5 `<section>` elements to help define the individual news stories.

1 If necessary, open **news.html** in Live view.

Adding the section elements first requires you to select the various paragraphs that comprise the story. This is a great place to introduce the new multiselect feature in Live view.

2 Position the cursor before the text *Green Buildings earn more Green.*

3 Drag down to select the next four paragraphs ending with the text *"Energy Waster"?*

The first news story is selected and highlighted in blue.

4   Press Ctrl+T/Cmd+T to open the Quick Tag Editor.

The Quick Tag Editor appears in Wrap mode.
You can now type any tag name to wrap the selection.

Note: At the time of this writing, only the Quick Tag Editor allows you to wrap Live view selections.

5   Type `section` and press Enter/Return twice to create the new element.

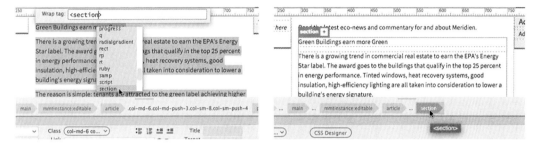

The new element appears in the tag selector interface wrapping the first news story. You can also use the DOM panel to create semantic structures.

6   Choose Window > DOM to display the DOM panel, if necessary.

7   In Live view, click the text *Shopping green saves energy*.

The element HUD appears in Live view focused on the p element. In the DOM panel, the p element is also highlighted.

8   Holding the Shift key, select the next three p elements in the DOM panel.

All four paragraphs are selected.

9   Right-click the selection and choose **Wrap Tag**.
Enter `section` in the element field.
Press Enter/Return as necessary to complete the new element.

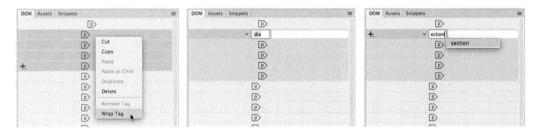

10 Wrap the remaining stories in new `<section>` elements.

When you're finished, you should have four `<section>` elements, one for each news story.

11 Save **news.html**.

Each of the news stories has headings, but they are currently formatted as paragraph elements. In the next exercise, you'll apply the proper tag to them.

Creating headings

In HTML, the tags `<h1>`, `<h2>`, `<h3>`, `<h4>`, `<h5>`, and `<h6>` create headings. Any browsing device, whether it is a computer, a Braille reader, or a cellphone, interprets text formatted with any of these tags as a heading. On the web, headings are used to introduce distinct sections with helpful titles, just as they do in books, magazine articles, and even term papers.

You are using one `<h1>` element per page as the primary page title. Any other headings used on the page should descend in order from the `<h1>`. Since each news story has equal importance, they all can begin with a second-level heading, or `<h2>`. At the moment, all the pasted text is formatted as `<p>` elements. Let's format the story headings as `<h2>` elements.

1 In Live view, select the text *Green Buildings earn more Green*. Choose **Heading 2** from the Format menu in the Property inspector, or press Ctrl+2/Cmd+2.

> **Tip:** If the Format menu is not visible, select the HTML mode of the Property inspector.

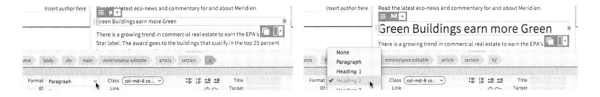

The text is formatted as an `<h2>` element.

2 Repeat step 1 with the text *Shopping green saves energy*, *Recycling isn't always Green*, and *Fireplace: Fun or Folly?*

All the selected text should now be formatted as `<h2>` elements. Let's create a custom rule for this element to set it off from the other headings with a unique style.

3 Insert the cursor in any of the newly formatted `<h2>` elements. Choose Window > CSS Designer to open the CSS Designer, if necessary.

4 Choose **green_styles.css** > GLOBAL.
Click the Add Selector icon ✚.

A new selector appears that targets the <h2> element but contains all the Bootstrap classes styling the parent elements too. There's no need for such a complex selector, so you should simplify these names whenever they appear.

5 Edit the selector to say this:

`section h2`

This name will target only <h2> elements used in the main content area.

6 Create the following specifications:

```
margin-top: 15px
margin-bottom: 5px
color: #090
font-size: 170%
font-weight: bold
```

● **Note:** By default, each heading tag—<h1>, <h2>, <h3>, and so on—is formatted smaller than the preceding tag. This formatting reinforces the semantic importance of each tag. Although size is an obvious method of indicating hierarchy, it's not a requirement; feel free to experiment with other styling techniques, such as color, indenting, borders, and background shading, to create your own hierarchical structure.

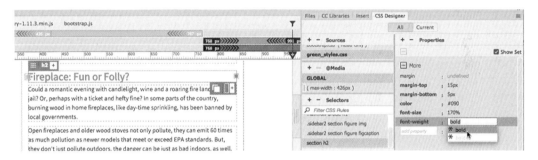

7 Save all files.

Adding other HTML structures

Descendant selectors are often sufficient for styling most elements and structures in a webpage. But not all the structural elements are available from the Insert menu or panel. In this exercise, you will learn how to build a custom HTML structure for a quotation and an attribution using the Quick Tag Editor.

1 Open **news.html** in Live view, if necessary.

2 In the Files panel, open **quotes09.txt** from the lesson09 resources folder.

```
 1   ----------------------- News.html -----------------------
 2
 3   "Keep close to Nature's heart... and break clear away, once in awhile, and climb a mountain or spend a week in
     the woods. Wash your spirit clean."
 4
 5   John Muir
 6
 7   "Try to leave the Earth a better place than when you arrived."
 8
 9   Sidney Sheldon
10
```

Since this is a plain-text file, Dreamweaver can open it. The file contains quotations you will insert in the various pages that will be created in this lesson.

3 Select the text of the first quotation, excluding the author name.
Press Ctrl+X/Cmd+X to cut the text.

4 Switch to **news.html**. Select the first quotation placeholder.
Press Ctrl+V/Cmd+V.

● **Note:** Remember to double-click the placeholder to open the orange editing box.

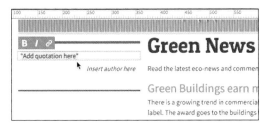 

The quotation has replaced the placeholder.

5 Switch to **quotes09.txt**.
Select and cut the author name, *John Muir*.

6 Switch to **news.html**.
Select the *Add Author Name* placeholder text and paste the text.

John Muir has replaced the author name placeholder.

Since there was only one quotation placeholder in the template, you'll have to create the other quotation structures from scratch.

7 Switch to **quotes09.txt**.
Select and cut the next two quotations and authors.

8 In **news.html**, click to select the first quotation.
Click the `blockquote` tag selector.

When an element is selected in Live view, Dreamweaver will paste new content directly after the selection.

9 Press Ctrl+V/Cmd+V to paste the new quotations and authors.

The text appears inserted in the `<aside>` element but after the `blockquote`.
The new text is not styled properly.

10 Using the cursor and the tag selector interface, compare the structure of the three quotations and note the differences.

The new quotations and author names appear in two separate p elements. Part of the styling problem is because of the missing parent `blockquote` element. Dreamweaver has no menu option for adding this specific tag, but you can use the Quick Tag Editor to build all types of custom structures in a pinch.

11 Drag to select the text for the second quotation, including the author name, *Sidney Sheldon*. Press Ctrl+T/Cmd+T.

Tip: Press Ctrl+T/ Cmd+T to toggle between modes in the Quick Tag Editor, if necessary.

The Quick Tag Editor appears. Since you have more than one element selected, it should default to Wrap mode.

12 Type `blockquote` and press Enter/Return twice to add the element as a parent to the two paragraphs.

The quotation text is now formatted properly, but the author name needs one more tweak: You need to change the tag applied to it. As with `blockquote`, there's no menu option for the `<cite>` tag.

13 Insert the cursor in the author name, *Sidney Sheldon*.
Select the tag selector for the `<p>` element.
Press Ctrl+T/Cmd+T.

The Quick Tag Editor appears. Since you have only one element selected, it should default to Edit mode. If the correct mode is not visible, press Ctrl+T/Cmd+T until it is.

Note: In HTML5, the cite element is used to identify the attribution of a quotation.

14 Press the Backspace key to delete "p" from the selected tag.
Type `cite` and press Enter/Return twice to complete the change.

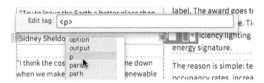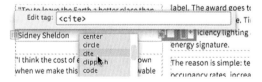

The author name now appears in a `<cite>` element and is styled identically to the other author.

15 Repeat steps 11 through 14 to create the `blockquote` and `cite` structure for the third quotation in **news.html**.

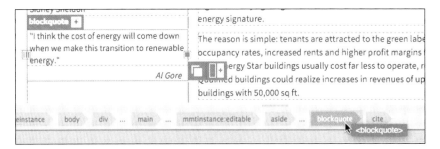

All three quotations are now structured properly in the first column.

16 Save and close **news.html**.

When you close **news.html**, Dreamweaver may prompt you to save **green_styles.css**. It is vital that you remember to save changes to the style sheet, especially when the file itself is not open. If you forget, you will lose any styling that was created in the previous exercises.

17 Click Save if necessary.

18 Close **quotes09.txt**. Do not save changes.

Closing the text file without saving the changes will preserve the original content in case you want to repeat this exercise later.

Creating lists

Formatting should add meaning, organization, and clarity to your content. One method of doing this is to use the HTML list elements. Lists are the workhorses of the web because they are easier to read than blocks of dense text; they also help users find information quickly.

In this exercise, you will learn how to make an HTML list.

● **Note:** The Template category is not visible in Live view. To create, edit, or use Dreamweaver templates, you must switch to Design or Code view or close all open documents.

1 Choose Window > Assets to bring the Assets panel to the front. In the Template category, right-click **mygreen_temp**. From the context menu, choose New From Template.

A new page is created based on the template.

2 Save the file as **tips.html** in the site root folder. Switch to Live view, if necessary.

3 In the Property inspector, select the placeholder text *Add Title Here* in the Document Title field. Type **Green Tips** to replace the text and press Enter/Return.

4 Switch to Code view. Locate the meta description element.
Select the text *add description here.*

5 Type **Learn the best eco-tips for your home, office and your community** and save the file.

The new description replaces the placeholder.

6 In the Files panel, double-click **green_tips.rtf** in the resources folder of lesson09.

The file will open outside Dreamweaver. The content consists of three individual lists of tips on how to save energy and money at home, at work, and in the community. As in the news page, you will insert each list into its own `<section>` element.

7 In **green_tips.rtf**, press Ctrl+A/Cmd+A.
Press Ctrl+X/Cmd+X to cut the text.
Close but do not save changes to **green_tips.rtf**.

You have selected and cut all the text.

8 Switch back to Dreamweaver.
Switch to Live view.

9 Select *Add main heading here.*
Type **Green Tips** to replace it.

10 Select and delete the entire `<h2>` element *Add subheading here.*

⬤ **Note:** When removing the placeholder text, be sure to delete the HTML tags too. The best way to select and delete entire elements is by using the tag selectors.

11 Double-click to edit the text *Add content here.*
Type **Here are some important ways to save energy and money in your home, office and in your community.**

The new text replaces the placeholder.

12 Click outside the orange editing box.

The orange box disappears.

13 Click to select the new paragraph.
Press Ctrl+V/Cmd+V.

The text for all three lists appears.

14 Drag to select the text starting at *At Home* and ending with *Buy fruits and vegetables locally.*

15 Press Ctrl+T/Cmd+T.
Type `section` and press Enter/Return.

The `<section>` element appears, wrapping the first list.

16 Select the text starting at *At Work* and ending with *Buy natural cleaning products.*

17 Insert the selection into a `section` as in step 15.

18 In Dreamweaver, repeat steps 14 and 15 to create the third list and `section` structure with the remaining text.

All three lists now appear in their own `<section>` elements.

As you did with the titles of the news stories, apply HTML headings to introduce the list categories.

19 Apply `<h2>` formatting to the text *At Home*, *At Work*, and *In the Community*.

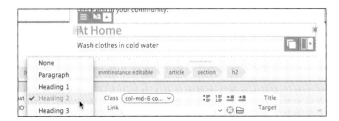

The remaining text is currently formatted entirely as HTML paragraphs. Dreamweaver makes it easy to convert this text into an HTML list. Lists come in two flavors: *ordered* and *unordered.*

20 Select all the <p> elements under the heading *At Home*. In the Property inspector, click the Ordered List icon ▦.

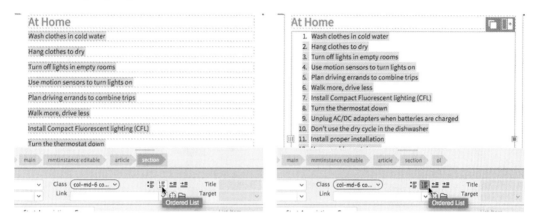

An ordered list adds numbers automatically to the entire selection. Semantically, it prioritizes each item, giving them intrinsic values relative to one another. However, this list doesn't seem to be in any particular order. Each item is more or less equal to the next one, so it's a good candidate for an unordered list—used when the items are in no particular order. Before you change the formatting, let's take a look at the markup.

21 Switch to Split view. Observe the list markup in the Code section of the document window.

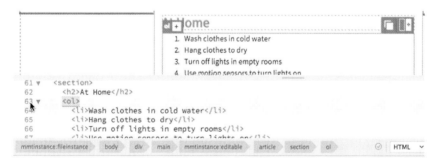

The markup consists of two elements: <ol> and <li>. Note that each line is formatted as an <li> (list item). The <ol> parent element begins and ends the list and designates it as an ordered list. Changing the formatting from numbers to bullets is simple and can be done in Code or Design view.

Before changing the format, ensure that the formatted list is still entirely selected. You can use the <ol> tag selector, if necessary.

▶ **Tip:** The easiest way to select the entire list is to use the <ol> tag selector.

Tip: You could also change the formatting by editing the markup manually in the Code view window. But don't forget to change both the opening and closing parent elements.

22 In the Property inspector, click the Unordered List icon .

All the items are now formatted as bullets.

If you observe the list markup, you'll notice that the only thing that has changed is the parent element. It now says <ul>, for *un*ordered list.

23 Select all the <p> formatted text under the heading *At Work*. In the Property inspector, click the Unordered List icon.

24 Repeat step 21 with all the text following the heading *In the Community*.

All three lists are now formatted with bullets.

25 In Dreamweaver, save and close **tips.html**.

Creating indented text

You're using the <blockquote> element in the semantically correct way to identify sections of text quoted from other sources, as in Sidebar 1, but some designers still use the element as an easy way to indent headings and paragraph text. Normally, text formatted this way will appear indented and set off from the regular paragraphs. If you want to comply with web standards, you should leave this element for its intended purpose and instead use custom CSS classes to indent text, as you will in this exercise.

1 Create a new page from the template **mygreen_temp**. Save the file as **contact_us.html** in the site root folder.

2 Switch to Design view, if necessary. Enter **Contact Meridien GreenStart** to replace the placeholder text *Add Title Here*.

3 In Code view, select the meta description placeholder text and type **Meet the amazing staff of Meridien GreenStart** to replace it.

4 In the Files panel, open **contact_us.rtf** from the lesson09/resources folder.

The text consists of five department sections, including headings, descriptions, and email addresses for the managing staff of GreenStart. You will insert each department into its own `<section>` element.

5 In **contact_us.rtf**, select all the text and cut it.
Close the file and do not save the changes.

6 In Dreamweaver, switch to Live view. Select and type **Contact Meridien GreenStart** to replace the placeholder heading *Add main heading here.*

7 Select and delete the entire heading *Add subheading here.*

8 Select and delete the text *Add content here.*

9 Click to select the heading Contact Meridien GreenStart.
Press Ctrl+V/Cmd+V to paste the content.

All the content cut from **contact_us.rtf** appears.

10 Format the text *Association Management* as a Heading 2.

As before, you need to wrap each content group in a `<section>` element.

11 Drag to select the heading and the rest of the text for this section including Elaine's email address.

12 Press Ctrl+T/Cmd+T.
Type `section` and press Enter/Return to create the element.

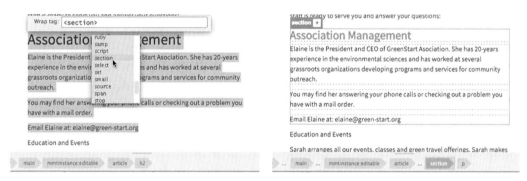

When the `<section>` element is created, the `<h2>` element formats in green as specified by the rule you created earlier.

13 Repeat steps 9 through 11 to structure and format the content for the *Education and Events, Transportation Analysis, Research and Development*, and *Information Systems* sections.

With all the text in place, you're ready to create the indent styling. If you wanted to indent a single paragraph, you would probably create and apply a custom class to the individual `<p>` element. In this instance, you want to indent the entire `<section>` element to produce the desired visual effect.

To make sure the styling is applied only to these employee profiles, you'll need to create a custom class that you can assign to them and style separately. First, let's create a `class` and add it to the style sheet.

14 In the CSS Designer, select **green_styles.css**.
Select GLOBAL.
Click the Add Selector icon ✚.

15 Type `.profile` and press Enter/Return to create the class selector.

You will create the styling after you apply it to the section.

16 Click any element in *Association Management*.
Click the `<section>` tag selector.

The element HUD appears focused on the `<section>` tag.

17 Click the Add Class/ID icon ⊞.

The Code Hinting window appears, displaying the appropriate attributes for the `<section>` element.

● **Note:** Don't forget to type the period at the beginning of the class name.

18 Type `.profile` as the class name and press Enter/Return to apply the class.

The hinting list appears and displays existing rules that match the name. Feel free to use the mouse or keyboard to select the name from the list.

19 Display the CSS Designer.
Click the Current button.

The class `.profile` appears at the top of the list of selectors. If you look at the Properties pane, you can see that no styles are set.

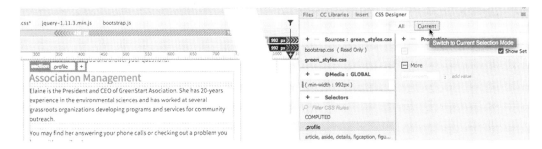

20 Enable the Show Set option, if necessary.

Enter the following properties:

```
margin: 0px 25px 15px 25px
padding-left: 10px
```

As with margins, border specifications can be entered individually or all at once.

21 Enter the following specifications for the left and bottom borders:

```
border-left: solid 2px #CADAAF
border-bottom: solid 10px #CADAAF
```

▶ **Tip:** When creating specifications manually, enter the property name in the field and press Tab. A value field will appear to the right. When Show Set is enabled, hinting may not appear in the values field.

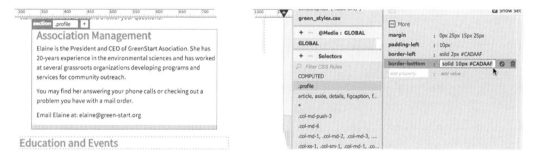

The borders appear on the left and bottom of the `section` element. The borders help to visually group the indented text under its heading.

22 Insert the cursor anywhere in the *Education and Events* section.
Click the `<section>` tag selector.

The HUD appears focused on the `section` element.

23 In the HUD, click the Add Class/ID icon and type `.profile` in the text field.

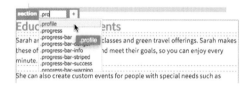

As you type, a hinting menu will show the matching class names. Feel free to select the name from the list. As soon as you add the class to the element, the formatting is applied to match the first section.

24 Repeat steps 23 and 24 to apply the `profile` class to the remaining `<section>` elements.

Each section is indented and displays the custom border.

25 Save all files.

Whenever you add new components or styling to a site, you need to make sure the elements and styling work well on all screen sizes and devices.

Making it responsive

In this exercise, you will test the new *profile* elements at multiple screen sizes and adapt them as needed.

1 If necessary, switch to Live view.

2 Drag the Scrubber to the left to make the document window narrower. Observe how the new components respond to the changing widths.

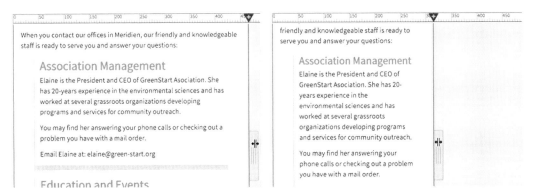

The `.profile` section looks fine until you get down to widths less than 450 pixels. At those sizes the left indent and border waste too much space. You can fix this situation easily by simply adding alternate styling in the appropriate media query.

● **Note:** Insert the new rule in the custom media query you created in Lesson 8, if it is different than the one described in step 4.

3 In the CSS Designer, click the All button.
Choose **green_styles.css** > (max-width: 426px).
Create the following selector:
`.profile`

4 Create the following properties in the new rule:
```
padding: 5px 0px
margin: 5px 0px
border-top: solid 10px #CADAAF
border-bottom: solid 10px #CADAAF
border-left-style: none
```

5 Save all files.

6 Test the new styles by dragging the Scrubber left and right to change the size of the document window.

7 Close all files.

● **Note:** You may need to click the Refresh button to see the changes in the layout properly.

When the screen drops down to your custom media query, the `.profile` section expands nearly to the full width of the screen and drops the indents and the left border. Remember to test all new components at every screen size and orientation and make changes to the styling as needed.

Creating and styling tables

Before the advent of CSS, HTML tables were often used to create page layouts. It was the only way to create multicolumn layouts and maintain some control over the content elements. But tables proved to be inflexible and hard to adapt to the changing Internet as well as just being a bad design choice. CSS styling provides so many more options for designing and laying out a webpage that tables were quickly dropped from the designer's toolkit.

That doesn't mean tables are no longer used on the web at all. Although tables are not good for page layout, they are good, and necessary, for displaying many types of data, such as product lists, personnel directories, and timetables, to name a few.

Dreamweaver enables you to create tables from scratch, to copy and paste them from other applications, and to create them instantly from data supplied from other sources, including database and spreadsheet programs such as Microsoft Access or Microsoft Excel.

Creating tables from scratch

In this exercise, you will learn how to create an HTML table.

1 Create a new page from the **mygreen_temp** template.
Save the file as **events.html** in the site root folder.

2 Enter **Green Events and Classes** to replace the *Title* placeholder text in the Property inspector.

3 Select the meta description placeholder and type **Meridien GreenStart hosts and sponsors a variety of eco events and classes for anyone interested in learning more about the environment or their community** to replace it.

4 Switch to Live view, select the *Add main heading here* placeholder heading and type **Green Events and Classes** to replace it.

5 Delete the *Add subheading here* placeholder.

6 Select the text *Add content here.*

7 Type the following text: **Want to get involved? Want to learn a new skill? There's no time like the present. Check out our list of Green Events and Classes. The schedule is updated on a regular basis, so you may want to bookmark this page and check it often. Hope to see you soon!**

8 Click outside the orange editing box.

The orange box closes, completing the paragraph.

9 Click the new paragraph to select it.
Choose Insert > Table.

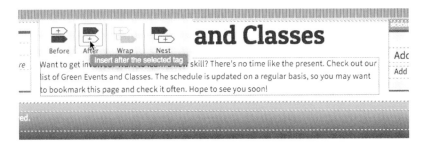

The Position Assist HUD appears.

10 Select After.

The Table dialog appears.

Although CSS has taken over most of the design tasks formally done by HTML attributes, some aspects of the table may still be controlled and formatted by those attributes. The only advantage HTML has is that the attributes continue to be well supported by all popular browsers, both old and new. When you enter values in this dialog, Dreamweaver still applies them via HTML attributes. But whenever you have a choice, avoid using HTML to format tables.

11 Enter the following specification for the table:
Rows: **2**
Columns: **4**
Width: **100%**
Border thickness: **1**

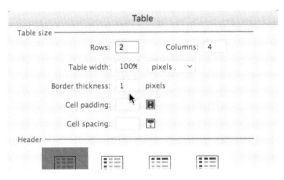

12 Click OK to create the table.

A four-column, two-row table appears below the main heading. Note that it fills the column from left to right. Let's wrap it in a `<section>` element.

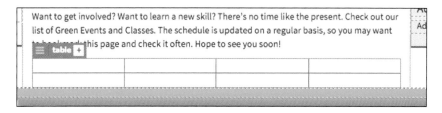

13 Select the table tag selector.
Select Insert > Section.

The Position Assist HUD appears.

14 Select Wrap.

The table is wrapped in a `<section>` element. The table is ready to accept input, but Live view is not optimized for data entry. If you have large amounts of data to enter, you're better off using Design view.

15 Switch to Design view.

16 Insert the cursor in the first cell of the table.
Type **Date** and press the Tab key.

▶ **Tip:** While in a table cell in Design view, pressing the Tab key moves the cursor to the next cell on the right. Hold the Shift key before pressing the Tab key to move to the left, or backward, through the table.

The cursor moves into the next cell of the same row.

17 In the second cell, type **Event** and press Tab.

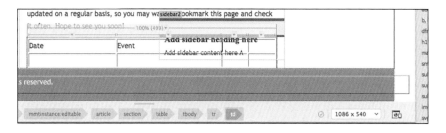

● **Note:** Design view does not display complex CSS styling properly. The sidebars may overlap the tables. If the preview is too hard to work with, try adjusting the width of the document window.

The text appears and the cursor moves to the next cell, but you may find it hard to see it. Depending on the width of the document window, Sidebar 2 may be overlapping the table structure visually, making it difficult to see or select the cells and their contents. Design view cannot accurately display modern CSS styling, so you end up with situations like this. In some cases, you can fix the display a bit by changing the size of the document window.

18 Drag the right edge of the document window to the left to make it narrower.

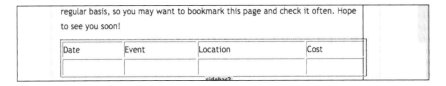

When you get to the correct width, Sidebar 2 will shift down below the table allowing you see the entire structure. The cursor should still be in the third column.

19 Type **Location** and press Tab.
Type **Cost** and press Tab.

Date	Event	Location	Cost

regular basis, so you may want to bookmark this page and check it often. Hope to see you soon!

The cursor moves to the first cell of the second row.

20 In the second row, type **May 1** (in cell 1), **May Day Parade** (in cell 2), **City Hall** (in cell 3), and **Free** (in cell 4).

When the cursor is in the last cell, inserting additional rows in the table is easy.

21 Press Tab.

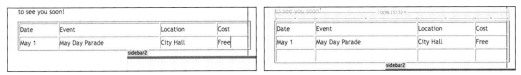

A new blank row appears at the bottom of the table. Dreamweaver also allows you to insert multiple new rows at once.

22 Select the `<table>` tag selector at the bottom of the document window.

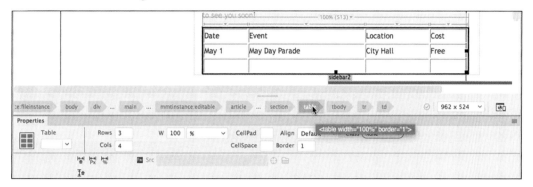

The Property inspector fields create HTML attributes to control various aspects of the table, including table width, cell width and height, text alignment, and so on. It also displays the current number of rows and columns and even allows you to change the number.

▶ **Tip:** If the Property inspector is not visible, select Window > Properties. Dock the panel to the bottom of the document window.

23 Select the number 3 in the Rows field.
Type **5** and press Enter/Return.

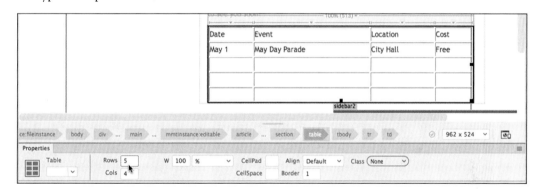

Dreamweaver adds two new rows to the table. You can also add rows and columns to the table interactively using the mouse.

24 Right-click the last row of the table.
Choose Table > Insert Row from the context menu.

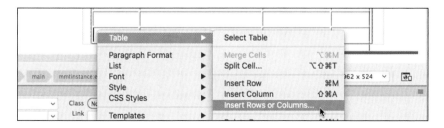

Another row is added to the table. The context menu can also insert multiple rows and/or columns at once.

25 Right-click the last row of the table.
Choose Table > Insert Rows or Columns from the context menu.

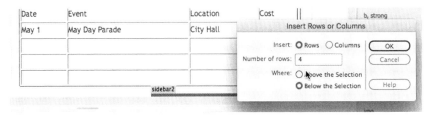

The Insert Rows or Columns dialog appears.

26 Insert four rows below the selection and click OK.

Four more rows are added to the table, for a total of ten rows.

27 Save all files.

Copying and pasting tables

● **Note:** Dreamweaver allows you to copy and paste tables from some other programs, such as Microsoft Word. Unfortunately, it doesn't work with every program.

Although Dreamweaver allows you to create tables manually inside the program, you can also move tables from other HTML files or even other programs by using copy and paste.

1 Open the Files panel and double-click **calendar.html** in the lesson09/resources folder to open it.

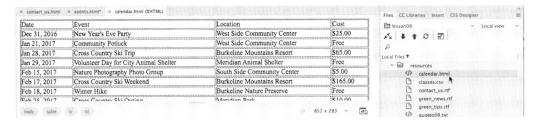

This HTML file opens in its own tab in Dreamweaver. Note the table structure—it has four columns and numerous rows.

When moving content from one file to another, it's important to match views in both documents. Since you were working in Design view in **events.html**, you should use Design view in this file too.

2 Switch to Design view, if necessary.

3 Insert the cursor in the table. Click the `<table>` tag selector.
Press Ctrl+C/Cmd+C to copy the table.

4 Close **calendar.html**.

5 Click the **events.html** document tab.

6 Insert the cursor in the table.
Select the `<table>` tag selector.
Press Ctrl+V/Cmd+V to paste the table.

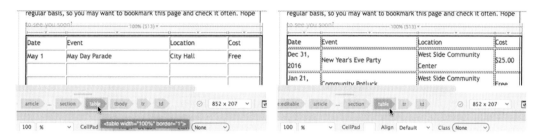

The new table element completely replaces the existing table. This workflow will work in Design and Code views. But you must match views in both documents before you copy and paste.

7 Save the file.

Styling tables with CSS

Currently, the formatting for the table is a mixed bag. Some is being supplied by HTML defaults and some by the Bootstrap framework. Whenever CSS styles conflict with HTML attributes, CSS wins. In the following exercise, you will create CSS rules to override any HTML styling.

1 Switch to Live view. Click the table.
Select the `table` tag selector.

2 In the CSS Designer, select the All button.
Choose **green_styles.css** > GLOBAL.
Create a new selector: `section table`

3 In the CSS Designer Properties window, deselect the option Show Set, if necessary.

4 In the Type category, click to open the font-family property.
Select Manage Fonts, and create the following custom font stack:
`Arial Narrow, Arial, Verdana, sans-serif`

▶ **Tip:** If you need a reminder how to create a custom font stack, check out Lesson 6, "Working with a Web Framework."

5 Create the following specifications for the new rule:

```
width: 95%
margin-bottom: 2em
font-family: Arial Narrow, Arial, Verdana, sans-serif
font-size: 90%
border-bottom: solid 3px #060
```

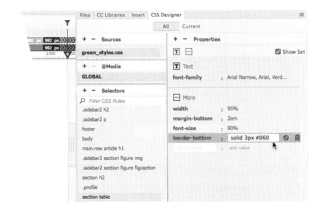

The table displays a dark green border at the bottom, and the content has been reduced in size and styled with Arial Narrow.

You have applied styling to one aspect of the table properties, but there are plenty of things you still need to address within this element.

6 Save all files.

The data in the table appears a bit crowded, and if your screen is narrower than the one shown, the content may wrap to two lines. It could use some extra spacing and other highlighting. The rule you just created formats only the overall structure of the table, but it can't control or format the individual rows and columns. In the next exercise, you will turn your attention to a table's inner workings.

Styling table cells

Just as for tables, column styling can be applied by HTML attributes or CSS rules. Formatting for columns can be applied via two elements that create the individual cells: `<th>` for table header and `<td>` for table data.

It's a good idea to create a generic rule to reset the default formats of the `<th>` and `<td>` elements. Later, you will create custom rules to apply more specific settings.

1 Choose **green_styles.css** > GLOBAL in the CSS Designer.

2 Create a new selector:

```
section td, section th
```

This simplified selector will work fine. Since `td` and `th` elements have to be in tables anyway, there's really no need to put `table` in the selector name.

3 In the Properties window, select the Show Set option.

4 Create the following properties for the new rule:
```
padding: 4px
text-align: left
border-top: solid 1px #090
```

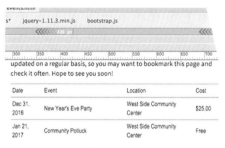 

A thin green border appears above each row of the table, making the data easier to read. You may not be able to see the border properly unless you use Live view.

Long columns and rows of undifferentiated data can be tedious to read and hard to decipher. Headers are often used to help the reader identify data. By default, the text in header cells is formatted in bold and centered to help it stand out from the normal cells, but some browsers do not honor this default styling. So don't count on it. You can make the headers stand out by giving them a touch of color of your own.

5 Choose **green_styles.css** > GLOBAL.
Create a new rule: `section th`

6 Create the following properties in the `section th` rule:
```
color: #FFC
text-align: center
border-bottom: solid 6px #060
background-color: #090
```

Note: The stand-alone <th> rule for the <th> element must appear after the rule styling th and td elements in the CSS or some of its formatting will be reset.

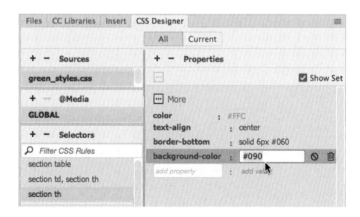

The rule is created, but it still needs to be applied. Dreamweaver makes it easy to convert existing `<td>` elements into `<th>` elements.

7 Click the first cell of the first row of the table.

In the Property inspector, select the Header option. Note the tag selector.

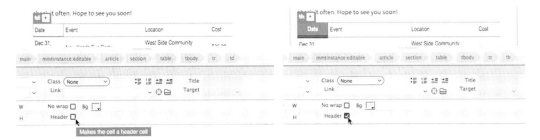

The cell background is filled with green.

When you click the Header checkbox, Dreamweaver automatically rewrites the markup, converting the existing `<td>` tags to `<th>` and thereby applying the CSS formatting. This functionality will save you lots of time over editing the code manually. In Live view, to select more than one cell, you have to use the enhanced table-editing function.

8 Select the `table` tag selector.

The element HUD appears focused on the `table` element. To enable the special editing mode for tables, you must first click the sandwich icon in the HUD.

9 Click the sandwich icon ▤.

When you click the icon, Dreamweaver enables an enhanced table-editing mode. Now you can select two or more cells, entire rows, or columns.

10 Click the second cell of the first row and drag to select the remaining cells in the first row. Or you can select an entire row at once by positioning the cursor at the left edge of the table row and clicking when you see the black selection arrow appear to the left of the row.

11 In the Property inspector, select the Header option to convert the table cells to header cells.

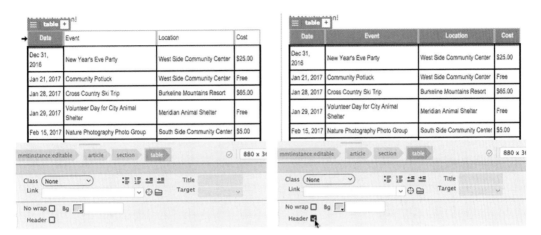

The whole first row is filled with green as the table cells are converted to header cells.

12 Save all files.

Controlling table display

Unless you specify otherwise, empty table columns will divide the available space between them equally. But once you start adding content to the cells, all bets are off—tables seem to get a mind of their own and divvy up the space in a different way. In most cases, they'll award more space to columns that contain more data, but that's not guaranteed to happen.

To provide the highest level of control, you'll assign unique classes to the cells in each column. But first you have to create the CSS rules. You can create them one at a time or all at once. If the rules already exist in the style sheet, it makes it easier to assign them to the various elements later.

1 Choose **green_styles.css** > GLOBAL.
   Create the following new selectors:

```
section .date
section .event
section .location
section .cost
```

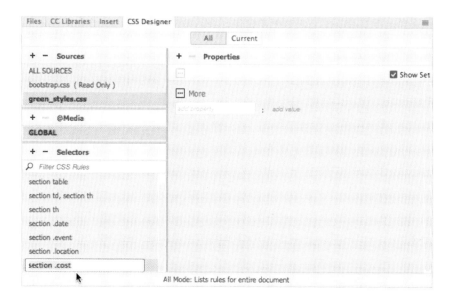

Four new rules appear in the Selectors window but contain no styling information. Even without styling, the classes can be assigned to each column. Dreamweaver makes it easy to apply classes to an entire column.

Note: If you have difficulty working with tables in Live view, you can perform all these actions in Design view.

2 Using the enhance table editing mode, position the cursor over the first column of the table until you see a black arrow. Click to select the entire column.

3 Click to open the Class menu in the Property inspector.

A long list of classes appears in alphabetical order. Most of these are coming from the Bootstrap style sheet. So you're going to have to carefully scroll through the list looking for the specific names using your mouse or keyboard.

4 Choose `date` from the list.

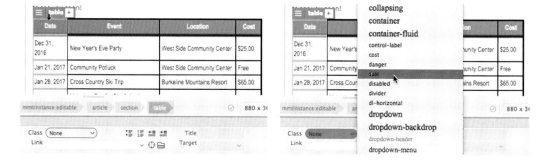

The cells in the first column should now have the class `.date` applied to them. But, after applying the class to the first column you may notice that Dreamweaver has returned the table to normal mode again.

5 Click the Sandwich icon  again.

Apply the `.event` class to the second column.

6 Repeat step 5 to apply the appropriate classes to the remaining columns.

Controlling the width of a column is quite simple. Since the entire column must be the same width, you have to apply a width specification to only one cell. If cells in a column have conflicting specifications, typically the largest width wins. Since you just applied a class to the entire Date column, settings will affect every cell at once. This will make it easier to get the table to adapt to any screen.

7 Add this property to the rule `section .date`:

`width: 6em`

The Date column resizes. The remaining columns automatically divvy up the space left over. Column styling can also specify text alignment as well as width. Let's apply styling to the contents of the Cost column.

8 Add these properties to the rule `section .cost`:

`width: 4em`
`text-align: center`

> **Note:** Even if you apply a width that's too narrow for the existing content, by default a cell can't be any smaller than the largest word or graphic element contained within it.

The Cost column resizes to a width of 4 ems, and the text aligns to the center. Now if you want to control the styling of the columns individually, you have the ability to do so. Note that the tag selector shows the class names with each element, such as `th.cost` or `td.cost`.

> **Note:** The event and location classes will be used later in the lesson.

9 Save all files.

Inserting tables from other sources

In addition to creating tables by hand, you can also create them from data exported from databases and spreadsheets. In this exercise, you will create a table from data that was exported from Microsoft Excel to a comma-separated values (CSV) file. As with the other content models, you will first create an `<section>` element in which to insert the new table. At the time of this writing, this function does not work with Live view.

1 Switch to Design view.

Insert the cursor in the existing Events table.

Select the `<section>` tag selector.

2 Press the right arrow key.

This technique moves the cursor after the closing `</section>` tag within the code.

3 Choose File > Import > Tabular Data.

The Import Tabular Data dialog appears.

4 Click the Browse button and select **classes.csv** from the lesson09/resources folder. Click Open. Comma should be automatically selected in the Delimiter menu.

5 Select the following options in the Import Tabular Data dialog:
Table width: **100%**
Border: **0**

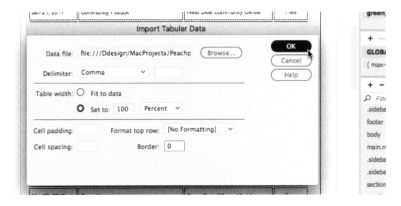

Although you set the width in the dialog, remember that the table width will actually be controlled by the table rule created earlier. HTML attributes will be honored in browsers or devices that do not support CSS. Because this is the case, make sure that the HTML attributes you use don't break the layout.

6 Click OK.

A new table—containing a class (course) schedule—appears below the first. To conform to the structure you created for the first table, you should insert the new one into an `<section>` element.

7 Select the `table` tag selector for the new table.

8 Choose Insert > Section.

Select **Wrap Around Selection** from the Insert menu.

Click OK to insert the `<section>` element.

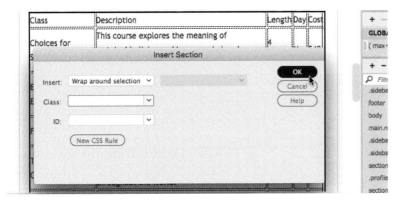

The new table is inserted into the `<section>` element. Green lines appear between the rows, but the header cells are not styled the same as in the first table.

9 Select the first row of the Class schedule.

In the Property inspector, select the Header option.

The header cells now display in green with reversed text.

The new table has an extra column, and the text is wrapping awkwardly in the last three columns. You will fix this display by using the `.cost` class created earlier and by creating additional custom classes, too.

10 Select the entire Cost column as you did in the previous exercise.

In the Property inspector, choose `cost` from the Class menu.

The two Cost columns are now the same width.

11 In the CSS Designer, right-click the rule `section .cost`.

Choose Copy All Styles from the context menu.

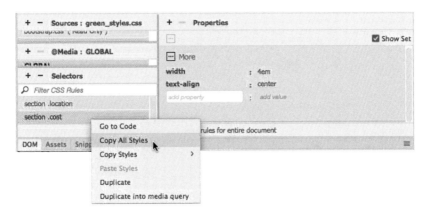

12 Create a new selector: `section .day`
Right-click the new selector.
Select Paste Styles from the context menu.

The new rule now has the same styling as the `section .cost` rule.

13 Repeat step 10 to apply the day class to the Day column in the Classes table.

Dreamweaver also provides an option for duplicating rules.

14 Right-click the rule `section .cost`.
Choose Duplicate from the context menu.
Enter `section .length` as the new selector.

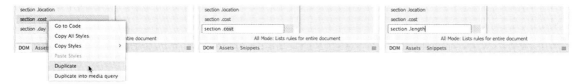

15 Apply the `.length` class to the Length column in the Classes table, as in step 10.

By creating and applying custom classes to each column, you have the means to modify each column individually. You need to make two more rules: one to format the Class column and the other to format the Description column.

16 Duplicate the rule `section .date`.
Enter `section .class` as the new rule name.
Change the width to `10em`.

17 Duplicate the rule `section .event`.
Enter `section .description` as the new name.

18 Apply the `.class` class to the Class column.
Apply the `.description` class to the Description column.

All columns in both tables now have classes assigned to them.

19 Save all files.

Adding and formatting caption elements

The two tables you inserted on the page contain different information but don't feature any differentiating labels or titles. To help users distinguish one set of data from the other, let's add a title to each and a bit of extra spacing. The `<caption>` element was designed to identify the content of HTML tables. This element is inserted as a child of the `<table>` element itself.

1 Open **events.html** in Live view, if necessary.

2 Insert the cursor in the first table.
Select the `<table>` tag selector.
Switch to Code view.

```
57 ▼    <section>
58 ▼      <table width="100%" border="0">
59          <tr>
60 ▼          <th class="date">Date</th>
61            <th class="event">Event</th>
62            <th class="location">Location</th>
63            <th class="cost">Cost</th>
64          </tr>
```

By selecting the table first in Live view, Dreamweaver automatically highlights the code in Code view, making it easier to find.

3 Locate the opening `<table>` tag.
Insert the cursor directly after this tag.
Press Return/Enter to insert a new line.

4 Type `<caption>` or select it from the code-hinting menu when it appears.

5 Type **2017 Event Schedule** and then type `</` to close the element, if necessary.

```
61 ▼    <section>
62 ▼      <table width="100%" border="0">
63            <caption>2017 Event Schedule</caption>
64 ▼        <tr>
```

6 Switch to Live view.

The caption is complete and inserted as a child element of the table.

7 Repeat steps 2 through 4 for the Classes table.
Type **2017 Class Schedule**
Then, type `</` to close the element, if necessary.

8 Switch to Live view.

The captions are relatively small, and they're lost against the color and formatting of the table. Let's beef them up a bit with a custom CSS rule.

9 Choose **green_styles.css** > GLOBAL.

Create a new selector: `table caption`

10 Create these properties for the rule `section caption`:

```
margin-top: 20px
padding-bottom: 10px
color: #090
font-size: 160%
font-weight: bold
line-height: 1.2em
text-align: center
```

The captions now appear sufficiently large and impressive above each table.

11 Save all files.

Formatting the tables and the captions with CSS has made them much easier to read and understand. Feel free to experiment with the size and placement of the caption and specifications affecting the tables.

Making tables responsive

The tables are finished and ready to go. They work fine for normal desktop displays and larger tablets, but the underlying page design is built to work seamlessly all the way down to smartphones. On the other hand, tables are notoriously ill-suited to smaller screens because they don't naturally adapt to them. To understand this concept, let's see how the current elements function on smaller screens.

1 If necessary, open **events.html** in Dreamweaver CC (2017 release) or later.

Design view doesn't provide an accurate rendition of the tables. Live view is a better choice, but the best option is to view the page in a browser.

2 Choose File > Real Time Preview.
Choose your favorite browser from the list.

The page opens in the browser, displaying all the colors, fonts, background images, and other CSS specifications set by the style sheet. To see how the tables will react to a smaller screen, just resize the browser window.

Note: The list will show only the browsers that are already installed on your computer. If you add new browsers, you will have to add them to this list manually.

3 Drag the right edge of the browser window to the left to make it narrower. Watch carefully how the tables respond, or don't respond, to the changing environment.

As the screen becomes narrower, the media queries will kick in and reformat the page and components to adapt to the smaller screen. Since the table widths are set to 95%, they mostly scale down with the page. But at the smallest sizes, the text within the table is trying to fit by wrapping in very narrow columns.

We need to rethink the whole concept of table design and display. You need to change the basic nature of the elements that compose tables so you can display them in a completely different way. During this process, you may sometimes find it easier to work in the CSS Designer; at other times you may want to enter the settings directly in Code view. Feel free to use whichever method feels more comfortable to you.

4 In Dreamweaver, switch to Live view and open the CSS Designer, if necessary. Click the custom media query in the VMQ you created in Lesson 7.

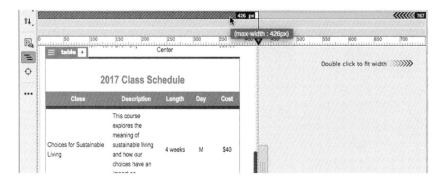

5 Choose **green_styles.css** > (max-width:426px) in the CSS Designer.

Your media query may differ from the one described. Choose the one you created in **green_styles.css**.

6 Create a new selector: `section td, section th`

7 Add the `display: block` property to the new rule.

The cells are now displayed vertically, stacking one atop the other when the width of the document window is narrower than 426 pixels.

This rule resets the default behavior of the table elements so that you can control their appearance on smaller screens. Some cells appear narrower than others because formatting is still being inherited from other parts of the style sheet. You'll have to create additional rules to override these specifications.

Note: Be sure that all subsequent rules and properties are added only to the custom media query.

8 Create a new rule: `section table`
Give the new rule the following properties:
`margin-right: auto`
`margin-left: auto`

With the data stacking vertically, it doesn't make much sense now to have a header row. You could set the header row to the `display:none` property to hide it, but that's not recommended for accessibility standards. The next best thing would be to simply format it to take up no space.

9 Create a new rule: `section th`
Give the new rule the following properties:
`height: 0`
`margin: 0`
`padding: 0`
`font-size: 0`
`border: none`
`overflow: hidden`

The header rows disappear visually but are still accessible to visitors using screen readers or other assistive devices. But now that they are invisible, you have to address the fact that there are no headers describing the data being displayed.

For this purpose, you'll resort to a new CSS3 property that can actually create labels based on the CSS class applied to the cell. Some of the latest CSS3 properties are not directly available in the CSS Designer, but you can enter them manually in the Properties window or in Code view, and Dreamweaver may provide hinting support for them as well.

10 Create a new rule: `td.date:before`

> ● **Note:** This type of selector is called a pseudo-class and is related to the classes you created for link behaviors in Lesson 6, "Working with a Web Framework."

11 Enable the Show Set option.
Enter the following property:value combo:
`content: "Date: "`

> ● **Note:** Make sure you add a space after the colon in the label. This will ensure that there is a space between the label and the cell content.

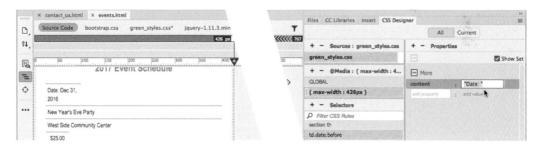

Notice that the label `Date:` appears in all the cells styled by the `date` class. You need to make a similar rule for each of the data elements.

Note: Be sure that all subsequent rules and properties are added only to the custom media query.

12 Repeat steps 10 and 11 to create the following rules and properties:

Rule	Property: Value
`td.event:before`	`content: "Event: "`
`td.location:before`	`content: "Location: "`
`td.cost:before`	`content: "Cost: "`
`td.class:before`	`content: "Class: "`
`td.description:before`	`content: "Description: "`
`td.day:before`	`content: "Day: "`
`td.length:before`	`content: "Length: "`

Each data cell now shows the appropriate labels. CSS can also style the data and labels.

Note: If you make a single selector as shown in step 13, do not add a comma on the last selector, which would disable the rule altogether. If you don't make a single selector, be sure to remove the comma from each one.

13 Create the following selector:

```
section .date,
section .event,
section .location,
section .cost,
section .class,
section .description,
section .length,
section .day
```

Tip: Creating long selectors may be easier to do in Code view. You can access the **green_styles.css** file by clicking its name in the Referenced file interface at the top of the document window.

I typed this rule on separate lines to make it easier to read, but you should enter it as one long string in the selector name field or in Code view. As long as the styling for all the data cells is identical, you can combine all the selectors into a single rule, separated by commas. Remember to mind the punctuation and spelling carefully. Even a tiny error in the code can cause the formatting to fail. If you want the styling to be different in one or more of the elements, then create eight separate rules.

Next, let's apply some styling to the labels themselves to help make them stand out more distinctly.

14 Apply the following properties to the new rule or in each of the separate rules:

```
width: 100%
padding-left: 30%
position: relative
text-align: left
```

● **Note:** Although the formatting is identical for these classes at this point, you may want to adjust the styling for one or more items later. Making separate rules can add flexibility even though it adds to the amount of code that has to be downloaded.

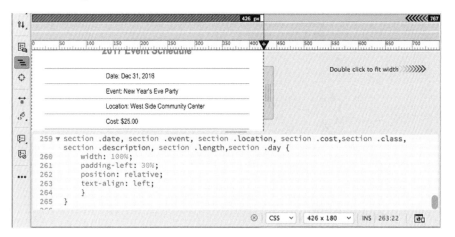

The event and class entries are now indented, and all appear at the same width. Next, you'll add a rule to differentiate the labels from the content of the tables themselves.

15 Create a new rule: `td:before`

Give the new rule the following properties:

```
width: 25%
display: block
padding-right: 10px
position: absolute
top: 6px
left: 1em
color: #060
font-weight: bold
white-space: nowrap
```

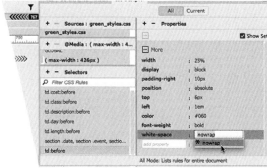

The labels now appear separated from the data and are styled in boldface and dark green. The only thing left to do now is to differentiate one record from the next. One way is to simply add a darker border between each table row.

16 Create a new rule: `section tr`

Give the new rule the following property:

`border-bottom: solid 2px #060`

Using a CSS3 selector you will add a little more pizzazz to the table.

17 Create a new rule: `section tr:nth-of-type(even)`

Give the new rule the following property:

`background-color: #D4EAD4`

◆ **Warning:** Advanced selectors like `nth-of-type(even)` may not be supported by older browsers.

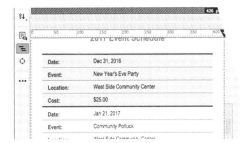 

This CSS3-based selector actually applies the background only on even rows of the table.

Both tables are now slickly styled and responsive to any changes in the screen size. Although they look good in Live view, don't get complacent; it's vital to test the design in a variety of browsers and mobile devices too.

18 Save all files. Preview the page in the default browser. Test the media queries and the responsive table styling by changing the size of the browser window.

Congratulations! You've learned not only how to insert HTML tables into your webpages but also how to make them adapt to almost any screen environment. It's likely that everything you tried in this exercise worked perfectly in both Dreamweaver and any browser you tested it in. But you have to remember that CSS3 is still fairly new and has not been fully adopted within the industry.

The good news is that most of the mobile devices you're targeting should support the various settings used in this exercise. And you can be sure Dreamweaver will stay current with the latest updates.

Spell-checking webpages

It's important to ensure that the content you post to the web is error-free. Dreamweaver includes a robust spell-checker capable of identifying commonly misspelled words and creating a custom dictionary for nonstandard terms that you might use on a regular basis.

1 Open **contact_us.html**, if necessary.

2 Switch to Design view. Insert the cursor at the beginning of the heading *Contact Meridien GreenStart.* Choose Tools > Spell Check.

Note: The spell-checker runs only in Design view. If you are in Code view, Dreamweaver will switch to Design view automatically. If you are in Live view, the command will be unavailable.

The spell-checker starts wherever the cursor has been inserted. If the cursor is located lower on the page, you will have to restart the spell-checker at least once to examine the entire page. It also does not check content locked in noneditable template regions.

The Check Spelling dialog highlights the word *Meridien*, which is the name of the fictional city where the GreenStart association is located. You could click the option Add To Personal to insert the word into your custom dictionary, but for now you will skip over other occurrences of the name during this check.

3 Click Ignore All.

Dreamweaver's spell-checker highlights the word *GreenStart*, which is the name of the association. If GreenStart were the name of your own company, you'd want to add it to your custom dictionary. However, you don't want to add a fictional company name to your dictionary.

4 Click Ignore All again.

Dreamweaver highlights the domain for the email address info@greenstart.org.

5 Click Ignore All.

Dreamweaver highlights the word *Asociation*, which is missing an "*s.*"

6 To correct the spelling, locate the correctly spelled word (*Association*) in the Suggestions list and double-click it.

7 Continue the spell-check to the end.
Correct any misspelled words and ignore proper names, as necessary.
If a dialog prompts you to start the check from the beginning, click Yes.

Dreamweaver will start spell-checking from the top of the file to catch any words it may have missed.

8 Click OK when the spell-check is complete. Save the file.

It's important to point out that the spell-checker is designed to find only words that are *spelled* incorrectly. It will not find words that are *used* incorrectly. In those instances, nothing takes the place of a careful reading of the content.

Finding and replacing text

The ability to find and replace text is one of Dreamweaver's most powerful features. Unlike other programs, Dreamweaver can find almost anything, anywhere in your site, including text, code, and any type of whitespace that can be created in the program. You can search the entire markup, or you can limit the search to just the rendered text in Design view or to just the underlying tags. Advanced users can enlist powerful pattern-matching algorithms known as *regular expressions* to perform sophisticated find-and-replace operations. And then Dreamweaver takes it one step further by allowing you to replace the targeted text or code with similar amounts of text, code, and whitespace.

In this exercise, you'll learn some important techniques for using the Find and Replace feature.

1 Select the **events.html** document tab, if necessary, or open it from the site root folder.

There are several ways to identify the text or code you want to find. One way is to simply type it in the Find field. In the Events table, the name *Meridien* was spelled incorrectly as *Meridian*. Since *Meridian* is an actual word, the spell-checker won't flag it as an error and give you the opportunity to correct it. So you'll use find and replace to make the change instead.

2 Switch to Code view, if necessary.

Click in the *Green Events and Classes* heading.

Choose Find > Find and Replace.

The Find and Replace panel appears at the top of the document window. If you have not used the feature before, the Find field should be empty.

3 Type **Meridian** in the Find field and press Enter/Return.

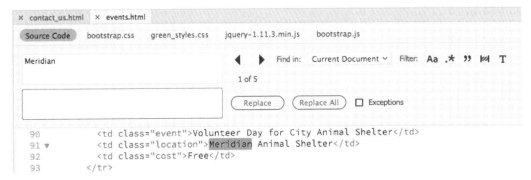

Dreamweaver finds the first occurrence of *Meridian* and indicates how many matches it has found in the document.

4 Type **Meridien** in the Replace field.

Choose Current Document from the Find In menu.

Choose Text from the Search menu.

5 Click Replace.

Dreamweaver replaces the first instance of *Meridian* and immediately searches for the next instance. You can continue to replace the words one at a time, or you can choose to replace all occurrences.

6 Click Replace All.

When you click Replace All, the Search report panel opens and lists all the changes made.

7 Right-click the Search report tab and select Close Tab Group from the context menu.

Another method for targeting text and code is to select it *before* activating the command. This method can be used in either Design or Code view.

8 In Code view, locate and select the first occurrence of the text *Burkeline Mountains Resort* in the Location column of the Events table. Choose Find > Find and Replace.

The Find and Replace dialog appears. The selected text is automatically entered into the Find field by Dreamweaver. This technique can be even more powerful when working with code.

9 With the cursor still inserted in the *Burkeline Mountains Resort* text, click the `<tr>` tag selector at the bottom of the document window.

10 Choose Find > Find and Replace.

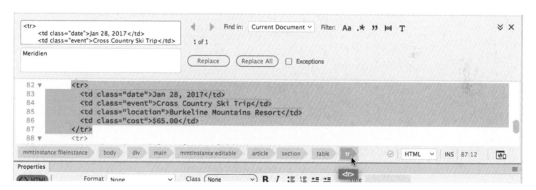

Observe the Find field. The selected code is automatically entered into the Find field in its entirety by Dreamweaver, including the line breaks and other white space. The reason this is so amazing is that there's no way to enter this type of markup in the dialog manually.

11 Select the code in the Find field. Press Delete to remove it.
Type `<tr>` and press Enter/Return to insert a line break. Observe what happens.

Pressing Enter/Return did not insert a line break; instead, it activated the Find command, which finds the next occurrence of the `<tr>` element. In fact, you can't manually insert any type of line break within the field.

You probably don't think this is much of a problem, since you've already seen that Dreamweaver inserts text or code when it's selected. Unfortunately, the method used in steps 8 and 10 don't work with large amounts of text or code.

12 In Code view, drag to select the code from line 70 to line 99.

13 Choose Find > Find and Replace. Observe the Find field.

Dreamweaver didn't transfer the selected code into the Find field. INote how the previous search text still remains and the field shows a red border, indicating that the expected behavior did not occur.

To get larger amounts of text or code into the Find field and to enter large amounts of replacement text and code, you need to use copy and paste.

14 Drag to select the code from line 70 to line 99 again.
Press Ctrl+C/Cmd+C to copy the code.

15 Insert the cursor into the Find field and press Ctrl+V/Cmd+V.

Superpowerfindelicious!

Note the Find and Filter option in the panel. The power and flexibility of Dreamweaver shine brightest here. The Find and Replace command can search in selected text, in the current document, in all open documents, in a specific folder, in selected files of the site, or in the entire current local site. But as if those options weren't enough, Dreamweaver also allows you to target, or limit, the search to the source code, to text only, based on case, and to whole words, as well as gives you the ability to use regular expressions and to ignore white space.

16 Insert the cursor in the Replace field.

Press Ctrl+A/Cmd+A to select the contents of the field.

Press Ctrl+V/Cmd+V.

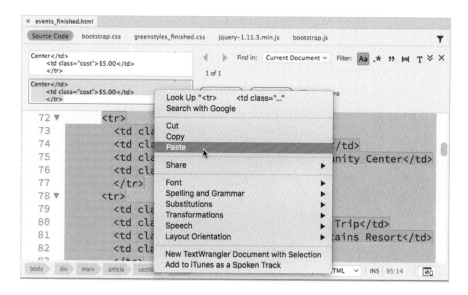

The entire selection is pasted into the Find and Replace fields. Obviously, the two fields contain identical markup, but it illustrates how easy it would be to change or replace large amounts of code when needed.

17 Close the Find and Replace panel. Save all files.

In this lesson, you created four new pages and learned how to import text from multiple sources. You formatted text as headings and lists and then styled it using CSS. You inserted and formatted two tables, added captions to each one, and styled them to make them responsive. And you reviewed and corrected text using Dreamweaver's spell-checker and Find and Replace tools.

Optional self-paced exercise

At the end of the lesson, the four pages created are only partially completed. Before proceeding to the next lesson, go ahead and finish each page using the resources in the files **quotes09.txt** and **sidebar2_09.txt**, located in the resources folder. If you have any questions about how the content should be created or formatted, check out the finished files with the same names within the finished_files folder for lesson09. Be sure to save all your changes when you are finished.

Review questions

1 How do you format text to be an HTML heading?

2 Explain how to turn paragraph text into an ordered list and then an unordered list.

3 Describe two methods for inserting HTML tables into a webpage.

4 What element controls the width of a table column?

5 What items will not be found by Dreamweaver's spell-check command?

6 Describe three ways to insert content in the Find field.

Review answers

1 Use the Format field menu in the Property inspector to apply HTML heading formatting, or press Ctrl+1/Cmd+1, Ctrl+2/Cmd+2, Ctrl+3/Cmd+3, and so on.

2 Highlight the text with the cursor and click the Ordered List button in the Property inspector. Then click the Unordered List button to change the numbered list to bullets.

3 You can copy and paste a table from another HTML file or a compatible program. Or you can insert a table by importing the data from a delimited file.

4 The width of a table column is controlled by the widest `<th>` or `<td>` element that creates the individual table cell within the specific column.

5 The spell-checker command finds only words *spelled* incorrectly, not the ones *used* incorrectly.

6 You can type text into the Find field; you can select text before you open the panel and then allow Dreamweaver to insert the selected text; or you can copy the text or code and then paste it into the field.

10 WORKING WITH IMAGES

Lesson overview

In this lesson, you'll learn how to work with images to include them in your webpages in the following ways:

• Insert an image into a webpage

• Use Photoshop Smart Objects

• Copy and paste an image from Photoshop

• Make images responsive to different device and screen sizes

• Use tools in Dreamweaver to resize, crop, and resample web-compatible images

This lesson will take about 2 hours to complete. If you have not already done so, download the project files for this lesson from the Lesson & Update Files tab on your Account page at www.peachpit.com, store them on your computer in a convenient location, and define a site based on the lesson10 folder as described in the "Getting Started" section at the beginning of this book. Your Account page is also where you'll find any updates to the lessons or to the lesson files. Look on the Lesson & Update Files tab to access the most current content.

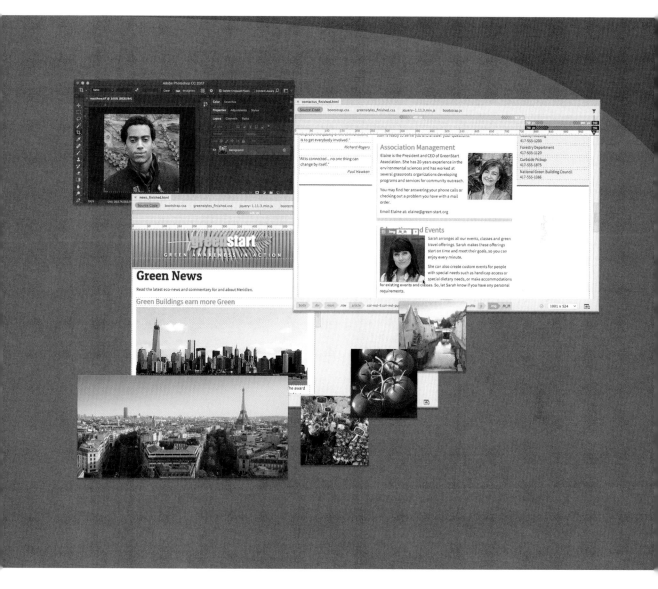

Dreamweaver provides many ways to insert and adjust graphics, both within the program and in tandem with other Creative Suite tools, such as Adobe Fireworks and Adobe Photoshop.

Web image basics

The web is not so much a place as it is an experience. Essential to that experience are the images and graphics—both still and animated—that populate most websites. In the computer world, graphics fall into two main categories: vector and raster.

Vector graphic formats excel in line art, drawings, and logo art. Raster technology works better for storing photographic images.

Vector

Raster

Vector graphics

Vector graphics are created by math. They act like discrete objects, which you can reposition and resize as many times as you want without affecting or diminishing their output quality. The best application of vector art is wherever geometric shapes and text are used to create artistic effects. For example, most company logos are built from vector shapes.

Vector graphics are typically stored in the AI, EPS, PICT, or WMF file formats. Unfortunately, most web browsers don't support these formats. The vector format that is supported is SVG (Scalable Vector Graphic). The simplest way to get started with SVG is to create a graphic in your favorite vector-drawing program—such as Adobe Illustrator or CorelDRAW—and then export it to this format. If you are a good programmer, you may want to try creating SVG graphics using XML (Extensible Markup Language). To find out more about creating SVG graphics, check out http://www.w3schools.com/html/html5_svg.asp.

Raster graphics

Although SVG has definite advantages, web designers primarily use raster-based images in their web designs. Raster images are built from *pixels,* which stands for *picture elements*. Pixels have three basic characteristics:

- They are perfectly square in shape.

- They are all the same size.

- They display only one color at a time.

Raster-based images are composed of thousands, even millions, of pixels arranged in rows and columns, in patterns that create the illusion of an actual photo, painting, or drawing. It's an illusion, because there is no real photo on the screen, just a bunch of pixels that fool your eyes into seeing an image. And, as the quality of the image increases, the more realistic the illusion becomes. Raster image quality is based on three factors: resolution, size, and color.

The inset image shows an enlargement of the flowers, revealing the pixels that compose the image itself.

Resolution

Resolution is the most well-known of the factors affecting raster image quality. It is the expression of image quality, measured in the number of pixels that fit in 1 inch (ppi). The more pixels you can fit in 1 inch, the more detail you can depict in the image. But better quality comes at a price. An unfortunate byproduct of higher resolution is larger file size. That's because each pixel must be stored as bytes of information within the image file—information that has real overhead in computer terms. More pixels means more information, which also means larger files.

● **Note:** Printers and printing presses use round "dots" to create photographic images. Quality on a printer is measured in dots per inch, or dpi. The process of converting the square pixels used in your computer into the round dots used on the printer is called *screening*.

Resolution has a dramatic effect on image output. The web image on the left looks fine in the browser but doesn't have enough quality for printing.

72 ppi   **300 ppi**

Luckily, web images have to appear and look their best only on computer screens, which are based mostly on a resolution of 72 ppi. This is low compared to other applications or output—like printing—where 300 dpi is considered the lowest acceptable quality. The lower resolution of the computer screen is an important factor in keeping most web image files to a reasonable size for downloading from the Internet.

Size

Size refers to the vertical and horizontal dimensions of the image. As image size increases, more pixels are required to create it, and therefore the file becomes larger. Since graphics take more time to download than HTML code, many designers in recent years have replaced graphical components with CSS formatting to speed up the web experience for their visitors. But if you need or want to use images, one method to ensure snappy downloads is to keep image size small. Even today, with the proliferation of high-speed Internet service, many websites still avoid using full-page graphics, although that too is changing.

Although these two images share the identical resolution and color depth, you can see how image dimensions can affect file size.

500KB

1.6MB

Color

Color refers to the color space, or *palette*, that describes each image. Most computer screens display only a fraction of the colors that the human eye can see. And different computers and applications display varying levels of color, expressed by the term *bit depth*. Monochrome, or 1-bit color, is the smallest color space, displaying only black and white, with no shades of gray. Monochrome is used mostly for line-art illustrations, for blueprints, and to reproduce handwriting.

The 4-bit color space describes up to 16 colors. Additional colors can be simulated by a process known as *dithering*, where the available colors are interspersed and juxtaposed to create an illusion of more colors. This color space was created for the first color computer systems and game consoles. Because of its limitations, this palette is seldom used today.

The 8-bit palette offers up to 256 colors or 256 shades of gray. This is the basic color system of all computers, mobile phones, game systems, and handheld devices. This color space also includes what is known as the *web-safe* color palette. Web-safe refers to a subset of 8-bit colors that are supported on both Mac and Windows computers. Most computers, game consoles, handheld devices, and even phones now support higher color palettes, so 8-bit is not as important anymore. Unless you need to support noncomputer devices, you can probably disregard the web-safe palette altogether.

Today, only a few older cellphones and handheld games support the 16-bit color space. This palette is named *high color* and sports a grand total of 65,000 colors. Although this sounds like a lot, 16-bit color is not considered good enough for most graphic design purposes or professional printing.

The highest color space is 24-bit color, which is named *true color*. This system generates up to 16.7 million colors. It is the gold standard for graphic design and professional printing. Several years ago, a new color space was added to the mix: 32-bit color. It doesn't offer any additional colors, but it provides an additional 8 bits of data for an attribute known as *alpha transparency*.

Alpha transparency enables you to designate parts of an image or graphic as fully or even partially transparent. This trick allows you to create graphics that seem to have rounded corners or curves and can even eliminate the white bounding box typical of raster graphics.

24-bit color   **8-bit color**   **4-bit color**

Here you can see a dramatic comparison of three color spaces and what the total number of available colors means to image quality.

As with size and resolution, color depth can dramatically affect image file size. With all other aspects being equal, an 8-bit image is more than seven times larger than a monochrome image. And the 24-bit version is more than three times larger than the 8-bit image. The key to the effective use of images on a website is finding the balance of resolution, size, and color to achieve the desired optimal quality.

Raster image file formats

Raster images can be stored in a multitude of file formats, but web designers have to be concerned with only three: GIF, JPEG, and PNG. These three formats are optimized for use on the Internet and compatible with virtually every browser. However, they are not equal in capability.

GIF

GIF (Graphics Interchange Format) was one of the first raster image file formats designed specifically for the web. It has changed only a little in the last 20 years. GIF supports a maximum of 256 colors (8-bit palette) and 72 ppi, so it's used mainly for web interfaces—buttons and graphical borders and such. But it does have two interesting features that keep it pertinent for today's web designers: index transparency and support for simple animation.

JPEG

JPEG, also written JPG, is named for the Joint Photographic Experts Group that created the image standard back in 1992 as a direct reaction to the limitations of the GIF file format. JPEG is a powerful format that supports unlimited resolution, image dimensions, and color depth. Because of this, most digital cameras use JPEG as their default file type for image storage. It's also the reason most designers use JPEG on their websites for images that must be displayed in high quality.

This may sound odd to you, since "high quality" (as described earlier) usually means large file size. Large files take longer to download to your browser. So, why is this format so popular on the web? The JPEG format's claim to fame comes from its patented user-selectable image compression algorithm, which can reduce file size as much as 95 percent. JPEG images are compressed each time they are saved and then decompressed as they are opened and displayed.

Here you see the effects of different amounts of compression on the file size and quality of an image.

**Low Quality
High compression
130K**

**Medium Quality
Medium compression
150K**

**High Quality
Low compression
260K**

Unfortunately, all this compression has a downside. Too much compression damages image quality. This type of compression is called *lossy*, because it loses quality. In fact, the loss in quality is great enough that it can potentially render the image totally useless. Each time designers save a JPEG image, they face a trade-off between image quality and file size.

PNG

PNG (Portable Network Graphics) was developed in 1995 because of a looming patent dispute involving the GIF format. At the time, it looked as if designers and developers would have to pay a royalty for using the .gif file extension. Although that issue blew over, PNG has found many adherents and a home on the Internet because of its capabilities.

PNG combines many of the features of GIF and JPEG and adds a few of its own. For example, it offers support for unlimited resolution, 32-bit color, and full alpha and index transparency. It also provides lossless compression, which means you can save an image in PNG format and not worry about losing any quality when you save the file.

The only downside to PNG is that its most important feature—alpha transparency—is not fully supported in older browsers. These browsers are retired year after year, so this issue is becoming of little concern to most web designers.

But as with everything on the web, your own needs may vary from the general trend. Before using any specific technology, it's always a good idea to check your site analytics and confirm which browsers your visitors are actually using.

Previewing the completed file

To get a sense of the files you will work on in this lesson, let's preview the completed pages in a browser.

Note: If you have not already downloaded the project files for this lesson to your computer from your Account page, make sure to do so now. See "Getting Started" at the beginning of the book.

1 Launch Adobe Dreamweaver CC (2017 release) or later.

2 If necessary, select lesson10 from the Site drop-down menu in the Files panel.

3 Open **contactus_finished.html** from the lesson10/finished folder.

   The page includes several images, as well as a Photoshop Smart Object.

4 Drag the Scrubber to the left to resize the window. Observe how the layout and images adapt to the changing screen size.

The images align alternately to the left and the right down the page and are small enough to fit any size screen, but they also move within the text as the screen narrows. When the browser window gets to the size of a smartphone, the images move to a separate line and center above the text.

5 Open **news_finished.html** from the lesson10/finished folder. Preview the page in your favorite browser.

6 Drag the right edge of the browser to resize the window. Observe how the layout and images adapt.

The first image stretches across the main content area. As the screen gets smaller, the image scales along with it to match the width of the area. As the screen gets wider, the picture fills the space again.

7 Close your browser and return to Dreamweaver.

The sample files display images of varying sizes and composition. Some images are small enough to fit any size screen; others scale responsively as the size of the page changes. In the following exercises, you will insert these images into these pages using a variety of techniques and format them to work on any screen.

Inserting an image

Note: When working with images in Dreamweaver, you should be sure that your site's default images folder is set up according to the directions in the "Getting Started" section at the beginning of the book.

Images are key components of any webpage, both for developing visual interest and for telling stories. Dreamweaver provides numerous ways to populate your pages with images, using built-in commands and even using copy and paste from other Adobe apps. Let's start with some of the tools built into Dreamweaver itself, such as the Assets panel.

1 In the Files panel, open **contact_us.html** in Live view.

2 Click the first paragraph under the heading *Association Management*.

The HUD appears focused on the p element.

3 Choose Window > Assets to display the Assets panel, if necessary. Click the Images category icon 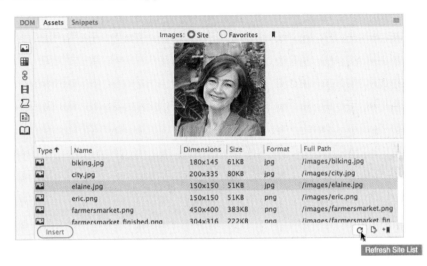 to display a list of all images stored within the site.

4 Locate and select **elaine.jpg** in the list.

Tip: The Assets panel should be populated as soon as you define a site and Dreamweaver creates the cache. If the panel is empty, click the Refresh Site List icon **C**.

A preview of **elaine.jpg** appears in the Assets panel. The panel lists the image's name, dimensions in pixels, size in kilo- or megabytes, and file type, as well as its full directory path.

5 Note the dimensions of the image: 150 pixels by 150 pixels.

⬤ **Note:** You may need to drag the edge of the panel to widen it to see all the asset information.

6 At the bottom of the panel, click the Insert button.

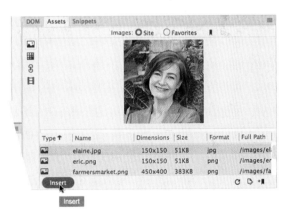

⬤ **Note:** The Images window shows all images stored anywhere in the defined site—even ones outside the site's default images folder—so you may see listings for images stored in the lesson subfolders too.

The position assist dialog appears.

7 Click Nest.

The image appears at the beginning of the paragraph. The HUD now focuses on the img element. You can use the HUD to add alt text to the image.

8 Click the Edit HTML Attribute icon ▤.

The HTML Attribute dialog appears.

9 In the Alt text field in the Element HUD, enter **Elaine, Meridien GreenStart President and CEO** as the alternate text.

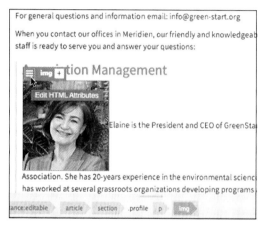
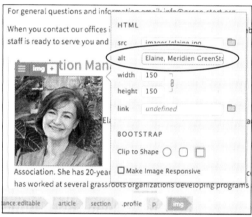

Note: Alt text provides descriptive metadata about images; alt text may be seen if the image doesn't load properly in the browser, or it may be accessed by individuals with visual disabilities.

10 Choose File > Save.

You inserted Elaine's picture in the text, but it doesn't look very nice at its current position. In the next exercise, you will adjust the image position using a CSS class.

Adjusting image positions with CSS classes

The <img> element is an inline element by default. That's why you can insert images into paragraphs and other elements. When the image is taller than the font size, the image will increase the vertical space for the line in which it appears. In the past, you could adjust its position using either HTML attributes or CSS, but many of the HTML-based attributes have been deprecated from the language as well as from Dreamweaver. Now you must rely completely on CSS-based techniques.

In this instance, the employee photos will alternate from right to left going down the page and the text will wrap around the image to use the space more effectively. To do this, you'll create a custom CSS class to provide options for left and right alignment. You can use the HUD to create and apply the new class all at once.

1   If necessary, open **contact_us.html** in Live view.

2   Click the image for Elaine in the first paragraph of the Association Management section.

The HUD appears focused on the `img` element.

3   Click the Add Class/ID icon ⊞ .

4   Type `.flt_rgt` in the text field.

The new class name is short for "float right," hinting at what CSS command you're going to use to style the images.

5   Press Enter/Return.

The CSS Source HUD appears.

6   If necessary, select **green_styles.css** from the source drop-down menu. Leave the media query drop-down menu empty.

7   Press Enter/Return to complete the class.

The CSS Source HUD disappears, and a new class is created in the style sheet. Let's take a look.

8   Select **green_styles.css** > GLOBAL > `.flt_rgt` in the CSS Designer.

The new rule appears at the bottom of the list of selectors. But there may be a problem lurking in the style sheet that will come back to bite you later.

9 Right-click the new selector `.flt_rgt`.
Select Go To Code from the context menu.

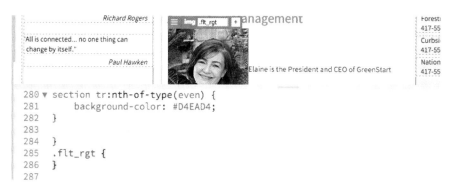

```
280 ▼ section tr:nth-of-type(even) {
281        background-color: #D4EAD4;
282   }
283
284   }
285   .flt_rgt {
286   }
287
```

Dreamweaver opens Split view and loads **green_style.css** in the window focused on the rule `.flt_rgt`.

CSS SNAFU

When you look at the new rule, was it inserted at the very end of the style sheet, as shown in the screenshot after step 9? Normally, this would not be an issue, but the section directly above this rule defines the custom media query you added in Lesson 7, "Designing for Mobile Devices." The purpose of the custom media query is to reset styling applied by the global specifications. Inserting any global rules after the media query could conflict with its purpose altogether.

The problem is that Dreamweaver doesn't create new rules the same way when using the Add Class/ID icon ⊞ from the Element HUD as it does when you use the Add Selector icon ✚ in the CSS Designer. When you use the CSS Designer, Dreamweaver honors any existing media queries and inserts global rules before them in the targeted style sheet. At the time of this writing, the bug was reported but still existed. It may still exist when you try to complete this exercise.

So this means you'll have to do two things unless or until this bug is fixed: First, you need to move any global rules that appear after your custom media queries to a position before them. Second, avoid using the Add Class/ID icon to create any new classes or ids that will need to have both global and mobile styling.

Instead, create rules first in CSS Designer, and then add them to the elements using the Element HUD or class menu in the Property inspector.

10 If the rule appears after the custom media query, select the entire markup and press Ctrl+X/Cmd+X to cut it; otherwise, skip to step 12.

```
284   }
285 ▾ .flt_rgt {
286   }      I
287
```

```
283
284   }
285
286
```

11 Scroll up to a position above the media query.
Insert a new line and press Ctrl+V/Cmd+V to paste the code.

```
187        ▸
188
189 ▾ @media (max-width: 426px){
190 ▾ header.row p {
```

```
187   .flt_rgt {
188   }
189
190 ▾ @media (max-width: 426px){
```

The rule appears on the new line above the media query. No properties are defined yet.

12 Create the following properties:

```
float: right
margin-left: 10px
```

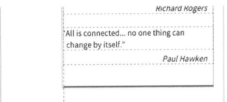

Richard Rogers

"All is connected... no one thing can change by itself."

Paul Hawken

Association Management

Elaine is the President and CEO of GreenStart Association. She has 20-years experience in the environmental sciences and has worked at several grassroots organizations developing programs and services for community outreach.

You may find her answering your phone calls or checking out a problem you have with a mail

```
187 ▾ .flt_rgt {
188       float: right;
189       margin-left: 10px;
190   }
191
192 ▾ @media (max-width: 426px){
193 ▾ header.row p {
```

● **Note:** If you write the properties in Code view, don't forget to add the proper punctuation after each line.

The image moves to the right side of the section element; the text wraps around on the left. As you learned in "CSS Basics Bonus Online Lesson 3," applying a float property removes an element from the normal flow of the HTML structure, although it still maintains its width and height.

The margin setting keeps the text from touching the edge of the image. You will create a similar rule to align images to the left in the next exercise.

Working with the Insert panel

The Insert panel duplicates key menu commands and makes inserting images and other code elements both quick and easy.

1 In Live view, click the first paragraph under the heading *Education and Events.*

   The Element HUD appears focused on the p tag.

2 Choose Window > Insert to display the Insert panel, if necessary.

3 In the Insert panel, choose the HTML category.

4 Click Image.

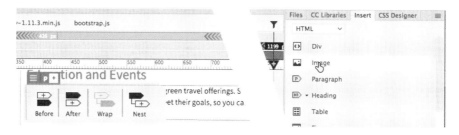

   The position assist HUD appears.

5 Click Nest.

   The Select Image Source dialog appears.

6 Select **sarah.jpg** from the site images folder. Click OK/Open.

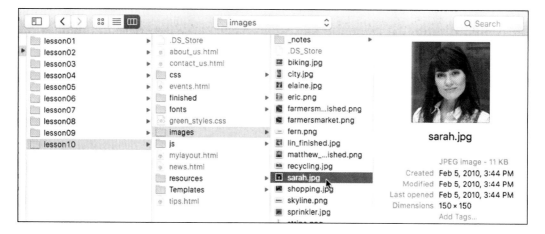

7 In the Property inspector, enter **Sarah, GreenStart Events Coordinator** in the Alt text field.

Now you'll create a new rule for images aligned to the left. For new classes, remember to use the CSS Designer first.

8 In CSS Designer, choose **green_styles.css** > GLOBAL.
Create a new selector.
Type `.flt_lft` and press Enter/Return.

The name is short for "float left."

9 Create the following properties in the new rule:
`float: left`
`margin-right: 10px`

10 Click the Add Class/ID icon on Sarah's image.
Type `.flt_lft` in the field and press Enter/Return.

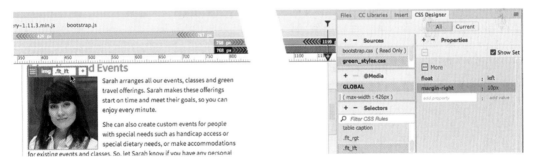

The image drops down into the paragraph on the left side, with the text wrapping to its right.

11 Save the file.

Another way to insert images in your webpage is by using the Insert menu.

Using the Insert menu

The Insert menu duplicates all the commands you'll find in the Insert panel. Some users find the menu faster and easier to use. Others prefer the ready nature of the panel, which allows you to focus on one element and quickly insert multiple copies of it at once. Feel free to alternate between the two methods as desired or even use the keyboard shortcut. In this exercise, you will use the Insert menu to add images.

1 Click the first paragraph under the heading *Transportation Analysis*.

2 Choose Insert > Image or press Ctrl+Alt+I/Cmd+Option+I.

The position assist dialog appears.

3 Click Nest.

The Select Image Source dialog appears.

4 Navigate to the images folder in lesson10.
Select the file **eric.png** and click Open.

The **eric.png** image appears in the Dreamweaver layout. Once the classes have been created and defined, you simply have to add the appropriate class using the HUD.

5 Click the Add Class/ID icon and type: `.flt_rgt`

As you type, the class will appear in the hinting menu. You can click the name or use the arrow keys to highlight it, and you can press Enter/Return to select it. As soon as the class is selected, the image floats to the right side of the paragraph.

6 In the Property inspector, type **Eric, Transportation Research Coordinator** in the Alt text field.

7 Save all files.

So far, you have inserted only web-compatible image formats. But Dreamweaver is not limited to the file types GIF, JPEG, and PNG; it can work with other file types too. In the next exercise, you will learn how to insert a Photoshop document (PSD) into a webpage.

Inserting nonweb file types

Although most browsers will display only the web-compliant image formats described earlier, Dreamweaver also allows you to use other formats; the program will then automatically convert the file to a compatible format on the fly.

1 Click the first paragraph under the heading *Research and Development*.

2 Choose Insert > Image. Nest the image in the first paragraph.
Navigate to the lesson10/resources folder. Select **lin.psd**.

3 Click OK/Open to insert the image.

The image appears in the layout, and the Image Optimization dialog opens; it acts as an intermediary that allows you to specify how and to what format the image will be converted.

4 Observe the options in the Preset and Format menus.

The presets allow you to select predetermined options that have a proven track record for web-based images. The Format menu allows you to specify your own custom settings from among five options: GIF, JPEG, PNG 8, PNG 24, and PNG 32.

5 Choose JPEG High For Maximum Compatibility from the Presets menu. Note the Quality setting.

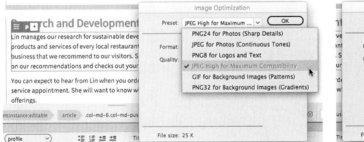
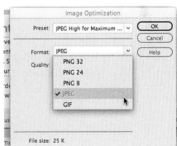

This Quality setting produces a high-quality image with a moderate amount of compression. If you lower the Quality setting, you automatically increase the compression level and reduce the file size; increase the Quality setting for the opposite effect. The secret to effective design is to select a good balance between quality and compression. The default setting for the JPEG High preset is 80, which is sufficient for your purposes.

Note: The Image Optimization dialog displays the final file size of the image at the bottom of the dialog.

6 Click OK to convert the image.

● **Note:** When an image has to be converted this way, Dreamweaver usually saves the converted image into the site's default images folder. This is not the case when the images inserted are web-compatible. So before you insert an image, you should be aware of its current location in the site and move it to the proper folder first, if necessary.

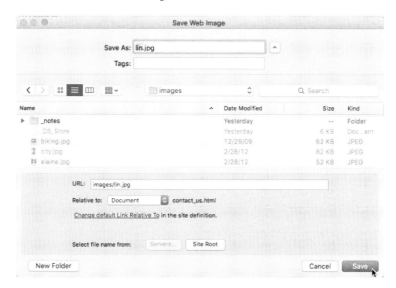

The Save Web Image dialog appears with the name *lin* entered in the Save As field. Dreamweaver will add the .jpg extension to the file automatically. Be sure to save the file to the default site images folder. If Dreamweaver does not automatically point to this folder, navigate to it before saving the file.

7 Click Save.

The Save Web Image dialog closes. The image in the layout is now linked to the JPEG file saved in the default images folder.

▷ **Tip:** The image HUD and the Property inspector can be used interchangeably to enter alt text.

8 Enter **Lin, Research and Development Coordinator** in the Alt text field.

The image appears in Dreamweaver at the cursor position. The image has been resampled to 72 ppi but still appears at its original dimensions, so it's larger than the other images in the layout. You can resize the image in the Property inspector.

9   If necessary, click the Toggle Size Constrain icon 🔒 to display the closed lock. Change the Width value to **150px** and press Enter/Return.

When the lock icon appears closed 🔒, the relationship between width and height is constrained, and the two change proportionally to each other: Change one and they both change. The change to the image size is only temporary at the moment, as indicated by the Reset ⊘ and Commit ✔ icons. In other words, the HTML attributes specify the size of the image as 150 pixels by 150 pixels, but the JPEG file holds an image that's still 300 pixels by 300 pixels—four times as many pixels as it needs to have.

⬤ **Note:** Whenever you change HTML or CSS properties, you may need to press Enter/ Return to complete the modification.

10 Click the Commit icon ✔.

The image is now resized to 150 by 150 pixels permanently.

11 Apply the flt_lft class to this image using the HUD. Save all files.

In Live view, the image now appears like the others in the layout; however, this image has a difference. But you can't see it in Live view.

12 Switch to Design view.

Live view

Design view

In Design view you can now see an icon in the upper-left corner of the image that identifies this image as a Photoshop Smart Object.

Right size, wrong size

Until the latest mobile devices appeared on the scene, deciding what size and resolution to use for web images was pretty simple. You picked a specific width and height and saved the image at 72 pixels per inch. That's all you needed to do.

But today, web designers want their sites to work well for all visitors, no matter what type or size device they want to use. So the days of picking one size and one resolution may be gone forever. But what's the answer? At the moment, there isn't one perfect solution.

One trend simply inserts an image that is larger or higher resolution and resizes it using CSS. This allows the image to display more clearly on high-resolution screens, like Apple's Retina display. The downside is that lower-resolution devices are stuck downloading an image that's larger than they need. This not only slows the loading of the page for no reason, but it can incur higher data charges for smartphone users.

Another idea is to provide multiple images optimized for different devices and resolutions and use JavaScript to load the proper image as needed. But many users object to using scripts for such basic resources as images. Others want a standardized solution.

So W3C is working on a technique that uses a new element named `<picture>`, which will not require JavaScript at all. Using this new element, you would select several images and declare how they should be used, and then the browser would load the appropriate image. Unfortunately, this element is so new that Dreamweaver doesn't support it yet, and few browsers even know what it is.

Implementing a responsive workflow for images is outside the scope of this course. For the purposes of these lessons, you will simply learn how to adapt standard web images to the current responsive template using CSS and media queries.

Working with Photoshop Smart Objects (optional)

Unlike other images, Smart Objects maintain a connection to their original Photoshop (PSD) file. If the PSD file is altered in any manner and then saved, Dreamweaver identifies those changes and provides the means to update the web image used in the layout. The following exercise can be completed only if you have Photoshop installed on your computer along with Dreamweaver.

1 If necessary, open **contact_us.html** in Design view.
   Scroll down to the **lin.jpg** image in the *Research and Development* section. Observe the icon in the upper-left corner of the image.

   The icon indicates that the image is a Smart Object. The icon appears only within Dreamweaver itself; visitors see the normal image in the browser as you saw originally in Live view. If you want to edit or optimize the image, you can simply right-click the image and choose the appropriate option from the context menu.

   To make substantive changes to the image, you will have to open it in Photoshop. (If you don't have Photoshop installed, copy lesson10/resources/smartobject/**lin.psd** into the lesson10/resources folder to replace the original image, and then skip to step 6.) In this exercise, you will edit the image background using Photoshop.

2 Right-click the **lin.jpg** image.
   Choose Edit Original With > Adobe Photoshop CC 2017 from the context menu.

Photoshop launches—if it is installed on your computer—and loads the file.

● **Note:** Dreamweaver and Photoshop can work only with the existing quality of an image. If your initial image quality is unacceptable you may not be able to fix it in Photoshop. You will have to re-create the image from scratch or pick another.

● **Note:** The exact name of the apps appearing in the menu may differ depending on what version of Photoshop you have installed and your operating system. If no version of Photoshop is installed at all you may see no program listed.

3 In Photoshop, choose Window > Layers to display the Layers panel, if necessary. Observe the names and states of any existing layers.

The image has two layers: Lin and New Background. New Background is turned off.

4 Click the eye icon ◉ for the New Background layer to display its contents.

The background of the image changes to show a scene from a park.

5 Save the Photoshop file.

6 Switch back to Dreamweaver.
Position the cursor over the Smart Object icon.

A tool tip appears indicating that the original image has been modified. You don't have to update the image at this time, and you can leave the out-of-date image in the layout for as long as you want. Dreamweaver will continue to monitor its status as long as it's in the layout. But for this exercise, let's update the image.

7 Right-click the image and choose Update From Original from the context menu.

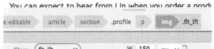

This Smart Object, and any other instances of it, changes to reflect the new background. You can check the status of the Smart Object by positioning the pointer over the image. A tool tip will appear showing that the image is synced. You can also insert the same original PSD image multiple times in the site using different dimensions and image settings under different filenames. All the Smart Objects will stay connected to the PSD and will allow you to update them as the PSD changes.

8 Save the file.

As you can see, Smart Objects have several advantages over a typical image work-flow. For frequently changed or updated images, using a Smart Object can simplify updates to the website in the future.

Copying and pasting images from Photoshop (optional)

As you build your website, you will need to edit and optimize many images before you use them in your site. Adobe Photoshop is an excellent program for performing these tasks. A common workflow is to make the needed changes to the images and then manually export the optimized GIF, JPEG, or PNG files to the default images folder in your website. But sometimes simply copying images and pasting them directly into your layout is faster and easier.

1   Launch Adobe Photoshop, if necessary. Open **matthew.tif** from the lesson10/ resources folder. Observe the Layers panel.

The image has only one layer. In Photoshop, by default you can copy only one layer at a time to paste into Dreamweaver. To copy multiple layers, you have to merge or flatten the image first, or you have to use the command Edit > Copy Merged to copy images with multiple active layers.

2   Choose Select > All, or press Ctrl+A/Cmd+A, to select the entire image.

3   Choose Edit > Copy, or press Ctrl+C/Cmd+C, to copy the image.

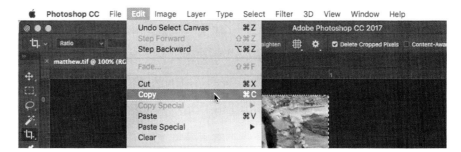

4   Switch to Dreamweaver. Scroll down to the Information Systems section in **contact_us.html**. Insert the cursor at the beginning of the first paragraph in this section and before the name *Matthew*.

5 Press Ctrl+V/Cmd+V to paste the image from the clipboard.

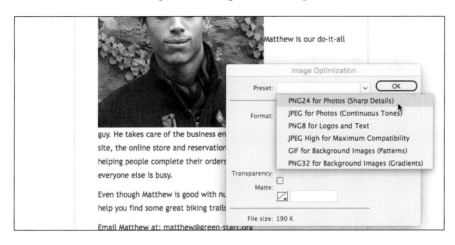

The image appears in the layout, and the Image Optimization dialog opens.

6 Choose the preset PNG24 for Photos (Sharp Details) and choose PNG24 from the Format menu. Click OK.

The Save Image dialog appears.

7 If necessary, navigate to the site default images folder.
Name the image **matthew.png** and select the default site images folder, if necessary. Click Save.

▶ **Tip:** When inserting images that are outside the site default images folder, Dreamweaver may try to save the image in its original location, which may be, in fact, outside the site folder. When in doubt, use the Site Root button in the Save As dialog to focus the dialog on the site folder. Then select the images folder from there.

You have now saved the image as a web-compatible PNG file in the site images folder. As with the image of Lin, Matthew's image is larger than the others.

Note: Raster images can be scaled down in size without losing quality, but the opposite is not true. Unless a graphic has a resolution higher than 72 ppi, scaling it larger without noticeable degradation may not be possible.

8   In the Property inspector, change the image dimensions to **150px** by **150px**. Click the Commit ✔ icon to apply the change. Click OK in the dialog that appears, acknowledging that the change is permanent.

9   If necessary, select the image for Matthew and enter **Matthew, Information Systems Manager** in the Alt text field in the Property inspector.

10 Apply the `flt_rgt` class to **matthew.png** using the Class menu in the Properties inspector.

The image appears in the layout at the same size as the other images and aligned to the right. Although this image came from Photoshop, it's not "smart" like a Photoshop Smart Object and can't be updated automatically. It does, however, give you an easy way to load the image into Photoshop or another image editor to perform any modifications.

Tip: If no image-editor program is displayed, you may need to browse for a compatible editor. The executable program file is usually stored in the Program Files folder in Windows and in the Applications folder on a Mac.

Note: The exact name displayed in the menu may differ depending on the program version or operating system installed.

11 In the layout, right-click **matthew.png**. Choose Edit With > Photoshop CC 2017 from the context menu. If Photoshop CC 2017 is not installed, select the program that is displayed.

The program launches and displays the PNG file from the site images folder. If you make changes to this image, you merely have to save the file to update the image in Dreamweaver.

12 In Photoshop, press Ctrl+L/Cmd+L to open the Levels dialog. Adjust the brightness and contrast. Save and close the image.

Note: This exercise is geared specifically to Photoshop, but the changes can be made in most image editors.

13 Switch back to Dreamweaver. Scroll down to view the **matthew.png** image in the Information Systems section.

The image should be updated in the layout automatically. Since you saved the changes under the original filename, no other action is necessary. This method saves you several steps and avoids any potential typing errors.

14 Save all the files.

Note: Although Dreamweaver automatically reloads any modified file, most browsers won't. You will have to refresh the browser display before you see any changes.

Today, the modern web designer has to contend with a multitude of visitors using different browsers and devices. Depending on the size of the images and how they are inserted, you may need to use several different strategies to get them to work effectively in your page design.

For example, the images used on the *Contact Us* page are small enough that they should be usable all the way down to the size needed on a smartphone, but they'll need some assistance to make them adapt better to smaller screens.

Adapting images to smaller screens

To get the current images to make the most of the available space as the pages respond to the size of the screen, you can create a few specific rules in the appropriate media queries. The first step is to observe how images adapt to the current design, and then you'll create an effective strategy for reformatting them.

1 Open **contact_us.html** in Live view.

2 Drag the Scrubber to the left to engage each of the existing media queries. Observe how the images adapt to the different dimensions.

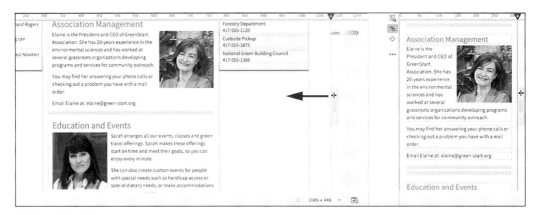

The images are small enough that they adapt well to desktop and tablet screen sizes. On the smallest screens, the text is starting to get crowded, wrapping around the edges of the images. One fix would be to remove the float and center the images.

3 In Dreamweaver, switch to Live view if necessary and click your custom media query, (max-width: 426px), at the top of the document window.

Tip: For this new rule to work, it must appear within the media query markup and after the rules it is designed to reset. If your layout does not look like the screen shot, check the structure and order of your CSS rules.

4 Choose **green_styles.css** > (max-width:426px) in CSS Designer. Create a new rule: `.flt_lft, .flt_rgt`

5 Add the following properties to the new rule:

```
max-width: 95%
height: auto
display: block
margin: 0px auto
float: none
```

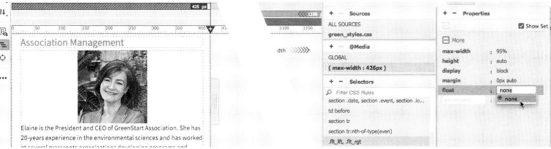

These new settings put the images on their own line and center them. The `max-width` property makes sure that larger images automatically scale down with the screen.

6 Save all files.

In the next exercise, you will insert a much larger image that will have to use a different responsive strategy.

Inserting images by drag and drop

Most of the programs in the Creative Suite offer drag-and-drop capabilities. Dreamweaver is no exception.

1 Open **news.html** from the site root folder in Live view.

2 Choose Window > Assets to display the Assets panel, if necessary.

The Assets panel is no longer opened by default in the Dreamweaver workspace. You can leave it as a floating dialog or dock it to keep it out of the way.

3 Drag the Assets panel to dock it beside the Files or DOM tab, if necessary.

4 In the Assets panel, click the Images category icon .

5 Drag the **skyline.png** icon from the panel and position the cursor between the first paragraph and the heading *Green Buildings earn more Green.*

Tip: If you don't see specific image files listed in the Assets panel, click the Refresh icon to reload site images.

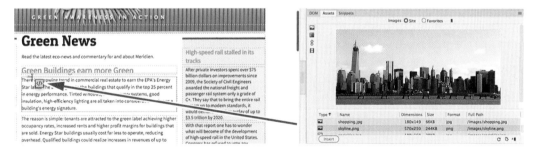

If you position the cursor correctly, you will see a green line between the heading and the paragraph, indicating where the image will be inserted once you release the mouse.

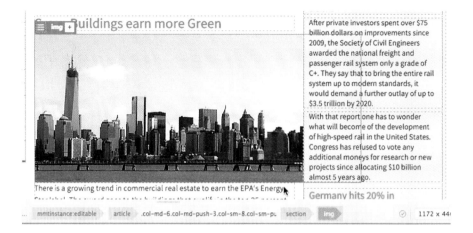

Unlike the images used in the previous exercises, **skyline.png** was inserted between the <h2> and <p> elements. The image is also too large for the column. Part of it is obscured behind Sidebar 2. Luckily, Dreamweaver has a new built-in way to deal with just this situation.

6 Click the Edit HTML Attributes icon ▤ on the new image.

The HTML Attributes HUD appears.

7 Select the Make Image Responsive checkbox.

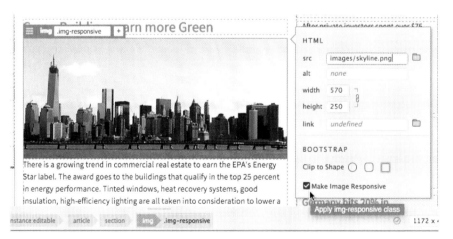

The image now conforms to the width of the column. But what happens when the screen gets smaller? You can check the behavior in Live view, or you can preview the page in a browser window.

8 Enter **Green buildings are top earners** in the Property inspector's Alt text field.

9 Save all files.

10 Drag the Scrubber to the left and observe how the image adapts to the changes to the layout.

The image scales automatically as the document window changes sizes. The option in the HTML Attributes HUD selected in step 7 applies the Bootstrap `.img-responsive` class to the image. This class forces the image to fit within the existing element and to scale as needed.

Optimizing images with the Property inspector

Optimized web images try to balance image dimensions and quality against file size. Sometimes you may need to optimize graphics that have already been placed on the page. Dreamweaver has built-in features that can help you achieve the smallest possible file size while preserving image quality. In this exercise, you'll use tools in Dreamweaver to scale, optimize, and crop an image for the web.

1 If necessary, open **news.html** in Live view or switch to it.
   Drag the Scrubber to the right to open the document window fully.

2 Click to select the first paragraph of the *Shopping green saves energy* heading.

3 Choose Insert > Image.
   Click Nest in the Position Assist HUD.
   Select **farmersmarket.png** from the site images folder.
   Click Open and nest the image in the paragraph.

4 Enter **Buy local to save energy** in the Alt text field.

5 Apply the `.flt_rgt` class to the image.

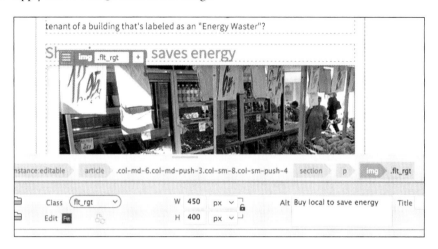

The image is too large. There is barely any room for the image in the column. It could really use some cropping. You're in luck, Dreamweaver provides built-in tools that can fix the image right in the page itself. The tools work only in Design view.

6 Switch to Design view and observe the Property inspector.

Whenever an image is selected, image-editing tools appear below the Class menu in the Property inspector. The icons allow you to edit the image in Photoshop **Ps** or Adobe Fireworks **Fw** or to adjust several aspects in place. See the sidebar "Dreamweaver's graphic tools" at the end of the lesson for an explanation of each tool.

There are two ways to reduce the dimensions of an image in Dreamweaver. The first method changes the size of the image temporarily by imposing user-defined dimensions.

7   Select **farmersmarket.png**. If necessary, click the Toggle Size Constrain icon 🔒 in the Property inspector to lock the image proportions. Change the image width to **350 pixels** and press the Tab key.

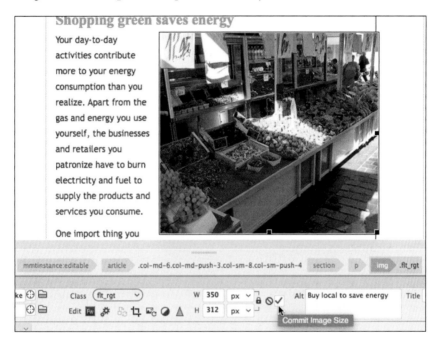

When the size constraint is locked, the height automatically conforms to the new width. Note that Dreamweaver indicates that the new size is not permanent by displaying the current specifications in bold and the Reset and Commit icons.

8   Click the Commit icon ✔. A dialog appears that indicates the change will be permanent.

9   Click OK.

Dreamweaver can also crop images.

10 With the image still selected, click the Crop icon ⛶ in the Property inspector.

A dialog appears indicating that the action will permanently change the image.

11 Click OK. Crop handles appear slightly inset from the edges of the image. You want to crop the width but not the height.

Tip: Dimensions may also be entered manually if you know the final proportions.

12 Drag the crop handles to set the image to a width of 300 pixels and a height of 312 pixels.

13 Press Enter/Return to apply the change.

14 Save all files.

Most designers will edit and resize images prior to bringing them into Dreamweaver, but it's nice to know that these tools are available for any last-minute changes or fast turnarounds.

In this lesson, you learned how to insert images and Smart Objects into a Dreamweaver page, copy and paste from Photoshop, and use the Property inspector to edit and resample images.

There are numerous ways to create and edit images for the web. The methods examined in this lesson show but a few of them and are not meant to recommend or endorse one method over another. Feel free to use whatever methods and workflow you desire based on your own situation and expertise.

Dreamweaver's graphic tools

All Dreamweaver's graphic tools appear in the Property inspector when an image is selected in Design view. Here are the seven tools:

 Edit—Opens the selected image in the defined external graphics editor if you have one installed. You can assign a graphics-editing program to any given file type in the File Types/Editors category of the Preferences dialog. The button's image changes according to the program chosen. For example, if Fireworks is the designated editor for the image type, a Fireworks icon is shown; if Photoshop is the editor, you'll see a Photoshop icon. If neither app is installed, you will see a generic edit icon.

 Edit Image Settings—Opens the Image Optimization dialog, allowing you to apply user-defined optimization specifications to the selected image.

 Update from Original—Updates any placed Smart Object to match any changes to the original source file.

 Crop—Permanently removes unwanted portions of an image. When the Crop tool is active, a bounding box with a series of control handles appears within the selected image. You can adjust the bounding box size by dragging the handles or by entering the final dimensions. When the box outlines the desired portion of the image, press Enter/Return or double-click the graphic to apply the cropping.

 Resample—Permanently resizes an image. The Resample tool is active only when an image has been resized.

Brightness and Contrast—Offers user-selectable adjustments to an image's brightness and contrast; a dialog presents sliders for each value that can be adjusted independently. A live preview is available so that you can evaluate adjustments before committing to them.

Sharpen—Affects the enhancement of image details by raising or lowering the contrast of pixels on a scale from 0 to 10. As with the Brightness and Contrast tool, Sharpen offers a real-time preview.

You can undo most graphics operations by choosing Edit > Undo until the containing document is closed or you quit Dreamweaver.

Review questions

1   What are the three factors that determine raster image quality?

2   What file formats are specifically designed for use on the web?

3   Describe at least two methods for inserting an image into a webpage using Dreamweaver.

4   True or false: All graphics have to be optimized outside of Dreamweaver.

5   What is the advantage of using a Photoshop Smart Object over copying and pasting an image from Photoshop?

Review answers

1 Raster image quality is determined by resolution, image dimensions, and color depth.

2 The compatible image formats for the web are GIF, JPEG, PNG, and SVG.

3 One method to insert an image into a webpage using Dreamweaver is to use the Insert panel. Another method is to drag the graphic file into the layout from the Assets panel. Images can also be copied and pasted from Photoshop and Fireworks.

4 False. Images can be optimized even after they are inserted into Dreamweaver by using the Property inspector. Optimization can include rescaling, changing format, or fine-tuning format settings.

5 A Smart Object can be used multiple times in different places on a site, and each instance of the Smart Object can be assigned individual settings. All copies remain connected to the original image. If the original is updated, all the connected images are immediately updated as well. When you copy and paste all or part of a Photoshop file, however, you get a single image that can have only one set of values applied to it.

11 WORKING WITH NAVIGATION

Lesson overview

In this lesson, you'll apply several kinds of links to page elements by doing the following:

- Creating a text link to a page within the same site
- Creating a link to a page on another website
- Creating an email link
- Creating an image-based link
- Creating a link to a location within a page
- Creating and styling a Bootstrap drop-down menu

 This lesson will take about 3 hours to complete. If you have not already done so, download the project files for this lesson from the Lesson & Update Files tab on your Account page at www.peachpit. com and store them on your computer in a convenient location, as described in the "Getting Started" section at the beginning of this book. Your Account page is also where you'll find any updates to the lessons or to the lesson files. Look on the Lesson & Update Files tab to access the most current content. Before you begin this lesson, define a new site based on the lesson11 folder using the method described in the "Getting Started" section.

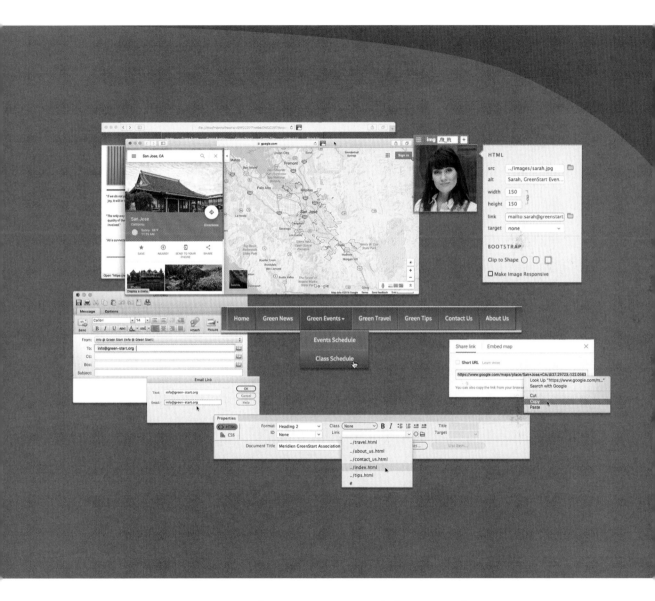

Dreamweaver can create and edit many types of
links—from text-based links to image-based links—
and does so with ease and flexibility.

Hyperlink basics

The World Wide Web, and the Internet in general, would be a far different place without the hyperlink. Without hyperlinks, HTML would simply be ML (markup language). The *hypertext* in the name refers to the functionality of the hyperlink. So what is a hyperlink?

A hyperlink, or *link*, is an HTML-based reference to a resource available on the Internet or within the computer hosting a web document. The resource can be anything that can be stored on and displayed by a computer, such as a webpage, an image, a movie, a sound file, a PDF—in fact, almost any type of computer file. A hyperlink creates an interactive behavior specified by HTML and CSS, or by the programming language you're using, and is enabled by a browser or other application.

An HTML hyperlink consists of the anchor <a> element and one or more attributes.

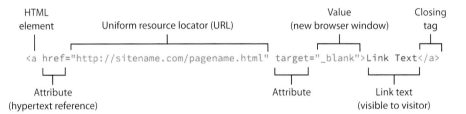

Internal and external hyperlinks

The simplest hyperlink—an internal hyperlink—takes the user to another part of the same document or to another document stored in the same folder or hard drive on the web server that hosts the site. An external hyperlink is designed to take the user to a document or resource outside your hard drive, website, or web host.

Internal and external hyperlinks may work differently, but they have one thing in common: They are enabled in HTML by the <a> *anchor* element. This element designates the address of the destination of the hyperlink and can then specify how it functions using several attributes. You'll learn how to create and modify the <a> element in the exercises that follow.

Relative vs. absolute hyperlinks

A hyperlink address can be written in two ways. When you refer to a target by where it is stored in relation to the current document, it is known as a *relative* link. This is like telling someone that you live next door to the blue house. If she were driving down your street and saw the blue house, she would know where you live. But those directions don't really tell her how to get to your house or even to your neighborhood. A relative link frequently will consist of the resource name and perhaps the folder it is stored within, such as `logo.jpg` or `images/logo.jpg`.

Sometimes you need to spell out precisely where a resource is located. In those instances, you need an *absolute* hyperlink. This is like telling someone you live at 123 Main Street in Meridien. This is typically how you refer to resources outside your website. An absolute link includes the entire uniform resource locator, or URL, of the target and may even include a filename—such as http://forums.adobe.com/index.html—or just a folder within the site.

Both types of links have advantages and disadvantages. Relative hyperlinks are faster and easier to write, but they may not work if the document containing them is saved in a different folder or location in the website. Absolute links always work no matter where the containing document is saved, but they can fail if the targets are moved or renamed. A simple rule that most web designers follow is to use relative links for resources within a site and absolute links for resources outside the site. Of course, whether you follow this rule or not, it's important to test all links before deploying the page or site.

Previewing the completed file

To see the final version of the file you will work on in this lesson, let's preview the completed page in the browser.

● **Note:** Before beginning this exercise, download the project files and define a new site based on the lesson11 folder using the instructions in the "Getting Started" section at the beginning of the book.

1 Launch Adobe Dreamweaver CC (2017 release) or later.

2 If necessary, press F8 to open the Files panel. Select lesson11 from the site list.

3 In the Files panel, expand the lesson11 folder.

4 In the Files panel, right-click **aboutus_finished.html** in the lesson11/finished folder. Choose Open in Browser from the context menu and select your favorite browser.

The **aboutus_finished.html** file appears in your default browser. This page features only internal links in the horizontal menu.

5   Position the cursor over the horizontal navigation menu. Hover over each button and examine the behavior of the menu.

The menu is the same one created and formatted in Lesson 5, "Creating a Page Layout," with a few changes.

6   Click the *Green News* link.

The browser loads the finished *Green News* page.

7   Position the cursor over the *About Us* link.
Observe the browser to see whether it's displaying the link's destination anywhere on the screen.

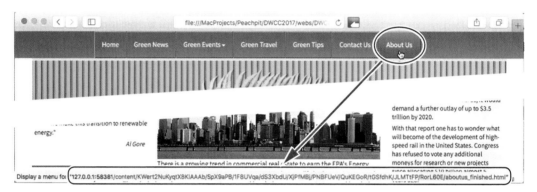

Typically, the browser shows the link destination in the status bar.

8   Click the *Contact Us* link.

The browser loads the finished *Contact Us* page, replacing the *Green News* page. The new page includes internal, external, and email links.

9   Position the cursor over the *Meridien* link in the second paragraph of the main content area. Observe the status bar.

▶ **Tip:** Most browsers will display the destination of a hyperlink in the status bar at the bottom of the browser window. In some browsers, this status bar may be turned off by default.

The status bar displays the http://google.com/maps link.

10 Click the *Meridien* link.

● **Note:** The display in Google Maps may differ from the one pictured.

A new browser window appears and loads Google Maps. The link is intended to show the visitor where the Meridien GreenStart Association offices are located. If desired, you can even include address details or the company name in this link so that Google can load the exact map and directions.

Note that the browser opens a separate window or document tab when you click the link. This is a good behavior to use when directing visitors to resources outside your site. Since the link opens in a separate window, your own site is still open and ready to use. This practice is especially helpful if your visitors are unfamiliar with your site and may not know how to get back to it once they click away.

11 Close the Google Maps window.

The *Contact Us* page is still open in the browser. Note that each employee has a link applied to their email address.

12 Click an email link for one of the employees.

● **Note:** Many web visitors don't use email programs installed on their computers. They use web-based services like AOL, Gmail, Hotmail, and so on. For these visitors, email links like the one you tested won't work. The best option is to create a web-hosted form on your site that sends the email to you via your own server.

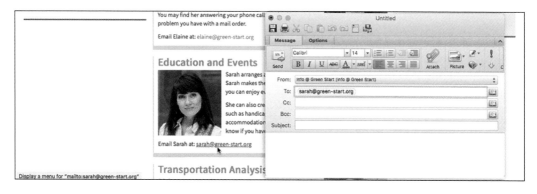

The default mail application launches on your computer. If you have not set up this application to send and receive mail, the program will usually start a wizard to help you set up this functionality. If the email program is set up, a new message window, similar to the one pictured in the screen shot, appears with the email address of the employee automatically entered in the To field.

13 Close the new message window, if necessary, and exit the email program.

14 Scroll down to the *Education and Events* section.

Note how the menu sticks to the top of the page as you scroll down.

15 Click the *events* link.

The browser loads the *Green Events and Classes* page. The browser focuses on the table containing the list of upcoming events near the top of the page. Notice how the horizontal menu is still visible at the top of the browser.

16 In the horizontal menu, click the *Green Events* link.

The menu opens showing two sublinks: one for the event schedule and one for class schedule.

17 Click the *Class Schedule* link.

The browser jumps down to the list of upcoming classes at the bottom of the page.

18 Click the *Return to Top* link that appears above the class schedule. You may need to scroll up or down the page to see it.

The browser jumps back to the top of the page.

19 Close the browser and switch to Dreamweaver, if necessary.

You have tested a variety of different types of hyperlinks: internal, external, relative, and absolute. In the following exercises, you will learn how to build each type.

Creating internal hyperlinks

Creating hyperlinks of all types is easy with Dreamweaver. In this exercise, you'll create relative text-based links to pages in the same site, using a variety of methods. You can create links in Design view, Live view, and Code view.

Creating relative links

Dreamweaver provides several methods for creating and editing links. Links can be created in all three program views.

1 Open **about_us.html** from the site root folder in Live view.

2 In the horizontal menu, position the cursor over any of the horizontal menu items. Observe the type of cursor that appears.

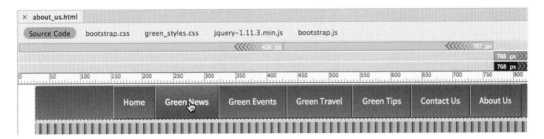

The pointer indicates that the menu item is structured as a hyperlink. In addition to changing the cursor icon, the styling of the link itself changes as you position the cursor over each one and then move it away. The links in the horizontal menu are not editable in the normal way, but this is something you can actually see only in Design view.

3 Switch to Design view. Position the cursor over any item of the horizontal menu again.

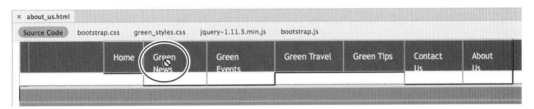

The "no" symbol ⊘ appears indicating that this section of the page is uneditable. The horizontal menu was not part of one of the editable regions you created in Lesson 8, "Working with Templates." That means it's considered part of the template and is locked within Dreamweaver. To add hyperlinks to this menu, you'll have to open the template.

4 Choose Window > Assets. In the Assets panel Template category, right-click **mygreen_temp** and choose Edit from the context menu.

5 Switch to Design view, if necessary.
In the horizontal menu, insert the cursor into the *Green News* link.

> **Tip:** When editing or removing an existing hyperlink, you don't need to select the entire link; you can just insert the cursor anywhere in the link text. Dreamweaver assumes you want to change the entire link by default.

The horizontal menu is editable in the template.

> **Note:** The Template category is not visible in Live view. You will see it only in Design and Code views and when no document is open.

6 If necessary, choose Window > Properties to open the Property inspector. Examine the contents of the Link field in the Property inspector.

To create links, the HTML tab must be selected in the Property inspector. The Link field shows a hyperlink placeholder (#).

7 In the Link field, click the Browse for File icon 📁.

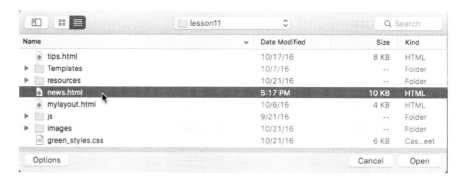

A file selection dialog appears.

8 Navigate to the site root folder, if necessary. Select **news.html** from the site root folder.

9 Click Open.

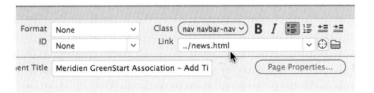

● **Note:** The link won't have the typical hyper-link appearance—a blue underscore—because of the special formatting you applied to this menu in Lesson 5.

The link `../news.html` appears in the Link field in the Property inspector.

You've created your first text-based hyperlink. Since the template is saved in a subfolder, Dreamweaver adds the path element notation (`../`) to the filename so that the link properly resolves once the template pages are updated. This notation tells the browser or operating system to look in the parent directory of the current folder. When you create a page from the template, Dreamweaver then rewrites the link simply to `"news.html"` or adds whatever additional path information that is needed. If necessary, you can type links in the field manually too.

10 Insert the cursor in the *Home* link.

The home page does not exist yet. But that doesn't stop you from entering the link text by hand.

11 In the Properties inspector Link field, select the hash (#) symbol, type `../index.html` to replace the placeholder, and press Enter/Return.

At any time, you may insert a link by typing it manually just this way. But, enter-ing links by hand can introduce a variety of errors that can break the very link you are trying to create. If you want to link to a file that already exists, Dream-weaver offers other interactive ways to create links.

12 Insert the cursor in the *Green Tips* link.

13 Click the Files tab to bring the panel to the top or choose Window > Files.

You need to make sure you can see the Property inspector and the target file in the Files panel.

▶ Tip: If a folder in the Files panel contains a page you want to link to but the folder is not open, drag the Point to File icon over the folder and hold it in place to expand that folder so that you can point to the desired file.

14 In the Property inspector, drag the Point to File icon ⊕—next to the Link field—to **tips.html** in the site root folder displayed in the Files panel.

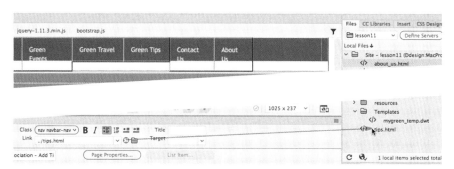

Dreamweaver enters the filename and any necessary path information into the Link field.

◐ Note: You will create the Green Events link later. The **travel.html** file has not been created yet. You'll have to create the link manually as you did with **index.html**.

15 Modify the rest of the menu as shown using any of the methods you've learned:

Green Travel: **../travel.html**

Contact Us: **../contact_us.html**

About Us: **../about_us.html**

For files that have not been created, you will always have to enter the link manually. Remember that all the links added to the template pointing to files in the site root folder must include the **../** notation so that the link resolves properly. Remember also that Dreamweaver will modify the link as needed once the template is applied to the child page.

Creating a home link

Most websites display a logo or company name, and this site is no different. The GreenStart logo appears in the header element—a product of two background graphics, a gradient, and some text. Frequently, such logos are used to create a link back to the site home page. In fact, this practice has become a virtual standard on the web. Since the template is still open, it's easy to add such a link to the Green-Start logo.

1 Open **mygreen_temp.dwt** in Design view.
Insert the cursor in the *GreenStart* text in the <header> element.

The text component of the logo is highlighted. Dreamweaver keeps track of links you create in each editing session until you close the program. You can access these previously created links from the Property inspector.

2 Click the h2 tag selector.

In the Property inspector Link field, choose `../index.html` from the drop-down menu.

Note: You can select any range of text to create a link—from one character to an entire paragraph or more; Dreamweaver will add the necessary markup to the selection.

Note: Design view will not render all the styling properly, but it will appear correctly in Live view and in a browser.

This selection will create a link to the home page that you will create later. The <a> tag now appears in the tag selector interface, and the logo has changed color to match the default styling of hyperlinks. Although you may want normal hyperlinks to be styled this way, the logo is not supposed to be blue. It's a simple fix with CSS.

3 In the CSS Designer, choose **green_styles.css** > GLOBAL. Create the following selector:

`header h2 a:link, header h2 a:visited`

This selector will target the "default" and "visited" states of the link within the logo.

4 Add the following properties to the rule:

`color: inherit`
`text-decoration: none`

5 Switch to Live view.

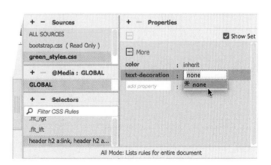

These properties will cancel the hyperlink styling and return the text to its original appearance. By using `inherit` for the color value, the color applied by the `header h2` rule will be passed automatically to the text. That way, any time the color in the `header h2` rule changes, the hyperlink will be styled in turn without any additional work or redundant code.

So far, all the links you've created and the changes you've made are only on the template. The whole purpose of using the template is to make updating pages in your site easy.

Updating links in child pages

To apply the links you've created to all the existing pages based on this template, all you have to do is save it.

1 Choose File > Save.

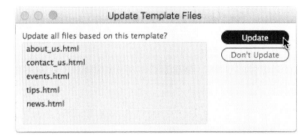

The Update Template Files dialog appears. You can choose to update pages now or wait until later. You can even update the template files manually, if desired.

2 Click Update.

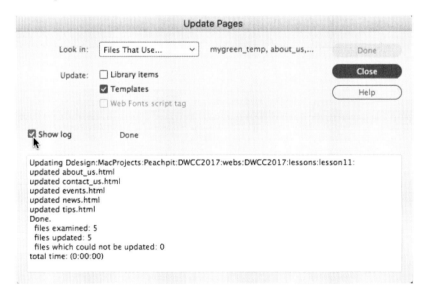

Dreamweaver updates all pages created by this template. The Update Pages dialog appears and displays a report listing the updated pages. If you don't see the list of updated pages, click the Show Log option in the dialog.

3   Close the Update Pages dialog.
    Close **mygreen_temp.dwt**.

Dreamweaver prompts you to save **green_styles.css**.

4   Click Save.

    The file **about_us.html** is still open. Note the asterisk in the document tab; this indicates that the page has been changed but not saved.

5   Save **about_us.html** and preview it in a browser.
    Position the cursor over the *Home* and *Green News* links.

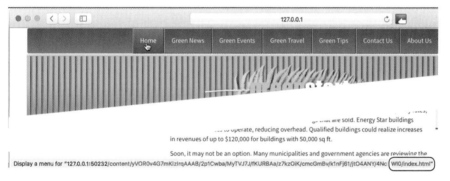

If you display the status bar in your browser, you can see the links applied to each item. When the template was saved, it updated the locked regions of the page, adding the hyperlinks to the horizontal menu. Child pages that are closed at the time of updating are automatically saved. Open pages must be saved manually or you will lose changes applied by the template.

6   Click the *Contact Us* link.

    The *Contact Us* page loads to replace the *About Us* page in the browser.

7   Click the *About Us* link.

    The *About Us* page loads to replace the *Contact Us* page. The links were added even to pages that weren't open at the time.

8   Close the browser.

Note: When you close templates or webpages, Dreamweaver may ask you to save changes to **green_styles.css**. Whenever you see these warnings, always save the changes; otherwise you could lose all your newly created CSS rules and properties.

▶ **Tip:** Thoroughly test every link you create on every page.

You learned three methods for creating hyperlinks with the Property inspector: typing the link manually, using the Browse for File function, and using the Point to File tool.

Creating an external link

The pages you linked to in the previous exercise were stored within the current site. You can also link to any page—or other resource—stored on the web if you know the URL.

Creating an absolute link in Live view

In the previous exercise, you used Design view to build all your links. As you build pages and format content, you'll use Live view frequently to preview the styling and appearance of your elements. Although some aspects of content creation and editing are limited in Live view, you can still create and edit hyperlinks. In this exercise, you'll apply an external link to some text using Live view.

▶ **Tip:** For this exercise, you can use any search engine or web-based mapping application.

1 Open **contact_us.html** from the site root folder in Live view.

2 In the second <p> element in the MainContent region, note the word *Meridien*.

You'll link this text to the Google Maps site.

◉ **Note:** In some browsers, you can type the search phrase directly in the URL field.

3 Launch your favorite browser.
In the URL field, type **google.com/maps** and press Enter/Return.

Google Maps appears in the browser window.

4 Type **San Jose, CA** into the search field and press Enter/Return.

◉ **Note:** We're using Adobe's headquarters in place of the fictional city of Meridien. Feel free to use your own location or another search term in its place.

San Jose appears on a map in the browser. In Google Maps, somewhere on the screen you should see a settings or share icon.

5   Open the settings interface as appropriate for your chosen mapping application.

Search engines and browsers may display their link-sharing and embedding interface slightly differently than the one pictured. Google Maps, MapQuest, and Bing usually offer at least two separate code snippets: one for use within a hyperlink and the other to generate an actual map that you can embed in your site.

Note: The technique for sharing map links is implemented differently in various browsers and search engines and may change over time.

Note how the link contains the entire URL of the map, making it an *absolute* link. The advantage of using absolute links is that you can copy and paste them anywhere in the site without worrying whether the link will resolve properly.

6   Select and copy the link.

7   Switch to Live view in Dreamweaver. Select the word *Meridien*.

In Live view, you can select an entire element or insert the cursor within the element to edit or add text or apply hyperlinks, as desired. When an element or section of text is selected, the Text HUD will appear. The Text HUD allows you to apply `<strong>` or `<em>` tags to the selection or (as in this case) to apply hyperlinks.

Tip: Double-click to select text in Live view.

8   Click the Hyperlink icon in the Text HUD.
Press Ctrl+V/Cmd+V to paste the link in the Link field.
Press Enter/Return to complete the link.

The selected text displays the default formatting for a hyperlink.

9 Save the file and preview it in the default browser. Test the link.

When you click the link, the browser takes you to the opening page of Google Maps, assuming you have a connection to the Internet. But there is a problem: Clicking the link replaced the *Contact Us* page in the browser; it didn't open a new window like when you previewed the page at the beginning of the lesson. To make the browser open a new window, you need to add a simple HTML attribute to the link.

10 Switch to Dreamweaver.
Click the *Meridien* link in Live view.

The Element HUD appears. The Property inspector displays the value of the existing link.

▶ **Tip:** You can access the Target attribute in the Property inspector in Live, Design, and Code views whenever a link is selected.

11 Choose _blank from the Target field menu in the Property inspector.

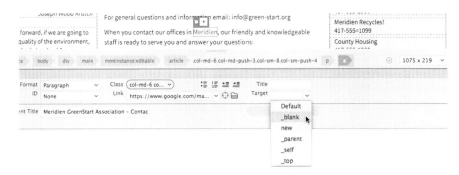

12 Save the file and preview the page in the default browser again. Test the link.

This time when you click the link, the browser opens a new window or document tab.

13 Close the browser windows and switch back to Dreamweaver.

As you can see, Dreamweaver makes it easy to create links to both internal and external resources.

Setting up email links

Another type of link doesn't take the visitor to another page; it opens the visitor's email program. Email links can create automatic, pre-addressed email messages from your visitors for customer feedback, product orders, or other important communications. The code for an email link is slightly different from the normal hyperlink, and—as you probably guessed already—Dreamweaver can create the proper code for you automatically.

1   If necessary, open **contact_us.html** in Design view.

2   Select the email address (info@green-start.org) in the first paragraph underneath the heading and press Ctrl+C/Cmd+C to copy the text.

3   Choose Insert > HTML > Email Link.

Tip: The Email Link menu cannot be accessed in Live view. But you can use the menu in Design view or Code view or just create the links by hand in any view.

The Email Link dialog appears. The text selected in the document window in step 2 is automatically entered into the Text field.

4   Insert the cursor in the Email field and press Ctrl+V/Cmd+V to paste the email address, if necessary.

5   Click OK. Examine the Link field in the Property inspector.

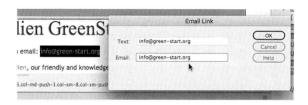

Tip: If you select the text before you access the dialog, Dreamweaver enters the text in the field for you automatically.

Dreamweaver inserts the email address into the Link field and also enters the `mailto:` notation, which tells the browser to automatically launch the visitor's default email program.

6   Save the file and preview it in the default browser. Test the email link.

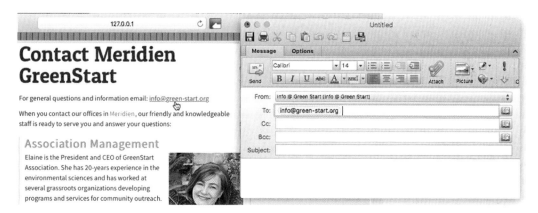

If your computer has a default email program installed, it will launch and create a new email message using the email address provided in the link. If there is no default email program, your computer's operating system may ask you to identify or install one.

7 Close any open email program, related dialogs, or wizards. Switch to Dreamweaver.

You can also create email links manually.

8 Select and copy the email address for Elaine.

● **Note:** Be sure that there are no spaces between the colon and the link text.

9 Type `mailto:` in the Property inspector link field. Paste Elaine's email address directly after the colon. Press Enter/Return to complete the link.

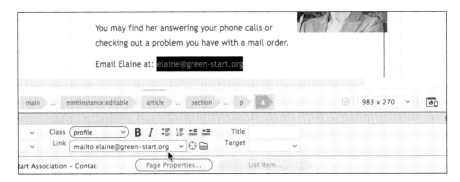

The text `mailto:elaine@green-start.org` appears in the Text HUD link field in Live view.

10 Save the file.

You can use the Element HUD to add links to images too.

Creating an image-based link

Image-based links work like any other hyperlink and can direct users to internal or external resources. You can use the Insert menu in Design or Code views or apply links and other attributes using the Element HUD interface in Live view.

Creating image-based links using the Element HUD

In this exercise, you will create and format an image-based link using the email addresses of each GreenStart employee via the Element HUD.

1 If necessary, open **contact_us.html** in Live view from the site root folder.

2 Select the image of Elaine in the *Association Management* section.

To access the hyperlink option, you must open the Edit HTML Attributes menu.

3 In the Element HUD, click the Edit HTML Attributes icon 🗒.

The menu opens and displays options for the image attributes `src`, `alt`, `link`, `width`, and `height`.

4   If the email address is still in memory from the previous exercise, simply enter `mailto:` and paste the address in the Link field. Otherwise, enter `mailto:elaine@green-start.org` in the link field after the colon and press Enter/Return to complete the link. Press the Esc key to close the HUD.

● **Note:** Normally, an image formatted with a hyperlink displays a blue border, similar to the blue underscore that text links get. But the predefined Bootstrap CSS turns this styling off. In non-Bootstrap sites, you may want to create a similar rule.

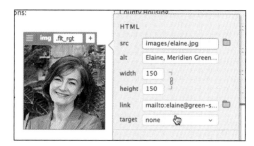

The hyperlink that is applied to the image will launch the default email program in the same fashion as it did with the text-based link earlier.

5   Select and copy the email address for Sarah.

Repeat steps 2 through 4 to create an email link for Sarah's image.

6   Create image links for the remaining employees using the appropriate email address for each.

All the image-based links on the page are complete. You can create text-based links using the Text HUD too.

Creating text links using the Text HUD

In this exercise, you will create text-based email links as needed for the remaining employees.

1   If necessary, open **contact_us.html** in Live view.

2   Select and copy the email address for Sarah.

The Text HUD appears around the selected text.

3   Click the Link icon ✐ .

A link field appears. A folder icon displays on the right side of the link field. If you were linking to a file on the website, you could click the folder to target the file. In this case, we're creating an email link.

4   Insert the cursor in the link field, if necessary.

Enter `mailto:` and paste Sarah's email address.

Press Enter/Return.

▶ **Tip:** You may need to double-click the text to be able to select and copy it.

5 Using the Text HUD, create email links for the remaining email addresses displayed on the page.

6 Save and close all files.

Attack of the killer robots

Although on the surface it sounds like a good idea to add email links to make it easier for your customers and visitors to communicate with you and your staff, email links are a double-edged sword. The Internet is awash in bad actors and unethical companies that use intelligent programs, or robots, to constantly search for live email addresses that they can flood with unsolicited email and spam. Putting a plain email address on your site as shown in these exercises is like putting a sign on your back that says "kick me."

In place of active email links, many sites use a variety of methods for limiting the amount of spam they receive. One technique uses images to display the email addresses, since robots can't read data stored in pixels (yet). Another leaves off the hyperlink attribute and types the address with extra spaces, like this:

```
elaine @ green-start .org
```

However, both of these techniques have drawbacks; if visitors try to use copy and paste, it forces them to go out of their way to remove the extra spaces or try to type your email address from memory. Either way, the chances of you receiving any communication decreases with each step the user has to accomplish without additional help.

At this time, there is no foolproof way to prevent someone from using an email address for nefarious purposes. Coupled with the fact that fewer users actually have a mail program installed on their computers anymore, the best method for enabling communication for your visitors is to provide a means built into the site itself. Many sites create web-hosted forms that collect the visitor's information and message and then pass them along using server-based email functionality.

Targeting page elements

As you add more content, the pages get longer, and navigating to that content gets more difficult. Typically, when you click a link to a page, the browser window loads the page and displays it starting at the top. But it can be helpful when you provide convenient methods for users to link to a specific point on a page.

HTML 4.01 provided two methods to target specific content or page structures: a *named anchor* and an *id* attribute. In HTML5, the named anchor method has been deprecated in favor of ids. If you have used named anchors in the past, don't worry, they won't suddenly cease to function. But from this point on, you should start using ids exclusively.

Creating internal targeted links

In this exercise, you'll work with id attributes to create the target of an internal link. You can add ids in Live, Design, or Code view.

1 Open **events.html** in Live view.

2 Scroll down to the table containing the class schedule.

When users move down this far on the page, the navigation menus are out of sight and unusable. The farther down the page they read, the farther they are from the primary navigation. Before users can navigate to another page, they have to use the browser scroll bars or the mouse scroll wheel to get back to the top of the page.

Older websites dealt with this situation by adding a link to take visitors back to the top, vastly improving their experience on your site. Let's call this type of link an *internal targeted* link. Modern websites simply freeze the navigation menu at the top of the screen. For our design you will learn how to do both techniques. First, let's create an internal targeted link.

Internal targeted links have two parts: the link itself and the target. Which one you create first doesn't matter.

3 Click the *2017 Class Schedule* table.
Select the `section` tag selector.

The HUD appears focused on the `section` element.

4 Open the Insert panel. Select the HTML category. Click the Paragraph item.

 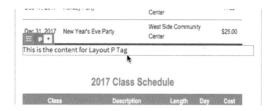

The position assist interface opens.

5 Click Before.

A new paragraph element appears in the layout, with the placeholder text *This is the content for Layout P Tag.*

6 Select the placeholder text.
Type **Return to Top** to replace it.

The text is inserted between the two tables, formatted as a <p> element. The text would look better centered.

7 Choose **green_styles.css** > GLOBAL in the CSS Designer.
Create a new selector: `.ctr`

8 Create the following properties for `.ctr`:
`text-align: center`
`margin-top: 15px`

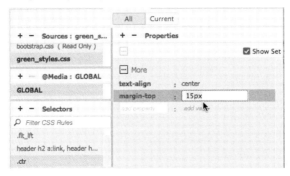

9 Click the Add Class/ID icon ⊞ for the selected <p> element.

10 Type `.ctr` in the text field, or choose `.ctr` from the hinting menu, and press Enter/Return.

The *Return to Top* text is aligned to the center. The tag selector now displays `p.ctr`.

11 Select the text *Return to Top*. Click the Edit HTML Attributes icon ☰ and type `#top` in the Link field. Press Enter/Return to complete the link.

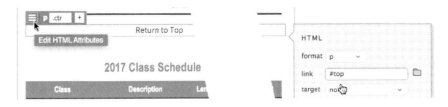

By using `#top`, you have created a link to a target within the current page. When users click the *Return to Top* link, the browser window jumps to the position of the target. This target doesn't exist yet. For this link to work properly, you need to insert the destination as high on the page as possible.

12 Save all files. Switch to Design view.

13 Scroll to the top of **events.html**.
Position the cursor over the header element.

The "no" symbol ⊘ indicates that this part of the page (and its related code) is uneditable, because the header and horizontal navigation menu are based on the site template. Putting the target at the top is important, or a portion of the page may be obscured when the browser jumps to it. Since the top of the page is part of an uneditable region, the best solution is to add the target directly to the template.

Creating a link destination using an id

By adding a unique id to the template, you will be able to access it automatically throughout the site wherever you want to add a link back to the top of a page.

1 Open the template **mygreen_temp.dwt f**rom the Templates folder in Design view.

The horizontal navigation menu is the highest point of the page. Let's add the destination target to this element.

2 Click any link in the horizontal menu.
Select the div.row tag selector.

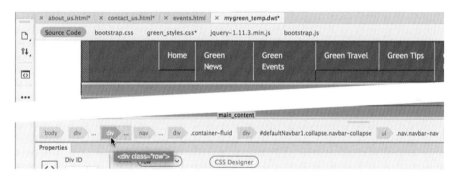

3 Press Ctrl+T/Cmd+T to open the Quick Tag Editor.

4 Insert id="top" after the div tag and press Enter/Return as necessary to complete the change..

Note: An id can be created and applied to any HTML element. They don't have to be referenced in the style sheet at all.

The tag selector changes to div#top.row; otherwise, the page shows no visible difference. The big difference is in how the page reacts to the internal hyperlink.

5 Save the file and update all template child pages. Close the template.

6 Switch to or open **events.html**, if necessary.
Save the file, and preview it in a browser.

7 Scroll down to the Class table.
Click the *Return to Top* link.

The browser jumps back to the top of the page.

Now that the id has been inserted in every page of the site by the template, you can copy the *Return to Top* link and paste it anywhere in the site you want to add this functionality.

8 In Dreamweaver, switch to Live view.
Select and copy the <p> element containing the text *Return to Top* and its link.

9 Insert the cursor in the Class table.
Using the tag selector, select the <section> element.
Press Ctrl+V/Cmd+V to paste.

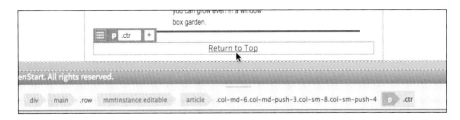

A new p.ctr element and link appear at the bottom of the page.

10 Save the file and preview it in the browser.
Test both *Return to Top* links.

Both links can be used to jump back to the top of the document. In the next exercise, you'll learn how to create link targets using element attributes.

Creating a destination link in the Element HUD

In the past, destinations were often created by inserting a stand-alone element known as a *named anchor* within the code. In most cases, there's no need to add any extra elements to create hyperlink destinations since you can simply add an id attribute to a handy element nearby. In this exercise, you will use the Element HUD to add an id.

1 Open **events.html** in Live view.
Click the *2017 Events Schedule* table.
Select the table tag selector.

The Element HUD and the Property inspector display the attributes currently applied to the Events table. You can add an id using either tool.

2 Click the Add Class/ID icon. Type a hash mark (#).

If any ids were defined in the style sheet but unused on the page, a list would appear. Since nothing appears, it means that there are no unused ids. Creating a new one is easy.

3 Type `calendar` and press Enter/Return.

The CSS Source HUD appears. You do not need the id in any style sheet.

4 Press Esc to close the HUD.

The tag selector now displays `table#calendar`, but no entry was made in the style sheet. Since ids are unique identifiers, they are perfect for targeting specific content on a page for hyperlinks. You also need to create an id for the Class table.

5 Repeat steps 1 through 4 to create the id `#classes` on the Class table.

Note: When creating ids, remember that they need to have names that are used only once per page. They are case sensitive, so look out for typos.

Note: If you add the id to the wrong element, simply delete it and start over.

The tag selector now displays `table#classes`.

6 Save all files.

You'll learn how to link to these ids in the next exercise.

Targeting id-based link destinations

By adding unique ids to both tables, you have provided an ideal target for internal hyperlinks to navigate to a specific section of your webpage. In this exercise, you will create a link to each table.

1 If necessary, open **contact_us.html** in Live view.
Scroll down to the *Education and Events* section.

2 Select the word *events* in the first paragraph of the section.

Tip: You can select single words by double-clicking them.

3 Using the Text HUD, create a link to the file **events.html**.

This link will open the file, but you're not finished. You now have to direct the browser to navigate down to the Events table.

● **Note:** Hyperlinks cannot contain spaces; make sure the id reference follows the filename immediately.

4 Type `#calendar` at the end of the filename to complete the link and press Enter/Return.

The word *events* is now a link targeting the Events table in the **events.html** file.

5 Select the word *classes*. Create a link to the **events.html** file.
Type `#classes` to complete the link and press Enter/Return.

6 Save the file and preview the page in a browser.
Test the links to the *Events* and *Class* tables.

The links open the *Events* page and navigate to the appropriate tables. You've learned how to create a variety of internal and external links. The last things you need to do are to learn how to freeze the horizontal navigation menu at the top of the screen and how to build special kinds of hyperlinks for the Green Events button.

Freezing a navigation menu

All elements usually move along with the page as you scroll down to view the content. But CSS has the ability to freeze elements so that they don't follow this normal behavior. Since our basic page layout was built using a Bootstrap framework, you'll use a predefined CSS class to apply the styling.

1   Open **mygreen_temp.dwt** in Live view.

To control the styling, you have to add a new class to the existing horizontal navigation menu.

2   Click any of the links in the menu.
Select the nav tag selector.

At the time of this writing, the Element HUD does not appear on elements within a Dreamweaver template. So, to add the new class, you'll have to use the Quick Tag Editor.

3   Press Ctrl+T/Cmd+T. Insert the cursor after the last class displayed in the Quick Tag Editor and press the spacebar.

4   Type `navbar-fixed-top` to insert the new class name and press Enter/Return.

This is a class predefined in the Bootstrap style sheet to format these kinds of menus. The horizontal navigation menu now stretches across the entire screen. The menu is no longer in the normal page flow. As a result, the rest of the content moves up to take up its original space and part of the header element is now obscured underneath the menu. To make sure no content is lost or unseen, you'll need to add some spacing above the header to make sure it's fully visible.

5   Select **green_styles.css** > GLOBAL > `header.row` in the CSS Designer.

6   Add the following properties to the rule:
    `margin-top: 52px`

The header element shifts down on the screen so you can see the yellow top border.

7   Save all files.

The Update Template Files dialog appears.

8   Click Update.

The Update Pages dialog appears and should report that all five pages are now updated. The new fixed menu now appears on all existing site pages.

The *Green Events* link is the only item in the menu that has not been modified yet. Since you have two destinations already defined in the page, this is a good opportunity to add a drop-down menu to the navigation options.

Creating a drop-down menu

Drop-down menus are a good option whenever you have known destinations set up on a particular page. This bit of customization gets your visitors to the information they desire quickly and efficiently. And, when you have analytics set up on a page, it also provides a handy way to track the interests and activities of visitors on your pages.

The easiest way to add drop-downs to a menu is to use one of the prebuilt options provided in the Bootstrap category of the Insert menu or panel. Since you're working in a template, you'll have to perform a few workarounds to get the code you need.

1 Open **mygreen_temp.dwt** in Split view.

In a normal document, you could simply delete the menu item and replace it with a drop-down element. But at the time of this writing, Dreamweaver templates were not fully supported in Live view. So, you will have to use a little workaround to achieve the same results.

2 Create a new document based on the site template.

You will use this new file to stage the modifications for the horizontal menu. Before you can edit the menu, you'll need to save the file, but you don't want to save the file to the site root folder.

You learned earlier in this lesson that the links in the menu in the site template display the `../` path notation indicating that the template is saved in a subfolder. When the template creates a new file, the paths in these links are rewritten by Dreamweaver based on where the page is then saved. To build the replacement menu efficiently, you'll want to reproduce the same types of paths in your work file. This can be done by saving the file in the same subfolder as the site template.

3 Save the file as **dropdown.html** in the Templates subfolder.

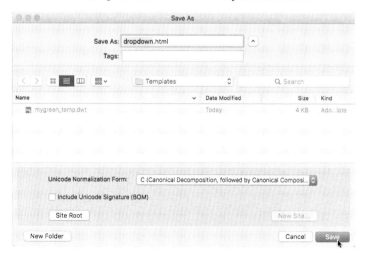

The horizontal menu is part of the template structure and uneditable in a child page. To modify it, you'll have to detach the page from the template.

4   Switch to Design view.

Select Tools > Templates > Detach From Template.

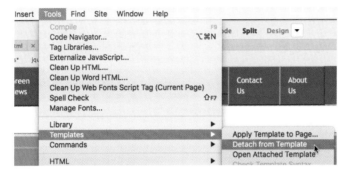

The new page is no longer connected to the template. You should now be able to edit the horizontal menu directly in Live view.

5   Switch to Live view in **dropdown.html**.

Click the *Green Events* item in the menu.

In most cases, the HUD will appear focused on the <a> element.

6   Select the <li> tag selector.

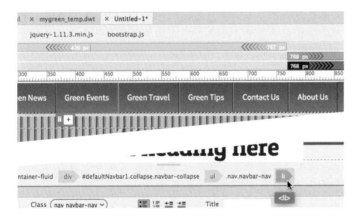

7   Open the Insert panel and select the Bootstrap category.

8 Select Navigation: > Nav Pills With Dropdown from the Bootstrap Components category in the Insert panel.

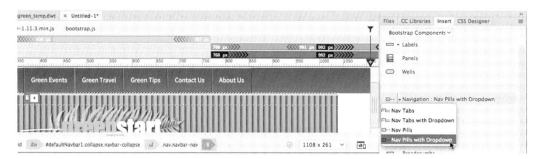

9 Select **After** in the Position Assist HUD.

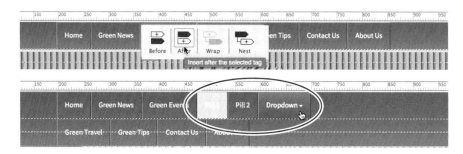

Note: The names *nav pill* and *nav tab* simply refer to the way a menu option is styled in Bootstrap. Otherwise, they function identically as hyperlinks.

Two nav pills and one drop-down menu option are added to the horizontal menu. You need the drop-down menu only so you can delete the nav pills.

10 Select Pill 1 and Pill 2 and delete them.

You also no longer need the original *Green Events* menu item.

11 Select and delete the `<li>` element containing the *Green Events* menu item.

Tip: Each pill is based on an `<li>` element. If you use the tag selector for each item, you should be able to delete the entire element by pressing the Delete key.

The Dropdown item has taken the place of the *Green Events* item. To change the text in the menu item, you'll find that Code view offers the easiest option.

12 Switch to Split view. In the Code view window, select the text "Dropdown" and type **Green Events** to replace it.

The new text has now replaced the original content. But there's something odd about the menu. Although you have deleted the additional items, the menu still appears in two rows. If you examine the code, you may discover why.

13 In Code view window, scroll down through the menu and examine the code structure.

Do you see anything odd or out of place?

```
41                    </ul>
42                  </li>
43 ▼           </ul>
44 ▼           <ul class="nav navbar-nav">
45  ▶             <li><a href="../travel.html">Green Travel </a></li>
46                <li><a href="../tips.html">Green Tips </a></li>
```
body div div .row nav #top.navbar.navbar-default.navbar-fixed-top div .container-fluid div #defaultNavbar1.collapse.navbar-collapse   HTML ✓   1204 x 341 ✓   INS 45:1

Around line 43 you will see a closing `</ul>` tag and then a new `<ul class="nav navbar-nav">` tag directly following it. In fact, Dreamweaver for some reason added these tags when you inserted the new drop-down menu. There's no reason for these tags, and they are causing the menu to break into two lines.

14 Select the two tags and delete them.

▷ **Tip:** If you click the line number, you can select and delete the tags and remove blank lines in the code at the same time.

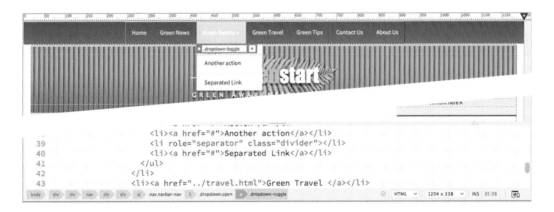

```
                      <li><a href="#">Another action</a></li>
39                    <li role="separator" class="divider"></li>
40                    <li><a href="#">Separated Link</a></li>
41                  </ul>
42                </li>
43              <li><a href="../travel.html">Green Travel </a></li>
```
body div div nav div div ul .nav.navbar-nav || .dropdown.open ▶ .dropdown-toggle   HTML ✓   1204 x 338 ✓   INS 35:38

The menu now collapses to one line.

15 Save all files.

The drop-down is ready for the final modifications, but the styling of the main item and the suboptions doesn't match the overall site theme. In the next exercise, you'll learn how to target the components of the drop-down menu for custom styling.

Styling a drop-down menu

The styling of the drop-down menu doesn't match the color theme of the rest of the navbar. Using the CSS Designer and a couple of other tools it will make it easy to style these items.

1 Open **dropdown.html** in Split view, if necessary.

When the drop-down menu is closed, it matches the other items, but it doesn't when it's open.

2 Position the cursor over the *Green Events* menu item.

The hover effect kicks in. The menu item still matches the others.

3 Click *Green Events* and move the cursor away from the menu item.

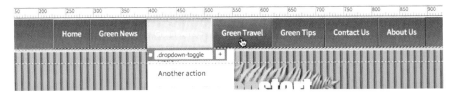

The menu opens. The submenu has a light-gray background. The background of the *Green Events* item turns gray when you move the cursor away from it. The first step is to identify the formatting on the element and the rules that provide it. Let's start with the submenu.

4 Click the Current button in the CSS Designer.

5 Click *Green Events* to open the menu, if necessary.
Click one of the submenu items.

By clicking the submenu item, the tag selector interface shows the menu structure. The menu has three basic elements: ul, li, and a.

6 Select the <a> tag selector.
Examine the rules in the CSS Designer.

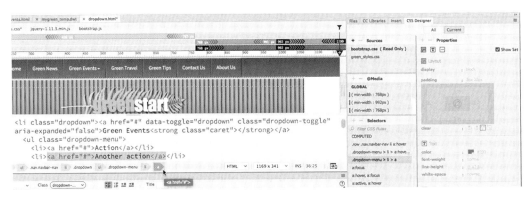

The CSS Designer shows the rules formatting the <a> element. The first rule is one you created yourself to style the hover behavior. But the second and third rules are coming from the Bootstrap style sheet and are supplying a lot of the styling. Let's create a rule to reset the Bootstrap styles.

7   Click the All button in the CSS Designer.
Choose **green_styles.css** > Global.
Create a new selector: `#top .dropdown-menu > li > a`

This selector matches the existing Bootstrap rule but adds the id attribute `#top` to increase its specificity.

8   Create the following properties:
```
padding: 10px
color: #ffc
text-align: center
background-color: #08A
border-top: solid 1px #09E
border-bottom: solid 1px #069
```

9   Click to open the drop-down menu again.

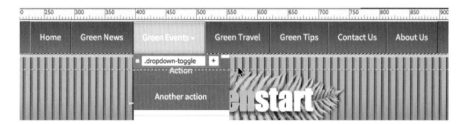

The new styling formats much of the submenu, but there is a gap at the top and bottom. Since the gap is only at the top and bottom, the styling is probably applied to the parent of the menu: the <ul> element. Since the drop-down is based on a child element of the *Green Events* menu item, you can't select any part of the structure when the menu is closed.

10 Click one of the submenu items.

Clicking the subitem exposes the structure of the submenu in the tag selector interface.

11 Click the Current button in the CSS Designer.
Select the `<ul>` tag selector for the submenu.
Examine the rules in the CSS Designer.

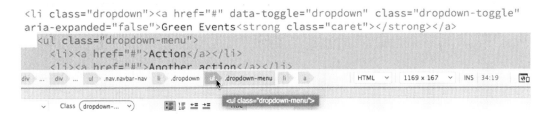

The second rule in the list `.dropdown-menu` applies 5 pixels of padding to the top and bottom of the `<ul>` element. You'll have to reset this spacing with a custom rule.

12 Click the All button in the CSS Designer.
Choose **green_styles.css** > Global.
Create a new selector: `#top .dropdown-menu`

13 Create the following property:
`padding: 0px`

14 Save all files.

15 Click to open the submenu.

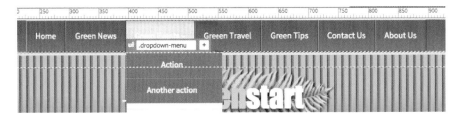

The gap at the top and bottom of the submenu is gone. The last step in styling the new drop-down menu is to reformat the color of the menu item itself whenever the submenu is open. In cases like this, working with Split view provides an important advantage.

16 Select the `<li>` tag selector for the *Green Events* item.

Note the code selected in Code view.

Pay special attention to the classes assigned to the menu item. Notice that the `<li>` element shows two classes, `dropdown` and `open`, in the HUD and in the tag selector but not in the code. That's because the class appears only when the visitor clicks the menu to open it. This class is assigned and removed via JavaScript dynamically.

17 Click to close the *Green Events* submenu.

Examine the classes again in Code view.

The `open` class disappears when the menu closes. This class is added and removed by a Bootstrap JavaScript behavior when a user clicks to open and close the dropdown menu. Dynamic or interactive elements present a unique challenge when you want to style them. Since the class does not appear in the code, it's difficult to identify and target the proper structure using normal methods. You'll have to learn some new techniques to work with and style such interactive elements.

Identifying styling on an interactive element

Identifying CSS styling on interactive elements is hard because the styling changes through user interaction. In this case, it looks one way by default and then changes when clicked. So, how do you track down styling on an element that changes whenever you click it?

You freeze the JavaScript, of course.

1 Open **dropdown.html** in Split view, if necessary.

2 Click the Current button in CSS Designer.

To identify the styling of the open menu, you first have to open it.

3 Click to open the *Green Events* submenu again.
Examine the classes assigned to the `<li>` and `<a>` elements.

When the submenu is open, the class `open` appears on the `<li>` element in the Element HUD and tag selector. This class is added and removed by JavaScript each time you click the menu item. For this reason, Dreamweaver provides a method to disable JavaScript temporarily.

4 Right-click the *Green Events* menu item.
Note the option Freeze JavaScript in the context menu.

▶ **Tip:** If you don't see the Common toolbar, you can display it by choosing Window > Toolbars > Common.

The Freeze JavaScript option is grayed out. Before you can enable it, you first have to disable a specific function in Live view.

5 Click the Live View Options icon ▣ in the Common toolbar.

6 Select Hide Live View Displays in Live View Options.

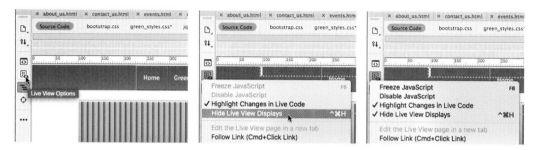

When Live View Displays are disabled, various behaviors and Live View features are turned off, such as the Element and Text HUDs. Now you should be able to freeze the JavaScript.

7 Click to open the *Green Events* submenu again.

You have to make sure the menu is open before you freeze JavaScript.

8 Right-click the *Green Events* menu item.
Choose Freeze JavaScript from the context menu.

The submenu is now locked open. Dreamweaver displays a message at the top of the document window indicating the JavaScript is frozen.

9 If necessary, click the *Green Events* menu item.
Select the `a.dropdown-toggle` tag selector.

The CSS Designer display focuses on the rules formatting the *Green Events* menu item. Examine the list to see whether any of the rules use the `.open` class. In fact, the fifth rule down says this: `.nav .open > a, .nav .open > a:hover, .nav .open > a:focus`. Now that the styling is frozen, it's easy to see the contents of the rule.

10 Select the rule `.nav .open > a, .nav .open > a:hover, .nav .open > a:focus` and examine the properties.

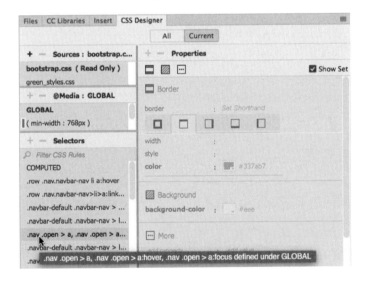

The properties in the rule should be grayed out since it's part of the read-only Bootstrap style sheet but you can still see that it formats borders, text color, and the background color. The four rules above it reset the border and text properties but not the background color. To reset the color, you'll need to create a more specific rule that will affect the *Green Events* menu item, but only when it's open.

11 Click the All button in the CSS Designer.
Choose **green_styles.css** > `Global`.

Create a new selector:

```
#top .open > a, #top .open > a:visited
```

This rule is based on the original BootStrap rule and targets the default and visited state of the menu only when it's open. By adding the id #top, the rule makes it more specific.

12 Create the following property:

```
background-color: #069
```

That did it. When the *Green Event* drop-down menu is open, it will display a dark blue background. Before you move on, don't forget to unfreeze JavaScript and enable Live View Displays.

13 Right-click the horizontal menu.

A check mark should appear on the Freeze JavaScript option in the context menu. To unfreeze JavaScript, you click the option a second time or you can press the function key F6.

14 Click Freeze JavaScript to enable JavaScript or press F6.

Now you can turn on the Live View Displays.

15 Click the Live View Options icon 🔲.

A check mark should appear on the Hide Live View Displays option indicating that Live View Displays are hidden.

16 Choose Hide Live View Displays to remove the check mark and enable the displays again.

17 Save all files.

The *Green Events* menu item and drop-down menu are fully styled. But before the menu is complete, you'll have to add the needed hyperlinks.

Adding hyperlinks to a drop-down menu

The drop-down menu offers a bit of challenge for adding hyperlinks. You may find it easier to work in Code view.

1 Open **dropdown.html** in Split view, if necessary.

2 Click the *Green Events* menu item in Live view.

The Element HUD appears focused on the <a> element, and the submenu opens.

3 Select the `a.dropdown-toggle` tag selector.

In the Code view window, the entire structure of the *Green Events* link is selected. You should be able to see the hash (#) symbol in the `href` attribute for the main menu item. Because of the animation that opens the submenu, a URL added to the *Green Events* link will be ignored. Instead, you'll add destinations to the submenu items. Dreamweaver's hyperlink tools work in Code view, too.

> **Tip:** To see some changes in the code, you may have to refresh the display in the Live view window.

4 In Code view, select the text "Action".
Type `Events Schedule` to replace it.

```
<ul class="dropdown-menu">
  <li><a href="#">Action</a></li>
  <li><a href="#">Another action</a></li>
  <li role="separator" class="divider"></li>
  <li><a href="#">Separated Link</a></li>
```

```
<ul class="dropdown-menu">
  <li><a href="#" Event Schedule</a></li>
  <li><a href="#">Another action</a></li>
  <li role="separator" class="divider"></li>
  <li><a href="#">Separated Link</a></li>
```

The cursor should still appear within the <a> element.

5 In the Property inspector, click the Browse For File icon 🗂 next to the Link field.

6 Navigate to the site root folder, if necessary.
Select **events.html** and click Open.

The filename **events.html** appears in the `href` attribute in Code view. You can target the Events table in the link specifically by adding the id assigned to it.

7 Insert the cursor at the end of the filename in the `href` attribute.

8 Type `#calendar` to insert the id.

```
<ul class="dropdown-menu">
  <li><a href="../events.html#calendar">Events Schedule</a></li>
  <li><a href="#">Another action</a></li>
  <li role="separator" class="divider"></li>
  <li><a href="#">Separated Link</a></li>
```

Let's do the same for the class schedule.

9 Select the text "Another Action" in the submenu.
Type `Class Schedule` to replace it.

10 Create a link to **events.html** and add the **#classes** id to it.

```
<ul class="dropdown-menu">
  <li><a href="../events.html#calendar">Events Schedule</a></li>
  <li><a href="../events.html#classes">Class Schedule</a></li>
  <li role="separator" class="divider"></li>
  <li><a href="#">Separated Link</a></li>
```

The submenu has two additional `<li>` elements that are unneeded at this time.

11 Select and delete the two unneeded `<li>` elements, around lines 39 and 40.

```
38      <li><a href="../events.html#classes">Class Schedule</a></
39 ▼    <li role="separator" class="divider"></li>
40      <li><a href="#">Separated Link</a></li>

        <li><a href="../events.html#classes">Class Schedule</a></
39  |
40    </ul>
```

12 Save all files.

The last step now is to move the modified menu into the site template so you can add it to every page.

Replacing the site navigation menu

Once you're finished editing the code, it's time to move the completed menu to the site template.

1 Open **dropdown.html** in Split view, if necessary.

The file contains the completed menu in a file based on but detached from the original site template. Because of the conflicts between Live view and editable regions, you'll need to use Code view to select and move the menu from this file to the site template.

2 In Live, view click the horizontal menu.

Selecting the menu in Live view should focus the Code view display on the menu structure.

3 In Code view, insert the cursor anywhere in the menu.

4 Select the `<nav>` element tag selector.

Note: You must reselct the nav element in Code view to copy it properly.

The entire menu is selected.

5 Press Ctrl+C/Cmd+C to copy the menu code.

6 Switch to or open **mygreen_temp.dwt**.
Switch to Split view, if necessary.

Before you can swap out the menu in the template, you must select it in the same way you did in the source file.

7 Click the horizontal menu in Live view.

Code view focuses on the menu structure. Using Live view helps you to identify the code creating the menu. The tag selectors display the structure of the menu.

8 In Code view, insert the cursor anywhere in the menu.

The cursor must be inserted in the Code view window before you use the tag selector.

9 Select the `<nav>` element tag selector.

The entire menu is selected. Once selected, you can now paste the new menu to replace the existing one.

Note: It is imperative that you use the same view in source and target documents when copying and pasting content in Dreamweaver. You copied the menu from Code view, so you must paste it in Code view, too.

10 Press Ctrl+V/Cmd+V to paste the menu.

The menu is now replaced with the modified code. You may need to click in the Live view window to see the new drop-down menu.

11 Position the cursor over each menu item to test the hover effect. Click the Green Events menu item to open the submenu. Check the menu structure in Code view to confirm the menu was replaced properly.

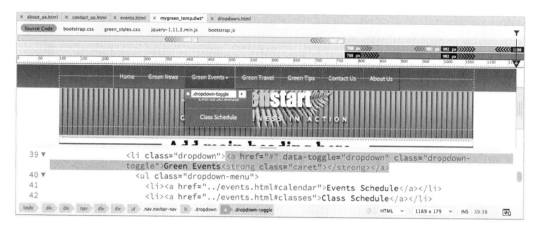

Once you are satisfied that the menu was replaced properly, it's time to update all the child pages.

12 Save **mygreen_temp.dwt**.

Click to update the template files.

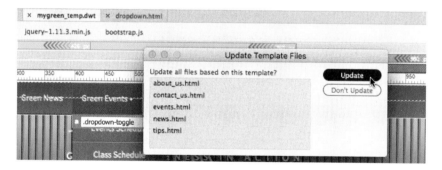

The Update dialog reports that all five child pages were updated successfully.

13 Save and close all open files.

You used **dropdown.html** to help you modify the horizontal menu, but there's no need to keep it any longer.

14 In the Files panel, select and delete **dropdown.html**.

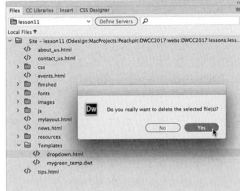

Once the menu has been updated in all the site pages, the next step is to check to see whether the links throughout your site are working properly.

Checking your page

Dreamweaver can check your page, as well as the entire site, for valid HTML, accessibility, and broken links. In this exercise, you'll learn how to check your links sitewide.

1 If necessary, open **contact_us.html** in Design view.

2 Choose Site > Site Options > Check Links Sitewide.

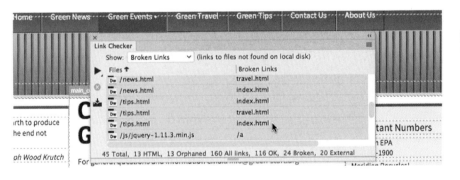

● **Note:** The Link Checker may find some suspicious links in a Bootstrap JavaScript file. Ignore any of these errors.

● **Note:** The total number and types of missing and broken links may vary from that pictured.

A Link Checker panel opens. The Link Checker panel reports broken links to the files **index.html** and **travel.html** you created for nonexistent pages. You'll make these pages in another lesson, so you don't need to worry about fixing these broken links now. The Link Checker will also find broken links to external sites, should you have any.

3 Close the Link Checker panel or, if it's docked, right-click the Link Checker tab and choose Close Tab Group from the context menu.

You've made big changes to the pages in this lesson by creating the main navigation menu with links to specific positions on a page, to email, and to an external site. You also applied links to images and learned how to check your site for broken links.

Adding destination links to the same page (optional)

Using the skills you have just learned, open **events.html** and create destination links for the words *Events* and *Classes* that appear in the first paragraph.

Remember that the words will link to the tables on the same page. Can you figure out how to construct these links properly? If you have any trouble, check out the **events_finished.html** file for the answer.

Review questions

1 Describe two ways to insert a link into a page.

2 What information is required to create a link to an external webpage?

3 What's the difference between standard page links and email links?

4 What attribute is used to create destination links?

5 What limits the usefulness of email links?

6 Can links be applied to images?

7 How can you check to see whether your links will work properly?

Review answers

1 Select text or a graphic and then, in the Property inspector, click the Browse for File icon next to the Link field and navigate to the desired page. A second method is to drag the Point to File icon to a file within the Files panel.

2 Link to an external page by typing or copying and pasting the full web address (a fully formed URL including http:// or other protocol) in the Link field of the Property inspector or the Text HUD.

3 A standard page link opens a new page or moves the view to a position somewhere on the page. An email link opens a blank email message window if the visitor has an email application installed.

4 You can apply unique id attributes to any element to create a link destination, which can appear only once in each page.

5 Email links may not be very useful because many users do not use built-in email programs, and the links will not automatically connect with Internet-based email services.

6 Yes, links can be applied to images and used in the same way text-based links are.

7 Run the Link Checker report to test links on each page individually or sitewide. You should also test every link in a browser.

12

ADDING INTERACTIVITY

Lesson overview

In this lesson, you'll add Web 2.0 functionality to your webpages by doing the following:

- Use Dreamweaver behaviors to create an image rollover effect
- Insert a Bootstrap Accordion widget

 This lesson will take about 2 hours to complete. If you have not already done so, download the project files for this lesson from the Lesson & Update Files tab on your Account page at www.peachpit.com, store them on your computer in a convenient location, and define a new site based on the lesson12 folder as described in the "Getting Started" section at the beginning of this book. Your Account page is also where you'll find any updates to the lessons or to the lesson files. Look on the Lesson & Update Files tab to access the most current content.

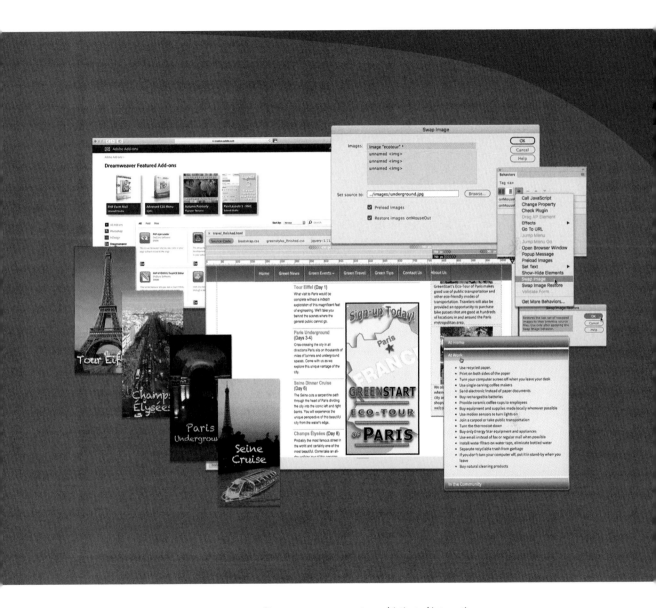

Dreamweaver can create sophisticated interactive effects with behaviors and accordion panels using Adobe's Bootstrap and jQuery frameworks.

Learning about Dreamweaver behaviors

Note: If you have not already downloaded the project files for this lesson to your computer from your Account page, make sure to do so now. See "Getting Started" at the beginning of the book.

Note: To access Dreamweaver behaviors, you must have a file open.

The term *Web 2.0* was coined to describe a major change in the user experience on the Internet—from mostly static pages, featuring text, graphics, and simple links, to a new paradigm of dynamic webpages filled with video, animation, and interactive content. Dreamweaver has always led the industry in providing a variety of tools to drive this movement, from its tried-and-true collection of JavaScript behaviors, jQuery, jQuery Mobile, and Bootstrap widgets. This lesson explores two of these capabilities: Dreamweaver behaviors and Bootstrap widgets.

A Dreamweaver *behavior* is predefined JavaScript code that performs an action, such as opening a browser window or showing or hiding a page element, when it is triggered by an event, such as a mouse click. Applying a behavior is a three-step process.

1 Create or select the page element that you want to trigger the behavior.

2 Choose the behavior to apply.

3 Specify the settings or parameters of the behavior.

The triggering element often involves a hyperlink applied to a range of text or to an image. In some cases, the behavior is not intended to load a new page, so it employs a dummy link enabled by the hash sign (#), similar to ones you used in Lesson 11, "Working with Navigation." The Swap Image behavior you will use in this lesson does not require a link to function, but keep this in mind when you work with other behaviors.

Dreamweaver offers more than 16 built-in behaviors, all accessed from the Behaviors panel (Window > Behaviors). You can download hundreds of other useful behaviors from the Internet for free or a small fee. Some are available from the Adobe Add-ons website, which you can add to the program by clicking the Add Behavior icon in the Behaviors panel and choosing Get More Behaviors from the pop-up menu. You can obtain other tools or features from third-party developers and install them in Dreamweaver as extensions. You can access the Adobe Add-ons website also by choosing Window > Extensions > Browse Extensions.

When the Adobe Add-ons page loads in the browser, click the link to download the plug-in, extension, or other add-on. Often you can simply double-click the add-on to install it.

The following are some examples of the functionality available to you using the built-in Dreamweaver behaviors:

* Opening a browser window

* Swapping one image for another to create what is known as a *rollover effect*

* Fading images or page areas in and out

- Growing or shrinking graphics

- Displaying pop-up messages

- Changing the text or other HTML content within a given area

- Showing or hiding sections of the page

- Calling a custom-defined JavaScript function

Not all behaviors are available all the time. Certain behaviors become available only in the presence and selection of certain page elements, such as images or hyperlinks. For example, the Swap Image behavior must target an image.

Each behavior invokes a unique dialog that provides relevant options and specifications. For instance, the dialog for the Open Browser Window behavior enables you to open a new browser window; set its width, height, and other attributes; and set the URL of the displayed resource. After the behavior is defined, it is listed in the Behaviors panel with its chosen triggering action. As with other behaviors, you can modify these specifications at any time.

Behaviors are extremely flexible, and you can apply multiple behaviors to the same trigger. For example, you could swap one image for another and change the text of the accompanying image caption—and do it all with one click. Although some effects may appear to happen simultaneously, behaviors are actually triggered in sequence. When multiple behaviors are applied, you can choose the order in which the behaviors are processed.

Check out https://creative.adobe.com/addons to learn more about Adobe Add-ons.

The Adobe Add-ons website offers tons of resources for many of the applications in Creative Cloud, including both free and paid add-ons.

Previewing the completed file

In the first part of this lesson, you'll create a new page for GreenStart's travel services. Let's preview the completed page in a browser.

1 Launch Adobe Dreamweaver CC (2017 release) or later.
Define a site based on the lesson12 folder. Name the site **lesson12**.

2 Open **travel_finished.html** directly in your favoriate browser. Some of the interactively may not preview properly in Dreamweaver.

The page includes Dreamweaver behaviors.

3 If Microsoft Internet Explorer is your default browser, a message may appear in the browser window indicating that it has prevented scripts and ActiveX controls from running. If so, click Allow Blocked Content.

This message appears only when the file is previewed from your hard drive. It doesn't appear when the file is actually hosted on the Internet.

4 Position the cursor over the *Tour Eiffel* heading. Observe the image to the right of the text.

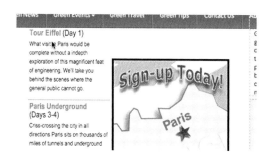
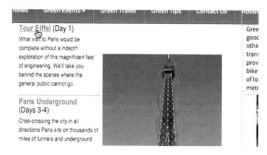

The existing image swaps for one of the Eiffel Tower.

5 Move the pointer to the *Paris Underground* heading.
Observe the image to the right of the text.

As the pointer moves off the *Tour Eiffel* heading, the image reverts to the Eco-Tour ad. Then, as the pointer moves over the heading *Paris Underground*, the ad image swaps for one of underground Paris.

6 Pass the pointer over each <h3> heading, and observe the image behavior.

The image alternates between the Eco-Tour ad and images of each of the tours. This effect is the Swap Image behavior.

7 When you're finished, close the browser window and return to Dreamweaver.

8 Close **travel-finished.html**.

In the next exercise, you'll learn how to work with Dreamweaver behaviors.

Working with Dreamweaver behaviors

Adding Dreamweaver behaviors to your layout is a simple point-and-click operation. But before you can add the behaviors, you have to create the travel page.

1 Create a new page from **mygreen_temp**.

2 Save the file as **travel.html** in the site root folder.
Switch to Design view, if necessary.

3 Open **sidebars12.html** in Design view from the lesson12/resources folder.
Insert the cursor into the first paragraph. Examine the tag selectors.

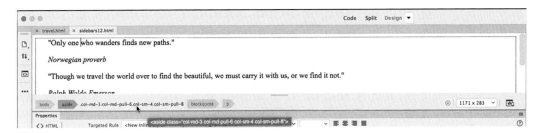

The paragraph is a child of a `<blockquote>` within an `aside` element. The classes and structure in the new file are identical to Sidebar 1 in the site template.

4 Select the `aside` tag selector.

5 Copy the `aside` element from **sidebars12.html**.

6 Switch to **travel.html**. Insert the cursor into the first quotation.
Select the `aside` tag selector.

7 Paste the content from step 5.

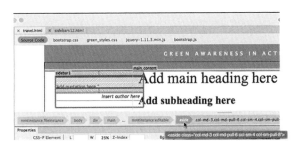
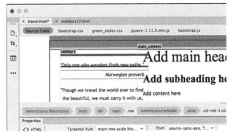

The new content replaces the placeholder.

8 Close **sidebars12.html**.

9 Open **travel-text.html** in Design view from the lesson12/resources folder.

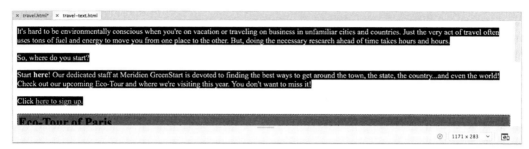

Note: It's vital that you use the same document view when copying and pasting content from one document to another in Dreamweaver.

The **travel-text.html** file contains content in some paragraphs and a table for the travel page. Note that the text and table are unformatted.

10 Press Ctrl+A/Cmd+A to select all the text.
Press Ctrl+C/Cmd+C to copy the contents.
Close **travel-text.html**.

11 In **travel.html**, select the text *Add main heading here*.
Type **Green Travel** to replace the text.

12 Select the heading placeholder *Add subheading here*.
Type **Eco-Touring** to replace it.

13 Select the p tag selector for the text *Add content here*.
Press Ctrl+V/Cmd+V to paste.

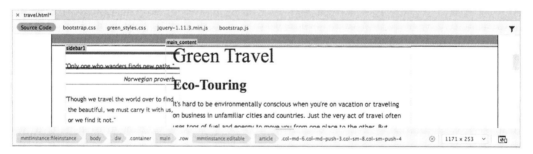

The content from **travel-text.html** appears, replacing the placeholder text. It assumes the default formatting for text and tables applied by the style sheet you created in Lesson 9, "Working with Text, Lists, and Tables."

Next, let's insert the Eco-Tour ad, which will be the base image for the Swap Image behavior.

14 In the table, double-click the *SideAd* placeholder.
Select **ecotour.png** from the images folder.
Click OK/Open.

The placeholder is replaced by the Eco-Tour ad. But before you can apply the Swap Image behavior, you have to identify the image you want to swap. You do this by giving the image an id.

15 Select **ecotour.png** in the layout.
In the Property inspector, select the existing id `SideAd`.
Type `ecotour` and press Enter/Return.
Enter `Eco-Tour of Paris` in the Alt field.

▶ **Tip:** Although it takes more time, giving all your images unique ids is a good practice.

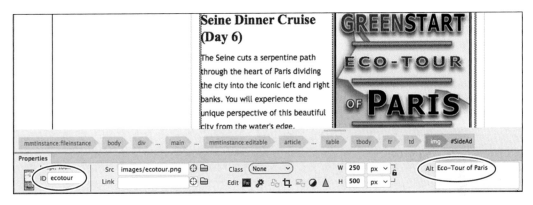

16 Save the file.

Next, you'll create a Swap Image behavior for **the new image**.

Applying a behavior

As described earlier, many behaviors are context sensitive, based on the elements or structure present. A Swap Image behavior can be triggered by any document element, but it affects only images displayed within the page.

1 Choose Window > Behaviors to open the Behaviors panel.

2 Insert the cursor in the *Tour Eiffel* text and select the <h3> tag selector.

● **Note:** You will be able to access only the Behaviors panel when you are in Design or Code view.

● **Note:** Feel free to dock the Behaviors panel with the other panels in the interface.

3 Click the Add Behavior icon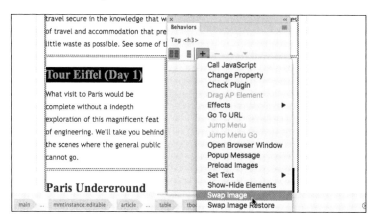
Choose Swap Image from the behavior menu.

The Swap Image dialog lists any images on the page that are available for this behavior. This behavior can replace one or more of these images at a time.

4 Select the `image "ecotour"` item and click Browse.

5 In the Select Image Source dialog, select **tower.jpg** from the site images folder. Click OK/Open.

Note: The Preload Images option forces the browser to download all images necessary for the behavior when the page loads. That way, when the user clicks the trigger, the image swap occurs without any lags or glitches.

6 In the Swap Image dialog, select the Preload Images option, if necessary, and click OK.

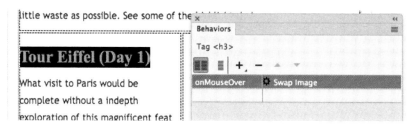

A Swap Image behavior is added to the Behaviors panel with an attribute of onMouseOver. Attributes can be changed, if desired, using the Behaviors panel.

7   Click the onMouseOver attribute to open the pop-up menu and examine the other available options.

The menu provides a list of trigger events, most of which are self-explanatory. For now, however, leave the attribute as onMouseOver.

8   Save the file. Switch to Live view to test the behavior.
Position the cursor over the *Tour Eiffel* text.

When the cursor passes over the text, the Eco-Tour ad is replaced by the image of the Eiffel Tower. But there is a small problem. When the cursor moves away from the text, the original image doesn't return. The reason is simple: You didn't tell it to return. To bring back the original image, you have to add another command—Swap Image Restore—to the same element.

Applying a Swap Image Restore behavior

In some instances, a specific action requires more than one behavior. To bring back the Eco-Tour ad once the mouse moves off the trigger, you have to add a restore function.

1   Switch to Design view. Insert the cursor in the *Tour Eiffel* heading and examine the Behaviors panel.

The inspector displays the currently assigned behavior. You don't need to select the element completely; Dreamweaver assumes you want to modify the entire trigger.

2 Click the Add Behavior icon.

Choose Swap Image Restore from the drop-down menu.

Click OK in the Swap Image Restore dialog to complete the command.

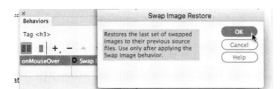

The Swap Image Restore behavior appears in the Behaviors panel with an attribute of onMouseOut.

3 Switch to Code view and examine the markup for the *Tour Eiffel* text.

```
100 ▼    <tr>
101         <td scope="col"><h3 onMouseOver="MM_swapImage('ecotour','','images/tower.jpg',1)"
          onMouseOut="MM_swapImgRestore()">Tour Eiffel (Day 1)</h3>
102           <p>What visit to Paris would be complete without a indepth exploration of this
```

The trigger events—onMouseOver and onMouseOut—were added as attributes to the <h3> element. The rest of the JavaScript code was inserted in the document's <head> section.

4 Save the file and switch to Live view to test the behavior. Test the text trigger *Tour Eiffel*.

When the pointer passes over the text, the Eco-Tour image is replaced by the one of the Eiffel Tower and then reappears when the pointer is withdrawn. The behavior functions as desired, but nothing is visibly "different" about the text. In other words, there is nothing here to prompt a user to roll their pointer over the heading. The result will be that many users will miss the swap image effect altogether.

Users sometimes need to be encouraged or directed to these types of effects. Many designers use hyperlinks for this purpose since users are already familiar with how they function. Let's replace the current effect with one based on a hyperlink.

Removing applied behaviors

Before you can apply a behavior to a hyperlink, you need to remove the current Swap Image and Swap Image Restore behaviors.

1 Switch to Design view. Open the Behaviors panel, if necessary.

Insert the cursor in the *Tour Eiffel* text.

The Behaviors panel displays the two applied events. Which one you delete first doesn't matter.

2 Select the Swap Image event in the Behaviors panel.
Click the Remove Event icon 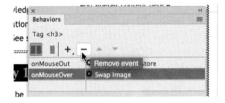.

The Swap Image event is removed.

3 Select the Swap Image Restore event.
In the Behaviors panel, click the Remove Event icon.

Both events are now removed. Dreamweaver also removes any unneeded JavaScript code.

4 Save the file and check the text in Live view again.

The text no longer triggers the Swap Image behavior. To reapply the behavior, you need to add a link or link placeholder to the heading.

Adding behaviors to hyperlinks

Behaviors can be added to hyperlinks even if the link doesn't load a new document. For this exercise, you'll add a link placeholder (#) to the heading to support the desired behavior.

1 Select only the text *Tour Eiffel* in the <h3> element.
Type # in the Property inspector Link field.
Press Enter/Return to create the link placeholder.

The text displays with the default hyperlink styling. The tag selector for the a tag appears.

2 Insert the cursor in the *Tour Eiffel* link.
Click the Add Behavior icon ➕.
Choose Swap Image from the pop-up menu.

As long as the cursor is still inserted anywhere in the link, the behavior will be applied to the entire link markup.

3 In the Swap Image dialog, select the item `image "ecotour"`.
Browse and select **tower.jpg** from the images folder.
Click OK/Open.

4 In the Swap Image dialog, select the **Preload Images** option and the **Restore Images onMouseOut** option, if necessary, and click OK.

The Swap Image event appears in the Behaviors panel along with a Swap Image Restore event. Since the behavior was applied all at once, Dreamweaver provides the restore functionality as a productivity enhancement.

5 Apply a link placeholder (#) to the text *Paris Underground*.
Apply the Swap Image behavior to the link.
Use **underground.jpg** from the images folder.

6 Repeat step 5 for the *Seine Dinner Cruise* text.
Select the image **cruise.jpg**.

7 Repeat step 5 for the *Champs Élysées* text.
Select the image **champs.jpg**.

The Swap Image behaviors are now complete, but the text and link appearances don't match the site's color scheme. Let's create custom CSS rules to format them accordingly. You will create two rules: one for the heading element and another for the link itself.

8 In the CSS Designer, select **green_styles.css** > GLOBAL. Create the new selector:
`article table h3`

9 Create the following properties in the new rule:
```
margin-top: 0px
margin-bottom: 5px
font-size: 130%
font-family: "Arial Narrow", Verdana, "Trebuchet MS",
sans-serif
```

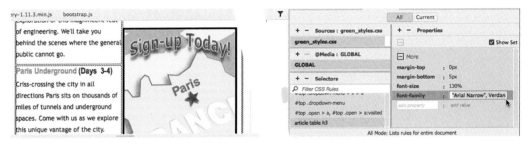

10 Select **green_styles.css** > GLOBAL. Create a new selector:

```
table h3 a:link, table h3 a:visited
```

11 Create the following properties in the new rule:

```
color: #090
font-weight: bold
```

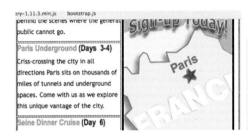 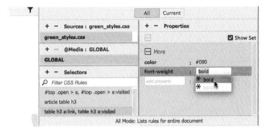

The headings are now more prominent and styled to match the site theme.

12 Save all files. Test the behaviors in Live view.

Note how the links are underlined when the mouse moves over them. The Swap Image behavior should work successfully on all links. If one or more of the links do not function, check to make sure the behavior was assigned to the link successfully.

Making it responsive

Once you're satisfied that all the rollover effects are functioning properly, you should check to make sure that the new components adapt properly to the responsive page design too. You can check the functionality in Dreamweaver or in any modern browser installed on your computer.

1 If necessary, open **travel.html**.
Switch to Live view.

2 Drag the Scrubber to the left to test how the new table responds to the existing set of media queries.

The table adapts to the changing screen in a fashion similar to the tables created and styled in Lesson 9. Everything seems to display fine, although the Eco-Tour ad does not scale or resize in any way.

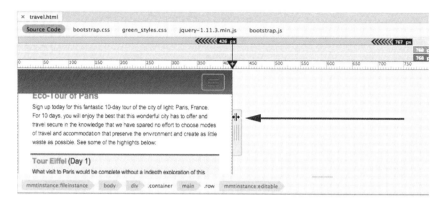

At a width of 426 pixels, the two columns merge, and the cells begin to stack one atop the other, including the cell containing the ad. The image does not appear beside the text describing the tours. At this point, the purpose of the rollover effect will be lost completely, as does the need for the ad itself. The simplest plan would be just to hide the ad on smaller screens and allow the text to speak for itself.

At this moment, there's a custom id applied to the ad image but nothing applied to the cell containing it. CSS can hide the image, but it will leave the blank cell behind. Instead, let's create a custom class to hide the entire cell and its contents.

3 Drag the Scrubber all the way to the right to restore the table layout to two columns.

4 Select the Eco-Tour image.

5 Select the td tag selector.

The HUD appears focused on the td element.

6 Click the Add Class/ID icon ⊞.

7 Enter .hide_ad in the HUD text field.
If the CSS Source HUD appears, press the Esc key to close it.

8 If necessary, open the CSS Designer.

Select **green_styles.css** > (max-width: 426px).

Create a new selector: `table .hide_ad`

This rule limits the styling to elements within a table when the screen drops down to the smallest media query.

9 Create the following property:

`display: none.`

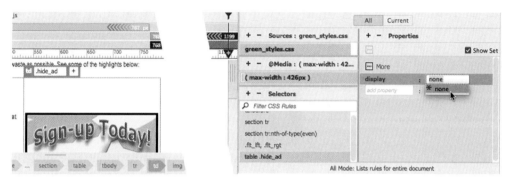

The table cell and ad will hide whenever the screen is 426 pixels or narrower.

10 Drag the Scrubber to 426 pixels or narrower.

Observe the changes to the table and its content.

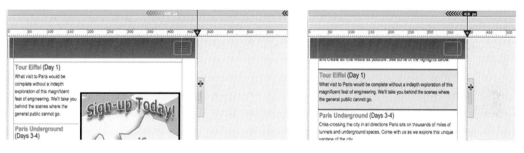

The Eco-Tour ad hides once the screen is narrower than 426 pixels. It reappears as soon as the screen gets wider than 426 pixels.

11 Save all files.

12 Close **travel.html**.

In addition to eye-catching effects, such as the dynamic behaviors you've just been learning about, Dreamweaver also provides structural components—such as jQuery and Bootstrap widgets—that conserve space and add more interactive flair to your website.

Working with Bootstrap Accordion widgets

The Bootstrap Accordion widget allows you to organize a lot of content into a compact space. In the Accordion widget, the tabs are stacked, and when opened, they expand vertically rather than side by side. Let's preview the completed layout.

1 In the Files panel, select **tips_finished.html** from the finished folder in lesson12 and preview it directly in your primary browser.

The page content is divided among three panels using the Bootstrap Accordion widget.

2 Click each panel in turn to open and close each.

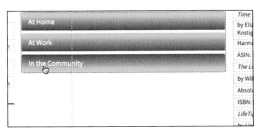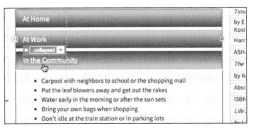

When you click a tab, the panel slides open with a smooth action. The panels are set to a specific height; if the content is taller than the default panel size, the panel adjusts its height automatically. When the panels open and close, the bulleted lists of green tips are revealed. The accordion panel allows you to display more content in a smaller, more efficient footprint.

3 Close your browser and return to Dreamweaver.
Close **tips_finished.html**.

In the next exercise, you'll learn how to create and format a Bootstrap Accordion widget.

Inserting a Bootstrap Accordion widget

In this exercise, you'll incorporate a Bootstrap Accordion widget into one of your existing layouts.

1 Open **tips.html** in Live view.

The page consists of three bulleted lists separated by <h2> headings. These lists take up a lot of vertical space on the page, requiring the user to scroll down two or more screens to read them. Keeping content on one screen as much as possible will make it easier to access and read.

One technique to maximize screen real estate is using tabbed or accordion panels. Dreamweaver 2017 offers these types of components in both jQuery and Bootstrap frameworks. Since you're using a Bootstrap layout here, let's use a Bootstrap Accordion widget.

2 Insert the cursor in the *At Home* heading and select the <h2> tag selector.

3 Open the Insert panel.
Select the Bootstrap category.
Click the Accordion item.

The position assist HUD appears.

4 Click Before.

Dreamweaver inserts the Bootstrap Accordion widget element above the heading but inside the <section> element. The default element is a three-panel Accordion widget that appears with the top panel (*Collapsible Group 1*) open. The HUD appears above the new object, focused on a div element with a class of .panel-group and an id of #accordion1.

The next step is to move the existing lists into the panel. Since two of the panels are hidden by default, the easiest way to work with the content will be in Code view.

5 Switch to Code view.

6 Scroll down and insert the cursor in the first bullet: <li>Wash clothes in cold water.</li> (around line 96).

7 Select the ul tag selector.
Press Ctrl+X/Cmd+X to cut the whole list.

8 Delete the code ~~<h2>At Home</h2>~~.

```
92          </div>
93        </div>
94 ▼  <h2>At Home</h2>
95
96        </section>
97 ▼   <section>
98        <h2>At Work</h2>
```

```
92          </div>
93        </div>
94
95        </section>
96 ▼   <section>
97        <h2>At Work</h2>
98 ▼    <ul>
```

9 Scroll up and select the heading *Collapsible Group 1* (around line 71).
Edit the heading to say: `At Home`

```
71 ▼      <h4 class="panel-title"><a data-toggle="collapse"
          data-parent="#accordion1"
          href="#collapseOne1">Collapsible Group 1</a></h4>
72      </div>                                    I
73 ▼    <div id="collapseOne1" class="panel-collapse collapse in">
74        <div class="panel-body">Content for Accordion Panel 1</div>
```

```
71 ▼      <h4 class="panel-title"><a data-toggle="collapse"
          data-parent="#accordion1"
          href="#collapseOne1">At Home</a></h4>
72      </div>
73 ▼    <div id="collapseOne1" class="panel-collapse collapse in">
74        <div class="panel-body">Content for Accordion Panel 1</div>
```

The new heading structure is based on an `<h4>` element.

10 Select and delete the text placeholder *Content for Accordion Panel 1* (approximately line 74).

The text appears in the `<div>` without any other structure. Make sure you do not delete the `<div>`.

11 Press Ctrl+V/Cmd+V to paste the list.

```
73 ▼    <div id="collapseOne1" class="panel-collapse collapse in">
74 ▼      <div class="panel-body">Content for Accordion Panel 1</div>
75      </div>
76    </div>
77 ▼  <div class="panel panel-default">
78 ▼    <div class="panel-heading">
```

```
73 ▼    <div id="collapseOne1" class="panel-collapse collapse in">
74 ▼      <div class="panel-body"><ul>
75      <li>Wash clothes in cold water</li>
76      <li>Hang clothes to dry</li>
77      <li>Turn off lights in empty rooms</li>
78      <li>Use motion sensors to turn lights on</li>
```

The list markup appears in `<div class="panel-body">`. The first Accordion panel group is complete. You have to repeat this process for the other two lists.

12 Scroll down to the *At Work* tip list (around line 120).

13 Select the `ul` tag selector as in step 7.
Cut the list.

14 Click the `<section>` tag selector. Press Delete.

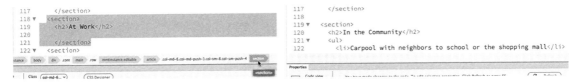

The `<section>` and the heading *At Work* are deleted.

15 Select the heading *Collapsible Group 2* and type **At Work** to replace it (approximately line 101).

16 Delete the placeholder text *Content for Accordion Panel 2* and paste the list you cut in step 13 (around line 104).

```
100 ▼       <div class="panel-heading">
101           <h4 class="panel-title"><a data-toggle="collapse" data-parent="#accordion1"
              href="#collapseTwo1">At Work</a></h4>
102         </div>
103 ▼       <div id="collapseTwo1" class="panel-collapse collapse">
104 ▼         <div class="panel-body"><ul>
105       <li>Use recycled paper.</li>
106       <li>Print on both sides of the paper</li>
107       <li>Turn your computer screen off when you leave your desk</li>
108       <li>Use single-serving coffee makers</li>
```

17 Repeat steps 12–16 to create the content section for *In the Community*.

When you're finished, all three lists are now contained within Accordion 1, and all the empty `<section>` elements have been deleted.

18 Switch to Live view.

You inserted a Bootstrap Accordion widget and added content to it.

19 Test the panels by clicking each heading.

When clicked, the panel should open, revealing the list contained within. When you click a different heading, the new panel opens, closing the old one.

20 Save all files.

In the next exercise, you'll learn how to apply the site color scheme to the Accordion widget.

Styling a Bootstrap Accordion

As with the basic layout and the other Bootstrap components created by Dreamweaver, the accordion is formatted by the Bootstrap CSS and JavaScript files. You should avoid editing these files directly unless you know what you are doing. Instead, you'll apply the site design theme to Accordion 1 using your own custom style sheet as before. Let's start with the tabs.

1 Click the *At Home* tab. Examine the tag selectors.

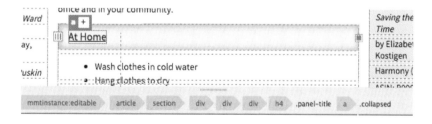

Tip: As you work in Code view, you may need to click the Refresh button from time to time in the Property inspector to see the tag selectors.

The tab is composed of three main elements: `<div.panel-heading>`, `<h4.panel-title>`, and `<a>`. But that's only on the surface. Behind the scenes, the Bootstrap JavaScript and CSS functions are manipulating the HTML and CSS to produce the various behaviors controlling the accordion. As you move your mouse over the tabs and click them, class attributes are being changed on the fly to produce the hover effects and animated panels.

As you learned earlier, hyperlinks exhibit four basic behaviors: link, visited, hover, and active. The Bootstrap framework is taking advantage of these default states to apply the various effects you see when interacting with Accordion 1 for the *At Home* list.

Your job will be to create several new rules that will override the default styling and apply the GreenStart theme instead. The first step is to format the default state of the tabs. Since only one tab can be open at a time, the closed state is considered the default state.

2 Click the *At Home* tab heading to close the tab content.

The tabs are currently styled a light gray. You need to identify any rules that format the background color of the Accordion tab. Be aware that there may be more than one rule affecting these properties and, as you learned in Lesson 11, "Working with Navigation," some of the styling is being applied dynamically. So you have to distinguish rules that apply by default and ones that work only by user interaction.

One trick that can help you identify rules that are styling a specific element is to notice how the selected element is displayed in the document window. For example, when you clicked the heading initially, only the `<a>` element was selected, as shown here.

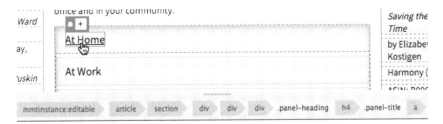

You can see how the HUD outlines the heading text but nothing else. If the element doesn't extend to the height and width of the tab, its CSS can't be responsible for the styling of the tab. Tracking down the right element is a simple matter of elimination.

3 Click the h4 tag selector for the closed tab.

When you click the h4 tag selector, the HUD outlines the <h4> element but does not extend to the full size of the tab.

● **Note:** When you click various elements, the classes displayed may differ than the ones pictured.

The outline is a literal indication of how far the styling of the heading extends. That means you can ignore rules styling the a and h4 elements if you want to set the background of the entire tab.

4 Click the next element in the tag selector interface.

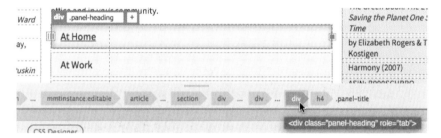

The element <div.panel-heading> is selected. Note how the HUD outlines the entire tab.

5 Click the Current button in the CSS Designer.
Examine the rules and properties applied to this element.

The very first rule displayed in the Selectors window, .panel-default > .panel-heading, applies a background color. To apply the site color theme, you need to override this rule.

6 Click the All button. Choose **green_styles.css** > GLOBAL. Create a new selector:
section .panel-default > .panel-heading

Since some elements already feature the site theme, it's a simple matter to grab this styling using the CSS Designer. Let's format the tabs the same way the footer is styled.

7 Select the footer rule in **green_styles.css** in the Selectors window.

8 Right-click the `footer` rule. Select Copy Styles > Copy Background Styles from the context menu.

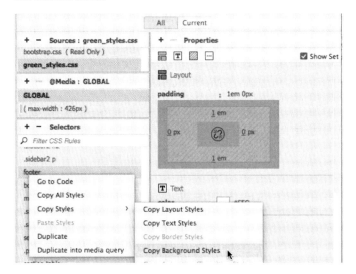

9 Right-click the rule `section .panel-default > .panel-heading` and select Paste Styles from the context menu.

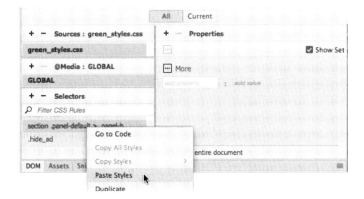

The background color and gradient properties are added to the new rule.

10 Add the following property:

`color: #FFC`

This styling will apply to the default state of the Accordion tabs. You'll add some interactive styling later, but first let's flesh out the styling of the accordion.

11 In **green_styles.css** > GLOBAL, create a new selector:

`section #accordion1`

12 Create the following properties:

```
border: solid 1px #060
border-radius: 5px
```

This new rule defines a border around the entire accordion.

13 Create a new selector: `section .panel-body`

Create the following property: `background-color: #CFC`

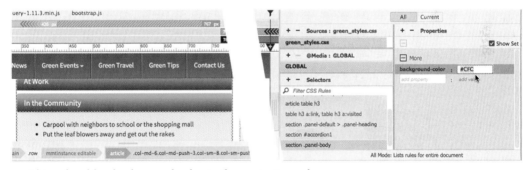

This rule adds a background color to the content panels.

Finally, let's give the accordion a little flair by adding a rollover behavior to the tabs. Although it's mainly used for links, the `:hover` pseudo-class can be used any time you want to create interactive effects.

14 Right-click the rule
   `section .panel-default > .panel-heading`.
   Select Duplicate from the context menu.

A duplicate of the rule appears in the Selectors window, complete with the same styling.

15 Edit the new selector as highlighted:
   `article .panel-default > .panel-heading:hover`

The new rule will format the tabs whenever you position the cursor over the tab. But at the moment, the styling is identical to the original.

16 Edit the background gradient property.
   Change the degree to 0

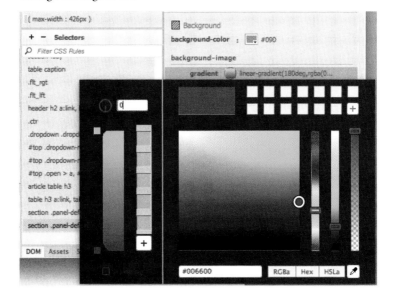

17 Change the `color` property to `#FFF`

18 Save all files.

19 Position the cursor over each tab to test the new behavior.

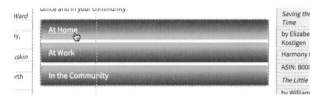

The gradient background inverts as the cursor moves over and away from each tab. There is only one distraction in the overall effect. The default hyperlink styling adds an underline to the heading when the cursor passes over it.

Although this may be an acceptable behavior in a normal text-based link, it's rather distracting in the Accordion tab. To turn this effect off, you first have to find the rule that's responsible for creating it.

20 Select the Current button in the CSS Designer.

21 Click the heading *At Home* in the first tab. Examine the rules listed in the Selectors window. Try to identify any rules adding the underline effect.

The third rule, `a:hover, a:focus`, applies the underline effect. You don't want to turn this styling off for all hyperlinks, just for links in the Accordion tabs.

22 Click the All button in CSS Designer. In **green_styles.css** > GLOBAL, create a new selector.

The name `.panel-heading .panel-title a` appears in the window.

23 Press the up arrow key once to make the selector less specific.

24 Add the highlighted markup to the name:

```
.panel-title a:hover,
.panel-title a:focus
```

This rule will style the hover state of the tab heading.

25 Create the following property:

```
text-decoration: none
```

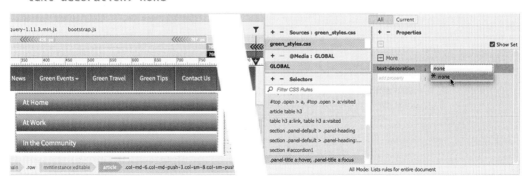

26 Test the rollover effect.

The underline no longer appears in the Accordion tabs.

27 Save all files.

The accordion is just one of more than 100 Bootstrap and jQuery widgets and components offered by Dreamweaver. They allow you to incorporate advanced functionality into your website, while requiring little or no programming skill. All of these components can be accessed via either the Insert menu or the Insert panel.

Adding interactivity to your webpages opens new possibilities of interest and excitement for your visitors, engaging them in new ways. It can easily be overdone, but a wise use of interactivity can help bring in new visitors and keep your frequent visitors coming back for more.

Review questions

1 What is a benefit of using Dreamweaver behaviors?

2 What three steps must be used to create a Dreamweaver behavior?

3 What's the purpose of assigning an id to an image before applying a behavior?

4 What does the Bootstrap Accordion widget do?

5 What Dreamweaver tools are helpful in troubleshooting CSS styling on dynamic elements?

Review answers

1 Dreamweaver behaviors add interactive functionality to a webpage quickly and easily.

2 To create a Dreamweaver behavior, you need to create or select a trigger element, select a desired behavior, and specify the parameters.

3 The id is essential for selecting the specific image during the process of applying a behavior.

4 A Bootstrap Accordion widget includes multiple collapsible panels that hide and reveal content in a compact area of the page.

5 The Current mode of the CSS Designer helps identify any existing CSS styling and create new specifications.

13 PUBLISHING TO THE WEB

Lesson overview

In this lesson, you'll publish your website to the Internet and do the following:

- Define a remote site
- Define a testing server
- Put files on the web
- Cloak files and folders
- Update out-of-date links sitewide

This lesson will take about 1 hour to complete. If you have not already done so, download the project files for this lesson from the Lesson & Update Files tab on your Account page at www.peachpit.com, store them on your computer in a convenient location, and define a new site based on the lesson13 folder, as described in the "Getting Started" section at the beginning of this book. Your Account page is also where you'll find any updates to the lessons or to the lesson files. Look on the Lesson & Update Files tab to access the most current content.

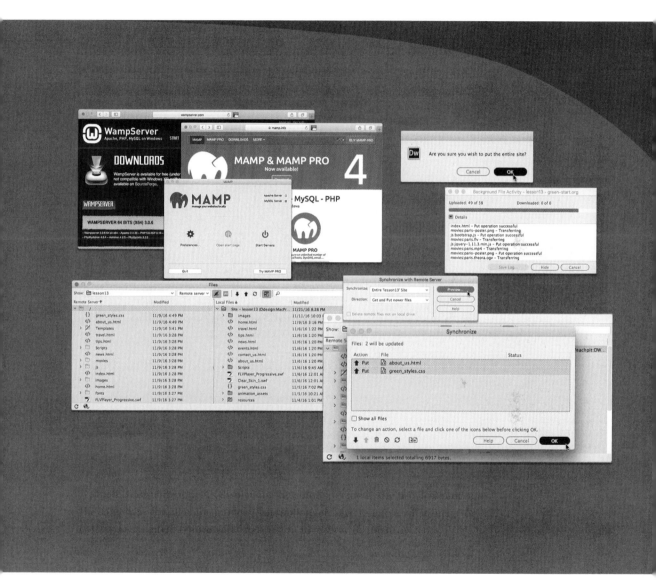

The goal of all the preceding lessons is to design, develop, and build pages for a remote website. But Dreamweaver doesn't abandon you there. It also provides powerful tools to upload and maintain any size website over time.

Defining a remote site

● **Note:** If you have not already down-loaded the project files for this lesson to your computer from your Account page and defined a site based on this folder, make sure to do so now. See "Getting Started" at the beginning of the book.

Dreamweaver's workflow is based on a two-site system. One site is in a folder on your computer's hard drive and is known as the *local site*. All work in the previous lessons has been performed on your local site. The second site, known as the *remote site*, is established in a folder on a web server, typically running on another computer, and is connected to the Internet and publicly available. In large companies, the remote site is often available only to employees via a network-based intranet. Such sites provide information and applications to support corporate programs and products.

Dreamweaver supports several methods for connecting to a remote site.

- **FTP** (File Transfer Protocol)—The standard method for connecting to hosted websites.

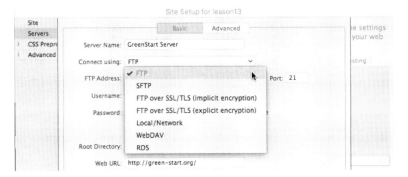

- **SFTP** (Secure File Transfer Protocol)—A protocol that provides a method to connect to hosted websites in a more secure manner to preclude unauthorized access or interception of online content.

- **FTP over SSL/TLS** (implicit encryption)—A secure FTP (FTPS) method that requires all clients of the FTPS server be aware that SSL is to be used on the session. It is incompatible with non-FTPS-aware clients.

- **FTP over SSL/TLS** (explicit encryption)—A legacy-compatible, secure FTP method where FTPS-aware clients can invoke security with an FTPS-aware server without breaking overall FTP functionality with non-FTPS-aware clients.

- **Local/network**—A local or network connection is most frequently used with an intermediate web server, known as a *staging server*. Staging servers are typically used to test sites before they go live. Files from the staging server are eventually published to an Internet-connected web server.

- **WebDav** (Web Distributed Authoring and Versioning)—A web-based system also known to Windows users as Web Folders and to Mac users as iDisk.

- **RDS** (Remote Development Services)—Developed by Adobe for ColdFusion and primarily used when working with ColdFusion-based sites.

Dreamweaver now can upload larger files faster and more efficiently and as a background activity, allowing you to return to work more quickly. In the following exercises, you'll set up a remote site using the two most common methods: FTP and Local/Network.

Setting up a remote FTP site

The vast majority of web developers rely on FTP to publish and maintain their sites. FTP is a well-established protocol, and many variations of the protocol are used on the web—most of which are supported by Dreamweaver.

1 Launch Adobe Dreamweaver CC (2017 release) or later.

2 Choose Site > Manage Sites or choose Manage Sites from the site list drop-down menu in the Files panel.

◆ **Warning:** To complete the following exercise, you must have a remote server already established. Remote servers can be hosted by your own company or contracted from a third-party web-hosting service.

In the Manage Sites dialog is a list of all the sites you may have defined.

3 Make sure that the current site, lesson13, is selected.

Click the Edit icon ✏.

4 In the Site Setup dialog for lesson13, click the Servers category.

The Site Setup dialog allows you to set up multiple servers so you can test several types of installations, if desired.

5 Click the Add New Server icon ➕.
Enter **GreenStart Server** in the Server Name field.

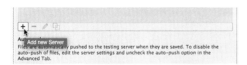

6 From the Connect Using pop-up menu, choose FTP.

▶ **Tip:** If you are in the process of moving an existing site to a new Internet service provider (ISP), you may not be able to use the domain name to upload files to the new server. In that case, the IP address can be used to upload files initially.

7 In the FTP Address field, type the URL or IP (Internet protocol) address of your FTP server.

If you contract a third-party service as a web host, you will be assigned an FTP address. This address may come in the form of an IP address, such as 192.168.1.100. Enter this number into the field exactly as it was sent to you. Frequently, the FTP address will be the domain name of your site, such as **ftp.green-start.org**. But don't enter the characters *ftp* into the field.

8 In the Username field, enter your FTP username.
In the Password field, enter your FTP password.

Usernames may be case sensitive, but password fields almost always are; be sure you enter them correctly. Often, the easiest way to enter them is to copy them from the confirmation email from your hosting company and paste them into the appropriate fields.

▶ **Tip:** Check with your web-hosting service or IS/IT manager to obtain the root directory name, if any.

9 In the Root Directory field, type the name of the folder that contains documents publicly accessible to the web, if any.

Some web hosts provide FTP access to a root-level folder that might contain nonpublic folders—such as cgi-bin, which is used to store common gateway interface (CGI) or binary scripts—as well as a public folder. In these cases, type the public folder name—such as public, public_html, www, or wwwroot—in the Root Directory field. In many web-host configurations, the FTP address is the same as the public folder, and the Root Directory field should be left blank.

10 Select the Save checkbox if you don't want to reenter your username and password every time Dreamweaver connects to your site.

11 Click Test to verify that your FTP connection works properly.

Dreamweaver displays an alert to notify you that the connection was successful or unsuccessful.

12 Click OK to dismiss the alert.

If Dreamweaver connects properly to the webhost, skip to step 14. If you received an error message, your web server may require additional configuration options.

13 Click the More Options triangle to reveal additional server options.

Tip: If Dreamweaver does not connect to your host, first check the username and password, as well as the FTP address and root directory for any errors.

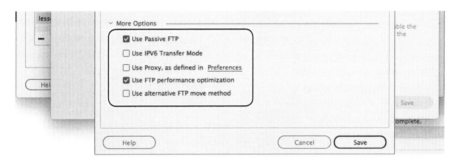

Consult the instructions from your hosting company to select the appropriate options for your specific FTP server:

- **Use Passive FTP**—Allows your computer to connect to the host computer and bypass a firewall restraint. Many web hosts require this setting.

- **Use IPV6 Transfer Mode**—Enables connection to IPV6-based servers, which use the most recent version of the Internet transfer protocol.

- **Use Proxy**—Identifies a secondary proxy host connection as defined in your Dreamweaver preferences.

- **Use FTP Performance Optimization**—Optimizes the FTP connection. Deselect this option if Dreamweaver can't connect to your server.

- **Use Alternative FTP Move Method**—Provides an additional method to resolve FTP conflicts, especially when rollbacks are enabled or when moving files.

Once you establish a working connection, you may need to configure some advanced options.

Troubleshooting your FTP connection

Connecting to your remote site can be frustrating the first time you attempt it. You can experience numerous pitfalls, many of which are out of your control. Here are a few steps to take if you have issues connecting:

• If you can't connect to your FTP server, double-check your username and password and reenter them carefully. Remember that usernames may be case sensitive on some servers, while passwords frequently are. (This is the most common error.)

• Select Use Passive FTP and test the connection again.

• If you still can't connect to your FTP server, deselect the Use FTP Performance Optimization option and click Test again.

• If none of these steps enables you to connect to your remote site, check with your IS/IT manager or your remote site administrator or web-hosting service.

14 Click the Advanced tab. Select among the following options for working with your remote site:

• **Maintain Synchronization Information**—Automatically notes the files that have been changed on the local and remote sites so that they can be easily synchronized. This feature helps you keep track of your changes and can be helpful if you change multiple pages before you upload. You may want to use cloaking with this feature. You'll learn about cloaking in an upcoming exercise. This feature is usually selected by default.

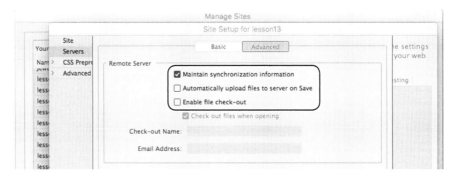

• **Automatically Upload Files To Server On Save**—Transfers files from the local to the remote site when they are saved. This option can become annoying if you save often and aren't yet ready for a page to go public.

• **Enable File Check-Out**—Starts the check-in/check-out system for collaborative website building in a workgroup environment. If you choose this option, you'll need to enter a check-out name and, optionally, an email address. If you're working by yourself, you do not need to select this option.

It is acceptable to leave any or all these options unselected, but for the purposes of this lesson, select the Maintain Synchronization Information option, if necessary.

15 Click Save to finalize the settings in the open dialogs.

The server setup dialog closes, revealing the Servers category in the Site Setup dialog. Your newly defined server is displayed in the window.

16 Click the Remote radio button to the right of the server name if necessary.

17 Click Save to finish setting up your new server.

A dialog appears, informing you that the cache will be re-created because you changed the site settings.

18 Click OK to build the cache. When Dreamweaver finishes updating the cache, click Done to close the Manage Sites dialog.

You have established a connection to your remote server. If you don't currently have a remote server, you can substitute a local testing server instead as your remote server.

Establishing a remote site on a local or network web server (optional)

If your company or organization uses a staging server as a "middleman" between web designers and the live website, it's likely you'll need to connect to your remote site through a local or network web server. Local/network servers are often used as testing servers to check dynamic functions before pages are uploaded to the Internet.

◆ **Warning:** To complete the following exercise, you must have already installed and configured a local or network web server as described in the sidebar "Installing a testing server."

1 Launch Adobe Dreamweaver CC (2017 release) or later.

2 Choose Site > Manage Sites.

3 In the Manage Sites dialog, make sure that lesson13 is selected. Click the Edit icon ✐.

4 In the Site Setup for lesson13 dialog, select the Servers category.

5 If you have already installed a local testing server, click the Add New Server icon. In the Server Name field, enter **GreenStart Local**.

Installing a testing server

When you produce sites with dynamic content, you need to test the functionality before the pages go live on the Internet. A testing server can fit that need nicely. Depending on the applications you need to test, the testing server can simply be a subfolder on your actual web server, or you can use a local web server such as Apache or Internet Information Services (IIS) from Microsoft.

For detailed information about installing and configuring a local web server, check out the following links:

- Apache/ColdFusion—http://tinyurl.com/setup-coldfusion
- Apache/PHP—http://tinyurl.com/setup-apachephp
- IIS/ASP—http://tinyurl.com/setup-asp

Once you set up the local web server, you can use it to upload the completed files and test your remote site. In most cases, your local web server will not be accessible from the Internet or be able to host the actual website for the public.

6 From the Connect Using pop-up menu, choose Local/Network.

7 In the Server Folder field, click the Browse icon [icon].

Select the local web server's HTML folder, such as C:\wamp\www\lesson13.

8 In the Web URL field, enter the appropriate URL for your local web server. If you are using WAMP or MAMP local servers, your web URL will be something like http://localhost:8888/lesson13 or http://localhost/lesson13.

You must enter the correct URL or Dreamweaver's FTP and testing features may not function properly.

● **Note:** The paths you enter here are contingent on how you installed your local web server and may not be the same as the ones displayed.

9 Click the Advanced tab, and as with the actual web server, select the appropriate options for working with your remote site: Maintain Synchronization Information, Automatically Upload Files To Server On Save, and/or Enable File Check-Out.

Although leaving these three options unselected is acceptable, for the purposes of this lesson, select the Maintain Synchronization Information option if necessary.

10 If you'd like to use the local web server as the testing server too, select the server model in the Advanced section of the dialog. If you are creating a dynamic site using a specific programming language, like ASP, ColdFusion, or PHP, select the matching Server Model from the drop-down menu so you'll be able to test the pages of your site properly.

11 Click Save to complete the remote server setup.

12 In the Site Setup dialog for lesson13, select Remote. If you want to use the local server as a testing server too, select Testing. Click Save.

13 In the Manage Sites dialog, click Done. If necessary, click OK to rebuild the cache.

Only one remote and one testing server can be active at one time, but you may have multiple servers defined. One server can be used for both roles, if desired. Before you upload files for the remote site, you may need to cloak certain folders and files in the local site.

Cloaking folders and files

Not all the files in your site root folder may need to be transferred to the remote server. For example, there's no point in filling the remote site with files that won't be accessed or that will remain inaccessible to website users. Minimizing files stored on the remote server may also pay financial dividends since many hosting services base part of their fee on how much disk space your site occupies. If you selected Maintain Synchronization Information for a remote site using FTP or a network server, you may want to cloak some of your local materials to prevent them from being uploaded. *Cloaking* is a Dreamweaver feature that allows you to designate certain folders and files that will not be uploaded to or synchronized with the remote site.

▶ **Tip:** You might consider uploading the template files to the server as means of creating a backup.

Folders you don't want to upload include the Templates and resource folders. Some other non-web-compatible file types used to create your site, such as Photoshop (.psd), Flash (.fla), or Microsoft Word (.doc or docx) files, also don't need to be on the remote server. Although cloaked files will not upload or synchronize automatically, you may still upload them manually, if desired. Some people like to upload these items to keep a backup copy of them off-site.

The cloaking process begins in the Site Setup dialog.

1 Choose Site > Manage Sites.

2 Select lesson13 in the site list, and click the Edit icon ✐.

3 Expand the Advanced Settings category and select the Cloaking category. Select the Enable Cloaking and Cloak Files Ending With checkboxes, if necessary.

The field below the checkboxes displays several extensions and may differ from those pictured.

◉ **Note:** Add any extension you may be using for your source files.

4 Insert the cursor after the last extension, and insert a space, if necessary. Type **.doc .txt .rtf**

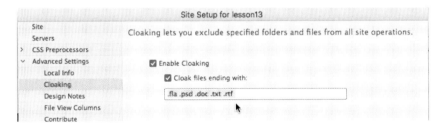

Be sure to insert a space between each extension. By specifying the extensions of file types that don't contain desired web content, you prevent Dreamweaver from uploading and synchronizing these file types automatically no matter where they appear in the site.

5 Click Save. If Dreamweaver prompts you to update the cache, click OK. Then, click Done to close the Manage Sites dialog.

Although you have cloaked several file types automatically, you can also cloak specific files or folders manually from the File panel.

6 Open the Files panel. The Files panel appears.

In the site list, you will see a list of the files and folders that make up the site. Some of the folders are used to store the raw materials for building content. There's no need to upload these items to the web. One of these items is the resources folder.

7 Right-click the resources folder.
From the context menu, choose Cloaking > Cloak.

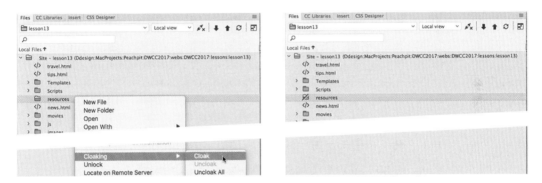

The select folder now shows a red slash, indicating that it is now cloaked.

The Templates folder is not needed on the remote site because your webpages do not reference these assets in any way. If you work in a team environment, it may be handy to upload and synchronize these folders so that each team member has up-to-date versions of each on their own computers. For this exercise, let's assume you work alone.

8 Apply cloaking to the Templates folder.

9 In the warning dialog that appears, click OK.

Using the Site Setup dialog and the Cloaking context menu, you cloaked file types, folders, and files. The synchronization process will ignore cloaked items and will not upload or download them automatically.

Wrapping things up

Over the last 12 lessons, you have built an entire website, beginning with a starter layout and then adding text, images, movies, and interactive content, but a few loose strings remain for you to tie up. Before you publish your site, you'll need to create one important webpage and make some crucial updates to your site navigation.

The file you need to create is one that is essential to every site: a home page. The home page is usually the first page most users see on your site. It is the page that loads automatically when a user enters your site's domain name into the browser window. Since the page loads automatically, there are a few restrictions on the name and extension you can use.

Basically, the name and extension depend on the hosting server and the type of applications running on the home page, if any. Today, the majority of home pages will simply be named *index*. But *default*, *start*, and *iisstart* are also used.

Extensions identify the specific types of programming languages used within a page. A normal HTML home page will use an extension of .htm or .html. Extensions like .asp, .cfm, and .php, among others, are required if the home page contains any dynamic applications specific to that server model. You may still use one of these extensions—if they are compatible with your server model—even if the page contains no dynamic applications or content. But be careful—in some instances, using the wrong extension may prevent the page from loading altogether. Whenever you're in doubt, use .html, because it's supported in all environments.

The specific home page name or names honored by the server are normally configured by the server administrator and can be changed, if desired. Most servers are configured to honor several names and a variety of extensions. Check with your IS/IT manager or web-server support team to ascertain the recommended name and extension for your home page.

1   Create a new page from the site template.
    Save the file as **index.html** or use a filename and extension compatible with your server model.

2   Open **home.html** from the lesson13 site root folder in Design view.

    The file contains content for the new home page.

3   Insert the cursor in the heading *Welcome to Meridien GreenStart.*
    Select the `article` tag selector and copy the content.

● **Note:** Moving content from one file to another is easier in Design or Code views. Remember, you must use the same view in both the source and target documents.

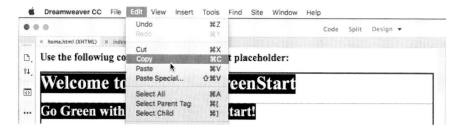

4 In **index.html**, select Design view.

Click the heading *Add main heading here.*

Select the `article` tag selector and paste.

The main content section in the new layout is replaced by the copied text and code.

5 Replace the quotation placeholder with the first `<aside>` element in **home.html**.

6 Replace Sidebar 2 with the second `<aside>` element in **home.html**.

Note the hyperlink placeholders in the `main_content` region.

7 Insert the cursor in the *News* link and in the `main_content` region.

In the Property inspector, browse and connect the link to **news.html**.

● **Note:** Pasting to replace an element works only in Design and Code views.

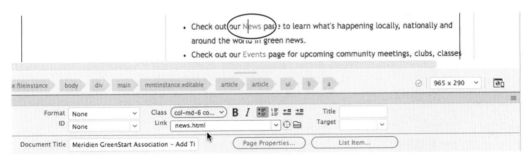

8 Repeat step 7 with each link. Connect the links to the appropriate pages in your site root folder.

9 Save and close all files.

The home page is nearly complete. For example, the title and meta description placeholders still need to be updated. Feel free to update them with the appropriate text.

In the meantime, let's assume you want to upload the site at its current state of completion. This happens in the course of any site development. Pages are added, updated, and deleted over time; missing pages will be completed and then uploaded at a later date. Before you can upload the site to a live server, you should always check for and update any out-of-date links and remove dead ones.

Prelaunch checklist

Take this opportunity to review all your site pages before publishing them to see whether they are ready for prime time. In an actual workflow, you should perform the following actions, which you learned in previous lessons, before uploading a single page:

- Spell-check (Lesson 9, "Working with Text, Lists, and Tables")
- Sitewide link check (Lesson 11, "Working with Navigation")

Fix any problems you find and then proceed to the next exercise.

Putting your site online (optional)

● **Note:** This exercise is optional since it requires that you set up a remote server beforehand.

For the most part, the local site and the remote site are mirror images, containing the same HTML files, images, and assets in identical folder structures. When you transfer a webpage from your local site to your remote site, you are publishing, or *putting*, that page. If you *put* a file stored in a folder on your local site, Dreamweaver transfers the file to the equivalent folder on the remote site. It will even automatically create the remote folder or folders if they do not already exist. The same is true when you download files.

◆ **Warning:** Dreamweaver does a good job trying to identify all the dependent files in a particular workflow. But in some cases, it may miss files crucial to a dynamic or extended process. It is imperative that you do your homework to identify these files and make sure they are uploaded.

Using Dreamweaver, you can publish anything—from one file to a complete site—in a single operation. When you publish a webpage, by default Dreamweaver asks if you would also like to put the dependent files too. Dependent files are the images, CSS, HTML5 movies, JavaScript files, server-side includes (SSI), and all other files necessary to complete the page.

You can upload one file at a time or the entire site at once. In this exercise, you will upload one webpage and its dependent files.

1 Open the Files panel and click the Expand icon ![expand icon], if necessary.

2 Click the Connect To Remote Server icon ![connect icon] to connect to the remote site.

If your remote site is properly configured, the Files panel will connect to the site and display its contents on the left half of the panel. When you first upload files, the remote site may be empty or mostly empty. If you are connecting to your Internet host, specific files and folders created by the hosting company may appear. Do not delete these items unless you check to see whether they are essential to the operation of the server or your own applications.

3 In the local file list, select **index.html**.
   In the Document toolbar, click the Put icon ![put icon].

By default, Dreamweaver will prompt you to upload dependent files. If a dependent file already exists on the server and your changes did not affect it, you can click No. Otherwise, for new files or files that have had any changes, click Yes. There is an option within Preferences where you can disable this prompt, if desired.

4 Click Yes.

Dreamweaver uploads **index.html** and all images, CSS, JavaScript, server-side includes, and other dependent files needed to properly render the selected HTML file. Although you chose only one file, you can see that 12 files and four folders were uploaded.

The Files panel enables you to upload multiple files as well as the entire site at once.

● **Note:** Dependent files include but are not limited to images, style sheets, and JavaScript used within a specific page and are essential to the proper display and function of the page.

5 Select the site root folder for the local site and then click the Put icon ⬆ in the Files panel.

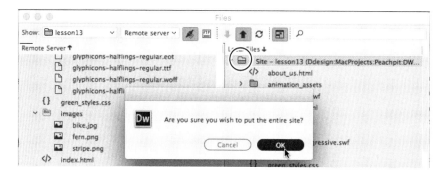

Dialogs appear, asking you to confirm that you want to upload dependent files and the entire site.

6 Click Yes and OK as appropriate.

▷ **Tip:** If you are using a third-party web-hosting service, be aware that they often create placeholder pages on your domain. If your home page does not automatically appear when you access your site, check to make sure that there is no conflict with the web host's placeholder pages.

Dreamweaver begins to upload the site. It will re-create your local site structure on the remote server. Dreamweaver uploads pages in the background so that you can continue to work in the meantime. If you want to see the progress of the upload, click the File Activity icon in the lower-left corner of the Files panel.

7 Click the File Activity icon 🐾.

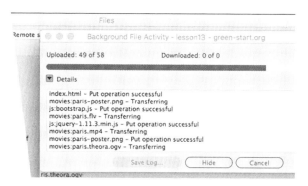

When you click the File Activity icon, you will see a list featuring the filenames and the status of the selected operation. You can even save the report to a text file, if desired, by clicking the Save Log button in the Background File Activity dialog.

Note that neither the cloaked lesson folders nor the files stored within them were uploaded. Dreamweaver will automatically ignore all cloaked items when putting individual folders or an entire site. If desired, you can manually select and upload individually cloaked items.

8 Right-click the Templates folder and choose Put from the context menu.

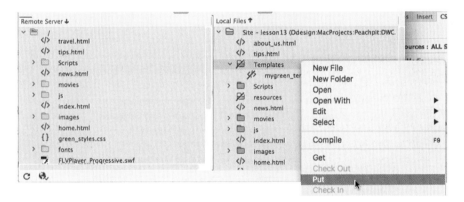

Note: A file that is uploaded or down-loaded will auto-matically overwrite any version of the file at the destination.

Dreamweaver prompts you to upload dependent files for the Templates folder.

9 Click Yes to upload dependent files.

The Templates folder is uploaded to the remote server. The log report shows that Dreamweaver checked for dependent files but did not upload the files that had not changed.

Note that the remote Templates folder displays a red slash, indicating that it, too, is cloaked. At times, you will want to cloak local and remote files and folders to prevent these items from being replaced or accidentally overwritten. A cloaked file will not be uploaded or downloaded automatically. But you can manually select any specific files and perform the same action.

The opposite of the Put command is Get, which downloads any selected file or folder to the local site. You can get any file from the remote site by selecting it in the Remote or Local pane and clicking the Get icon ⬇. Alternatively, you can drag the file from the Remote pane to the Local pane.

Note: When accessing Put and Get, it doesn't matter whether you use the Local or Remote pane of the Files panel. Put always uploads to Remote; Get always downloads to Local.

10 If you were able to successfully upload your site, use a browser to connect to the remote site on your network server or the Internet. Type the appropriate address in the URL field—depending on whether you are connecting to the local web server or to the actual Internet site—such as http://localhost/*domain_name* or http://www.*domain_name*.com.

The GreenStart site appears in the browser.

11 Click to test the hyperlinks to view each of the completed pages for the site.

Once the site is uploaded, keeping it up-to-date is an easy task. As files change, you can upload them one at a time or synchronize the whole site with the remote server.

Synchronization is especially important in workgroup environments where files are changed and uploaded by several individuals. You can easily download or upload files that are older, overwriting files that are newer in the process. Synchronization can ensure that you are working with only the latest versions of each file.

Synchronizing local and remote sites

Synchronization in Dreamweaver keeps the files on your server and your local computer up to date. It's an essential tool when you work from multiple locations or with one or more co-workers. Used properly, it can prevent you from accidentally uploading or working on out-of-date files.

At the moment, your local and remote sites are identical. To better illustrate the capabilities of synchronization, let's make a change to one of the site pages.

1 Open **about_us.html** in Live view.

2 Collapse the Files panel.

Clicking the collapse button re-docks the panel on the right side of the program.

3 Select **green_styles.css** > GLOBAL in the CSS Designer.
Create a new selector: .green

4 Add the following property to the new rule: `color: #090`

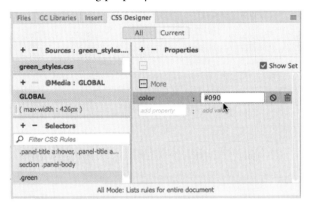

5 In the main heading, drag the cursor across the characters *Green* in the heading *About Meridien GreenStart.*

6 Apply the `green` class to this text.

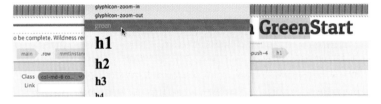

7 Apply the `green` class to each occurrence of the word *green* anywhere on the page where the text is not already green.

8 Save all files and close the page.

9 Open and expand the Files panel.
In the Document toolbar, click the Synchronize icon .

The Synchronize Files dialog appears.

● **Note:** The Synchronize icon looks similar to the Refresh icon but is located at the top-right side of the Files panel.

10 From the Synchronize pop-up menu, choose the option Entire 'lesson13' Site. From the Direction menu, choose the Get And Put Newer Files option.

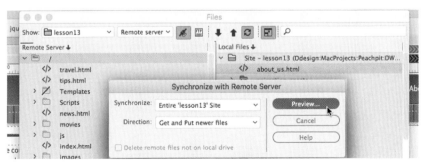

Choose specific options in this dialog that meet your needs and workflow.

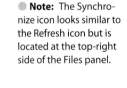

Note: Synchronize does not compare cloaked files or folders.

11 Click Preview.

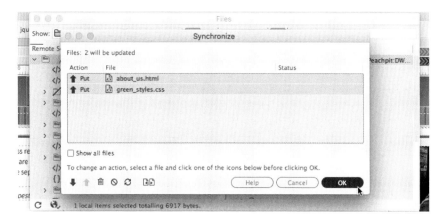

The Synchronize dialog appears, reporting what files have changed and whether you need to get or put them. Since you just uploaded the entire site, only the files you modified—**about_us.html** and **green_styles.css**—should appear in the list, which indicates that Dreamweaver wants to put them to the remote site. If you see any other files listed, select them and click the Synchronized icon ⟳ to tell Dreamweaver that these files are okay as is.

Synchronization options

During synchronization, you can choose to accept the suggested action or override it by selecting one of the other options in the dialog. Options can be applied to one or more files at a time.

⬇ **Get**—Downloads the selected file(s) from the remote site

⬆ **Put**—Uploads the selected file(s) to the remote site

🗑 **Delete**—Marks the selected file(s) for deletion

🚫 **Ignore**—Ignores the selected file(s) during synchronization

⟳ **Synchronized**—Identifies the selected file(s) as already synchronized

🔲🔲 **Compare**—Uses a third-party utility to compare the local and remote versions of a selected file

12 Click OK to upload the two files.

If other people access and update files on your site, remember to run synchronization *before* you work on any files to be certain you are working on the most current versions of each file in your site. Another technique is to set up the check-out/check-in functionality in the advanced options of the server's setup dialog.

In this lesson, you set up your site to connect to a remote server and uploaded files to that remote site. You also cloaked files and folders and then synchronized the local and remote sites.

Congratulations! You've designed, developed, and built an entire website and uploaded it to your remote server. By finishing all the exercises in this book, you have gained experience in all aspects of the design and development of a standard website compatible with desktop computers and mobile devices. Now you are ready to build and publish a site of your own. Good luck!

Review questions

1 What is a remote site?

2 Name two types of file transfer protocols supported in Dreamweaver.

3 How can you configure Dreamweaver so that it does not synchronize certain files in your local site with the remote site?

4 True or false: You have to manually publish every file and associated image, JavaScript file, and server-side include that are linked to pages in your site.

5 What service does synchronization perform?

Review answers

1   A remote site is typically the live version of the local site stored on a web server connected to the Internet.

2   FTP (File Transfer Protocol) and local/network are the two most commonly used file transfer methods. Other file transfer methods supported in Dreamweaver include Secure FTP, WebDav, and RDS.

3   Cloaking the files or folders prevents them from synchronizing.

4   False. Dreamweaver can automatically transfer dependent files, if desired, including embedded or referenced images, CSS style sheets, and other linked content, although some files may be missed.

5   Synchronization automatically scans local and remote sites, comparing files on both to identify the most current version of each. It creates a report window to suggest which files to get or put to bring both sites up to date, and then it will perform the update.

14

WORKING WITH CODE

In this lesson, you'll learn how to work with code and do the following:

- Write code using code hinting and Emmet shorthand
- Set up a CSS preprocessor and create SCSS styling
- Use multiple cursors to select and edit code
- Collapse and expand code entries
- Use Live Code to test and troubleshoot dynamic code
- Use the Inspect mode to identify HTML elements and associated styling
- Access and edit attached files using the Related Files interface

 This lesson will take about 90 minutes to complete. Download the project files for this lesson from the Lesson & Update Files tab on your Account page at www.peachpit.com and store them on your computer in a convenient location, as described in the "Getting Started" section at the beginning of this book. Your Accounts page is also where you'll find any updates to the lessons or to the lesson files. Look on the Lesson & Update Files tab to access the most current content.

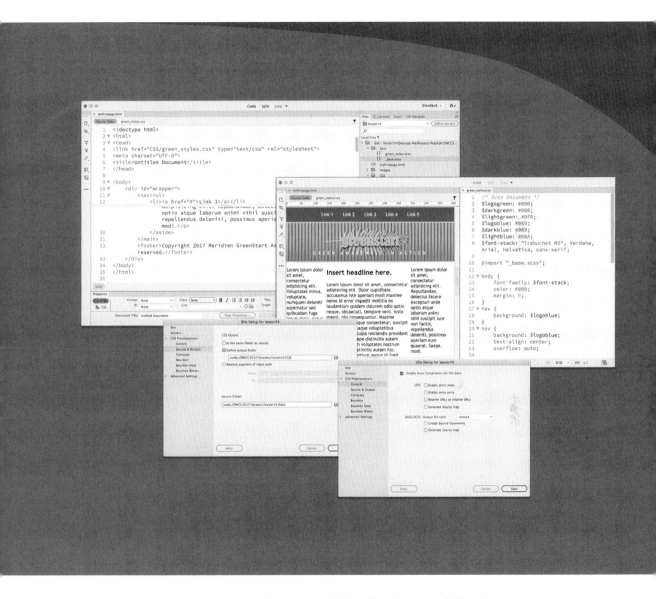

Dreamweaver's claim to fame is as a visually based HTML editor, but its code-editing features don't take a backseat to its graphical interface and offer few compromises to professional coders and developers.

Creating HTML code

Note: If you have not already downloaded the project files for this lesson to your computer from your Account page, make sure to do so now. See "Getting Started" at the beginning of the book.

Note: Some tools and options are available only when Code view is active.

As one of the leading WYSIWYG HTML editors Dreamweaver allows users to create elaborate webpages and applications without touching or even seeing the code that does all the work behind the scenes. But for many designers, working with the code is not only a desire but also a necessity.

Although Dreamweaver has always made it as easy to work with a page in Code view as in Design or Live views, some developers believed that the code-editing tools took a backseat to the visual design interface. Although in the past this was partially true, it is no longer the case with Dreamweaver CC (2017 release). The latest release is unveiling new and vastly improved tools and workflows for coders and developers. In fact, Dreamweaver CC (2017 release) can now unify the entire web development team as never before by providing a single platform that can handle almost any needed task.

You'll often find that a specific task is actually easier to accomplish in Code view than in Live or Design views alone. In the following exercises, you'll learn more about how Dreamweaver makes working with the code an effortless and surprisingly enjoyable task.

Writing code manually

If you completed the previous 13 lessons, you have had numerous opportunities to view and edit code by hand. But for anyone jumping directly to this lesson, this exercise will provide a quick overview of the topic. The first step to experiencing Dreamweaver's code writing and editing tools is to create a new file.

1   Define a site based on the lesson14 folder downloaded from your account page, as described in the "Getting Started" section at the beginning of the book.

2   Select Developer from the Workspace menu.

All the code-editing tools work identically in either workspace, but the Developer workspace focuses on the Code view window and will provide a better experience for the following exercises.

3   Choose File > New.

The New Document dialog appears.

4 Choose New Document > HTML > None.
Click Create.

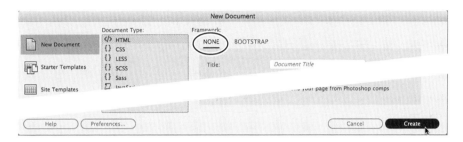

Dreamweaver creates the basic structure of a webpage automatically. The cursor will probably appear at the beginning of the code.

As you can see, Dreamweaver provides color-coded tags and markup to make it easier to read, but that's not all. It also offers code hinting for ten different web development languages, including but not limited to HTML, CSS, JavaScript, and PHP.

5 Choose File > Save.

6 Name the file **myfirstpage.html** and save it in the lesson14 folder.

7 Insert the cursor after the <body> tag and press Enter/Return.
Type <

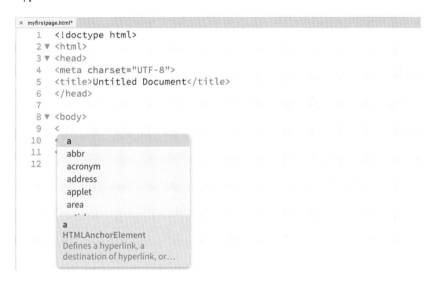

A code-hinting window appears showing you a list of HTML-compatible codes you can select from.

8 Type **d**

The code-hinting window filters to code elements that start with the letter *d*. You can continue to type the tag name directly or use this list to select the desired element. By using the list, you can eliminate simple typing errors.

9 Press the down arrow.

The **dd** tag in the code-hinting window is highlighted.

10 Continue pressing the down arrow until the tag **div** is highlighted. Press Enter/Return.

```
 8   <body>                          8   <body>
 9   <d                              9   <div
10   </      del                    10   </body>
11   <,      details                11   </html>
12           dfn                     12
             div
             dl
```

The tag name **div** is inserted in the code. The cursor remains at the end of the tag name waiting for your next input. For example, you could complete the tag name or enter various HTML attributes. Let's add an **id** attribute to the **div** element.

11 Press the spacebar to insert a space.

The hinting menu opens again displaying a different list; this time the list contains various appropriate HTML attributes.

12 Type **id** and press Enter/Return.

Dreamweaver creates the **id** attribute complete with equal sign and quotation marks. Note that the cursor appears within the quotations marks ready for your entry.

13 Type **wrapper** and press the right arrow key once.

The cursor moves outside the closing quotation mark.

14 Type ></

```
 8   <body>                          8 ▼ <body>
 9   <div id=""                      9      <div id="wrapper"></div>
10   </body>                        10   </body>
11   </html>                        11   </html>
12                                   12
```

When you type the backslash (/), Dreamweaver closes the **div** element automatically. As you see, the program can provide a lot of help to assist you as you write code manually. But, it can help you write code automatically, too.

15 Choose File > Save.

Writing code automatically

Emmet is a web-developer toolkit that was added to the last version of Dream-weaver and enables you to supercharge your code-writing tasks. By entering short-hand characters and operators, Emmet enables you to create whole blocks of code with just a few keystrokes. To experience the power of Emmet, try this exercise.

1 If necessary, open **myfirstpage.html**.

2 In Code view, insert the cursor within the `div` element and press Enter/Return to create a new line.

   Emmet is enabled by default and works whenever you are typing in Code view. In our original site mock-up, the navigation menu appears at the top of the page. HTML5 uses the `<nav>` element as the foundation of site navigation.

3 Type **nav** and press the Tab key.

```
 8 ▼ <body>                              8 ▼ <body>
 9 ▼     <div id="wrapper">              9 ▼     <div id="wrapper">
10           nav                        10             <nav></nav>
11       </div>                         11       </div>
12   </body>                            12   </body>
```

   Dreamweaver creates the opening and closing tags all at once. The cursor appears inside the `nav` element ready for you to add another element, some content, or both.

   HTML navigation menus are usually based on an unordered list, which consists of a `<ul>` element with one or more child `<li>` elements. Emmet allows you to create more than one element at the same time, and by using an operator, you can specify whether the subsequent elements follow the first (+) or are nested one within the other (>).

4 Type **ul>li** and press Tab.

```
 9 ▼     <div id="wrapper">              9 ▼     <div id="wrapper">
10           <nav>ul>li|</nav>          10 ▼         <nav><ul>
11       </div>                         11                 <li>|</li>
12   </body>                            12             </ul></nav>
13   </html>                            13       </div>
```

   A `<ul>` element appears containing one list item. The greater-than symbol (>) is used to create the parent-child structure you see here. By adding another opera-tor, you can create several list items.

5 Choose Edit > Undo.

   The code reverts to the `ul>li` shorthand. It's easy to adapt this shorthand markup to create a menu with five items.

6 Edit the existing shorthand phrase as highlighted ul>li*5 and press Tab.

```
 9 ▼      <div id="wrapper">
10            <nav>ul*li*5</nav>
11        </div>
12   </body>
13   </html>
14
```

```
 9 ▼      <div id="wrapper">
10 ▼         <nav><ul>
11               <li>k</li>
12               <li></li>
13               <li></li>
14               <li></li>
15               <li></li>
16            </ul></nav>
17        </div>
```

A new unordered list appears this time with five <li> elements. The asterisk (*) is the mathematical symbol for multiplication, so this latest change literally says "<li> times 5."

To create a proper menu, you also need to add a hyperlink to each menu item.

7 Press Ctrl+Z/Cmd+Z or choose Edit > Undo.

The code reverts to the ul>li*5 shorthand.

8 Edit the existing shorthand phrase as highlighted: ul>li*5>a

If you guessed that adding the markup >a would create a hyperlink child element for each link item, you were correct. Emmet can also create placeholder content, too. Let's use it to insert some text in each link item.

9 Edit the shorthand phrase as highlighted: ul>li*5>a{Link}

Adding text within braces passes it to the final structure of the hyperlink, but we're not done yet. You can also increment the items, such as Link 1, Link 2, Link 3, and so on, by adding a variable character ($).

10 Edit the shorthand phrase as highlighted: ul>li*5>a{Link $}
Press Tab.

```
 9 ▼      <div id="wrapper">
10            <nav>ul*li*5>a{Link $}</nav>
11        </div>
12   </body>
13   </html>
14
```

```
 9 ▼      <div id="wrapper">
10 ▼         <nav><ul>
11               <li><a href="">Link 1</a></li>
12               <li><a href="">Link 2</a></li>
13               <li><a href="">Link 3</a></li>
14               <li><a href="">Link 4</a></li>
15               <li><a href="">Link 5</a></li>
16            </ul></nav>
17        </div>
```

The new menu appears fully structured with five link items and hyperlink placeholders incremented 1 through 5. The menu is nearly complete. The only thing missing are targets for the href attributes. You could add them now using another Emmet phrase, but let's save this change for the next exercise.

11 Insert the cursor after the closing </nav> tag.
Press Enter/Return to create a new line.

Note: Adding the new line makes the code easier to read and edit, but it has no effect on how it operates.

Let's see how easy it is to add a header element to your new page using Emmet.

12 Type **header** and press the Tab key.

Like the <nav> element you created earlier, the opening and closing header tags appear with the cursor positioned to insert the content. If you model this header on the one in the site completed in Lessons 4–13, you need to add two text components: an <h2> for the company name and a <p> element for the motto. Emmet provides a method for not only adding the tags but also the content.

13 Type **h2{greenstart}+p{Green Awareness in Action}** and press Tab.

```
17              <header>h2{greenstart}+p{Green Awareness in Action}</header>
18      </div>
19    </body>
20    </html>
```

```
17              <header><h2>greenstart</h2>
18              <p>Green Awareness in Action</p></header>
19      </div>
20    </body>
```

The two elements appear complete, containing the company name and motto. Note how you added the text to each item using braces. The plus (+) sign designates that the <p> element should be added as a peer to the heading.

14 Insert the cursor after the closing </header> tag.

15 Press Enter/Return to insert a new line.

Emmet enables you to quickly build complex multifaceted parent-child structures like the navigation menu and the header, but it doesn't stop there. As you string together several elements with placeholder text, you can even add id and class attributes. To insert an id, start the name with the hash (#) symbol; to add a class, start the name with a dot (.). It's time to push your skills to the next level.

16 Type **main#content>aside.sidebar1>p(lorem)^article>p(lorem100) ^aside.sidebar2>p(lorem)** and press Tab.

Note: The entire phrase may wrap to more than one line in Code view, but make sure there are no spaces within the markup.

```
17          <header><h2>greenstart</h2>
18          <p>Green Awareness in Action</p></header>
19          main#content>aside.sidebar1>p(lorem)^article>p(lorem100)^aside.sidebar2>p(lorem)|
20      </div>
21  </body>
22  </html>
23
```

```
17          <header><h2>greenstart</h2>
18          <p>Green Awareness in Action</p></header>
19 ▼        <main id="content">
20 ▼            <aside class="sidebar1">
21                  <p>Lorem ipsum dolor sit amet, consectetur adipisicing elit. Dolor
                    similique rem dolorum accusantium voluptatem? Nesciunt doloribus aperiam
                    nemo voluptatum ipsam libero, optio porro similique eaque. Explicabo, vitae
                    itaque architecto minima.</p>
22              </aside>
23 ▼            <article>
24                  <p>Lorem ipsum dolor sit amet, consectetur adipisicing elit. Adipisci neque
```

A <main> element is created with three child elements (aside, article, aside) along with id and class attributes. The caret (^) symbol in the shorthand is used to ensure the article and aside.sidebar2 elements are created as siblings of aside.sidebar1. Within each child element, you should see a paragraph of placeholder text. Emmet includes a *Lorem* generator to create blocks of placeholder text automatically. When you add lorem in parentheses after an element name, such as p(lorem), Emmet will generate 30 words of placeholder content. To specify a larger or smaller amount of text, just add a number at the end, such as p(lorem100) for 100 words.

Let's finish up the page with a footer element containing a copyright statement.

17 Insert the cursor after the closing </main> tag. Create a new line.
Type footer{Copyright 2017 Meridien GreenStart Association. All rights reserved.} and press Tab.

```
29          </main>
30          footer{Copyright 2017 Meridien GreenStart Association. All rights reserved.}
31      </div>
32  </body>
33  </html>
```

```
29          </main>
30          <footer>Copyright 2017 Meridien GreenStart Association. All rights reserved.
            </footer>
31      </div>
32  </body>
```

18 Save the file.

Using a few shorthand phrases, you have built a complete webpage structure and some placeholder content. Ideally, you can see how Emmet can supercharge your code-writing tasks. Feel free to use this amazing toolkit at any time to add a single element or a complex multifaceted component. It's there any time you need it.

This exercise has barely scratched the surface for what Emmet can do. It is simply too powerful to fully describe in just a few pages. But you got a good peek at its capabilities.

Check out http://emmet.io to learn more about Emmet.

Check out http://docs.emmet.io/cheat-sheet/ for a handy Emmet shorthand cheat sheet.

Working with multicursor support

Have you ever wanted to edit more than one line of code at a time? Another addition to Dreamweaver CC (2017 release) is multicursor support. This feature allows you to select and edit multiple lines of code at once to speed up a variety of mundane tasks. Let's take a look at how it works.

1   If necessary, open **myfirstpage.html** as it appears at the end of the previous exercise.

The file contains a complete webpage with `header`, `nav`, `main`, and `footer` elements. The content features classes and several paragraphs of placeholder text. The `<nav>` element includes five placeholders for links, but the `href` attributes are empty. For the menu and links to appear and behave properly, you need to add a filename, URL, or placeholder element to each link. In the previous lessons, the hash (#) mark was used as placeholder content until the final link destinations could be added.

2   Insert the cursor between the quotation marks in the `href=""` attribute in Link 1.

Normally, you would have to add a hash (#) mark to each attribute individually. Multicursor support makes this task much easier, but don't be surprised if it takes you a little practice. Note how all the link attributes are aligned vertically on consecutive lines.

3   Hold the Alt key (Windows) or Opt key (macOS) and drag the mouse down through all five links.

Using the Alt/Opt key enables you to select code or insert cursors in consecutive lines. Be careful to drag down in a straight line. If you slip a little to the left or right, you may select some of the surrounding markup. If that happens, you can just start over. When you are finished, you should see a cursor flashing in the `href` attribute for each link.

4 Type #

```
10 ▼      <nav><ul>                                    10 ▼      <nav><ul>
11            <li><a href="">Link 1</a></li>            11            <li><a href="#">Link 1</a></li>
12            <li><a href="">Link 2</a></li>            12            <li><a href="#">Link 2</a></li>
13            <li><a href="">Link 3</a></li>            13            <li><a href="#">Link 3</a></li>
14            <li><a href="">Link 4</a></li>            14            <li><a href="#">Link 4</a></li>
15            <li><a href="">Link 5</a></li>            15            <li><a href="#">Link 5</a></li>
16        </ul></nav>        I                          16        </ul></nav>
```

The hash (#) mark appears in all five attributes at the same time.

The Ctrl/Cmd key enables you to select code or insert cursors in nonconsecutive lines of code.

5 Hold the Ctrl/Cmd key and click to insert the cursor between the p and the > bracket in the three opening <p> tags in the <main> element.

6 Press the spacebar to insert a space and type class="first"

```
20 ▼      <aside class="sidebar1">              20 ▼      <aside class="sidebar1">
21            <p>Lorem ipsum dolor              21            <p class="first">.or
              minus, voluptate, nu                        voluptates minus, vc
              dicta, natus earum r                        ipsum dicta, natus e
              blanditiis sint adip                        blanditiis sint adip
22        </aside>                              22        </aside>
23 ▼      <article>                             23 ▼      <article>
24            <p>Lorem ipsum dolor              24            <p class="first">.or
              cupiditate accusamus                        Dolor cupiditate acc
              mollitia ex laudanti                        mollitia ex laudanti
              vero. Iusto magni, r                        vero. Iusto magni, r
              suscipit cum deserur                        suscipit cum deserur
              provident quo vel al                        provident quo vel al
              nostrum doloremque!                         nostrum doloremque!
              fugit aspernatur atc                        fugit aspernatur atc
              quibusdam omnis expe                        quibusdam omnis expe
              sit reprehenderit vi                        sit reprehenderit vi
              aspernatur, vel, per                        aspernatur, vel, per
25        </article>                            25        </article>
26 ▼      <aside class="sidebar2">              26 ▼      <aside class="sidebar2">
27            <p>Lorem ipsum dolor              27            <p class="first">.or
              delectus facere exce                        Repudiandae, detectu
```

The class appears simultaneously in all three <p> tags.

7 Save the file.

Multicursor support can save tons of time in repetitive code-editing tasks.

Customizing the Common toolbar

Some of the code-editing exercises in this lesson require tools that may not appear in the interface by default. The Common toolbar was previously called the Coding toolbar and appeared only in Code view. The new toolbar appears in all views, but some tools may be visible only when the cursor is inserted directly in the Code view window.

If the exercise calls for a tool that is not visible, even with the cursor in the proper position, you may need to customize the toolbar yourself. This can be done by first clicking the Customize Toolbar icon ••• and then enabling the tools within the Customize Toolbar dialog. At the same time, feel free to disable tools you don't use.

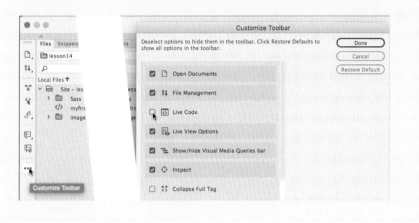

Commenting your code

Comments allow you to leave notes within the code—invisible in the browser—to describe the purpose of certain markup or provide important information to other coders. Although you can add comments manually at any time, Dreamweaver has a built-in feature that can speed up the process.

1 Open **myfirstpage.html** and switch to Code view, if necessary.

2 Insert the cursor after the opening tag `<aside class="sidebar1">`.

3 Click the Apply Comment icon.

```
16    </ul></nav>
17    <header><h2>greenstart</h2>
18    <p>Green Awareness in Action</p></header>
19 ▾  <main id="content">
20 ▾      <aside class="sidebar1"><!--|-->
21          <p class="first">Lorem ipsum dolor sit
              Voluptates minus, voluptate, numquam de
```

Apply HTML Comment
Apply /* */ Comment
Apply // Comment
Apply ' Comment
Apply Server Comment

A pop-up menu appears with several comment options. Dreamweaver supports comment markup for various web-compatible languages, including HTML, CSS, JavaScript, and PHP among others.

4 Choose Apply HTML Comment.

An HTML comment block appears with the text cursor positioned in the center.

5 Type `Insert environmental quotations into Sidebar 1`

The comment appears in gray between `<!--` and `-->` markup. The tool can also apply comment markup to existing text.

6 Insert the cursor after the opening tag `<aside class="sidebar2">`.

7 Type `Sidebar 2 should be used for content related to the Article section`

8 Select the text created in step 7.
Click the Apply Comment icon.

A pop-up menu opens.

9 Select Apply HTML Comment.

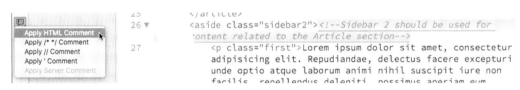

Dreamweaver applies the `<!--` and `-->` markup to the selection. If you need to remove existing comment markup from a selection, click the Remove Comment icon in the toolbar.

10 Save all files.

You've created a complete basic webpage. The next step is to style the page. Dreamweaver CC (2017 release) now supports CSS preprocessors for LESS, Sass, and SCSS. In the next exercise, you'll learn how to set up and create CSS styling using a preprocessor.

Working with CSS preprocessors

One of the biggest changes to the latest version of Dreamweaver was adding built-in support for LESS, Sass, and SCSS. These industry-standard CSS preprocessors are scripting languages that enable you to extend the capabilities of cascading style sheets with a variety of productivity enhancements and then compile the results in a standard CSS file. These languages provide a variety of benefits for designers and developers who prefer to write their code by hand, including speed, ease of use, reusable snippets, variables, logic, calculations, and much more. No other software is needed to work in these preprocessors, but Dreamweaver also supports other frameworks, such as Compass and Bourbon.

In this exercise, you'll get a taste of how easy it is use a preprocessor with Dreamweaver as well as what advantages they offer compared to a regular CSS workflow.

Enabling a preprocessor

Support for CSS preprocessors is site-specific and must be enabled for each site defined in Dreamweaver, as desired. To enable LESS, Sass, or SCSS, you first define a site and then enable the CSS Preprocessors option within the Site Definition dialog.

1 Select Site > Manage Sites.

The Manage Sites dialog appears.

2 Select **lesson14** in the Your Sites window.
Click the Edit icon ✎ at the bottom of the Your Sites window.

The Site Definition for lesson14 appears.

3 Select **CSS Preprocessors** option in Site Definition dialog.

The CSS Preprocessors option contains six subcategories, including General, Source & Output, as well as options for various Compass and Bourbon frameworks. You can check out the Dreamweaver Help topics for more information on these frameworks. For this exercise, you only need the features that are built into the program itself.

4 Select the General category.

When selected, this category features the on/off switch for the LESS, Sass, and SCSS compiler, as well as various options for how the languages operate. For our purposes, the default settings will work fine.

5 Click the Enable Auto Compilation on File Save checkbox to enable the preprocessor compiler, if necessary.

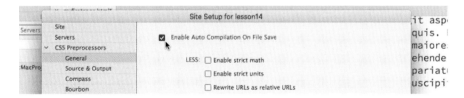

When this is enabled, Dreamweaver will automatically compile your CSS from your LESS, Sass, or SCSS source files whenever they are saved. Some designers and developers use the root folder of the site for compilation. In this case, we'll separate the source and output files in distinct folders.

LESS or Sass, the choice is yours

LESS and Sass offer similar features and functions, so which one should you choose? That's hard to say. Some think that LESS is easier to learn but that Sass offers more powerful functionality. Both make the chore of writing CSS faster and easier and more importantly provide significant advantages for maintaining and extending your CSS over time. There are lots of opinions on which preprocessor is better, but often you'll find it comes down to personal preferences.

Before you decide, check out the following links to get some informed perspectives:

- blog.udemy.com/less-vs-sass/
- css-tricks.com/sass-vs-less/
- zingdesign.com/less-vs-sass-its-time-to-switch-to-sass/
- keycdn.com/blog/sass-vs-less

6 Select the Source & Output category.

This category enables you to designate the source and output folders for your CSS preprocessor. The default option targets the folder where the source file is saved.

7 Select the Define Output Folder option.
Click the Browse for Folder icon 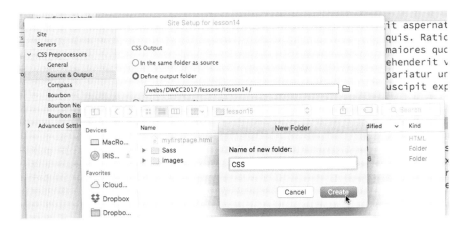.

A file browser dialog appears.

8 Navigate to the Site Root folder, if necessary.
Create a new folder.

9 Name the new folder **CSS.** Click Select Folder/Choose.

10 Click the Browse for Folder icon 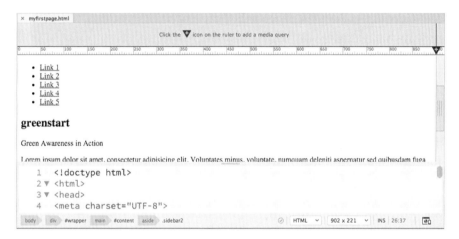 beside the Source Folder field.

11 Navigate to the Site Root folder.
Select the existing Sass folder and click Select Folder/Choose.

12 Save the changes and click Done to return to your site.

The CSS preprocessor is enabled, and the source and output folders are now designated. Next, you'll create the CSS source file.

Creating the CSS source file

When using a preprocessor workflow, you do not write the CSS code directly. Instead, you write rules and other code in a source file that is then compiled to the output file. For the following exercise, you'll create a Sass source file and learn some of functions of that language.

1 Select Standard from the Workspace menu.

2 Choose Window > Files to display the Files panel.
Select lesson14 from the Site List drop-down menu, if necessary.

3 Open **myfirstpage.html** and switch to Split view.

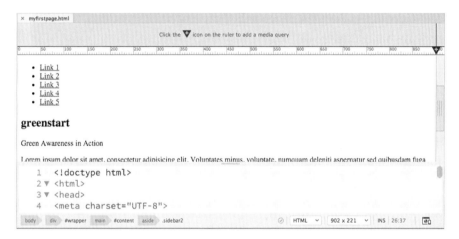

The webpage is unstyled at the moment.

4 Choose File > New.

The New Document dialog appears. This dialog allows you to create all types of web-compatible documents. In the Document Type section of the dialog, you will see the LESS, Sass, and SCSS file types.

5 Choose New Document > SCSS.
Click the Create button.

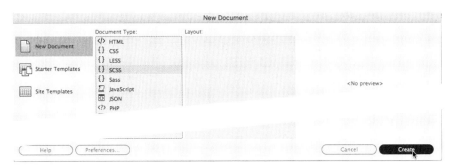

A new blank SCSS document appears in the document window. SCSS is a flavor of Sass that uses a syntax similar to regular CSS, which many users find easier to learn and work with.

6 Save the file as **green_styles.scss** in the Sass folder you targeted in the previous exercise as the Source folder.

There's no need to create the CSS file; the compiler in Dreamweaver will do that for you. You're all set to start working with Sass. The first step is to define variables. Variables are programmatic constructs that enable you to store CSS specifications you want to use multiple times, such as colors in your site theme. By using a variable, you have to define it only once. If you need to change it in the future, you can edit one entry in the style sheet and all the instances of the variable are updated automatically.

7 Insert the cursor into line 2 of **green_styles.scss**.
Type `$logogreen: #090;` and press Enter/Return.

You've created your first variable. This is the main green color of the site theme. Let's create the rest of the variables.

8 Type `$darkgreen: #060;`
`$lightgreen: #0F0;`
`$logoblue: #069;`

```
$darkblue: #089;
$lightblue: #08A;
$font-stack: "Trebuchet MS", Verdana, Arial, Helvetica,
sans-serif;
```

and press Enter/Return to create a new line.

```
 ×  myfirstpage.html    ×  green_styles.scss*
   1    /* Scss Document */
   2    $logogreen: #090;
   3    $darkgreen: #060;
   4    $lightgreen: #0F0;
   5    $logoblue: #069;
   6    $darkblue: #089;
   7    $lightblue: #08A;
   8    $font-stack: "Trebuchet MS", Verdana, Arial, Helvetica, sans-serif;
```

Entering the variables on separate lines makes them easier to read and edit but does not affect how they perform. Just make sure you add a semicolon (;) at the end of each variable.

Let's start the style sheet with the base or default styling of the body element. SCSS markup in most cases looks just like regular CSS, except in this case you'll use one of your variables to set the font-family.

9 Type **body** and press the spacebar.
Type { and press Enter/Return.

When you typed the opening brace ({), Dreamweaver created the closing brace automatically. When you created the new line, the cursor was indented by default, and the closing brace moved to the following line. You can also use Emmet to enter the settings more quickly.

10 Type `ff$font-stack` and press Tab.

```
   8    $font-stack: "Trebuchet MS", Verdana, Arial, Helvetica, sans-serif;
   9  ▼ body {
  10        ff$font-stack
  11    }
```

```
   8    $font-stack: "Trebuchet MS", Verdana, Arial, Helvetica, sans-serif;
   9  ▼ body {
  10        font-family: $font-stack;
  11    }
```

The shorthand expands to `font-family: $font-stack;`.

11 Press Enter/Return to create a new line.
Type c and press Tab.

The shorthand expands to `color: #000;`. The default color is acceptable.

12 Hold the Alt/Cmd and press the right arrow key to move the cursor to the end of the current line of code.

13 Press Enter/Return to create a new line.

Type `m0` and press Tab.

```
 9 ▼ body {
10        font-family: $font-stack;
11        color: #000;
12        margin: 0;
13    }
```

The shorthand expands to `margin: 0;`. This property completes the basic styling for the body element. Before you save the file, this a good time to see how preprocessors do their work.

Compiling CSS code

You have completed the specifications for the body element. But you have not created the styling directly in a CSS file. Your entries were made entirely in the SCSS source file. In this exercise, you will see how the CSS output is generated by the compiler built into Dreamweaver.

1 Display the Files panel, if necessary, and expand the list of site files.

The site consists of one HTML file and three folders: CSS, images, and Sass.

2 Expand the view of the CSS and Sass folders.

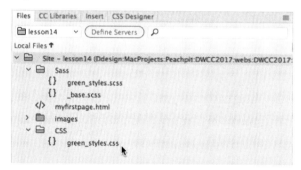

The Sass folder contains **green_styles.scss** and **_base.scss**. The CSS folder contains **green_styles.css**. This file did not exist when you started the lesson. It was generated automatically when you created the SCSS file and saved it into the site folder defined as the Source folder. At the moment, the CSS file should contain no CSS rules or markup. It's also not referenced in the sample webpage.

3 Select the document tab for **myfirstpage.html**.
Switch to Split view, if necessary.

The page shows only default HTML styling.

4 In Code view, insert the cursor after the opening `<head>` tag and press Enter/Return to insert a new line.

5 Type `<link` and press the spacebar.

The hinting menu appears. You'll link the webpage to the generated CSS file.

6 Type `href` and press Enter/Return.

```
3 ▼ <head>                          3 ▼ <head>
4    <link href|                    4    <link href=""
5    <meta char  href               5    <meta charse  Browse...
6    <title>Unt  hreflang  </title> 6    <title>Untit  CSS/       itle>
7    </head>                        7    </head>       images/
```

The complete `href=""` attribute appears, and the hinting menu changes to display the Browse command and list of pathnames to folders available in the site.

7 Press the down arrow to select the path `CSS/` and press Enter/Return.

The hinting menu now displays the path and file name to **green_styles.css**.

8 Press the down arrow to select `CSS/green_styles.css` and press Enter/Return.

```
3 ▼ <head>                              3 ▼ <head>
4    <link href="CSS/|                  4    <link href="CSS/green_styles.css"
5    <meta charset="  Browse...         5    <meta charset="UTF-8">
6    <title>Untitled  CSS/green_styles.css  6  <title>Untitled Document</title>
7    </head>                            7    </head>
```

The URL to the CSS output file appears in the attribute. The cursor is moved outside the closing quotation mark and ready for the next entry. For the style sheet reference to be valid, you need to create two more attributes.

9 Press the spacebar and type `type` and press Enter/Return.
Select `text/css` from the hinting menu and press Enter/Return.

10 Press the spacebar and type `rel` and press Enter/Return.
Select `stylesheet` from the hinting menu and press Enter/Return.

11 Move the cursor outside the closing quotation mark.
Type > to close the link.

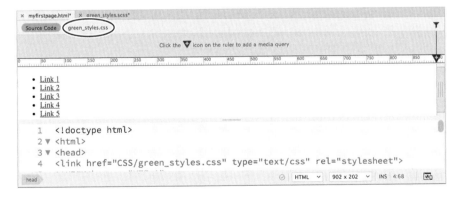

The CSS output file is now referenced by the webpage. In Live view, there should be no difference in the styling, but you should now see **green_styles.css** displayed in the Related Files interface.

12 Select **green_styles.css** in the Related Files interface.

Code view displays the contents of **green_styles.css** showing only the comment entry `/* Scss Document */`. An asterisk appears next to the filename in the document tab for **green_styles.scss**, indicating that file has been changed but has not been saved.

13 Choose Window > Arrange > Tile.

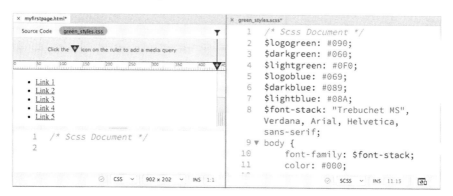

The webpage and the source file appear side by side in the program window.

14 Insert the cursor anywhere in **green_styles.scss** and choose File > Save.

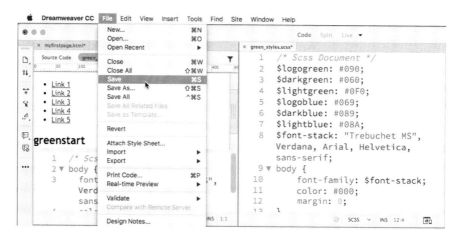

After a moment, the display of **myfirstpage.html** changes, showing the new font and margin settings. The Code view window also updates to display the new contents of **green_styles.css**. Each time you save the SCSS source file, Dreamweaver will update the output file.

Nesting CSS selectors

Targeting CSS styling to one element without accidentally affecting another is the constant bane of web designers everywhere. Descendant selectors are one method for ensuring the styling is applied correctly. But creating and maintaining the correct descendant structure becomes more difficult as the site and style sheets grow in size. All preprocessor languages offer some form of nesting for selector names.

In this exercise, you will learn how to nest selectors while styling the navigation menu. First, you'll set the basic styling for the <nav> element itself.

1 In **green_styles.scss**, insert the cursor after the closing brace (}) for the body rule.

2 Create a new line and type nav { and press Enter/Return.

The nav selector and declaration structure is created and ready for your entry. Emmet provides shorthand entries for all CSS properties.

3 Type bg$logoblue and press Tab.
Press Enter/Return.

● **Note:** From this point on all CSS rules and other markup will be made only in the SCSS file. The CSS file displayed in the Related Files interface is only for reference.

```
14 ▼ nav {
15       bg$logoblue
16  }
```

```
14 ▼ nav {
15       background: $logoblue;
16  }
```

The shorthand expands to background: $logoblue, which is the first variables you created in the SCSS source file. This will apply the color #069 to the nav element.

4 Type ta:c and press Tab.
Press Enter/Return.

The shorthand expands to text-align: center.

5 Type ov:a and press Tab.
Press Enter/Return.

The shorthand expands to overflow: auto.

6 Save the source file.

The <nav> element in **myfirstpage.html** displays the color #069. The menu doesn't look like much yet, but you've only just begun. Next, you'll format the <ul> element. Note how the cursor is still within the declaration structure for the nav selector.

7 Type `ul {` and press Enter/Return.

```
14 ▼  nav {
15        background: $logoblue;
16        text-align: center;
17        overflow: auto;
18 ▼      ul {
19
20        }
21    }
                    ⊘  SCSS  ∨   INS  18:9        🖥
```

The new selector and declaration are created within the `nav` rule.

8 Create the following properties:

```
list-style: none;
padding: 0;
```

These properties reset the default styling of the unordered list, removing the bullet and indent. Next, you'll override the styling of the list items.

9 Press Enter/Return and type `li {`
Press Enter/Return again.

As before, the new selector and declaration are fully within the `ul` rule.

10 Create the property `display: inline-block;` and press Enter/Return.

This property will display all the links in a single row, side by side. The last element to style is the <a> for the link itself.

11 Type `a {` and press Enter/Return.
Create the following properties:

```
margin: 0;
padding: 10px 15px;
color: #FFC;
text-decoration: none;
background: $logoblue;
```

The rule and declaration for `a` appear entirely within the `li` rule. Each of the rules styling the navigation menu has been nested one inside the other in a logical intuitive manner and will result in an equally logical and intuitive CSS output.

12 Save the file.

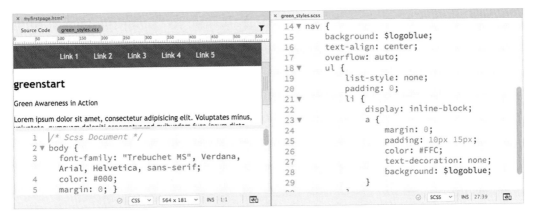

The navigation menu in **myfirstpage.html** is reformatted to display a single line of links, side by side. The CSS output file displays several new CSS rules. The new rules are not nested as in the source file. They are separate and distinct. And more surprising, the selectors have been rewritten to target the descendant structures of the menu, such as `nav ul li a`. As you can see, nesting rules in the SCSS source file eliminates the chore of writing complex selectors entirely.

Calculating CSS values

One advantage Sass has over LESS is its ability to derive CSS values through mathematical computations. For example, you can generate complementary or contrasting colors by multiplying a hex number by another number or percentage.

In this exercise, you will create a basic responsive page structure by generating the widths of the elements in the layout dynamically using a mathematical equation.

1   In **green_styles.scss**, insert the cursor after the `nav` rule.

Be sure to find the closing brace (}) for the `nav` rule. Remember, it includes the markup for four separate rules.

● **Note:** Remember to make all CSS entries only in the SCSS file.

2   Create a new line, if necessary.
Type `#wrapper {` and press Enter/Return.

3   Create the following properties:
`max-width: 1100px;`
`margin: 0 auto;`
Press Enter/Return.

```
32   }
33 ▼ #wrapper {
34       max-width: 1100px;
35       margin: 0 auto;
36   }
                        SCSS  ∨   INS  34:20
```

This rule sets the default width of the content on the webpage.

4 Type: `aside {` and press Enter/Return.

Make sure the new selector is fully nested in the `#wrapper` rule.

The two aside elements each start at 250 pixels in width, but you want them to scale down evenly as the screen size changes. You'll do that by creating an equation that takes the width of the element and divides it by the original size of the structure and then turns it into a percentage.

5 Create the following properties:

```
width: 250px / 1100px * 100%;
float: left;
```

The `width` property calculates a dimension that will maintain the proportions of the `<aside>` elements no matter what size the screen is. You'll also have to create a similar equation for the `<article>` element. But before you create the `article` rule, you have to move the cursor outside the `aside` rule. The two elements are of equal status, peers. The `article` rule should be inside the `wrapper` rule but outside the `aside` rule.

6 Move the cursor to the end brace (}) of the `aside` rule.
Press Enter/Return to create a new line.
Type `article {` and press Enter/Return.

7 Create the following properties:

```
width: 540px / 1100px * 100%;
margin-right: 10px/1100px * 100%;
margin-left: 10px/1100px * 100%;
float: left;
```

Along with calculating the width of `<article>`, you're also creating responsive margins for the left and right sides.

8 Save the file.

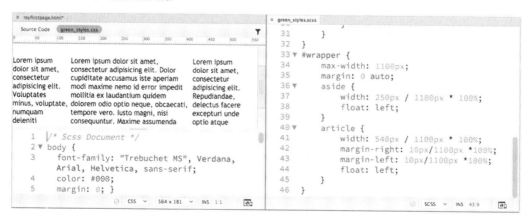

The three elements display side by side in **myfirstpage.html** subdividing the width of the #wrapper element.

Importing other style sheets

To make CSS styling more manageable, many designers split their style sheets into multiple separate files, such as one for navigation components, another for feature articles, and still another for dynamic elements. Large companies may create an overall corporate standard style sheet and then allow various departments or subsidiaries to write custom style sheets for their own products and purposes. Eventually, all these CSS files need to be brought together and called by the webpages on the site, but this can create a big problem.

Every resource linked to a page creates an HTTP request that can bog down the loading of your pages and assets. This is not a big deal for small sites or lightly traveled ones. But popular, heavily traveled sites with tons of HTTP requests can overload a webserver and even cause pages to freeze in a visitor's browser. Too many experiences like this can cause visitors to flee.

Reducing or eliminating superfluous HTTP calls should be the goal of any designer or developer, but especially those working on large enterprise or highly popular sites. One important technique is to cut down on the number of individual style sheets called by each page. If a page needs to link to more than one CSS file, it's usually recommended that you designate one file as the main style sheet and then simply import the other files into it, creating one large universal style sheet.

In a normal CSS file, importing multiple style sheets would not produce any benefit, because the import command creates the same type of HTTP request that you're trying to avoid in the first place. But, since you are using a CSS preprocessor, the import command happens *before* any HTTP request occurs. The various style sheets are imported and combined. Although this makes the resulting style sheet larger respectively, this file is downloaded only once by the visitor's computer and then cached for their entire visit, speeding up the process overall.

Let's see how easy it is to combine multiple style sheets in one file.

1   Open **myfirstpage.html** and switch to Split view, if necessary.
    Open **green_styles.scss** and choose Window > Arrange > Tile.

    The two files are displayed side by side to make it easier to edit the CSS and see the changes as they occur.

2   In **myfirstpage.html** click **green_styles.css** in the Related Files interface.

    Code view displays the content of **green_styles.css**. It contains the output of rules written in the SCSS Source file.

3   In **green_styles.scss**, insert the cursor at the beginning of the body rule.
    Type `@import "_base.scss";` and press Enter/Return to insert a new line.

    This command imports the contents of the file `_base.scss` stored in the Sass folder. The file was created ahead of time to style other portions of your page.

At the moment, nothing has changed because **green_styles.scss** has not been saved yet.

4 Save **green_styles.scss** and observe the changes in **myfirstpage.html**.

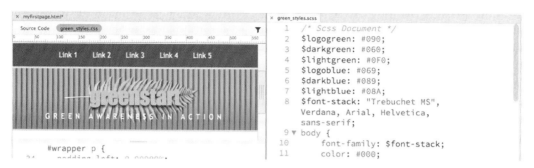

If you followed the instructions on how to create the HTML structure earlier in this lesson correctly, the page should be entirely formatted now. If you examine **green_styles.css**, you will see that several rules were inserted before the body rule. Imported content will be added starting at line 9, the position of the `@import` command. Once the content has been imported, normal CSS precedence and specificity take effect. Just make sure that all rules and file references appear after the variables; otherwise, the variables won't work.

5 Save and close all files.

Congratulations! You created an SCSS file and learned how to work with a CSS preprocessor. You experienced various productivity enhancements and advanced functionality and have glimpsed just a bit of the breadth and scope of what is possible.

Learn more about preprocessors

Check out the following books to learn more about CSS preprocessors and super-charging your CSS workflow:

Beginning CSS Preprocessors: With SASS, Compass.js, and Less.js, by Anirudh Prabhu, Apress (2015), ISBN: 978-1484213483

Instant LESS CSS Preprocessor How-to, by Alex Libby, Packt Publishing (2013), ISBN: 978-1782163763

Jump Start Sass: Get Up to Speed with Sass in a Weekend, by Hugo Giraudel and Miriam Suzanne, SitePoint (2016), ISBN: 978-0994182678

Linting support

Dreamweaver CC (2017 release) provides live code error checking. Linting support is enabled by default in Preferences, which means the program monitors your code writing and flags errors in real time.

1   Open **myfirstpage.html**, if necessary, and switch to Code view.
    If necessary, select Source Code in the Related Files interface.

2   Insert the cursor after the opening `<article>` tag and press Enter/Return to create a new line.

3   Type `<h1>Insert headline here.`

4   Save the file.

Note: Dreamweaver may create the opening and closing tags at once. If so, delete the closing `</h1>` tag before proceeding to step 4.

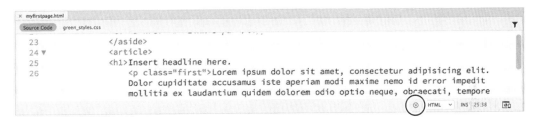

You failed to close the `<h1>` element in step 3. When an error occurs, a red X ✖ will appear at the bottom of the document window whenever the user saves the page.

5   Click the X ✖.

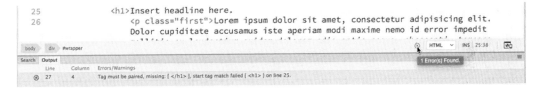

The Output panel opens automatically and displays the coding errors. In this case, the message says that the tag must be paired and identifies what line it thinks the error occurs on. The message erroneously targets line 32, but this can happen because of the nature of HTML tags and structures.

6   Double-click the error message.

Dreamweaver focuses on the line in the Code view window that it identifies as containing the error. Since Dreamweaver is looking for the closing tag for the `<h1>` element, the first closing tag it encounters is `</article>` and flags it, which is incorrect. This behavior will get you close to the error, but often you will have to track down the actual issue yourself.

7 Insert the cursor at the end of the code `<h1>Insert headline here.` Type `</`

Dreamweaver should close the `<h1>` tag automatically. If not, go ahead and finish it properly.

8 Save the file.

```
24 ▼        <article>
25              <h1>Insert headline here.</h1>|
26              <p class="first">Lorem ipsum dolor sit amet, consectetur adipisicing elit.
                                                            HTML  ∨   INS  25:47
 Search   Output
                                                            No Errors
```

Once the error is corrected, a red X is now replaced by a green checkmark ⊘.

9 Right-click the Output panel tab and select Close Tab Group from the context menu.

It's important to be wary of this icon as you save your work. No other error message will pop up indicating any problems, and you'll want to catch and correct any errors before uploading your pages to the web server.

Selecting code

Dreamweaver provides several methods for interacting with and selecting code in Code view.

Using line numbers

You can use your cursor to interact with the code several ways.

1 Open **myfirstpage.html**, if necessary, and switch to Code view.

2 Scroll down and locate the `<nav>` element (around line 11).

3 Drag the cursor across the entire element, including the menu items.

Using the cursor in this way, you can select the code in any portion or in its entirety. However, using the cursor in this way can be prone to error, causing you to miss vital portions of the code. At times, using line numbers to select whole lines of code is easier.

4 Click the line number beside the `<nav>` tag.

The entire line is selected within the window.

5 Drag down the line numbers to select the entire `<nav>` element.

```
10 ▼      <div id="wrapper">
11 ▼          <nav><ul>
12                <li><a href="#">Link 1</a></li>
13                <li><a href="#">Link 2</a></li>
14                <li><a href="#">Link 3</a></li>
15                <li><a href="#">Link 4</a></li>
16                <li><a href="#">Link 5</a></li>
17          </ul></nav>
18              <header><h2>greenstart</h2>
```

Dreamweaver completely highlights all seven lines. Using line numbers can save a lot of time and avoid errors during selection, but it doesn't take into account the actual structure of the code elements, which may begin and end in the middle of a line. Tag selectors provide a better way to select logical code structures.

Using tag selectors

One of the easiest and most efficient ways to select code is to use the tag selectors, as you have frequently done in previous lessons.

1 Scroll down and locate the following code: `<a href="#">Link 1</a>`

2 Insert the cursor anywhere in the text `Link 1`.
Examine the tag selectors at the bottom of the document window.

The tag selectors in Code view display the `<a>` tag and all its parent elements, the same way they do in Live or Design view.

3 Select the `<a>` tag selector.

```
11 ▼          <nav><ul>
12 ▼              <li><a href="#">Link 1</a></li>
13                <li><a href="#">Link 2</a></li>
14                <li><a href="#">Link 3</a></li>
15                <li><a href="#">Link 4</a></li>
16                <li><a href="#">Link 5</a></li>
```

The entire `<a>` element, including its content, is highlighted in Code view. It can now be copied, cut, moved, or collapsed. The tag selectors clearly reveal the structure of the code, even without referring to the Code view display. The `<a>` is a child of the `<li>` element, which is a child of `<ul>`, which is in turn a child of `<nav>`, which is a child of `<div#wrapper>`, and so on.

The tag selectors make it a simple chore to select any part of the code structure.

4 Select the `<ul>` tag selector.

The code for the navigation menu is entirely selected.

5 Select the `<nav>` tag selector.

The code for the entire menu is selected.

6 Select the `<div#wrapper>` tag selector.

The code for the entire page is now selected. Using the tag selectors allows you to identify and select the structure of any element on your page, but it requires you to identify and select the parent tag yourself. Dreamweaver offers another tool that can do it for you automatically.

Using parent tags

Using the Parent Tag selector in the Code view window makes the job of selecting the hierarchical structure of your page even simpler.

1   Choose Window > Toolbar > Common to display the Common toolbar, if necessary.

● **Note:** The Select Parent Tag icon may not be displayed by default in the Common toolbar. Click the Customize Toolbar icon and enable the tool before proceeding to step 3, if necessary.

2   Insert the cursor anywhere in the text `Link 1`.

3   In the Common toolbar, click the Select Parent Tag icon ⟨⟩ .

```
 9 ▼  <body>
10 ▼      <div id="wrapper">
11 ▼          <nav><ul>
                  <li><a href="#">Link 1</a></li>
                  <li><a href="#">Link 2</a></li>
14                <li><a href="#">Link 3</a></li>
```

The entire <a> element is highlighted.

4   Click the Select Parent Tag icon ⟨⟩ again or press Ctrl+[/Cmd+[(left square bracket).

The entire <li> element is selected.

5   Click the Select Parent Tag icon ⟨⟩ .

The entire <ul> element is selected.

6   Press Ctrl+[/Cmd+[until <div#wrapper> is selected.

Each time you click the icon or press the shortcut key, Dreamweaver selects the parent element of the current selection. Once you've selected it, you may find working with long sections of code unwieldy. Code view offers other handy options to collapse long sections to make them easier to work with.

Collapsing code

Collapsing code is a productivity tool that makes a simple process out of copying or moving large sections of code. Code sections are also collapsed when coders and developers are looking for a particular element or section of a page and they want to temporarily hide unneeded sections from view. Code can be collapsed either by selection or by logical element.

1 Select the first three Link items in the <nav> element.

Note the Collapse icon ▼ along the left edge of Code view. The Collapse icon ▼ indicates that the selection is currently expanded.

2 Click the Collapse icon ▼ to collapse the selection.

```
10 ▼    <div id="wrapper">                10 ▼    <div id="wrapper">
11 ▼        <nav><ul>                     11 ▼        <nav><ul>
12 ▼            <li><a href="#">Link 1</a></li>  12 ▶    <li><a href="#">Link 1</a...
13              <li><a href="#">Link 2</a></li>  16              <li><a href="#">Link 5</a></
14              <li><a href="#">Link 3</a></li>  17          </ul></nav>
15              <li><a href="#">Link 4</a></li>  18          <header><h2>greenstart</h2>
16              <li><a href="#">Link 5</a></li>  19          <p>Green Awareness in Action</p>
17          </ul></nav>                    20 ▼        <main id="content">
```

The selection collapses, showing only the first <li> element and a snippet of text from it.

You can also collapse code based on logical elements, like <ul> or <nav>.

3 Click the Collapse icon ▼ beside the line for the <nav> element.

```
10 ▼    <div id="wrapper">                10 ▼    <div id="wrapper">
11 ▼        <nav><ul>                     11 ▶        <nav><ul> <li><a href="#">...
12 ▶    <li><a href="#">Link 1</a...       18          <header><h2>greenstart</h2>
16              <li><a href="#">Link 5</a></  19          <p>Green Awareness in Action</p>
17          </ul></nav>                    20 ▼        <main id="content">
```

The entire <nav> element collapses in the Code window, showing only an abbreviated snippet of the entire element. In either instance, the code hasn't been deleted or damaged in any way. It still functions and operates as expected. Also, the collapse functionality appears only in Code view in Dreamweaver; on the web or in another application the code will appear normally. To expand the code, just reverse the process, as described in the following section.

Expanding code

When the code is collapsed, you can copy, cut, or move it like you would any other selected element. You can expand elements one at a time or all at once.

1 Click the Expand icon ▶ beside the line for the <nav> element.

```
10 ▼    <div id="wrapper">                10 ▼    <div id="wrapper">
11 ▶        <nav><ul> <li><a href="#">...  11 ▼        <nav><ul>
18          <header><h2>greenstart</h2>   12 ▶    <li><a href="#">Link 1</a...
19          <p>Green Awareness in Action</p>  16              <li><a href="#">Link 5</a></
20 ▼        <main id="content">            17          </ul></nav>
```

The <nav> element expands, but the three <li> elements collapsed in the previous exercise are still collapsed.

2 Click the Expand icon ▶ beside the line for the <li> elements.

All collapsed elements are now expanded.

Accessing split Code view

Why should coders be denied the ability to work in two windows at the same time? Split Code view enables you to work in two different documents or two different sections of the same document at once. Take your pick.

1 If necessary, switch to Code view.

2 Choose View > Split > Code-Code.

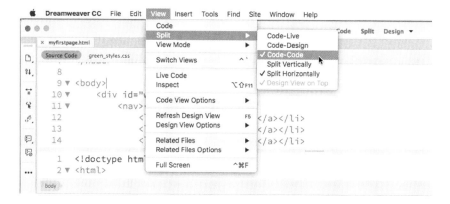

The document displays two Code view windows, both focusing on **myfirstpage.html**.

3 Insert the cursor in the top window and scroll down to the `<footer>` element.

Split Code view enables you to view and edit two different sections of the same file.

4 Insert the cursor in the bottom window and scroll to the `<header>` element.

You can also view and edit the contents of any related file.

5 In the Related Files interface, select **mygreen_styles.css**.

The window loads the style sheet into one of the windows.

Previewing assets in Code view

Although you may be a diehard coder or developer, there's no reason why you can't feel the love from Dreamweaver's graphical display, too. The program provides visual previews of graphic assets and certain CSS properties in Code view.

1 Open **myfirstpage.html** and switch to Code view.

The only graphical assets appear in the CSS file **green_styles.css**.

2 Click **green_styles.css** in the Related Files interface.

The style sheet appears in the window. Although it's fully editable, don't waste your time making any changes to it. Since the file is the output of the SCSS source file, any changes you make will be overwritten the next time the file compiles.

3 Locate the `header` rule (around line 3).

The `header` consists of two text elements and two images. You should be able to see the image references in the `background` property.

4 Position the cursor over the markup `url(../images/fern.png)` in the `background` property.

```
 3 ▼ header {
 4      text-align: center;
 5      padding: 20px 10px;
 6      background: url(../images/fern.png), url(../images/stripe.png);
 7      background-repeat: no-repeat, repeat-x;
 8      background-size                    o;
 9      background-posi              ft top;
10      background-colo
11      border-top: sol  597 × 206 pixels
12      border-bottom: solid 4px #FD5: }
```

A miniature preview of the fern image appears below the cursor.

5 Position the cursor over the markup `url(../images/stripe.png)` in the `background` property.

A miniature preview of the stripe image appears below the cursor. The preview function also works with color properties.

6 Position the cursor over the markup `#090` in the `background-color` property.

```
 6      background: url(../images/fern.png), url(../images/stripe.png);
 7      background-repeat            repeat, repeat-x;
 8      background-size:            0%, auto auto;
 9      background-position  47% center, left top;
10      background-color: #090;
11      border-top: solid 4px #FD5;
```

A small color chip appears displaying the color specified. The preview functions the same way for all color models. You no longer have to guess what image or color you specified before you can see it in Live view or the browser.

In this lesson, you learned a number of techniques to make working with code easier and more efficient. You learned how to write code manually using hinting and auto-code completion and automatically using Emmet shorthand. You learned how to select, collapse, and expand code, as well as how to create HTML comments and view code in different ways. Overall, you learned that whether you are a visual designer or a hands-on coder you can rely on Dreamweaver to offer vital features and power to create and edit HTML code without compromises.

Review questions

1   In what ways does Dreamweaver assist you in creating new code?

2   What is Emmet, and what functionality does it provide to users?

3   What do you have to install to create a LESS, Sass, or SCSS workflow in Dreamweaver?

4   What feature in Dreamweaver reports code errors when you save a file?

5   True or false: Collapsed code will not appear in Live view or the browser until it is expanded.

6   What Dreamweaver feature provides instant access to most linked files?

Review answers

1   Dreamweaver provides code hinting and auto-completion for HTML tags, attributes, and CSS styling as you type, along with support for ColdFusion, JavaScript, and PHP, among other languages.

2   Emmet is a scripting toolkit that creates HTML code by converting shorthand entries into complete elements, placeholders, and even content.

3   No additional software or services are needed to use LESS, Sass, or SCSS. Dreamweaver supports these CSS preprocessors out of the box. You merely have to enable the compiler in the Site Definition dialog.

4   Linting checks the HTML code and structure every time you save a file and displays a red X icon at the bottom of the document window when there is an error.

5   False. Collapsing code has no effect on the display or operation of the code.

6   The Related Files interface appears at the top of the document window and enables users to instantly access and review CSS, JavaScript, and other compatible file types linked to the webpage. In some cases, a file displayed in the interface will be stored on a remote resource on the Internet. While the Related Files interface enables you to view the contents all the files displayed, you will only be able to edit ones stored on your local hard drive.

APPENDIX

TinyURLs

PAGE	TINYURL	FULL URL
Lesson 3		
87	tinyurl.com/shorten-CSS	http://www.w3.org/community/webed/wiki/CSS_shorthand_reference
Lesson 6		
176	http://tinyurl.com/pseudo-class	http://www.w3schools.com/css/css_pseudo_classes.asp
Lesson 7		
226	tinyurl.com/adobe-media-queries	www.adobe.com/devnet/archive/dreamweaver/articles/introducing-media-qu
226	tinyurl.com/w3c-media-queries	www.w3.org/TR/css3-mediaqueries/
226	tinyurl.com/media-queries-smashing	www.smashingmagazine.com/2010/07/how-to-use-css3-media-queries-to-create-a-mobile-version-of-your-website/
Lesson 13		
424	http://tinyurl.com/setup-coldfusion	http://www.adobe.com/devnet/archive/dreamweaver/articles/setup_cf.html?PID=4166869
424	http://tinyurl.com/setup-apachephp	http://www.adobe.com/devnet/archive/dreamweaver/articles/setup_php.html?PID=4166869
424	http://tinyurl.com/setup-asp	http://www.adobe.com/devnet/archive/dreamweaver/articles/setup_asp.html?PID=4166869

PAGE	TINYURL	FULL URL
Lesson 15 Online		
15-12	http://tinyurl.com/fluid-width-animation	https://css-tricks.com/NetMag/FluidWidthVideo/Article-FluidWidthVideo.php
15-22	http://tinyurl.com/video-HTML5-1	http://www.w3schools.com/html/html5_video.asp
15-22	http://tinyurl.com/video-HTML5-2	http://tinyurl.com/fluid-width-animation
15-22	http://tinyurl.com/video-HTML5-3	http://tinyurl.com/video-HTML5-1
15-22	http://tinyurl.com/fluid-video	https://ulrich.pogson.ch/complete-responsive-videos-breakdown
15-22	http://tinyurl.com/fluid-video-1	https://css-tricks.com/NetMag/FluidWidthVideo/Article-FluidWidthVideo.php
15-23	http://tinyurl.com/do-not-host-video	https://www.wp101.com/10-reasons-why-you-should-never-host-your-own-videos/
15-23	http://tinyurl.com/video-hosting-overview	https://www.koozai.com/blog/social-media/video-marketing/video-distribution-vs-self-hosting-videos/

INDEX

borders
  accordion, 411
  indented text, 269
  navigation menu, 149–151
  table row, 279
box model, 72–73

 tag, 57, 255
Brightness and Contrast tool, 339
Browse for File icon, 350, 381, 387
Browse for Folder icon, 14, 15, 454, 455
browsers. *See* web browsers

C

<canvas> tag, 60
captions, table, 287–288
cascade theory, 74, 76
CC Files option, 22
cells, styling table, 278–281
character entities, 58–59
Check Spelling dialog, 295–296
child pages, 235–246
  adding content to, 237–241
  creating new, 236–237
  formatting content in, 241–243
  hyperlink updates in, 354–355
  updating, 243–246, 354–355
<cite> element, 172, 261
class attributes, 87–88
classes
  creating custom, 161–163, 176–178
  pseudo-classes and, 145
Classroom in a Book series, 1
clipboard, 255
cloaking process, 426–427
code, 440–475
  automatically writing, 445–449
  collapsing/expanding, 470–471
  comments added to, 451–452
  Common toolbar for, 451
  creating HTML, 442–449
  CSS preprocessors for, 452–466
  Emmet toolkit for, 445–449
  font in book indicating, 2
  Linting support for, 467–468

  manually writing, 442–444
  multicursor support for, 449–450
  review questions/answers on, 474–475
  selection options for, 468–470
  Split view option for, 472
  See also CSS; HTML
Code Hinting window, 268, 443–444
Code Navigator, 79–83
Code view, 26
  CSS styling in, 46
  Find and Replace feature, 299–300
  hyperlink tools used in, 381
  long selectors created in, 292
  previewing assets in, 472–473
  Refresh button, 407
  selecting code in, 468–470
  Split view option, 472
  writing code in, 442–449
collapsing/expanding code, 470–471
color
  background, 146–148, 167, 411
  text, 158–159
color picker, 148, 159
color space, 308–309
color themes, 11–12
column widths, 210–215
comma-separated values (CSV) file, 283
comments, 57, 451–452
Commit icon, 323, 330, 337
Common toolbar, 26, 451
Compare option, 436
compiling CSS code, 458–460
compression, image file, 310–311
COMPUTED option, 46, 85–86
Connect to Remote Server icon, 431
Container-fluid option, 118
content placeholders, 174–175
copying/pasting
  code to find/replace, 300–301
  consistent view required for, 383, 394
  CSS properties, 221–224
  images from Photoshop, 327–331
  styles, 285–286, 410
  tables, 276–277
Crop tool, 337–338, 339

cropping images, 337–338
CSS (cascading style sheets), 64–91
    bonus lesson on, 66, 68
    box model, 72–73
    cascade theory, 74, 76
    class and id attributes, 87–89
    code compilation, 458–460
    Code Navigator tool, 79–83
    copying/pasting properties, 221–224
    CSS Designer tool, 43–47, 83–86
    current version, 89–90
    descendant theory, 77
    HTML comparison, 66–68
    inheritance theory, 76
    multiple element formatting, 86
    positioning images using, 314–317
    preprocessors, 452–466
    pseudo-classes, 145
    rules and rule syntax, 73–74, 75, 219–220
    selector nesting, 461–463
    shorthand techniques, 87
    specificity theory, 77–78
    style sheet imports, 465–466
    styling tables with, 277–278
    support resources, 90
    values calculation, 463–464
CSS3, 89–90
CSS Designer, 43–47, 83–86
    All and Current modes, 46–47, 84
    copying/pasting properties, 221–222
    example of working with, 139–145
    @Media window, 44
    Properties window, 45–46, 85
    Selectors window, 44, 85
    Sources window, 43
    style sheet creation, 142–145
CSS preprocessors, 452–466
    code compilation, 458–460
    enabling, 453–455
    resources on, 454, 466
    selector nesting, 461–463
    source file creation, 455–458
    style sheet imports, 465–466
    values calculation, 463–464
CSS Property inspector, 40

Current mode, CSS Designer, 46, 47, 84, 415
custom classes, 161–163, 176–178
custom media queries, 217–218, 316
Customize Toolbar dialog, 451

D

declarations, 73
Delete icon, 223, 436
dependent files, 431
deprecated tags, 67
descendant theory, 77
Design view, 27, 255, 273, 282, 324
designing webpages. *See* web design
destination links
    adding to the same page, 386
    Element HUD for creating, 366–367
    id attribute for creating, 365–366
Developer workspace, 31, 442
Disable icon, 223
dithering process, 308
<div> element, 57, 106, 122, 127
Document toolbar, 25
DOM Viewer, 48, 170–174, 207–208
dpi (dots per inch), 307
dragging and dropping images, 333–335
Dreamweaver
    color themes, 11–12
    graphic tools, 339
    installing, 4
    introduction screens, 8–11
    resources, 17
    site setup, 13–16
    updating, 5, 16
    workspaces, 12
drop shadows, 160–161
drop zone, 35
drop-down menus, 370–385
    adding hyperlinks to, 381–382
    creating, 370–373
    identifying styling on, 377–381
    moving to site template, 382–385
    styling, 374–377
    See also navigation menus
.dwt file extension, 231
dynamic templates, 231

HTML (HyperText Markup Language), 52–63
    automatically writing, 445–449
    bonus exercises on, 56
    character entities, 58–59
    comments added to, 452
    CSS comparison, 66–68
    current version, 59–61
    defaults, 68–70
    Emmet toolkit for, 445–449
    historical origins, 54–55
    manually writing, 442–444
    structure of webpage using, 56
    table formatting and, 272
    tags, 55, 56–58, 443
HTML5, 59–61
    Bootstrap and, 122–125
    quote attribution in, 261
    semantic web design, 60–61
    tags, 59–60
HTML entities, 180–182
HTML Property inspector, 39
HTML structures, 259–262
<html> tag, 57
HUDs. *See* heads-up displays
Hyperlink icon, 357
hyperlinks, 342–387
    absolute, 345, 356–358
    adding behaviors to, 399–401
    checking on pages, 385–386
    destination, 365–368, 386
    drop-down menu, 381–382
    editing/removing, 349
    email, 347, 358–362
    external, 344, 356–358
    home page, 352–354
    image-based, 360–361
    internal, 344, 348–356
    navigation menu, 151–153
    placeholder for, 350, 399, 400
    pseudo-classes for, 145
    relative, 344, 345, 348–352
    targeted, 362–368
    text-based, 361–362
    updating in child pages, 354–355

I

id attributes
    creating, 88–89, 444
    targeted links and, 362, 365–366, 367–368
<iframe> tag, 57
Ignore option, 436
Image HUD, 49, 322
Image Optimization dialog, 321, 329, 339
Image Property inspector, 40
image-based links, 360–361
images, 304–341
    color spaces used for, 308–309
    copying/pasting from Photoshop, 327–331
    cropping with Crop tool, 337–338
    dragging and dropping, 333–335
    file formats for, 306, 310–311
    inserting on a webpage, 312–314, 318–324
    making responsive, 334–335
    non-web file type, 321–324
    optimizing with Property inspector, 335–338
    Photoshop Smart Objects as, 325–327
    positioning, 314–317
    Quality setting for, 321
    raster graphics, 306–311, 330
    resolution of, 307–308, 324
    screen size and, 331–333
    size of, 308, 324, 337
    tools for editing, 339
    vector graphics, 306
Images category icon, 313, 333
<img> element, 57, 314
.img-responsive class, 335
Import Tabular Data dialog, 284
importing
    CSS style sheets, 465–466
    text, 253–256
indented text, 266–269
inheritance theory, 76
inline formatting, 73
<input> tag, 57
Insert menu, 320–321
Insert panel, 118, 131, 318–319
Insert Row with Columns dialog, 119, 120–121

saving
    custom workspaces, 36
    pages as templates, 230
`<script>` tag, 58
Scrubber tool
    mobile device design and, 201–203
    resizing document windows with, 110, 113
SCSS documents, 456
`<section>` element, 60, 241, 256, 285
Select File dialog, 350
Select Image Source dialog, 318, 320, 396
selecting code, 468–470
    line numbers for, 468–469
    parent tags for, 470
    tag selectors for, 469–470
selectors
    CSS, 73–74, 75, 77, 461–463
    tag, 42, 132, 469–470
Selectors window, 44
semantic content, 169–178
    adding to Bootstrap, 122–125
    creating for text, 256–258
    custom element classes and, 176–178
    DOM panel for creating, 170–174
    main content placeholders and, 174–175
    steps for building, 169–170
semantic web design, 60–61
SFTP (Secure FTP), 418
Sharpen tool, 339
shorthand, CSS, 87
Show All option, 24
Show Set option, 45, 85, 142, 269, 278
Site Definition dialog, 453
Site menu, 13
Site Root button, 329
site root folder, 14, 109
Site Setup dialog, 13, 419, 426
Smart Objects, 325–327, 341
smartphones. *See* mobile device design
`<source>` tag, 60
`<span>` tag, 58, 161
special characters, 180–182
specificity theory, 77–78
spell-checking webpages, 295–297
Split Code view, 472
Split view, 28–29, 265

stacks, font, 184, 189–191
staging servers, 418, 423
Standard toolbar, 25
Standard workspace, 12, 30–31
Start Screen options, 21–24
starter templates, 23, 108
strikethrough formatting, 2
`<strong>` tag, 58, 357
`<style>` tag, 58
styling
    Accordion widgets, 407–414
    copying/pasting, 285–286, 410
    drop-down menus, 374–377
    identifying on interactive elements, 377–381
    navigational menus, 146–153
    tables and cells, 277–281
SVG graphics, 306
Swap Image behavior, 395–397
Swap Image Restore behavior, 397–398
synchronization process, 434–436
Synchronize icon, 435
syntax
    CSS rule, 75
    media query, 200

T

tabbed panels, 404
Table dialog, 272
Table Property inspector, 40
tables, 271–295
    caption elements in, 287–288
    cell styling for, 278–281
    controlling the display of, 281–283
    copying and pasting, 276–277
    creating from scratch, 271–276
    inserting from other sources, 283–286
    making responsive, 288–295
    moving between cells in, 273
    styling with CSS, 277–278
`<table>` tag, 58, 275, 287
tag selectors, 42, 132, 469–470
tags
    HTML, 55, 56–58
    HTML5, 59–60
targeted links, 362–368

web design, 92–101
   important questions for, 94
   page design and, 98–99
   responsive, 96, 198–200
   statistics relevant to, 95
   testing regimen for, 219
   thumbnails for, 97–98
   wireframes for, 99–100
Web Edition of book, 6
web fonts
   building font stacks with, 189–191
   Edge Web Fonts as, 185–188
WebDav system, 418
web-safe color palette, 309

Windows vs. macOS instructions, 3–4
wireframes, 99–100
workspaces
   customizing, 18–51
   interface components, 20
   prebuilt, 30–31
   saving custom, 36
   setting up, 12
writing code
   automatically, 445–449
   manually, 442–444
WYSIWYG view, 20